JUVENILE GANGS

Second Edition

JUVENILE GANGS

By

HERBERT C. COVEY, Ph.D.

Colorado Department of Human Services and
Colorado Juvenile Parole Board

SCOTT MENARD, Ph.D.

Institute of Behavioral Science
University of Colorado, Boulder

ROBERT J. FRANZESE, Ph.D.

Dean of the School of Arts and Sciences
Iowa Western Community College

CHARLES C THOMAS • PUBLISHER, LTD.
Springfield • Illinois • U.S.A.

Published and Distributed Throughout the World by
CHARLES C THOMAS • PUBLISHER, LTD.
2600 South First Street
Springfield, Illinois 62794-9265

©*1997 by* CHARLES C THOMAS • PUBLISHER, LTD.
ISBN 0-398-06716-3   (cloth)
ISBN 0-398-06717-1   (paper)

Library of Congress Catalog Card Number: 96-30243

First Edition, 1992

Second Edition, 1997

With THOMAS BOOKS *careful attention is given to all details of manufacturing
and design. It is the Publisher's desire to present books that are satisfactory as to their
physical qualities and artistic possibilities and appropriate for their particular use.*
THOMAS BOOKS *will be true to those laws of quality that assure a good name
and good will.*

Printed in the United States of America
SC-R-3

Library of Congress Cataloging-in-Publication Data

Covey, Herbert C.
    Juvenile gangs / by Herbert C. Covey, Scott Menard, Robert J.
Franzese. — 2nd ed.
        p.   cm.
    Includes bibliographical references and index.
    ISBN 0-398-06716-3 (cloth). — ISBN 0-398-06717-1 (paper)
    1. Gangs—United States.   2. Juvenile delinquency—United States.
I. Menard, Scott W.   II. Franzese, Robert J.   III. Title.
HV6439.U5C68   1997
364.3'6'06073—dc20   96-30243
                                                                        CIP

INTRODUCTION TO THE SECOND EDITION

This book is about juvenile gangs. It seems as though the threat posed by juvenile gangs is on the increase: the press, law enforcement, movies, television, and citizens have all recently expressed concerns about the rise of gangs and gang violence. The news media routinely carry accounts of drug gangs, random gang violence, and other gang-related phenomena (Huff, 1989). This has led some people to become very concerned about the safety of themselves and their families. In some segments of society, strong efforts are being made to curb the spread of juvenile gangs. The topic of juvenile gangs is of considerable interest to many Americans. Ironically, until recently, we knew relatively little about contemporary juvenile gangs, and much of what we did know was out of date. The comment that research on juvenile gangs is relatively rare was made in the late 1980s by several scholars (Hagedorn and Macon, 1988; Huff, 1989), but scholarly interest in juvenile gangs has increased since then.

Over the past five to ten years, there has been an explosion of research and scholarly publication on juvenile gangs and youth subcultures. Accompanying the plethora of studies has been a sizable increase in the number of efforts at gang prevention and intervention. Much of this concern is fueled by public perceptions of gang violence and loss of control of communities to gangs. Increasing pressure has been placed on public officials to "do something." For researchers and practitioners in the business of gang prevention and intervention, business has been booming and it shows no signs of slowing down. Whether current prevention and intervention efforts are effective remains a central and unresolved question facing gang researchers and policy makers. Recent changes in politics, unemployment rates, the economy, drug use, and gang violence all warrant careful examination of what we know about gangs and what we should be studying.

In the first edition of this book, we commented that our knowledge base on gangs had grown, but had not been integrated into a contemporary theoretical framework. The result was that students and scholars continued to return to theoretical frameworks developed in the 1950s and 1960s. It is still the case that gang studies tend to be comparatively weak on theory, but there has been some progress. We also noted that studies of gangs that have been undertaken have often been parochial, bound to small geographical areas and relatively short periods of time. Although ethnographic studies of gangs are rich in detail, they need to be placed into a broader historical and comparative context, one that goes beyond present-day American society, in order to more fully understand gangs and gang-related activities.

ORGANIZATION OF THE BOOK

The first chapter introduces the topic of juvenile gangs. Different proposed definitions of gangs are presented, and the distinctions among gangs, groups, and subcultures are examined. We also describe some characteristics of gangs in contemporary American society, and consider why the extent of gang activity and gang membership are so difficult to measure. Social reactions to gangs and the role of the media in publicizing gang activity are also discussed.

Chapters 2, 3, and 4 continue the focus on contemporary American gangs. Chapter 2 examines gang violence, with special attention to the relationships among juvenile gangs, drug use and the sale of illicit drugs, and violence. Chapter 3 focuses on differences among gangs with different ethnic composition, and the important role of ethnicity in gang membership in the United States. Chapter 4 examines female gangs and changes that have taken place in the nature and extent of female gang behavior over time. These chapters emphasize the variability that characterizes juvenile gangs across ethnic and gender boundaries. In addition, Chapter 2 emphasizes the different impressions we receive about juvenile gangs from the press, public agencies, and national statistics on crime and delinquency.

The fifth and sixth chapters place contemporary American gangs in historical and international perspective. Chapter 5 traces the history of gang activity in European and American society, and shows how juvenile gangs have evolved over time, from the Middle Ages to the twentieth century. Chapter 6 examines evidence on the nature and extent of juvenile gang activity in other countries. Important distinctions among patterns of gang activity in different countries are described. Chapters 5 and 6 emphasize the variability of juvenile gang behavior across different cultures and different times.

Chapters 7, 8, and 9 present different approaches to explaining juvenile gang behavior. Chapter 7 discusses typological approaches to crime, delinquency, and gangs, and considers their applicability to the study of juvenile gangs. Chapter 8 reviews theories of juvenile delinquency, crime, and gang behavior up to 1980, evaluates those theories, and emphasizes the different phenomena these theories attempted to explain. Chapter 9 considers the applicability of contemporary theories of crime and delinquency to the explanation of gang formation, persistence, membership, and gang delinquency.

Chapters 10 and 11 review major efforts to combat the influence of gangs and to reduce their illegal behavior. Chapter 10 centers on law enforcement and gang suppression approaches, and Chapter 11 focuses on what Klein (1995a) characterizes as "softer" interventions. Chapter 12 concludes by considering the future of juvenile gangs in the United States in light of historical and cross-sectional evidence, theory, and experience with intervention programs.

Throughout the book, a central theme is the wide variation in the nature of gangs and gang behavior. This theme may also be found in ethnographic studies of juvenile gangs and gang-like groups. At the same time, we have attempted to balance this theme of uniqueness and variability by providing a broad historical and comparative overview of juvenile gangs, and by emphasizing those features that are shared by most or all gangs, regardless of time, nationality, ethnicity, or gender. Ethnographic studies of gangs have provided a richness and depth of description that is indispensable to the study of gangs, but they have typically focused on a single gang or ethnic group (Horowitz, 1990). Klein (1995a) argues that our knowledge about gangs must encompass both city-specific and more generic information about gangs. Our goal in the present volume is different from but complementary to the city-specific ethnographic studies: to provide breadth and generality that may help to put separate studies of gangs in particular times and locations within an appropriate historical, comparative, and theoretical context.

Changes Since the First Edition

Chapter 1 has been revised to include additional material on gang definitions, gang migration and proliferation, and the emergence of tagger crews. The data on violent crimes and homicides in Chapter 2 have been updated, and information from more recent studies of the connections among gangs, drug , and violence have been included. In Chapter 3, there is more extensive information on ethnic gangs of all types, but especially Crips and Bloods (African American), Stoners and Skinheads (white), and Vietnamese (Asian) gangs. Chapters 4 and 5 have been slightly modified to include new material on female gangs and the history of gangs in Europe and the United States. Chapter 6 has been extensively revised and updated to include new material on gangs in other countries, including new material on countries covered in the first edition plus additional material on countries that were not covered in the first edition. Chapters 7, 8, and 9 include some minor additions on typologies, classical gang theories, and contemporary gang theory. The principal changes involve inclusion of additional material on psychological theories, gang cohesion, and alternative typologies. The typology (Chapter 7) we proposed in the first edition remains the same, and the theory (Chapter 9) we proposed in the first edition has been very slightly modified.

The material on interventions, Chapter 10 in the first edition, has been split into two chapters, 10 and 11, in the present edition. This was necessary because of the substantial increase in the literature on gang intervention programs since the first edition. Chapter 12 (formerly Chapter 11) has been updated, but the conclusions remain largely unchanged. Despite the increased interest in gangs and gang intervention programs, future prospects for the juvenile gang problem in the United States are as grim as ever.

CONTENTS

xi

JUVENILE GANGS

Chapter 1

CONTEMPORARY AMERICAN JUVENILE GANGS

The topic of juvenile gangs seems to breed disagreement. Some scholars (Hagedorn 1988; Huff 1989; Siegel and Senna 1988; Snyder and Sickmund 1995:54) have suggested that research on juvenile gangs is relatively rare, especially at the national level, and that we know little about juvenile gangs. Others (Campbell and Muncer 1989:271) comment that " . . . the most extensively researched and prominent form of youth group in the United States is the street gang." Most fundamentally, there is no consensus about what constitutes a gang, as opposed to a subculture or a group of individuals. Several terms have been used to refer to gangs, and the term *gang* has been broadly applied to a variety of different collections or aggregates of individuals (Bynum and Thompson 1988; Horowitz 1990; Johnstone 1981; Klein 1971; Loeb 1973; Reiss 1988; Siegel and Senna 1988; Stafford 1984; Spergel 1984; Spergel 1990).

In this chapter, we deal first with the issue of defining gangs and other collectivities. We then present an overview of contemporary juvenile gangs in the United States, including patterns of gang participation and membership and the extent of gang behavior. We conclude the chapter with a discussion of the role of the mass media in shaping our perceptions of the gang problem in America.

GANGS, GROUPS, AND SUBCULTURES

The difficulty of distinguishing between group and gang delinquency has been a major problem for gang research (Kornhauser 1978). Ever since social scientists began to study gangs, the definition of what constitutes a gang has been imprecise (Siegel and Senna 1988; Stafford 1984). Early uses of the term were very general, and the term *gang* has sometimes been used to signify a group of close associates or friends with no criminal intentions (Bynum and Thompson 1988). Almost 30 years ago, Empey (1967:33) observed that "The term 'gang' is so overworked and is so imprecise that its use in scientific discourse may very well be

3

questioned." More recently, Miller (1982) asserted that there has never been anything close to a consensus on the definition of a gang by scholars, criminal justice workers, or the general public.[1]

Underlying the imprecision in the use of the term *gang* is the finding that most juvenile delinquency is typically committed in the company of friends, and solitary acts are the exception, not the rule (Erickson and Jensen 1977; Harris 1988; Short 1968). The size of the group involved in group delinquency, however, is usually small. Miller (1982) estimated that of all crimes committed by groups, two-thirds were committed by pairs of individuals, and only one-third involved three or more perpetrators.

One of the earliest and most frequently cited definitions of a gang is that of Thrasher (1927). Thrasher defined a gang as a group that forms spontaneously and without any special attachment to existing parts of society. Gangs, according to Thrasher, are "interstitial"; they form in the "cracks" in the social fabric, the boundaries of society. Thrasher believed that conflict integrates gangs because it provides common labels and common enemies. Thrasher's definition is important because of its influence on decades of research and thinking on gangs and gang activities.

Box 1.1: Thrasher's definition of a gang

A gang is an interstitial group, originally formed spontaneously, and then integrated through conflict. It is characterized by the following types of behavior: meeting face to face, milling, movement through space as a unit, conflict, and planning. The result of this collective behavior is the development of tradition, unreflective internal structure, *esprit de corps*, solidarity, morale, group awareness, and attachment to a local territory. (Thrasher 1927:57)

Cartwright (1975:4) provided an updated version of Thrasher's original definition of a gang. A gang, according to Cartwright, is "an interstitial and integrated group of persons who meet face to face more or less regularly and whose existence and activities as a group are considered an actual or potential threat to the prevailing social order." Both Thrasher and Cartwright included meeting face to face, interstitial status, and awareness of gang membership of gang members among their criteria for the existence of a gang. For Cartwright, an additional element of the definition is that there is an assumption by nongang members that the gang is up to no good.

It would be little exaggeration to suggest that according to the definition originally proposed by Thrasher, the Harvard and Notre Dame football teams could be regarded as gangs. So, too, could groups of migrant workers (especially if they were unionized, thus increasing the potential for conflict, especially non-physical conflict) or Mardi Gras revelers. Cartwright's more restrictive definition would clearly exclude the football teams and migrant workers, and perhaps the Mardi Gras partiers, by specifying that element—threat—that most of us probably associate with gangs.

Box 1.2: Miller's definition of youth gangs

A youth gang is a self-formed association of peers, bound together by mutual interests, with identifiable leadership, well-developed lines of authority, and other organizational features, who act in concert to achieve a specific purpose which generally includes the conduct of illegal activity and control over a particular territory, facility, or type of enterprise. (Miller 1982:315–316)

Illegal activity is also an element of the definition of gangs proposed by Miller (1975). According to Miller, a gang is a group of recurrently associating individuals with identifiable leadership and internal organization, identifying with or claiming control over territory in the community and engaging either individually or collectively in violent or other forms of illegal behavior. Miller's definition distinguishes gangs from friendship groups, athletic teams, and the like, and is based on criteria used by criminal justice personnel with working contact with gangs (Campbell and Muncer, 1989).

Several other definitions of gangs have been proposed. Short (1987) proposed that characteristics of gangs included recurrent congregation outside the home, self-defined criteria of inclusion and exclusion, continuity of affiliation, a territorial basis consisting of customary hanging-out and ranging areas including self-defined use and occupancy rights, and organizational differentiation. These criteria are similar to Miller's, particularly with regard to territoriality and organization, but they do not include illegal behavior as a criterion for gang membership. Klein (1971:13) defined an adolescent gang as "any denotable adolescent group of youngsters who (a) are generally perceived as a distinct aggregation by others in their neighborhood; (b) recognize themselves as a denotable group (almost invariably with a group name); and (c) have been involved in a sufficient number of delinquent incidents to call forth a consistent negative response from neighborhood residents and/or enforcement agencies." Klein's definition would not clearly distinguish gangs from law-violating youth groups, as defined by Miller (see the section "Gang Delinquency and Group Delinquency" below).

Johnstone (1981:351) summarized the sociological characteristics of gangs to include "a specific locale; a formal structure; identifiable leaders; strong in-group loyalty combined with out-group hostility; [and] norms and taboos regarding certain behavior." Spergel (1984) distinguished gangs and particularly violent gangs from other delinquent and criminal groups by characterizing gangs as having (1) larger and better organization, (2) age-graded structure, (3) leaders and core members, (4) names, insignia, and other identifiers, (5) a sense of tradition, (6) a sense of turf, (7) primary use of violence to obtain objectives, and (8) involvement in activities other than crime and delinquency.

Ball and Curry (1995) argue against the inclusion of illegal behavior in the definition of gangs, and propose that if delinquency or crime is to be a defining characteristic of the group being studied, the qualified term *delinquent gangs* is appropriate. Bursik and Grasmick (1993) acknowledge the popularity of Klein's definition, but prefer not to include delinquency as a defining characteristic of gangs because it makes a possible outcome of gang activity one of the defining characteristics. Other scholars (Morash 1983; Thrasher 1927) have also argued that gang behavior can be delinquent or non-delinquent, that many non-delinquent formal and informal groups can be treated as gangs. Practically all of these definitions emphasize the existence of group integration or identity and involvement in illegal behavior as characteristics of gangs, and Johnstone and Spergel also emphasize turf (or locale) and formal structure. The definitions of Johnstone and Spergel are thus similar to Miller's definition.

Box 1.3: Ball and Curry's "heuristic" definition of a gang

The gang is a spontaneous, semisecret, interstitial, integrated but mutable social system whose members share common interests and that functions with relatively little regard for legality but regulates interactions among its members and features a leadership structure with processes of organizational maintenance and membership services and adaptive mechanisms for dealing with other significant social systems in its environment. (Ball and Curry 1995:240)

Gang Delinquency and Group Delinquency

Miller's definition of gangs includes illegal behavior and territoriality. It also expands the definitions of Thrasher and Cartwright to include organization (more organization than some scholars would agree exists for gangs). Miller contrasts gangs with *law violating youth groups,* which he defines as "an association of three or more youths whose members engage recurrently in illegal activities with the cooperation and moral support of their companions" (Miller 1982:313). This definition of law-violating youth groups does not include structure or territory, two important elements of Miller's definition of youth gangs. Spergel (1984:200) similarly defined delinquent groups as "an association of two or more youths, usually between the ages of ten and seventeen years, who are engaged in acts defined as illegal." Spergel's definition of delinquent groups is less restrictive than Miller's, insofar as "recurrent" activity and "cooperation and support" of others in the group are not included in Spergel's definition, but are in Miller's.

Delinquent acts often occur within a group context (Erickson and Jensen 1977; Giordano et al. 1986; Harris 1988; Short 1968; Zimring 1981). The distinction between group and gang delinquency is an area of disagreement among scholars and public authorities (Fagan 1989). Using the distinction proposed by Miller between gangs and law-violating youth groups, we know that most delinquency is conducted by groups, not gangs (Klein and Crawford 1967; Morash 1983; Reiss 1988; Yablonsky 1959). Campbell (1991:12) suggested that many of the gangs described by Thrasher (1927) were "little more than social clubs that from time to time engaged in some suspect activities." Lerman's (1967) research on juvenile delinquents in New York found that until the age of 14 or 15, most boys committed delinquent acts with small groups of close associates. This pattern continued in later years with increasing numbers of youths committing delinquent acts alone. Miller (1977) noted that street crime is often committed by small, informal groups of teenagers and not true gangs. Reiss (1988) suggested that offending groups are often inappropriately labeled as gangs.

Gangs as Near-Groups

Yablonsky (1959), based on his study of violent gangs, questioned the extent to which gangs are organized and have clear membership boundaries. He suggested that violent gangs are midway along a continuum between mobs and groups. Mobs, according to Yablonsky, are temporary, with an undetermined number of participants, no expectations for members, no clearly defined roles, and little social cohesion. Groups, on the other hand, are relatively permanent, with stable memberships, well-defined expectations, clearly identifiable leaders, clear role definitions, and a high degree of cohesion. Between mobs and groups lie gangs, which are impermanent, expand and contract in numbers of members, involve limited expectations, variable leadership, diffuse role definitions, and limited cohesiveness. Yablonsky suggested that the public often assumes more social organizational structure in gangs than is really present.

Some of the research on gangs supports Yablonsky's characterization of gangs. Gangs have been found to be loosely organized, with subgroups inadvertently breaking down group cohesion (Klein and Crawford, 1967; Short and Strodtbeck, 1965). The lack of contact among members, changing membership, and a core group of members seem to characterize most juvenile gangs. Other aspects of Yablonsky's description of gangs have been challenged, however. Klein (1971), for example, asserted that the majority of gang members are neither sociopathic nor suffering from emotional maladjustments, contrary to Yablonsky's description of violent gangs. Bynum and Thompson (1988) have indicated that gang members share common values, norms, and roles, which suggests that they may be closer to true groups than was suggested by Yablonsky. Horowitz (1990) concluded that more recent evidence on gangs supported the existence of more or less informal leadership positions and rules, and the existence of several different organizational patterns in different gangs.

Gangs and Youth Subcultures

In addition to a concern with gangs, some scholars have linked collective juvenile law violation to youth subcultures. At times, the terms "gang" and "subculture" have been used interchangeably. Subcultures characterize groups within a society, but not the whole society, and they have patterns of values, norms, and behaviors which have become traditional within the group (Short, 1968:11), but which may deviate from the values, norms, and behaviors of the larger society. Specific to youth, Campbell and Muncer (1989:272) defined youth subculture in terms of values, ideology, interaction, and membership criteria.[2] Based on their definition, gangs can be distinguished from subcultures because the latter are less dependent on face to face interaction among members, less geographically centralized, and have less rigid criteria of entry, membership, or obligation.

Box 1.4: Campbell and Muncer's definition of Youth Subculture

Youth subculture has come to denote a geographically diffuse social movement of teenagers and young people who share a common set of values, interests, and a tacit ideology, but who are not necessarily dependent on face-to-face interaction with other members and do not have any rigid criteria of entry, membership, or obligation. (Campbell and Muncer, 1989:272)

Subcultures may be important frames of reference that youths and other groups use to interpret their social worlds. Although gangs often reflect subcultures in values, norms, and behaviors, and although subcultures may have gangs as adherents, the two are nevertheless different. Subcultures are not organized to the same extent as gangs, and they lack the face to face interaction that characterizes gangs, according to most definitions of gangs (Pfautz, 1961). Gangs form within larger subcultures that may be organized racially, ethnically, politically, religiously, or economically. For example, Skinhead gangs may be regarded as part of a white supremacist (political and racial) subculture, but they are only one manifestation of that subculture. Not all white supremacists are members of skinhead gangs—indeed, not all skinheads are necessarily members of skinhead gangs.

Gangs and Mobs

In 1989, a group of youths assaulted, beat, and raped a young woman in New York City's Central Park (Cohen 1990). The media and others were quick to label the group a gang—but were they? The youths were not organized. There was no gang identity. There was no formal or informal structure. Their actions were spontaneous and unplanned. Only with a very broad definition of "gang" that includes all group behavior could we call this gang activity. By any of the definitions suggested above, this was not gang activity, but mob behavior.

Tagger Crews

A fairly new form of group that some would consider to be a juvenile gang are what has been labeled a tagger crew. Tagger crews, also known as "Toys," or "piecers," "housers," "graffiti bands," or "posses," are one of the newest and fastest rising delinquent groups to emerge in the United States. In Los Angeles alone, law enforcement estimated that there could be as many as 30,000 taggers and slightly over 400 tagger crews operating in 1993 (Glionna, 1995). Taggers are typically armed with cans of spray paint, felt pens, and increasingly weapons. They mark property with their tags. Tags are stylized initials of group members. Groups of taggers, most commonly referred to as crews go out on "bombing runs" and mark property with their tags. They also mark over the tags of others which forms a type of competition that can lead to conflict among taggers and tagger crews. Taggers are caught up in the competition with others to locate their tags in high risk and visible areas. The competition is to get the most tags in the most locations. Reputation and the accompanying respect are goals for taggers.

Tagger crews draw membership from every racial and ethnic group. Tagger crews are characterized by their spray painting initials or symbols on buildings and other publicly visible surfaces. The painting is usually done in groups called crews but is also done by individual members of crews acting independently of the group. Usually nonviolent, taggers may operate in the same areas as more violent, territorially oriented street gangs without serious conflict with those gangs (Klein 1995), but some have become more violent in nature, carrying weapons for defense, and some more violent gangs have added tagging to their repertoire of illegal activities. Tagger crews do not claim any specific "turf," and do not usually attempt to keep other taggers out of areas in which they have been active. Crossing out the tags of other taggers appears to be more the exception than the rule. Instead, any location is a fair target for taggers.

According to Wooden (1995) some of the characteristics of tagger crews are that they (a) do not have detailed organizational structures, (b) change names, (c) lack initiation rituals, (d) are not territorial, (e) come from all socioeconomic backgrounds and races, and (f) have changing membership as taggers move from crew to crew. All of these and other features, Woodson proposes, make tagger crews something other than a gang. But it is also true that taggers are involved in law violating behavior, have face-to-face interaction with each other that continues over time, associate for other reasons other than tagging, although tagging is the central reason, have a sense of group membership, may have a sense of identity, share common goals, and have a sense of status within the group (the reputations of successful taggers). Are taggers true gangs? The evidence is mixed and will require more research and a consistent use of the definition of what represents a gang.

Juvenile Gangs, Youth Gangs, Street Gangs, Ethnic Gangs, . . . What Kind of Gang?

The title of this book, juvenile gangs, reflects a focus on gangs made up primarily and sometimes exclusively of adolescents and preadolescents. Judging from the literature on American gangs, it appears that gang membership at older ages typically represents a continuity of gang membership that began in adolescence or earlier, rather than initiation of gang membership in adulthood (see the section on Age below). A possible exception to this is the prison gang; inmates who were not previously gang members may join a prison gang for protection in prison, but many members of prison gangs were also gang members before they were imprisoned (Jacobs 1974). Juvenile gangs are contrasted here with adult gangs, about whom there exists a separate literature in criminology, whose primary focus tends to be on organized crime and racketeering.

In speaking of adult gangs, the criminological literature focuses on groups of individuals whose ages typically range from the twenties through the fifties or sixties, although both older and younger ages are possible. These gangs are invariably criminal in nature, more or less organized, and range from small burglary rings (Shover 1973) to local "chop shops" (U.S. Senate 1980), to national and international criminal organizations that specialize in the illicit drug trade (Inciardi 1986) and other crimes (Albanese 1989). They characteristically avoid visibility, especially to law enforcement officials, but may attempt to maintain a reputation for efficiency, effectiveness, persistence, and dangerousness (Ianni 1972), not only in dealing with their victims but also in helping their allies. Regardless of the visibility of the gang as a collectivity, members of adult gangs do not advertise their membership in any way that might draw public attention to themselves as gang members. Instead, they attempt to keep their membership in the gang secret, and may deny, at least in public, that the gang exists. Some juvenile gangs also follow this pattern (see Chapters 3 and 7), but the most common types of juvenile gangs, and the ones with which public officials and criminological researchers appear to be most concerned, are more likely to advertise both the existence of the gang and their membership in the gang with tattoos, graffiti, clothing styles, hand signs, and other visible indications of gang involvement.

Other modifiers used in describing gangs include "youth" gangs (Spergel 1990), reflecting a concern with the increasing age of members in what were traditionally juvenile gangs; "delinquent" gangs (Goldstein 1991), reflecting an emphasis on juvenile or youth gangs involved in illegal behavior; various defined gangs defined in terms of ethnicity (White/African American/Chicano/etc.), gender (female gangs), subcultures or interest groups (bikers, stoners, skinheads, surfers). Klein (1995a) focuses on "street" gangs, which he describes as being aimless (as opposed to having well-defined objectives), publicly visible, and criminal in nature. (With the exception of aimlessness, this parallels his earlier definition of gangs, described above.)

All of these modifiers serve to specify the types of gangs in which different authors are interested. They should not, however, be taken as defining the more general term, *gang*. They denote specific types, not universal characteristics, of gangs. Our own interest in juvenile gangs reflects our interest with the earliest stage (and for most gang members, the only stage) of gang membership.

Conclusion: Definitions

The absence of consensus on the definition of the term *gang* has an impact on what we conclude about gang behavior. Decker and Kempf-Leonard (1991) suggest that public perception of the seriousness and scope of the gang problem is influenced by the definition being used. If a broad definition of the term is used, then a wide variety of groups, such as college fraternities, athletic teams, play groups, street corner groups, and other collections of individuals can be defined as gangs, and we are likely to conclude that gang activity is widespread in American society. Miller (1982) argues that the use of very narrow definitions of gangs have resulted in gross underestimation of the extent of gang behavior in the United States. For the remainder of this book, we will generally use Miller's definitions of gangs and law-violating youth groups, and Campbell and Muncer's definition of subcultures. Although there may be no consensus on proposed definitions of gangs, Miller's definition is reasonable, useful in distinguishing gangs from groups, and contains elements common to many other proposed definitions. It also provides a reasonable balance between excessively restrictive and overly broad definitions. Note that although we will try to adhere to these definitions, many of the works cited in this book will not; where discrepancies clearly exist, they will be pointed out.

THE STRUCTURE OF JUVENILE GANGS

Gangs, like other groups in society, must perform certain functions in order to survive. They must recruit members, provide for the well-being of their members, make decisions about immediate (and perhaps long-term) goals and lines of action, and settle internal disputes. There is considerable variability in how different gangs approach these tasks. According to Stafford (1984), most researchers have found that gang are loosely structured, not very cohesive, and without clearly defined leadership roles. Some gangs, however, are more highly structured, especially Hispanic and Asian-American gangs in the United States (Chin 1990; Harris 1988; Moore 1978; Vigil 1988). It also appears that gangs that focus on profitable property crime, as opposed to drug use, violence, or other activities, tend to be more formally organized (see Chapter 7).

Spergel (1990) and Klein (1971) have described patterns of *vertical* and *horizontal* structure or alliances in gangs. Vertical structure refers to hierarchy, and includes differentiation between leaders and followers, and differentiation between age groups, who may move from one level to another, or from one gang to another, as they get older. Horizontal structure refers to distinctions that are not vertical in nature, including linkages with the neighborhoods from which gang members are drawn and the combination of different, separate gangs into "nations," "super-gangs," alliances, or confederation. According to Spergel, horizontal structure is the more common pattern in contemporary American gangs. Within these broader structural patterns, Campbell (1984b) found that gangs tend to be imitative of structures in the larger society: families, businesses, the military.

Typically, gangs consist of a small *core* of five to twenty-five members who are most active in gang activities and from which the leadership of the gang is drawn, and a set of *peripheral* or *marginal* members, more or less strongly affiliated with the gang, more or less frequently involved in gang activities, and more or less committed to the gang (Hagedorn 1988; Hardman 1969; Harris 1988; Klein 1968a; Spergel 1990; Taylor 1990; Vigil 1988; Yablonsky and Haskell 1988). Counting only core members, most gangs are fairly small, typically twenty or fewer members (Davis 1978). Ice T (1994) suggests that there are three levels of membership, *hardcore* (totally focused on gang violence), *members* (highly involved in the gang, willing to stand up for it, usually involved in running the gang, but there primarily for the friendship and companionship), and *affiliates* (people who know the gang members, wear the colors, and abide by the rules, occasionally involved in running the gang; basically kids who go along to get along). If peripheral members or affiliates are included, gangs may number in the hundreds, and coalitions of gangs may have thousands of members (Spergel 1990).

Some gang research has studied how the inner city environment shapes the organizational structure of the gang. For example, Jankowski (1991) focused on the intense competition for and conflict over scarce resources that exists in gang areas. He argues that gangs are organized around this competition (See also Padilla 1992). Others such as Vigil (1988; 1990) stress the role culture conflict has on shaping the structure of gangs. The media and larger community reaction to gangs may also play roles in shaping gang structure (Klein 1967; 1971; Zatz 1987).

Gang Leadership

Yablonsky (1962) suggested that leaders of violent gangs were the most sociopathic and socially inept members of the gang, the members with the most severe psychological problems.[3] If the gang leader's status was threatened, the leader would respond with verbal threats or violence. Partially consistent with Yablonsky's position, other researchers have indicated that gang leaders may use violence and other delinquent activities to maintain status as the leader of the gang and to promote gang cohesiveness (Short and Strodtbeck 1965; Spergel 1990).

Short and Strodtbeck (1965) indicated that gang members generally suffered from social disability or ineptness, but disagreed with Yablonsky's view of gang leadership, and concluded instead that gang leaders were often the most socially adept members of the gang. Klein (1971) also suggested that gang leaders were more socially adept than other members of the gang. Horowitz and Schwartz (1974) found no evidence of social disability among members of Hispanic gangs. Campbell (1984b) and Harris (1988) found that gang members who were truly psychologically disturbed were systematically excluded from leadership roles and sometimes avoided entirely by gang members. Thrasher (1927) suggested that leaders in gangs held prestige by coming up with better ideas than other gang members and by suggesting activities that other gang members were likely to agree with. Hood and Sparks (1970) suggested that the apparent social disabilities and aggressiveness of gang leaders, as described by Yablonsky, may be expected of leaders as a rational tactic for maintaining leadership; Campbell (1984b) echoed a similar suggestion. According to Bartol and Bartol (1989), most gang theorists (other than Yablonsky and Short and Strodtbeck) view gang members as socially normal.

Yet a third perspective on gang leadership was suggested by Klein (1968a), who suggested that leadership is not a position, but a collection of functions. Leadership is situational, and varies with the type of activity in which the gang is engaged. DeFleur (1967a) viewed leadership similarly as being temporary, spontaneous, and reactive to changing situations. Spergel (1990) also suggested that leadership was variable, and Miller (1974) indicated that the leadership role is assumed by different gang members at different times. Bloch and Niederhoffer (1958) suggested that there is usually more than one leader in a gang. Labov (1982) found that there was no clear leadership, but instead a more egalitarian structure. Under some circumstances, gang members may pull back from leadership roles (Klein 1968a; Moore 1978; Vigil 1988), a situation Klein (1968a) described as "hesitant leadership."

Conclusion: Gang Structure

Although some patterns of gang structure, including loose organization, fluidity of leadership, and ambiguity of membership, appear to prevail in contemporary American gangs, there is considerable variation in the patterns. In particular, certain types of gangs, based on patterns of illegal behavior or on ethnicity, appear to have more formal, rigid, hierarchical organization than others. Leadership functions vary with the situation, and may be assumed by different individuals in the same gang and by individuals with different strengths or weaknesses in different types of gangs. Membership in some types of gangs is ambiguous; in others, there are clear distinctions between members and non-members (see Chapter 7). Altogether, the variability in gang structure is consistent with a more general pattern of variability in the juvenile gang phenomenon.

DEMOGRAPHIC CHARACTERISTICS
OF GANG MEMBERS

Although there is considerable variation among gangs, gang members, especially members of violent gangs, typically share some common characteristics. Some of those common characteristics are detailed here. Gender, ethnicity, and race receive extended treatment in Chapters 3 and 4.

Residence

One of the enduring themes in delinquency research is that delinquency, and especially gang delinquency, are most likely to occur in the cities. Fischer (1975) proposed that only in urban areas are delinquents present in sufficient numbers to establish a delinquent subculture. It may also be necessary for a *critical mass* (see Chapter 9) of youths to be present in some proximity to one another in order for a gang to form. Opportunities for joining gangs are therefore greater in urban areas than elsewhere. Others have questioned the critical mass theme (Erickson and Jensen 1971), but there is general agreement that gangs have historically been primarily an urban slum phenomenon (Short 1974; Miller 1975), although that pattern may be changing with present-day gangs.

Areas in which the community is rapidly changing have historically been more likely to have gangs than other areas of the city. Research on gangs dating back to the 1920s and 1930s has found that certain areas of the city are more likely to have gang activity (Shaw and McKay 1972). Curry and Spergel (1988) indicated that gang problems were concentrated in low-income public housing projects and in poor African and Hispanic American parts of cities. Miller (1975; 1977) reached similar conclusions. Although the gang problem may have been greatest in major American cities such as New York, Los Angeles, and Chicago, it is certainly not confined to those cities. The U.S. Department of Justice (1988b) underscored the existence of gangs in mid-sized American cities. Some of the gangs identified in this and other reports include the Creepers, Untouchables, and Down by Law in Atlanta, Georgia, the Folks in Jackson, Mississippi, and the Warriors and Black Angels in Chattanooga, Tennessee. Hagedorn (1988) identified over a dozen gangs in the Milwaukee area. Klein (1995a) estimates that there may now be over 1,000 American cities with street gangs.

One recent trend has been for the traditional inner city slum or barrio to move out from the center of the city toward the suburbs (Stover 1986). This outward movement has resulted in neighborhood gangs distancing themselves further from the core of the city (Miller 1975). To support this observation, Stover (1986:19) cited statistics that indicated "Of the estimated 50,000 gang members inside Los Angeles County, only between 15,000 to 18,000 still live within the city limits." Self-reported delinquency studies have indicated that gangs are present in suburban areas and are not restricted to the inner city. Hardman (1969) found evidence of juvenile gangs in a small college town. Johnstone (1981) found strong gang activity in suburban Chicago. The Simon City Royals of Chicago were linked to a string of suburban robberies (De Mott 1985). Chambliss (1973) and Myerhoff and Myerhoff (1964) provided evidence of gangs operating in suburban areas twenty to thirty years ago. Counter to this general trend, Miler (1977) noted that poor, unemployed, unskilled youths are becoming more concentrated in the inner cities. The traditional pool from which gangs have drawn their membership in the past is thus becoming more concentrated in the inner cities. It may be most accurate to suggest that gangs have become a metropolitan phenomenon, rather than just a central city phenomenon.

It has been suggested that the availability of automobiles and mass transportation have also allowed gangs to spread beyond the traditional neighborhoods known for gangs to other areas of the city (Hagedorn 1988). The national press reports that juvenile gangs have greater mobility in Los Angeles now than in the past (De Mott 1985; Leo et al. 1988). In one case that received national attention, four juveniles aged twelve to eighteen flew to Seattle, robbed a jewelry store of $300,000 in gems, then flew back to Los Angeles. Mobility for gangs occurs in other ways, however. Changes in population size or composition, or the failure of gangs to replace their members as they get older, may also lead to shifts in the location of gang activity. The South Bronx police station was for years known as "Fort Apache" because of the high levels of gang activity in the area. As early as 1980, however, the station was referred to as the "little house on the prairie" because gang activity in the area had declined (Rosario 1980).

It has also been suggested that court mandated busing may have played a role in spreading gangs and promoting gangs across neighborhood boundaries (Hagedorn 1988; Huff 1989). According to this model, prior to busing, youths were more closely linked to their neighborhoods and developed a strong sense of identity. Busing moved youths from their local neighborhoods to other parts of the metropolitan area that contained youths from rival gangs and neighborhoods. This created tension among youths in the schools which forced them either to join a gang for protection, or, if they were already members of a gang, caused them to strengthen their gang ties. This crystallization of juvenile gangs led to increased violence among gangs forced to share the same schools. Alternatively, a viable argument could be made that moving youths into different schools may have helped break down ties to gangs. It is entirely possible that gang membership has been neither increased nor decreased as a result of busing, but that the distribution of gang membership in the cities has been changed to include proportionally fewer individuals from the traditional gang neighborhoods and more from other neighborhoods.

Age

Gangs are mostly comprised of teenagers and, secondarily, of young adults in their early twenties. Klein's (1967) research found that most members were between the ages of twelve and the early twenties. Kantor and Bennett (1968) reported similar findings, and placed the ages of gang members at 10 to 25 years. Cooper (1967) reported the ages of 11 to 25 as most common. Huff (1989) found that Cleveland and Columbus members were between 10 and 30 years old, with most between 14 and 24. Esbensen, Huizinga, and Weiher (1993) using self-report data from the Denver Youth Survey found 47 percent of gang members aged from 12 to 14, 31 percent were aged 15 to 16 and the remainder up to and including age 18. The reason for the age ranges cited above may be linked to the age at which gangs recruit members. For example, youths aged 12 to 14 who are street-wise males appear to be the best target for recruitment into gangs (Johnstone 1983).

Miller (1975) and other researchers (Fagan 1990; Hagedorn 1988; Vigil 1990) have indicated that the average age of gang members may be increasing. There is also evidence that juvenile gangs are sometimes led by adults (Miller 1975). Some gang experts have departed from the notion of a "gang age" and have suggested that the "youth" gang may no longer be a valid concept with contemporary gangs (Horowitz 1990; Huff 1990; Klein and Maxson 1989). The aging of gang members is typically attributed to declining occupational opportunities, decaying institutional controls, and the profitability of drug trafficking (Lasley

1992). For example, Hagedorn (1988: 125) stated, "Rather than maturing out of the gang into a job, or raising a family, Milwaukee gang founders have just kept hanging out together." In contrast, Esbensen and Huizinga (1993) found that most self-reported gang members in a sample of Denver high-risk neighborhoods did not become gang members for long periods of time; instead, few of the adolescents they sampled stayed in the gang for more than one year over a five-year period. Snyder and Sickmund (1995:54) contended that the age structure of gangs is dependent on the length of time the gang has been in existence. "Cities with an emerging gang problem report that up to 90% of their gang members are juveniles. In cities with more established gangs, only about one-fourth of gang members are juveniles."

A study by Lasley (1992), which used Miller's definition of gangs, examined whether gang members are getting older, and the degree to which the growing underclass has contributed to this trend. Lasley sampled 435 Southern California gang members in Los Angeles and Orange counties and found that gang membership is still primarily an adolescent phenomenon. The results show that gang participation peaked during ages 16 and 17. Only 12–15 percent of gang members were 20 years old or older; over half were 14–17 years old, and if 18–19 year olds are included, over 80 percent are 14–19. Since Los Angeles is a city with a long history of gangs, this would seem to contradict the assertion by Snyder and Sickmund, above, that in cities with established gangs only a minority of gang members are juveniles. In addition, Lasley found no support for the notion that increases in urban deprivation resulted in longer involvement in gangs. Adult gang membership was statistically as rare in neighborhoods where opportunities were few as those where opportunities were higher. Small differences for race were also found. Lasley (1992:447) noted that, " . . . the immediate findings support the traditional notion that race and SES do not condition the length of time one spends in a street gang." Lasley concluded that when all things are considered, street gangs are still very much youth gangs.

Other evidence (Cartwright et al. 1975; Yablonsky 1988) suggests that gang members are being recruited at increasingly young ages. According to one Chicago authority, the average age of gang members dropped from 15 in 1984 to 13.5 in 1987. McKinney (1988) provided testimony from law enforcement officials that some gangs are recruiting children as young as eight, nine, and ten years old. Spanier and Fischel (1973) found that youths in low-income housing projects started to form gang-like groups as early as six or seven years old. This pre-teen period may also be the age at which some children begin their delinquent careers (Werthman 1967). Younger gang members are viewed by older gang members as ideal for some of the risky gang activities such as drug sales because they are insulated from serious criminal penalties that could be applied to older offenders.

Gender

Gangs are predominantly a male enterprise, as are crime and delinquency more generally. Adler (1975) has suggested that women have become more assertive and increasingly involved in traditionally male dominated forms of deviance. Following her argument, women could catch up with males and someday participate in gangs to the same extent as males, but others (Canter 1982) have criticized Adler's conclusions. Giallombardo (1980) concluded that the changes in female arrest rates were relatively small, and did little to reduce the gap between male and female delinquency, and perhaps less to reduce the gap between male and female adult crime.

Miller's (1975) national study found that over 90 percent of gang members were male. Campbell (1991) similarly concluded about 10 percent of New York City gang members were female. Higher percentages have been reported by Esbensen, Huizinga and Weiher (1993) and Fagan (1990), 20–46 and 33 percent respectively. Totally autonomous female gangs have been relatively rare in American society (Giordano 1978), but there is evidence that female auxiliaries are often important components of male gangs. In her study of Hispanic gangs in Los Angeles, Harris (1988) reported that girls are an important part of gangs and especially Hispanic gangs. She concluded that there is usually a female component to Hispanic gangs. There is some evidence that female gangs are more common in larger cities. Miller (1973) described an Anglo low-income female gang which was involved in theft, petty offenses, and occasionally violent crime. The issue of female gangs is examined more extensively in Chapter 4.

Socioeconomic Background and Ethnicity

The relationship between socioeconomic status and delinquency, including gang delinquency, is controversial. Short and Strodtbeck's (1965) research on Chicago gangs found that lower class boys were the most delinquent. Johnstone (1983) found that low income communities were more likely to serve as recruitment areas for gangs. In part, whether there are substantial differences by socioeconomic class may depend on whether official or self-report statistics are used (Elliott and Ageton 1980; Elliott and Huizinga 1983). The different data sources tend to show the same general pattern, but the differences are more pronounced for official arrest records than for self-report data (Huizinga and Elliott 1987). Although gangs appear to be primarily a lower class phenomenon, there is evidence of the existence of middle class gangs (Coleman 1970; Chambliss 1973; Karacki and Toby 1962; Vaz 1967). Stover (1986) noted that Los Angeles and Detroit police reported problems among middle class suburban youths, as well as lower class youths from the central city.

Huff (1989) and Hagedorn (1988) found that African American gang members were drawn predominantly from the African American underclass, as described by Wilson (1987) and Duster (1987). As formulated by Wilson (1984; 1987), the idea behind the underclass is that economic growth does not benefit everyone. Some people, because of race, or lack of access to transportation, or lack of integration into social networks, are more isolated from the mainstream of society than others. In particular, poorer and less educated African Americans may be concentrated in central city slum areas, where they are isolated from legitimate economic opportunity, education, and mainstream society generally. Others have also stressed the development of a African American underclass (Duster 1987; Lehmann 1986a; Lehmann 1986b) because of a decline in low-skill jobs in the United States. Fagan (1989) and Hagedorn (1988) have suggested that gangs may be more important in the context of the underclass because they provide an alternative to the increasingly unfamiliar and foreign mainstream society.

Minority group youths are more likely to be involved in gang activity than white, non-Hispanic youths (Miller 1975; Siegel and Senna 1988; Stafford 1984). One police department study of New York gangs found that 55 percent were Hispanic and 36 percent were African American, with the remainder being white non-Hispanic or Oriental (Collins 1979). Furthermore, gangs tend to be racially exclusive (Miller 1975), although some racial mixing does occur (Yablonsky 1962). All African American (Miller 1962; Short and Strodtbeck 1965), all Hispanic (Erlanger 1979; Horowitz and Schwartz 1974; Moore 1978; Moore et al. 1983), Vietnamese (Morgenthau 1982), and Chinese (Joe and Robinson 1980;

Takagi and Platt 1978) gangs have been well-documented. It is generally agreed that the racial and ethnic composition of the gangs reflects the racial and ethnic composition of the inner city neighborhoods from which gang members are drawn.

Whether gangs spread from established gang centers, such as Los Angeles and Chicago, to other areas, or develop independently from local youth is a question that has been raised by many concerned with the growth of gangs in the United States. The general public and law enforcement agencies typically assume that hard core gang members move to other communities and recruit local youth into the gang. The spread of gangs from this perspective is one that views gangs as forming franchises and branches across the country. Recent research by Klein, Maxson, and Miller (1995) found that most gangs that emerge are built from "home-grown" youth and not from the spread or branching out of gangs from central locations.

While it is true some gang members do move from centers to new locations and start new or join existing gangs, they typically are moving for family reasons rather than with the motive of building gangs (Zevitz and Takata, 1992). What seems to confuse this issue is the practice of many youth of adopting gang culture and terms that give the impression that they are branches of larger gangs. Many gangs call themselves Crips or Bloods without any formal or informal ties to either confederation. Klein, Maxson, and Miller (1995) observe the use of terms like Crip or Blood are more copy-cat phenomena than an indication of true gang migration or affiliation. The senior author's interviews with many gang members calling themselves Crips or Bloods supports this observation, as many of these gang youth don't have the slightest idea why they have either label other than they and others will think it is "cool" and adds legitimacy to their gang.

Increasing attention is being paid to the immigration of gangs to the United States (Leo et al. 1988). Immigrant groups from Asia and Latin America (see Chapter 3) such as the Marielito gangs from Cuba raise concerns that parallel issues raised in the 19th century concerning southern European immigration to America. A key question may be whether the new immigrant gangs will decline with the process of acculturation as other gangs did (Leo et al. 1988).

Conclusion: Gang Membership

Even with all of the variation in gangs, gangs can be characterized as predominantly male, young, urban, lower class, and minority. Although females participate in juvenile gangs, they have historically taken secondary roles (Campbell 1984b). Gangs may be getting both older and younger in terms of the typical age range of members, as gang members remain in the gang longer, and as younger members are recruited to insulate older members from more serious criminal penalties. Although gangs have increasingly moved to suburban areas and to smaller cities, they remain predominantly an urban, central city phenomenon. Finally, lower class minority group members are more likely to be identified as gang members, a fact which may at least in part reflect a bias in the way official statistics are produced, but which, even according to self-report data, accurately reflects a disproportionately high probability that lower class minority group youths will become involved in gangs.

THE EXTENT OF GANG BEHAVIOR

One of the most difficult questions to answer about gangs is how prevalent and extensive is current gang activity in the United States. Some suggest that it may be impossible to answer this question, given the diversity in definitions of what represents a gang (Bookin-Weiner and Horowitz 1983; Spergel 1990). Siegel (1989:177) typifies the common perception that "Today, the number of gang youths appears at least in these major cities (Philadelphia, Los Angeles, and Chicago) to be at an all-time high." Earlier research reported declines in gang activities in some cities and stability of gangs in other cities (Spergel 1990). Davis (1978) and Miller (1980) suggested that gang membership and activity had increased, and that the extent of the gang problem was underestimated in the 1970s. One more recent estimate is that there are about 800 cities with about 10,000 gangs and perhaps as many as a half-million members (Klein, 1995b). As indicated in Table 1.1, this represents a substantial increase from 1960. The increase, according to Klein (1995a) and Howell (1994), represents the independent emergence of gangs in different cities, sometimes as a result of normal family residential migration, rather than "unit relocation," the "migration" or "expansion" of gang franchises from one city to another.

Table 1.1: Growth in Gang Involved Cities (Klein 1995a:91)	
Year	*Number of Cities with Street Gangs*
Before 1961	54
Up to 1970	94
Up to 1980	172
Up to 1992	766

Very few recent studies have addressed this question on a national scale. Most current research focuses on individual gangs or ethnic groups (Horowitz 1990), rather than on national data. (A notable exception is Klein 1995a; 1995b.) This is to some extent understandable. The Department of Justice's (1988) *Report to the Nation on Crime and Justice* fails to even list gangs in its index. Most of what is known about the extent of gangs and their activities comes from large metropolitan areas, such as New York, Los Angeles, and Chicago. Varying methods used to define gangs and to count gang members may make estimates of their extent terribly unreliable. In addition, research indicates that gang membership fluctuates considerably over time. To complicate matters even more, media attention to gangs appears to be cyclic, and the media since the mid-1980s have show considerable interest in juvenile gangs. This has created a context in which it is difficult to determine whether gangs are as active, as prevalent, and growing as fast as the media would suggest. Gang activity is simply good press.

Bastian and Taylor (1991:8) presented data from the National Crime Survey (NCS) on juvenile gang activity in schools. Their data cannot be generalized outside the school setting (because many gang members are no longer in school when they are still active in gangs), and the data are cross-sectional, so they do not give us information about trends in gang activity. Nonetheless, the data do reflect the patterns of socioeconomic status, ethnicity, and age described above. In the NCS data, 15 percent of students reported that gangs were present in their schools; 5 percent were uncertain, and 79 percent said that there were no gangs at their schools. Higher percentages of students reported gang activity at their schools if they were from lower (but not the lowest) income families (17 percent at less than $7,500; 18–21 percent from $7,500 to $24,999; 13–16 percent at $25,000 to $50,000; and 11 percent with over $50,000 annual family income), if they were ethnic minorities (32 percent among

Hispanics, 20 percent among African Americans, 14 percent among whites), and if they were from central cities (25 percent) rather than suburbs (14 percent) or non-metropolitan areas (8 percent). There was, predictably, no difference by gender. Students at schools with gangs reported more fear of attack and greater availability of drugs than students at schools without gangs, although most students (56 percent) at schools with gangs reported that the gangs never fought at the school, or did so only once or twice a year.

Determining the extent of gang membership is difficult. Most researchers must depend on police records or court records, or in some cases self-report data. Klein (1971) has suggested that these sources of data may often be inaccurate. Official data is not systematically collected on gangs at the national level and at most local levels, it is based on incidents, and definitions of what constitutes gang activity or gang-related activity vary across jurisdictions. When they are picked up by the police, gang members may deny gang membership, and non-members may fear to become involved in the identification of gang members. Citizens have been reluctant to report on gang activities, serve as witnesses, or cooperate with authorities. Johnson, Webster, and Connors (1995) attribute this to three basic factors: fear of retaliation from the gang, not wanting to be labeled a "snitch," and involvement of the victim or witness in gang activities. Klein and Maxson (1989) noted that defining "gang-related offenses" by law enforcement agencies and other officials is likely to vary across jurisdictions. As an alternative to official statistics, researchers may be limited financially to using other secondary sources or small-scale, local studies (Bookin-Weiner and Horowitz 1983).

The study of contemporary gangs is beset with methodological problems. Gaining access to gangs and building rapport with gang members is difficult because gangs have a natural and justified mistrust of outsiders (Horowitz 1986; Kleiner et al. 1975). In addition, most gang researchers have come from dramatically different backgrounds than the members of the gangs (Parks 1995). Kleiner et al. (1975) noted that African American gangs tended to be particularly hostile to white gang researchers. Hopper and Moore (1989) reported similar reactions in non-Hispanic white adult motorcycle gangs. Gangs have also been known to exaggerate or minimize their activities for the press and for researchers (Miller 1977; Miller 1982; Spergel 1984). Separating facts from fiction may be difficult. Fleisher (1994) contends that the truth value of gang member responses is dependent on how long the researcher is in the field. One solution to the problems of access and honesty in reporting has been to involve gang members or former gang members, or individuals in the community who have access to the gangs in the research process (Hagedorn 1988; Hopper and Moore 1989; Kleiner et al. 1975; Moore 1977).

Some researchers have taken the bias of law enforcement when studying gangs (Miller 1975). They have used law enforcement definitions for understanding gangs, and law enforcement data (information from police contact sheets, arrest records, and court documents) for analysis. Few truly national studies have been conducted on gangs. Agencies do not typically collect information on gangs, and national data on youth crime and delinquency do not separate gang activities from group delinquency or delinquent acts committed by individuals.

Given the available evidence, there is some indication that the extent of gang membership and gang activity are growing. For example, Thompson and Jason (1987) concluded that several studies of Chicago indicated growth in gang activity. Davis (1978) contended that street gangs had increased in the 1970s. Numerous studies have acknowledged the existence of gangs in the nation's largest cities and in smaller cities as well (Kornblum 1985; Miller 1975; Needle and Stapleton 1983). The number of gangs in New York was reported in the early 1980s to have declined to about 4,300 gang members operating within 86 gangs (Needle and Stapleton 1983). This reported decline occurred, however, at a time when New York's Police Gang Intelligence Unit was being dissolved, and may be more reflective of a less sensitive measurement of the extent of gang activity than of any real decline in gang activity (Campbell 1984b).

Klein (1995b) suggests that street gangs operate in a variety of cycles. Sanders (1993) also observed a cyclical pattern to gang activities in San Diego. Block and Block (1993) found that gang violence in Chicago was cyclical over a 26-year period, with periodic increases, perhaps as gangs sought to expand territory. Gangs and gang activity fluctuate in cycles. For example, in the late 1960s gang activity decreased but increased in the 1980s. Klein pointed out that the extent of gang activity increases and decreases according to a number of factors including but not limited to seasonality, research attention, political climate, media attention, and gang members self-regulation.

SOCIAL REACTIONS TO GANGS
AND THE ROLE OF THE MASS MEDIA

Public reaction to gangs does much to shape the nature of gangs and gang behavior. Community perceptions may be critical to the definition and perception of groups as gangs. According to Miller (1974:263), "Put in general terms, if youth groups in a particular community appear clearly to present a problem, they are perceived as gangs; if they do not, that community has 'groups' but no 'gangs'." Every group, including a gang, is shaped by its external environment and community (Short 1976). Short and Moland (1976) found that the community context had a bearing on the politicization of gangs in the 1960s.

The perception of the nature and extent of gangs in society is a function of the mass media (Miller 1981). Media portrayals and false depictions of gangs have been criticized by a number of researchers (Decker and Kempf-Leonard 1991; Hagedorn 1988; Horowitz 1990; Zatz 1987). Parks (1995) and Prothrow-Stith and Weissmann (1991) have suggested that the nature of violence associated with gang behavior may have resulted in its being distorted and exaggerated by the media. Klein (1995a:55) suggests that "Most serious writers about gang affairs know better than to rely heavily on media reports." Ethnicity, social class, and cultural attributes of groups of youths may influence the extent to which they are perceived as problems. In a study of community perceptions of gangs, Takata and Zevitz (1990) found that social position influenced general perceptions about the degree and nature of the gang problem in Racine, Wisconsin. They concluded (p. 301) "Prior research on youth gangs reveals that the label, gang member, is a social status that defines the way certain young people within a community are perceived and dealt with by others in that community, including agents of the legal system."

Zatz's (1987) study of gangs in Phoenix found that law enforcement agencies, with the help of the press, were able to create an overreaction or "moral panic" over Hispanic gangs. Moore (1991) noted that Hispanic gangs originated and have existed in contexts of periodic moral panics that shape public perceptions of gangs. Cohen (1980) traced the development of mod and rocker youth cultures in England, and offered similar findings. Takagi and Platt (1978) studied Chinese juvenile gangs in San Francisco's Chinatown and contended that youth groups are incorrectly labeled as gangs by the press and the criminal justice system. Chambliss

(1973) found dramatic differences in how two gangs, one middle class and one lower class, were perceived by their community. The middle class "Saints" were less visible, had a more acceptable demeanor, and were subject to less community and police hostility than the "Roughnecks," the lower class gang. The "Roughnecks" received more negative community response even though they were involved in about the same amount of delinquent activity as the "Saints." Chambliss concluded that subjective assessments are important in defining gangs and gang activities.

Klein (1971) noted that the public nature of gangs and gang activity makes it difficult for gangs and members to back down from insults and attacks by individuals and members of other gangs. The desire and need to convey a tough image is important to the gang's status in the community. One relationship between the gang and the community is thus for the gang to reinforce and perpetuate its tough image so that it has status in the community. Gangs talk tough, dress tough, and otherwise behave in ways that reinforce the image of toughness.

Another relationship between gangs and the community is that the community may contribute to the gang's group cohesion (Klein and Crawford 1968; Yablonsky 1970). The more the community reacts to the gang and takes actions to undercut it, the more the gang solidifies into a cohesive group, becoming stronger in the face of adversity. Klein and Crawford (1967) proposed that eliminating external forces which contribute to gang cohesion may help reduce the gang problem and may even lead, at least temporarily, to the elimination of gangs (Klein 1995a; see discussion in Chapter 10). Gangs, they believe, are internally unstable and tend to break apart when external threats decline.

Some current research suggests that communities may pass through a series of stages in their relationship to gangs. The initial stage may be official denial, in which officials deny that gangs are present in their jurisdictions. Denial of the existence of gang problems by officials is well documented in the literature (Takata and Zevitz 1990). This was a pattern observed by Huff (1989) in his study of gangs in Cincinnati and Cleveland. Officials fear that acknowledging that gangs exist may influence business and industry to locate elsewhere, and politicians fear that the existence of gangs will be taken as evidence that they have lost control in the community. Huff (1989) asserts that denial of the existence of a gang problem may facilitate gang activity, by leading the community to avoid action and allowing the gangs to operate freely. In a similar vein, there is some evidence that school officials may deny the existence of gangs to protect the image of their schools. It should be noted that American society may have reached a point where denial of gangs is no longer a significant pattern. A recent survey of prosecutors found that 80 percent of respondents from major U.S. cities acknowledged a gang problem in their jurisdictions (Johnson, Webster, and Connors 1995). On the other hand, a city gang survey by Klein (1995a) suggested that in 40 percent of the cities surveyed, the initial response of the police departments to the emergence of gangs was to deny their presence in the city.

As gangs grow and gang incidents increase, the press and the community may realize that the community has a gang problem. This realization may lead to increased pressure on officials to do something about the gangs. Communities may begin to take actions such as holding community workshops, gang education programs, recreation programs for youths, and street patrols by parents and other citizens.

As random violence occurs and people other than gang members are victimized, the community may become less tolerant of gangs. The amount of publicity over gangs may increase, and officials may find it increasingly difficult to ignore gangs. As long as violence is restricted to gang members and poor youths, public outcry other than by those directly affected by gangs is not likely to be substantial. Miller (1977) noted that some officials and the public may view gang warfare cynically, and hope that the gangs kill each other off. As innocent people who are not involved with gangs also become victimized in suburban and affluent areas, public outrage and calls for action are likely to occur.

Once public outcry becomes sufficient to warrant a public response, officials are likely to become vocal about all they are doing to curb the gang problem. Officials publicly acknowledge that the gang problem exists and state their concern over the problem and their intention to take action. This leads to greater emphasis by law enforcement agencies on the gang problem. Budgets may change to reflect official concern about gangs, and schools, community action groups, and police all become involved in curbing the gangs. Aggressive behavior toward gangs and police crackdowns may backfire as gang youths become more cohesive in the face of the external threat (Huff 1989).

Another interface between the gang and the community is the relationship of gangs to the local schools (Dolan and Finney 1984; Huff 1989; Miller 1977; Stover 1986). Gangs are known to disrupt schools and can prove to be serious threats to students and staff members (Stover 1986).

Assaults, extortion, vandalism, gang wars, drug sales, and other illegal acts occur when gangs are active in the schools. Miller (1977) had documented cases of gangs demanding payment from students for protection or for use of school facilities. School officials may either deny that there is a gang problem or may take action by increasing security guards and cracking down on gang members. Locking doors and stricter security measures as well as anti-gang education are typical responses to school-based gang problems. Gang affiliations, such as wearing gang colors, has been prohibited in some schools in Los Angeles and other cities, with some reported success. School officials also have worked with parents and youths to make schools "gang-free zones" (Stover 1986).

The role of the mass media is important in understanding gangs and their relationships with the community. Hollywood and other sources of mass media have done much to shape our perceptions of gangs. In the decades since the 1950s, images of gangs have emerged from movies such as *The Outsiders, Colors, The Lords of Flatbush, West Side Story, Rumblefish,* and *The Wild Ones.* Another gang movie, *American Me,* portrayed an account of one gang member's experiences in a youth and prison gang in California. Some, such as Marlon Brando's leather-jacketed character from *The Wild Ones,* have created perceptions and stereotypes at the international level. More recently, the movie *Colors* caused considerable controversy, with some critics arguing that it glorified gang violence, and others believing that the violence in the film showed the horrors of gang warfare. Gang violence occurred at some showings of *Boyz 'n the Hood,* a movie with an anti-gang message, but one that attracted gang members as viewers. The violence that occurred may have been attributable not to the movie itself, but to the proximity of members of competing gangs as moviegoers.

Law enforcement agencies have become more aware of the important role of the mass media in affecting public opinion. Some researchers have suggested that gang behavior is played up by the police to maintain control of community resources (Takagi and Platt 1978; Zatz 1983). Law enforcement agencies, however, have sometimes been reluctant to release the names of gangs involved in homicides and other illegal acts, in order to avoid glorifying the gangs and contributing to their reputations in the community (Yablonsky 1988). In addition, some officials believe that naming gangs in press reports of gang violence may encourage gang rivalries and attempts at revenge.

CONCLUSION

Research on gangs presents us with a blurred picture, blurred because of the paucity of good information on gangs at both the national and the local level. Individual studies of gangs give us depth and richness of description that allow us something akin to an inside view of the workings of individual gangs, or of gangs of a particular ethnicity, within a narrowly defined area, but they give us little information about the extent of gang membership and activity. Official sources, too, give us a biased and inconsistent picture, not least of all because definitions of what constitutes a gang or gang activity may vary from one jurisdiction to another, and within one jurisdiction from one time to another. The best available evidence suggests that gangs are disproportionately drawn from the lower classes and ethnic minorities, but this may at least in part reflect how officials and the communities react differently to misbehaving groups of lower class minority youths and middle class white youths, as suggested by Chambliss' (1973) study of the Saints and the Roughnecks.

Most research on gangs consistently has found that gang members spend most of their time in non-delinquent activities (See Hagedorn 1988; Jankowski 1991; Klein 1971). However, the nature of gang activity appears to have changed somewhat over time, and there is evidence that gang violence and gang involvement in drug use and the sale of drugs has increased in the past decade. This evidence will be reviewed in the next chapter. Perhaps the most striking facet of our picture of gangs is the variability of gangs in their structure, their leadership, and in the way they are perceived and reacted to by the press and the community. Chapters 5 and 6 will further document that diversity within a broader historical and international context.

CHAPTER NOTES

[1]Horowitz (1990) suggested that it may not be desirable to have a consensus on the definition of juvenile gangs. Instead, the existence of divergent definitions may promote the exploration of diverse and distinct aspects of gang behavior. Goldstein (1991:3) takes a similar position, arguing that there "is not, nor should there be, a single, acceptable definition of gang. . . . " Ball and Curry (1995) discuss the different possible approaches to defining gangs, and note the difficulty of arriving at a consensus on any single definition. In discussing street gangs, Klein (1995a) eschews definition in favor of description. Rather than avoiding the difficulties of definition, it may be more appropriate to suggest first that the absence of consensus on what constitutes a gang promotes a

broader range of research that can be subsumed under the umbrella of gang research, and second that diversity in research could just as easily be encouraged with a consensus on definitions of gangs plus an interest in studying non-gang, group crime and delinquency.

We should also note at this point that we use the terms "juvenile" gang and "youth" gang interchangeably throughout this book. The two terms are sometimes used separately to distinguish gangs in which the oldest members are adolescents ("juvenile") and gangs in which there are some young adults ("youth"). More often, however, the terms as used in the literature on gangs are indistinguishable.

[2]Much of the literature on juvenile gangs takes the existence of subcultures for granted. From some theoretical perspectives, such as Hirschi's (1969) control theory, however, the existence of subcultures is problematic, and the use of the concept of subcultures as an explanation of gang behavior would be regarded as tautological. The need for subcultures as an explanation of gang behavior will be further examined in Chapter 8.

[3]Yablonsky indicates that this description of gang leaders as sociopathic applies specifically to violent gangs, not to all gangs. In social gangs, according to Yablonsky, leadership is likely to be based on popularity and constructive leadership qualities. In delinquent gangs, the leader is usually the most effective criminal, the best organizer and planner of criminal activities.

Chapter 2

JUVENILE GANG VIOLENCE

In a six-day period in Omaha, Nebraska in the summer of 1990, five people were gunned down in apparent gang related shootings. The shootings were indiscriminate, and there is evidence that they were undertaken for no more reason than meeting one expectation associated with dangerous gangs: go out and find someone to hurt, even kill, if necessary and feasible.

On the evening of July 31, 1990, an 18-year-old, African American male was shot in the chest with a .25 caliber handgun in what police believed to be an attempt by the youth and other youths to intimidate a 21-year-old street pedestrian. Police reports indicate that the youth was one of several teenagers who accused the man of belonging to the Bloods street gang. A fight between these youths and the pedestrian ensued, and the youth was accidentally shot by one of the other youths who had approached the intended victim.

The youth was fortunate: he lived. Another victim was not as fortunate. On August 1, 1990, just one day after the first youth was shot, a 37-year-old man was shot in the chest with a .22 caliber rifle and was killed instantly. The man was apparently indirectly involved in a dispute involving a friend. As the victim approached a car whose driver had called out to him, the assailant opened fire, killing the man.

On September 17, 1995, a car full of passengers returning home from a barbecue accidentally took a wrong turn onto a dead-end street in the Cypress Park section of Los Angeles. Without any provocation, a local Hispanic gang opened fire on the car and riddled it with bullets as it tried to escape from the ambush. A 3-year-old girl was killed and her 2-year-old brother sitting in his infant seat was wounded along with the driver of the car. The area is known for its gang battles among Hispanic gangs. The gang members could clearly see that the passengers were not rival gang members and included non-threatening small children. This event struck the nation as an act of ruthless and senseless violence.

Gang violence has increasingly become an important component of

33

our perceptions of juvenile gangs. Some authorities have even proposed that violence is at the core of understanding gangs (Sanders, 1994). There is some justification for this, because studies have found that gang members are disproportionately involved in the commission of violent offenses (Spergel 1990). Media reports of drive-by shootings of gang members by rival gang members (e.g., *New York Times,* April 4, 1988) or of former gang members by members of the same gang (e.g., *Boulder Daily Camera,* March 29, 1991) have become almost commonplace in large metropolitan areas. Fifteen years ago, Miller (1975) wrote, "The amount of lethal violence currently directed by youth gangs in major cities both against one another and against the general public is without precedent." For many people, this observation may appear to be even truer today than it was in 1975. Klein and Maxson (1989), in their study of homicide rates, concluded that gang violence is a more serious problem today than it has been in the past.

The nature of gang violence has evolved from small-scale confrontations and the rare but impressive large scale "rumbles" of the 1950s and 1960s into the more frequent and more heavily armed guerrilla forays, gang-bangs, and drive-by shootings of the 1980s and 1990s. Smaller, mobile groups with automobiles for transportation have become more common in gang violence. The press has attributed murders to gang violence or mistaken gang affiliation with increasing frequency. For example, in 1988, a Denver youth was shot to death while he rode his bicycle because the baseball cap he was wearing was the color used to identify one of two local rival gangs. Both the press and the entertainment industry may have contributed to the public's fear and apprehension about gang violence.

This chapter will cover gang violence from primarily an empirical-research perspective. The emphasis of all discussions will be on what the data say about the nature of juvenile gang violence. Juvenile gang violence has been a topic of study for over 50 years (Thrasher 1936; Shaw and McKay 1943; Whyte 1943; Karacki and Toby 1962; Miller 1962, 1976, 1980; Yablonsky 1962; Werthman and Piliavin 1967; Klein 1968, 1971; Klein and Maxson 1983; Maxson, Gordon, and Klein 1985; Klein, Gordon, and Maxson 1986; Curry and Spergel 1988; Sanders 1994). Researchers who have studied juvenile gang violence have emphasized different aspects of this phenomenon, such as the severity of the violence engaged in by gang members (Thrasher 1936; Whyte 1943; Klein 1971; Block 1985; Camp and Camp 1985) and trends in rates of violence attributable to juvenile gangs (Miller 1975; Stover 1986; Klein and Maxson 1989; Spergel 1990).

GANG VERSUS NON–GANG VIOLENCE

Differences in the rates of violence between gangs and groups other than gangs have been documented over time. Data have pointed to the greater involvement of gangs in serious violent acts (Klein and Myerhoff 1967; Cohen 1969; Friedman, Mann, and Friedman 1975; Tracy 1981, 1982, 1987; Maxson, Gordon, and Klein 1985; Klein, Gordon, and Maxson 1986; Rand 1987). Not only has the research consistently revealed that gang members are more violent than non-gang participants, but studies have also suggested that after incarceration gang members continue in careers of violence (Camp and Camp 1985). The Camps tracked the careers of 250 randomly selected gang members from the California prison system, and reported that after release nearly 80 percent (N = 195) had been rearrested, many for violent acts, including 24 arrests for murder.

In a study of homicides in Los Angeles, Maxson, Gordon, and Klein (1985) were able to differentiate between gang-related and non-gang homicide. Using data from the Los Angeles Police Department (LAPD) and the Los Angeles Sheriffs Department (LASD) the authors found that gangs were more likely to engage in homicides, and that two critical variables distinguishing gang from non-gang homicides were setting variables (where the offense took place, in this case usually in a public setting) and that the murders were generally associated with other offenses, such as burglaries. They found that gang homicides were more visible than non-gang homicides (a phenomenon that could result in higher probability of arrest and correspondingly higher arrest rates for gang homicides than for non-gang homicides) and more violent than non-gang homicides. A major difference between the findings from the two law enforcement organizations was the lower number of white victims in the LASD data. This led the authors to conclude that participant variables took precedence over all other influences on the murder rates for gangs and groups other than gangs.

In yet another study of the differences between gang and non-gang violence, Klein, Gordon, and Maxson (1986) studied the effects of police investigative procedures on the rates of gang-related homicides. They reported that the Philadelphia and Chicago police departments both used a restricted definition of gang homicides, limiting it to homicides involving gang members as both assailants and victims, or one in which there is a clear gang motive. In addition, the Philadelphia definition focused only on high profile gangs. The definition employed by the Los Angeles police and sheriff's departments is more broad in nature, and does involve violent acts committed against the general public. Given this approach, if a cab driver is assaulted by a juvenile gang it is recognized as an act of gang violence in Los Angeles, but not in either Philadelphia or Chicago.

The authors examined the gang and non-gang related homicide reporting practices of the Los Angeles Police Department (LAPD) and the Los Angeles Sheriffs Department (LASD) in an attempt to discover if the practices impacted the rates of murders associated with juvenile gangs. As they had done in previous research, Klein, Gordon, and Maxson used three categories of variables to study the effects of reporting on official rates of homicides: setting variables, such as location, if the murder was committed from an automobile, and the type of weapon used; offense characteristics, which included the issue of multiple offenses in the act of murder, and participant characteristics, such as the relationship between victim and assailant and if the victim was affiliated with a juvenile gang. These socially-oriented variables were then compared with the reporting practices of the LAPD and the LASD to ascertain which had the greatest impact on gang and non-gang homicide rates. Based on the application of these factors to the reporting practices of the two law enforcement organizations, the authors found that participant and setting variables were far more significant in the designation of gang-related homicides than the definitions used by the LAPD and the LASD. In other words, the official reporting policies used by the police organizations did not contribute to differences in official rates of gang and non-gang homicides.

These findings are supported by other studies that also reported the influence of non-procedural considerations on the differences in gang and non-gang violence. Friedman, Mann, and Friedman (1975) found that the rates of violent and non-violent crimes of gangs were greater than that for groups other than gangs, and that gangs engaged more frequently in substance abuse and truancy. Based on the use of official police data and self-report scales, Tracy (1987) reported higher average seriousness of offense scores for gangs. Bailey and Unnithan (1994), using a sample of all homicides known to police in California in 1989 found some support for gang homicides being different from non-gang homicides. They found that for homicides the age of gang perpetrators and victims tended to be younger than non-gang members. Gang homicides also involved more suspects, and perpetrators who had no prior contact with the victim. Gang homicides were in more public locations and firearms were more likely to be present during the crime than non-gang homicides.

In a study of gang and non-gang delinquency rates in Chicago, Spergel and Curry (1988) found that patterns of social disorganization had a major impact on the differences in the rates of gang and non-gang homicides. Using gang homicide rates, percentage of residents living below the poverty level, delinquency and unemployment data, and mortgage investment per dwelling as indicators of the quality of life, the authors found that ethnic groups with the highest rates of social disorganization had the greatest numbers of gang-related homicides. More specifically, Hispanic gangs were reported to have the highest rates of gang homicides. Spergel and Curry attributed this finding to the relative newness of Hispanics to Chicago. Their research confirmed the findings of previous studies, that gang violence is a far more extensive problem than violence by non-gang participants. In summary, the data strongly supported the notion that gang are more violent than other types of teenage social groups, and this holds true for juvenile gangs of different ethnic and racial backgrounds.

TRENDS IN JUVENILE GANG VIOLENCE

One of the most important questions facing gang researchers is "is juvenile gang violence on an increase, and if so what is the nature of the violence that gang members are involved with?" In the study of homicides committed by gang members, several authors have reported increases in both the numbers and rates of murders committed by juvenile gangs. Klein and Maxson (1989) have suggested that serious gang violence is on an increase, and Genelin (1989) has reported that in 1989 in Los Angeles County there were 515 gang-related homicides, up from 387 in 1987.

Although most students of gang violence report alarming figures concerning it, there isn't always total agreement on the question of trends in violence committed by juvenile gangs. For example, Spergel (1990) reported fluctuations in gang-related homicides in Chicago, Illinois, with the peak year occurring in 1981 when there were 84 gang reported homicides. Based on official statistics, Spergel (1990) reported sharp decreases in gang homicides from 1975 to 1990 for the cities of New York and Philadelphia. Other data reported by Spergel are also indicative of the variations in gang violence, not only over time, but also from one city to another.

The belief that gangs are more violent today than in the past may be a consequence of a number of factors. Klein and Maxson have suggested the perception of greater gang violence may be connected to more intense efforts on behalf of the police to curtail gang activities and that the greater number of gangs in our society may account for the belief that gangs are more violent (1990). In addition, Horowitz (1983) has reported that unplanned and spontaneous gang shootings are more common today, and Maxson, Gordon, and Klein (1985) have suggested that the advent of the older gang member is related to the use of more violent weapons among juvenile gangs.

It is important to exercise caution when using official measures of gang violence, as noted earlier in this chapter. Definitions of "gang-related" homicides differ between jurisdictions, for example, between Los Angeles and Chicago (Spergel 1989). Definitions of what constitutes a gang-related crime may also vary over time. The great attention given to gang violence by the media, coupled with the high profile types of crimes committed by juvenile gangs, such as drug offenses and drive-by shootings, has certainly made it appear that juvenile gangs are more violent than ever. National data on violent crimes, however, raise questions about whether the media images accurately reflect real trends in gang violence.

National Data on Trends in Violent Crime

Data from Bastian (1993) indicate that the evidence for increases in violent behavior attributable to gangs is mixed at best. National Crime Survey data indicate that violent crime rates have fluctuated during the past decade, and the rates of violence for the crimes of rape, robbery, and aggravated assault in 1992 were down 9 percent from their peak in 1981. Although rates of violent crime have increased over time according to Federal Bureau of Investigation (FBI) Uniform Crime Reports (UCR) of crimes known to the police, victimization data from the National Crime Survey (NCS) show fluctuation with no clear trend. This is illustrated in Figure 2.1. There are three series in Figure 2.1. "UCR" refers to crimes known to the police according to the Federal Bureau of Investigation's

(FBI) Uniform Crime Reports (UCR). This measure of crimes known to police officials is taken from the FBI (1993). "NCS" refers to the National Crime Survey, later renamed the National Crime Victimization Survey. NCS data span the period from 1973 to 1992, during which it was renamed the National Crime Victimization Survey. In 1992, the revised National Crime Victimization Survey (NCVS) began publishing data, and in 1993, data from the redesigned survey completely replaced data from the old design. The data from the new design are represented as "NCVS" in Figure 2.1. Note that the rates of violent crime indicated by data from the new design are higher than the rates suggested by the old design, by an amount about half as large as the amount by which the old NCS data exceeded the UCR data in their estimates of violent crime.[1] If the new rates are valid, they suggest that the old NCS design substantially underestimated the amount of violent crime in the United States.

Figure 2.1 indicates two important differences between the information provided by FBI Uniform Crime Report data and National Crime Survey victimization data. First, the rate of violent crimes is much higher according to victimization data than to Uniform Crime Report data in every year. This is because the National Crime Survey includes reports on crimes that have been committed, but have never been reported to the police. This is true despite the fact that the Uniform Crime Reports include data on homicides, but the National Crime Survey data do not. There are other technical reasons for differences between UCR and NCS data, as detailed in O'Brien (1985) and Menard and Covey (1988). In general, it is probable that the NCS victimization data provide a more complete accounting of violent crimes than the UCR data. The exception to this generalization is the crime of homicide, which is discussed in more detail below.

The second point to be noted about the difference in the data on crimes known to the police and victimizations reported in the National Crime Survey is that the trends in the two series are quite different. Uniform Crime Report data indicate a fairly consistent increase over time in the rate of violent crimes known to the police. National Crime Survey data indicate more fluctuation, but a general downward trend in violent crime in the 1980s. Together, these trends indicate that if juveniles in general, and juvenile gangs in particular, are committing violent crimes more frequently than in the past, then others (adults, non-gang members) are committing violent crimes *less* frequently than before. Either the commission of crime has been *displaced* to juvenile gang

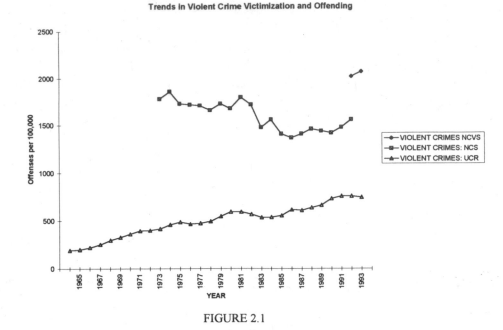

FIGURE 2.1

members, or juvenile gang members were really committing violent crimes no more frequently in the 1980s than they were before. If the latter is true, it suggests that the plague of juvenile gang violence is largely a creation of the press and perhaps of some official agencies, who are just paying more attention to the juvenile gang violence that has been going on for a long time.

In contrast to other crimes of violence, homicides are fairly completely covered in the FBI Uniform Crime Report statistics (O'Brien 1985). Figure 2.2 shows the trends in the rates of homicides known to the police from 1965 to 1989. Like crimes of violence in general, homicide rates appear to have *declined* during the 1980s, with some increase in the early 1990s, again suggesting that if juvenile gang homicides have in fact increased, then homicides by others must have decreased. From 1965 to 1974, on the other hand, homicide rates did increase substantially. Based on arrest statistics, this increase appears to have been driven by an increase in homicides committed by adults, not homicides committed by juveniles. This is illustrated in Figure 2.3.

In Figure 2.3, rates of homicide arrests are compared for two age groups, under 18 years old (juveniles) and over 18 years old. As the chart indicates, rates of homicide arrests for juveniles have increased, while

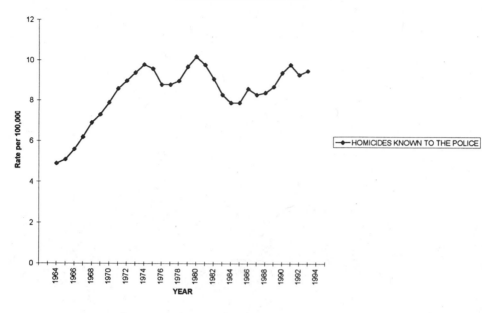

FIGURE 2.2

homicide arrest rates for adults have actually declined from 1980 to the early 1990s. This may either be because the actual rate of committing homicides is increasing for one group and decreasing for the other, because the police are more likely to arrest juvenile suspects for homicide as a result of crackdowns on gangs and other policy changes with regard to juvenile homicide arrests, or because homicides committed by juveniles are increasingly brazen and suspects are increasingly easy to identify, while adult homicide perpetrators are increasingly escaping detection by the police.

Given the gravity of the offense of homicide, it seems improbable that the police are somehow deliberately trying to blame homicides on juveniles. It is quite plausible, as outlined above, that homicides committed by juveniles, particularly gang members, are increasingly public and thus increasingly likely to lead to the identification and arrest of a suspect. A real decline in the rate of homicide committed by adults and an increase in the rate of homicide committed by juveniles cannot be ruled out. Figure 2.4 shows the trend in the ratio of juvenile to adult homicide arrest rates. The increasing trend in the ratio of juvenile to adult homicide arrest rates is a result of the decline in the adult homicide arrest rate, coupled with an increase in juvenile homicide arrest rates.

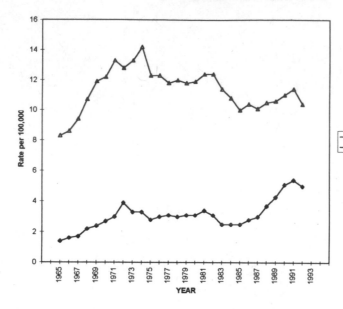

FIGURE 2.3

The net result is a dramatic increase in the ratio of juvenile to adult homicide arrest rates beginning in the mid-1980s.

It appears plausible, then, that juvenile violence in general and juvenile gang violence in particular may be increasing, but only if we accept the proposition that adult violence is, at the same time, declining. Moreover, adult violence must be declining about as rapidly as juvenile violence is increasing, in order to produce the generally stable to declining rates of violence indicated in the National Crime Survey data. From a consideration of adult and juvenile homicide arrest rates, this appears to be plausible. Another possibility is that juvenile gang violence is increasing, but only in central cities. Again, in order to maintain consistency with national statistics, this would suggest a countervailing decline in violence in rural and suburban areas. Caution must be made when giving more affirmative answers to the question since the issue of juvenile gang violence is so complex, and is affected by methodological as well as legal variables.

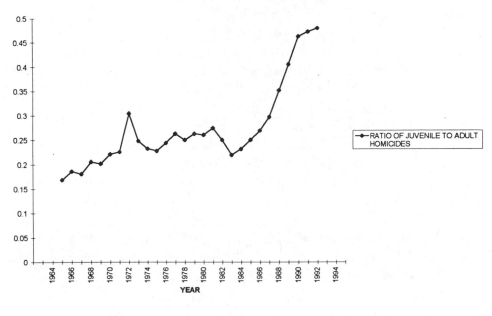

FIGURE 2.4

Estimating Recent Rates of Gang Violence

One crude estimate of the contribution of juvenile gangs to the overall level of violence is the proportion of serious violent offenses (homicides, aggravated assaults, robberies, and rapes, as contrasted with minor assaults) perpetrated by two or more juveniles. Not all offenses committed by two or more juveniles are gang-related; many may involve law violating youth groups rather than juvenile gangs. At the same time, some offenses committed by a single juvenile may represent actions taken by a single gang member, either representing the gang, or on her or his own behalf. (Note that in some jurisdictions, as discussed above, both would be classified as gang-related offenses, while in others, only the first would be.) Single-offender, gang-related offenses and multiple-offender non-gang offenses therefore tend to produce errors in opposite directions, and at least partially cancel each other out, when we use the proportion of offenses committed by two or more juveniles as an estimate of juvenile gang-related violence.

Based on 1991 National Crime Victimization Survey data, Snyder and Sickmund (1995) reported that 6 percent of all serious violent offenses in

1991 were committed by groups that victims reported as consisting of two or more juveniles. An additional 8 percent were committed by groups that included at least one juvenile and at least one adult, and 11 percent were committed by juveniles acting alone. The composition of the group of perpetrators varied considerably by the age of the victim: only 3 percent of adult victims, but 14 percent of juvenile victims, reported being victimized by a group of two or more adults. Three-fourths of all victims reported either a single adult perpetrator (53%) or two or more adult perpetrators (22%). Based on these data, it appears reasonable to estimate the proportion of serious violent offenses committed by juvenile gangs to be about 5–15 percent of the total number of serious violent offenses. The true percentage is probably closer to 5 than to 15.

Arrest data, also reported in Snyder and Sickmund (1995), indicate that approximately 10 percent of all crimes cleared by arrest in 1991 were attributed to juvenile offenders. For violent crimes cleared by arrest, 8 percent of homicides, 11 percent of aggravated assaults, and 13 percent each of rapes and robberies were attributed to juveniles. Again, it is not clear what proportion could be attributed to gangs as opposed to law violating youth groups or to individuals acting alone (Howell 1994). It is also unclear whether juvenile offenders have a higher (as seems likely) or lower risk of apprehension than adult offenders. Nevertheless, to the extent that arrest statistics tell us anything about actual behavior, they too suggest 5–15 percent as a reasonable estimate of the proportion of violent offenses attributable to juvenile gangs, again with the lower estimate more likely than the upper estimate to reflect the true level of juvenile gang involvement in serious violent offending at the national level.

Even more variation may be evident at the local level. Using official statistics on homicide (a crime for which official statistics tend to be more valid than for other offenses), Spergel noted that in 1987, gang homicides accounted for over one-fourth of all homicides that were reported in Los Angeles, but only comprised 7 percent of all murders in Chicago in that year. In addition, in 1987, gang felonious assaults were 11 percent of total serious assaults in Los Angeles, but were less than 5 percent of all felonious assaults in Chicago. Spergel (1990) reports the same pattern for robberies, with gang related robberies accounting for just under 7 percent of all such offenses in Los Angeles, but only one percent in Chicago. The contrast between Los Angeles and Chicago further illustrates the range of uncertainty in estimating the contributions of gangs to violent crime, but although the Los Angeles rates (which Klein 1995a suggests are probably among the highest in the U.S.) are higher than those suggested above, the rates for Chicago fall nicely within the 5–15 percent range. Allowing for cities with no juvenile gangs, and for cities in which gangs may contribute even less to the violent crime rate than in Chicago, Spergel's data are consistent with the national data on the contribution of gangs to violent crime in the United States.

GANG VIOLENCE: WEAPONS AND VICTIMS

The availability and use of guns by gangs has received increased attention over the past 20 years (Callahan and Rivara 1992; O'Donnell 1995). Victimization data indicate youth are increasingly using firearms and the rates of firearm related homicide in urban areas are dramatically increasing (Lizotte et al. 1994; Wintemute 1987). Between 1933 and 1982, one estimate shows that one million people had died in the United States due to firearm injuries (Wintemute 1987). Firearm death rates among youths using handguns are especially high (O'Donnell 1995). During the teen years, 72 percent of homicides for children 10 to 14 years old and 85 percent of homicides for adolescents 15 to 19 years old involved firearms. African American males have a firearm-related homicide victimization rate nine times higher than whites (Centers for Disease Control and Prevention 1992), and homicides involving firearms have been the leading cause of death for African American males 15–19 years old since 1969 (Snyder and Sickmund 1995:26). From 1979 to 1989, the rate of firearm homicide deaths more than doubled, from 40 to 85 per 100,000, for African American males; this rate is 6.5 times higher in metropolitan than in non-metropolitan areas. Block and Block (1993:7) found that Latino men had homicide rates comparable to African American men, and that most gang violence occurred between gangs of the same ethnicity.

One of the most important studies on gang violence was undertaken in the mid-1970s by Walter Miller and offers a broad perspective on the nature of juvenile gang violence. Miller undertook a nationwide study of juvenile gangs in twelve major American cities and reported the extent of juvenile gangs ranged from a low of 760 gangs and 28,500 gang members to a high of 2,700 gangs and 81,500 members. Additionally, the age range of gang members was 12 to 21 years of age, and members tended to reside in low rent or ghetto districts and were predominantly non-white (1975).

Of particular significance to this chapter are Miller's findings concerning the types of gang violence and who were most likely to be its victims. Miller identified four types of gang violence, beginning with normal gang violence, or inter-gang violence. Miller notes that this is the type of gang violence that receives the least amount of attention from the police. Miller's second type of gang violence involves the victimization of non-gang members from the same social backgrounds as the gang members. The characteristic police response in this case may be that the incident is unfortunate, but a more active police response may not be forthcoming. Miller's last two types of gang violence involve acts against the property of the general public, which receives both media and public attention, and violence against middle class citizens, especially women and children, which is met with strong action by the authorities.

In his study of gang violence, Miller narrowed his focus to four large American cities, Los Angeles, New York, Chicago, and Philadelphia, with the purpose of identifying the most common victims of gang violence. His data revealed that gang members themselves were the most likely target of juvenile gangs, with the rumble or the inter-gang fight the typical incident leading to the violence. However, Miller reported that the most common non-gang victims of gang violence were, as alluded to previously, women and children. Miller also identified the types of weapons that were confiscated by the police from juvenile gangs. These weapons included rifles of all calibers; shotguns of all calibers; handguns of all calibers; semi-automatic rifles, some of which were converted to automatic rifles; home made mortars; Molotov cocktails; and pipe bombs.

Horowitz and Schwartz (1974), during the mid-1970s, reached conclusions similar to Miller. They observed an increase in deadly gang conflicts and attributed this change to greater reliance on guns by gang members. A decade later Spergel (1983; 1984) reaffirmed earlier research with his conclusions that gangs were using more sophisticated weapons. More recent research by Tromanhauser (1994) reports that gang members are more likely to report carrying guns for protection. Tromanhauser's (1994) survey of youth in jail found street gang members reported they were three times as likely to carry guns, five times more likely to fire a gun during their commission of crimes, and seven times as likely to use assault rifles during the commission of a crime than their non-gang counterparts. Tromanhauser also found that gang members reported they carried or used weapons at an earlier age and continued to carry or use them more frequently as they aged. Callahan and Rivara's (1992) self-report study of high school students also found a strong association between gang membership and gang membership.

Block and Block (1993) found that street gangs in Chicago were becoming increasingly lethal and attributed this to their increased reliance on guns. They found an increase in the use of guns by gangs committing violent offenses. In almost all gang homicides, the weapon used was a gun. In addition, their research found that the proportion of murder weapons that were automatic or semi-automatic rose from 22 to 31 percent and large-caliber guns from 13 to 39 percent from 1987 to 1990. They concluded the almost the entire increase in the number of street gang-motivated homicides appeared to be attributed to the use of more deadly firearms.

Karacki and Toby's (1962) study of a middle-class gang, the Dukes, found that even this middle class gang was characterized by violence. Violence has reportedly been used by some gangs to coerce others into joining the gangs (Friedman et al. 1976). Writing years before the current and increased use of lethal automatic and semi-automatic weapons (MAC-10s, MAC-11s, 9mms, Uzis, and AK-47s), Horowitz and Schwartz (1974) proposed that greater use of guns by gangs resulted in more lethal encounters. Miller (1975; 1977) similarly concluded that gangs in the 1970s had begun to use more sophisticated weapons than had been the case in the past.

The increased accessibility, ownership, and use of firearms and in particular handguns by gang members indicated in much of the research is reflective of gun use patterns among youth in general (See Callahan and Rivara 1992; Prothrow-Stith and Weissmann 1991). Nationally, about 20 percent of high school students say that they carry weapons, but few (about 5%) carry guns, mostly handguns (Snyder and Sickmund 1995:52). Rates of carrying firearms were higher among males, ethnic minorities, and inner-city students. In a sample of youthful prisoners and 1,653 students in 10 inner city public high schools in 5 large cities, Wright et al. (1992; Sheley and Wright 1993) found that 83 percent of the inmates reported that they owned a gun just prior to confinement, and 22 percent of students owned a gun at the time of the survey; 55 percent of the inmates carried a gun at least most of the time in the year or two prior to incarceration, and 35 percent of students reported carrying guns regularly or occasionally; and most of the inmates had committed crimes with their guns (63%), obtained a gun for protection (74%), and had fired at someone at least once (about three-fourths).

Firebombings and Connections between Juvenile and Adult Gangs

Miller's study of gang violence included Molotov cocktails as one of the weapons used in gang assaults. Recently there have been reports of increased use of firebombings, using gasoline-soaked rags stuffed into bottles, as a method of attack in several cities, including Los Angeles, Denver, and Houston (Callahan 1996; Cortez and Robinson 1996; Fong et al. 1996). Denver gangs have allegedly been involved in over 50 firebombings in 1995, primarily mutual retaliation between two rival gangs. Journalistic accounts have suggested that difficulty in obtaining firearms, plus imitation of Los Angeles gangs, may be two of the reasons for the use of firebombings instead of drive-by shootings as the method of attack.

Interestingly, the reports of firebombings in some cities have involved linkages between juvenile gangs and adult gang members, but in contrasting ways. In Los Angeles, gang-related firebombings increased after the Mexican Mafia allegedly "outlawed" drive-by shootings among Latino street gang members because of the number of innocent bystanders being killed. According to Gilbert Sanchez, director of the Gang Violence Bridging Project at California State University—Los Angeles, " ... The punishment in Los Angeles was steep. If word spread that Latino gang members were involved in a drive-by, mobsters would come after them personally and settle the score" (Callahan 1996:1A). Here, the firebombings are an indirect result of pressure from adult gang members.

A more direct encouragement of firebombing by juvenile gangs is suggested by Fong et al. (1996:122) for Houston. They suggest an even closer linkage between the actions of the juvenile gang members and adult prison gang members.

> Recent police intelligence indicates that prison gangs are intensifying their efforts to carry out criminal activities on the streets by using juvenile street gangs. There are several reasons for this new development. First, juvenile street gangs are more

organized when compared to individual associates, want-to-be's, and sympathizers, thus, enabling them to carry out their activities more effectively. In one recent incident in Houston, a juvenile street gang was ordered by the Texas Syndicate to burn down the house of a person on a gang hit list. The fire killed the target as well as four other innocent victims (TDCJ [Texas Department of Criminal Justice] intelligence record). Second, prison gang members are aware that juveniles are more likely to be sanctioned by juvenile courts or, if bound over to adult courts, may receive more lenient sentences. Third, law enforcement officials do not scrutinize juvenile gang activities as closely as adult gangs. Fourth, juvenile gangs provide an abundant resource base upon which prison gangs can recruit their future members."

It remains to be seen whether firebombings will become a more general method of attack in cities other than Denver, Houston, and Los Angeles, and if so, whether involvement with adult gangs, similar to the patterns in Houston and Los Angeles, emerge elsewhere.

JUVENILE GANGS, DRUGS, AND VIOLENCE

The 1980s were marked by a number of violent crimes that were reported to be associated with juvenile gangs and drugs. The rise in media interest in the "Crips" and the "Bloods" and their alleged involvement in the illegal sale of hard drugs fueled the concerns and fears that juvenile gangs were becoming more dangerous as a result of their role in the illegal drug market. The fact that violent crimes were frequently linked to drug dealing juvenile gangs only facilitated beliefs that juvenile gangs had emerged as some of the most feared criminal organizations in American society. Before discussing the relationship of juvenile gangs, drugs, and violence specifically, we turn our attention to a more general issue, and that is the connection between delinquency and drug use.

Box 2.1: The U.S. Attorney General on Drugs and Violence

"Drug trafficking and its inevitable handmaiden of violence are the greatest threats to what I have always called the first civil right of every American—the right to be free from fear in our homes, in our streets, and in our communities." (Dick Thornburgh, Attorney General, The 1991 Crime Summit)

Delinquency and Drug Use

The relationship between delinquency and drug use has been examined in detail (Scott and Wilcox 1965; Hindelang and Weis 1972; Tinklenberg 1973; Dunnette 1975; Jessor 1976; Johnston, O'Malley, and Eveland 1978; Kandel 1975, 1978, 1980; Elliott and Ageton 1976; Gandossy, Williams, Cohen, and Harwood 1980; Dolan and Finney 1984; Elliott and Huizinga 1983, 1984, 1985; White et al. 1987; Huizinga et al. 1989). One of the most widely shared stereotypes is that the use of illegal drugs causes adolescents to engage in delinquent and criminal behaviors. There is disagreement in the literature concerning the actual relationship between the use of illegal substances among teenagers and anti-social behaviors. For example, Goldstein (1985) reported a positive correlation between the use of drugs and violence. However, few authors have been able to link the use of substances, such as marijuana with illegal behaviors (Goode 1970; Elliott and Ageton 1976; Gandossy, et al. 1980; Johnson 1973; Tinklenberg 1974).

Huizinga et al. (1989) used data from the National Youth Survey to further examine the relationship between drug use and juvenile delinquency. One major objective of the study was to discern the causal direction of the relationship between drug use and delinquency by ascertaining which comes first, the use of drugs or delinquency. The results from their research are consistent with many similar studies. The authors reported that in most instances delinquency precedes the use of drugs, and that this held true for both minor delinquency and delinquency of a more serious nature, even including assaults. When causality was clearly indicated in the data it normally involved the influence of drugs on other drugs. Huizinga et al. found that alcohol acts as a cause or precursor of marijuana and polydrug use, and that the onset of the use of marijuana too acted as a precursor to polydrug use. Similarly, Goode (1980), and Kandel (1980) reported that alcohol use among teenagers usually acts as the precursor to the use of other illegal drugs, such as marijuana.

The one exception to the findings concerning causality was that minor offending consistently occurred prior to index offending, or more serious criminality. The authors concluded that reducing the use of drugs among adolescents would probably not have a significant effect on reducing delinquency generally, but they did find that use of "hard" drugs such as heroin, cocaine, hallucinogens, amphetamines, and barbiturates appeared to prolong involvement in illegal behavior, once that behavior had been initiated.

Other studies have echoed the results of the research just discussed. Many authors have simply been unable to isolate drug use as a sufficient cause of delinquency. Even Gandossy et al. (1980) were only able to suggest that a moderate relationship exists between the use of hallucinogenic drugs and violent crimes committed by juveniles. Tinklenberg (1974) reported similar findings for alcohol use and delinquency. Huizinga et al. (1989) have argued that whether or not the use of illegal drugs actually affects delinquency may have more to do with how frequently the drugs are used than with simple prevalence of drug use.

Juvenile Gangs and Drug Trafficking

Juvenile gangs have been suspected of involvement in the distribution and sale of illegal drugs for years, although the earlier research was not able to confirm this without serious reservations. Some authors found limited involvement in drug trafficking by juvenile gangs, but they were unable to substantiate claims that these gangs were more heavily involved in the drug distribution enterprise (Chein et al. 1964; Spergel 1964). In addition to these earlier findings, there were reports that juvenile gangs looked down on drug abusers, and consequently prohibited use among their own gang members. Of particular concern to these gangs were individuals who used and sold heroin, since they were viewed as threats to their own neighborhoods (Spergel 1964; Short and Strodtbeck 1965).

By the late 1970s, the information on the role of juvenile gangs in drug trafficking began to change. Moore (1978) reported minor drug dealing was a method of socializing younger gang members into the overall gang milieu. For older gang members, Moore reported that drug trafficking acted as a source of income and social cohesion for the juvenile gang. Involvement in the selling of drugs was a cement that bound gang members together. Moore also suggested that drug trafficking was more common among gang than non-gang members, a finding also supported by other scholars (Dolan and Finney, 1984; Spergel, 1984).

A number of studies during the 1980's reported the increasing involvement of juvenile gangs in illegal drug trafficking. Hagedorn (1988), in his study of Milwaukee based gangs found that most gang founders and gang members had engaged in the selling of illegal substances. Klein et al. (1988) reported that juvenile gangs in Los Angeles are more heavily involved in selling rock cocaine than are groups other than gangs, although there is evidence that gangs may be less involved than groups other than gangs in trafficking cocaine. Cooper (1987) also found the connection between juvenile gangs and trafficking in rock cocaine. Taylor (1990) suggested that gangs have grown in membership due to the significant amounts of money members could make in drug trafficking (see also Fagan 1989; Padilla 1992). Rodriquez (1993) reported that Hispanic youths as young as 10 years old could make $80 to $100 a day serving as lookouts for drug dealers.

Terry Williams (1989) conducted an extensive ethnographic study of a juvenile gang's involvement in the cocaine trade. Williams study was of a Latino (mostly Dominican) gang (or crew) operating in New York City. Williams found that to some youth, cocaine sales was a safety net when other economic opportunities were not available. Most youth were drawn to cocaine sales because they wanted jobs. Youth were recruited into the trade if they showed promise. The cocaine trade was highly organized with specific roles, commissions, and informal rules. Actual wholesale rates for cocaine were determined by the Colombian drug bosses. Dealers and sellers often worked on consignment. Roles included runners, lookouts, catchers (caught drugs out of windows during drug busts), transporters, baby-sitters (who watched the inventory), mules (carried cocaine), swimmers (swam after drugs dropped off in the harbor) dealers, distributors, suppliers, and sellers. As youth moved up the hierarchy, their commissions increased until they found themselves "behind the scales." Being behind the scales meant that they were the leaders who made the business decisions, such as the size of the profits and levels of commissions. The operation had to be highly mobile to avoid robberies, competitors, and law enforcement. Youth needed to be constantly on the lookout for trouble and violence. Most of the youths in Williams' gang (crew) eventually moved out of the drug trade to adult and legitimate roles in society. In another study, Skolnick et al. (1990) interviewed incarcerated gang members in Northern California and found that gang members did not necessarily organize for the purpose of selling drugs. For cultural gangs, they found that drug sales develops almost as an afterthought due to use by gang members. However, sometimes a different type of gang-like "business organization" did organize primarily around drug sales.

Decker and Van Winkle (1994) report that gang members in St. Louis, Missouri, are heavily involved in drug sales, but that drug sales are seldom well organized. Of the 99 gang members they interviewed, representing 29 gangs (of which 16 claimed affiliation with the Crips and 13 claimed affiliation with the Bloods), approximately equal proportions reported that all gang members were involved in drug sales (27%) as reported that less than half or no gang members were involved in drug sales (24%). About half (49%) of the gang members reported that either half or most of the gang members were involved in drug sales. Over half (58%), however, could not identify any specific roles in selling drugs, suggesting that drug selling by gang members is largely informal and not highly organized. One-third of the gang members reported that the main suppliers of drugs were leaders in the gang, and 59 percent said that selling drugs increased a member's influence in the gang.

In Los Angeles, major local newspapers have reported the relationship of juvenile gangs to drug trafficking. In 1988, The Los Angeles News Service claimed that all 300 African American street gangs were involved in selling drugs, and that a rigid hierarchy existed, with younger gang members acting as the runners in the drug trafficking enterprise. The *Los Angeles Daily News* (1988) also suggested the role of juvenile gangs in drug trafficking by reporting that nearly 400 homicides in Los Angeles in 1987 were linked to juvenile gang drug trafficking.

Reporting of California gang activities by prominent print journalism has not been limited to that state. The *Minneapolis Star* (1988), in an article on the migratory drug trafficking practices of the Crips and the Bloods, claimed that these two juvenile gang organizations have affected most states with their drug selling enterprise, and with this has come a wave of violence necessitating a call for more serious drug laws. Articles such as these are also supported by research that examines the drug/violence connection. Mieczkowski (1986) and Cooper (1987) found evidence of juvenile gang drug trafficking and violence in Detroit, Michigan, with heroin and crack cocaine the two most dangerous substances sold by the gangs.

Chaiken and Johnson (1988) have developed a typology of juvenile gang drug dealers which includes the "lesser predatory" dealers, or the small time drug sellers who are unlikely to be involved in serious criminality; the "losers," or the type of dealer who will become addicted to hard drugs such as heroin and cocaine; and the "winners," recognized by Chaiken and Johnson as the middlemen in the drug distribution network. Of particular interest to their typology is that all three types of drug dealers are drug users themselves, a position that does run contrary to reports that gang members are discouraged from engaging in substance abuse (Fagan 1989; Chin 1990; Waldorf 1993).

Some authors have suggested that gang violence seems to be driven more and more by the economics of drug distribution (Bynum and Thompson 1988; Kleiman and Smith 1990; McKinney 1988). The money made from drug sales can be substantial, especially for youths from low-income communities. McKinney (1988) suggested that youths serving as lookouts for crack houses could earn $200 per week, a lot of money for a 9, 10, or 11 year old. As reported in the California "State Task Force on Youth Gang Violence" (1986) by Sgt. Jackson of the Los Angeles Police Department, "How can you tell a kid who's making $500 a week guarding a rock house that he really ought to be in school or that he ought to be getting up at 4 A.M. every day to ride his bicycle around his neighborhood to deliver the morning papers?" Given the high profits of illegal drug sales, it is easy to understand why the competition for drug markets and control of markets has led some gangs to open gang warfare reminiscent of the Prohibition era. The highly publicized warfare between the Bloods and the Crips in Los Angeles and other cities is evidence of the importance of drugs and sale of drugs to some gangs. Control over territory or turf has clear economic ramifications for many of today's gangs (Yablonsky 1988), and the stakes are high.

Blumstein (1995) has proposed that juveniles have been recruited into the illicit drug trade, partly because they work more cheaply than adults, partly because the sanctions they face are not as severe as the sanctions faced by adults, and partly because they tend to be willing to take greater risks than adults would take. Like other participants in the illicit drug trade, these juveniles tend to carry firearms, particularly handguns, for self-protection. Partly in response to the gun-toting juvenile drug traders, other juveniles arm themselves in self-defense, and guns proliferate in the juvenile population. Finally, because juveniles are less circumspect than adults in their behavior, they are more willing to use guns carelessly or recklessly. This, plus a lack of social skills for settling disputes without violence, leads to the use of guns in situations that in earlier years would have resulted in fistfights instead of gunfights. Thus, according to Blumstein, juvenile participation in the drug trade leads to proliferation of guns among juveniles, which in turn leads to increases in juvenile homicide rates. Although Blumstein does not focus exclusively on gangs, this analysis should be applicable to gang as well as non-gang adolescents.

Some gang research leads us to a different conclusion. In a rev[...] years worth of gang-related homicides in Chicago, Block a[...] (1993) found that few gang motivated homicides were related to dru[...] In one period, out of 288 gang-related homicides occurring from 1987 to 1990, they found that only 8 were tied to drugs. Most gang-motivated homicides were linked to conflicts over territory. This observation parallels that of Klein, Maxson, and Cunningham (1991) in Los Angeles who found a weak relationship between street gangs, drugs, and homicide. In addition, Moore (1991) suggests that the high number of homicides involving the sale of drugs should not be considered gang violence because the motive is competition for money and not traditional gang objectives. Finally, Sanders (1993) observed that gangs like the Crips were violent long before they became involved in cocaine distribution. Drug sales only added to the violence that was already occurring.

Juvenile Gangs and Drug Use

The use of illegal substances among America's teenage population is nothing new to any observer. In a major study of drug abuse among American high school students, Johnston, O'Malley, and Bachman (1986) reported widespread use of various illegal drugs. From 1975 to 1985, the authors found that alcohol was by far the most popular drug used by high school students, with marijuana/hashish and cigarettes the second drugs of choice. Neither cocaine nor heroin was said to have been used with much frequency in the study. Of significance to this research are the sample size and the scope of the research. Over 175,000 high school students were sampled during the 11 years reported here, representing 125 high schools nationwide. The data indicated very little change in the usage and preference patterns over the 11-year period.

Since drug use among teenagers as a general population is not uncommon, then it should come as no surprise that youthful law violators, whether gang members or not, are involved in the use of illegal drugs. The relationship between juvenile gangs and drug use is heavily documented in the literature on juvenile gangs (Campbell 1984; Dolan and Finney 1984; Feldman et al. 1985; Harris 1988; Klein and Maxson 1985). Klein and Maxson reported that Los Angeles police believe that two-thirds of gang violence is now drug related, because gangs are heavily involved in the sale and distribution of drugs. In a systematic study of drugs and gangs, Fagan (1989) found a positive association between drug use and serious violence by gangs. Drug use was wide-spread and violent behavior occurred, but violence was independent of drug use and sales. Serious crimes were committed by gangs regardless of the gang's involvement in sales of drugs. Conflicts over control of drug territories were the only reason for the positive association between gang violence and drugs, according to Fagan.

In their research on drug use and delinquency, Huizinga et al. (1989) reported moderate to high probabilities of having engaged in delinquent acts and using drugs. The chances of committing delinquent acts were greater when associated with alcohol than they were with the presence of marijuana or polydrug use. As reported earlier, their research was unable to establish causal direction between drug use and the commission of delinquent behaviors, but the issue under of concern here is whether or not members of juvenile gangs engage in the use of illegal drugs, as much as this is portrayed in American society.

Feldman et al. (1985) reported that the nature of drug use among Latino gangs in San Francisco varied according to their relationship to violence. The authors developed a typology of these gangs, classifying them as "fighting gangs," "entrepreneurial gangs," and "social gangs." The "fighting gangs" were reported to be occasional drug users, and drug use was said to have a minor relationship to violence. "Entrepreneurial gangs" were more concerned with drug trafficking as a method of attaining money for the purpose of social status, and only occasionally used drugs heavily. Violent behaviors were also only occasionally related to the presence of drugs. Finally, "social gangs" used drugs for strictly recreational purposes, and rarely if ever were involved in fighting or other forms of violence.

There is research that challenges the assumptions that gang members are frequent users of illegal substances. Fagan (1989), in his review of the literature on drugs and gangs, noted that although some gangs are actively involved in drug *sales,* they have strict codes against the use of addictive drugs like heroin by gang members. Mieczkowski's (1986) Detroit-based research found that heroin use by teenage drug runners was prohibited by gang norms, and that violence, along with sanctions that eliminated monetary rewards, were used to discourage gang use of heroin. Although gang members did use other illegal substances, such as cocaine and marijuana for recreational purposes, the abuse of heroin was definitely looked down upon and viewed as a threat to gang stability and security.

Chin's (1986) research on heroin trafficking Chinese juvenile gangs in New York City reported that gang members rejected the use of heroin, and that the gangs had rigid rules that included punishment by violence for using heroin. Cooper's (1987) research on juvenile gangs that were involved in selling crack cocaine in Detroit reported that gang members were prohibited from using drugs, since this was believed to pose a threat to gang economic efficiency, and well as exposing them to the police. These studies are also supported by earlier research that reported strong gang norms prohibiting the use of heroin among gang members. Members found to have used heroin were removed from the gangs, although other drugs, such as marijuana and alcohol, had legitimacy with gang leaders (Spergel, 1964; Short and Strodtbeck, 1965).

More recently, Waldorf (1993) studied gang drug use and sales by interviewing a sample of 300 gang members in San Francisco. He found that African American gang members reported almost universal participation in drug sales, predominantly sales of crack and marijuana. He also found that African American gang members believed that crack use was bad business and was dangerous because it is addictive. Waldorf (1993:5) wrote, "Black gang members tend to avoid injectable drugs (heroin, cocaine and methamphetamines) and psychedelics; they concentrate on alcohol and marijuana and only a small percentage use cocaine and crack." He (1993:5) also found, "Latino gang members use a broader range of drug-alcohol, marijuana, heroin, cocaine, and PCP (Known by the Spanish term "Maton" or killer) and seldom use crack as they consider it a Black drug." Latinos or Hispanics reported selling marijuana, cocaine, and heroin; only a small number reported selling crack. For all ethnic groups, large percentages of marijuana (88.8%), cocaine (64.3%), and heroin (80%) sellers reported they used the drugs they sold. However, only 18.2 percent of crack sellers said they used crack.

The use of drugs by gangs is not necessarily done for strictly utilitarian purposes. Vigil's (1988) study of Chicano gangs in east Los Angeles reported that drug use by gang members contributed to feelings of acceptance and social status among gang members. Other authors too have reported the varying meanings attached to drug use by gang members, noting its role as a source of social cohesion and gang identity (Stumphauzer et al. 1988; Dolan and Finney 1984; Campbell 1984).

Juvenile Gangs, Drugs, and Violence

The relationship of drugs to juvenile gang violence has been researched with increasing frequency in recent years. The greater attention given to gang violence by the media and law enforcement has drawn attention to the connection between drugs use and dealing by gang members, and their role in assaults and homicides.

In a study undertaken in Chicago on the relationship between gang member arrests and drug possession, Bobrowski (1988) found little evidence to support any belief that the presence of drugs contributed to gang violence. His data indicated that drug-related activity was only directly linked with 18 of 4,052 juvenile gang assaults over a year-and-a-half period. Moreover, Bobrowski reported that gang vice activity could only be attributed to two of 82 homicides and three of 362 robberies in that time span.

Research undertaken by Fagan (1988) and by Klein et al. (1988) also failed to demonstrate a clear causal relationship between gang violence and drugs. Fagan's (1988) research on African American and Hispanic juvenile gangs in Chicago, Los Angeles, and San Diego found that juvenile gang violence occurred independent of any connection with drug possession or trafficking, and that when juvenile gangs did engage in violent behaviors this was most likely to be associated with turf and status issues. Fagan (1989) also found that not all gangs were involved in drug trafficking.

Using self-report measures, Fagan interviewed 151 gang members from the three different cities, and was able to develop a typology of gangs that differentiated them on the basis of their relationships to drug use and criminality. Four types of gangs emerged from his data: Type I gangs rarely engaged in delinquency, drug dealing, and drug abuse; Type II gangs were more likely to have been involved in drug use and sales, and limited their delinquency to vandalism; Type III gangs were frequently involved in serious and non-serious delinquent acts, however, they were unlikely to have engaged in drug selling and usage; and Type IV gangs had extensive involvement in delinquencies of all levels of seriousness, as well as drug trafficking and use. Based on his research, Fagan concluded that drug use is widespread among juvenile gangs, but violent crimes did occur without a relationship to drug use or dealing.

The research by Klein, Maxson, and Cunningham (1991) in Los Angeles reported little violent activity in connection with cocaine sale arrests, and the authors also reported that homicides attributed to drugs were more likely to be linked with non-gang than gang activities. The increased sale of crack cocaine was found to be no more than normal drug dealing activity in the neighborhoods, and this occurred with or without the involvement of juvenile gangs. Klein et al. concluded that "The drug/homicide connection . . . is not basically a gang phenomenon." Their findings suggest that the mass media and official law enforcement agencies have overstated the extent to which street gangs have become involved in the drug trade, and the extent to which street gang violence has been motivated by drug involvement.

The research cited is not able to show a direct relationship between drug use, drug dealing, and juvenile gang violence. Spergel (1988) has argued that gang structure tends to break down when gangs become extensively involved in drug use and dealing. The drug enterprise appears to demand a different type of social organization, one that is antithetical to traditional gang objectives and issues. But perhaps the most important implication that comes out of the research is that drug use, dealing, and violence may be more a reality for groups other than gangs than it is for gangs.

CONCLUSION: DRUGS, VIOLENCE, AND JUVENILE GANGS

In 1977, *Time* reported on the "youth crime plague," including increased gang violence, excessive leniency in juvenile court, and the financial and psychological costs of the rapid increase in juvenile delinquency that was occurring at that time. For that period, as for the 1980s, official rates of violent crimes known to police were increasing, as were rates of juvenile arrest. It is undoubtedly true that the absolute number of juvenile crimes was increasing in the 1970s, yet evidence from victimization and self-report surveys (Gold and Reimer 1975; Menard 1987; Paez and Shenk 1983) indicated that rates of illegal behavior were stable or decreasing for all except minor substance use offenses among adolescents, particularly adolescent females (Gold and Reimer 1975). In short, the "youth crime plague" was a creation of the press, aided by selective use of official crime statistics.

It may well have been the case that juvenile delinquency and youth crime were, in fact, increasing both in absolute number of offenses and in rates (number of offenses per 1,000 or 100,000 population) in some areas. If so, however, it appears that rates were going down in other areas, enough to offset the increases, where they occurred. Our review of juvenile gang violence and involvement in drug use and drug sales suggests a similar pattern. Official rates of crimes known to the police and rates of juvenile arrests are on the increase, and many of these crimes and arrests are labeled by police or by the media as gang phenomena. Press reports focus on the innocent victims of gang violence (Carlson 1988; *U.S. News and World Report* 1979) or spectacular finds such as an anti-tank weapon found in a police raid in Chicago (Carney 1986), and conclude that gang violence is increasing (*Newsweek* 1988; *U.S. News and World Report* 1979). At the same time, however, rates of violent crime victimization and drug use, with the exception of "crack" cocaine, appear to have been stable or declining since 1980.

Once again, a plausible argument may be made for a displacement effect, a movement of crime from one location to another (for example, concentration of criminal activity in major urban centers), but not for a general, national increase in violence, drug dealing, and drug use by juvenile gangs. The present "juvenile gang plague" appears to be as much a creation of the press, once again with selective use of statistics, as its predecessor, the "youth crime plague" was a decade earlier.

This is not intended to minimize what we believe is a serious problem, or to suggest that the gang problem can be ignored. We do, indeed, have a juvenile gang plague, one that has been with us for a long time. The locations in which gangs are most active, the specific drugs used and sold by the gangs, the weapons used in gang violence, and the level of interest in juvenile gangs by the press and public officials may change over time. The total number of offenses committed by juvenile gangs and the total number of victims upon which their crimes have been perpetrated have surely increased, perhaps not because of any change in behavior, but as a simple result of population growth, particularly growth in urban areas. If the data indicate that the problems have not gotten appreciably worse, however, it is equally true that the problems of juvenile gang violence, drug use, and drug dealing do not appear to have gotten appreciably better in the 1980s and early 1990s.

CHAPTER NOTES

[1]Beginning with a half sample in 1992, the NCVS has substantially changed its data collection procedures as part of a deliberate attempt to uncover more victimizations. As

one individual involved in the redesign process put it, "more is better" from the perspective of the NCVS researchers. The results of this redesign, as noted in the text, can be seen in Figure 2.1 when we compare the NCS and NCVS data. (Note that for NCS/NCVS data, violent crime includes rape, robbery, and aggravated assault—the same offenses, less homicide, as are included in the UCR data—and excludes simple assault, which is commonly included in the "violent" crime category in NCVS reports.) As stated by Bastian (1995), "Comparisons of estimates of crime based on previous survey procedures with estimates from the data in the redesigned survey are not recommended. The improvements noted above and other fundamental changes introduced by the redesign make comparisons inappropriate." This warning is bolstered by the huge difference between the two victimization estimates for 1992, a disparity (as noted in the chapter) about half as large as the disparity between the original NCS and UCR data. Given past attention to such details among some criminological researchers, and even more so among journalists, it is safe to bet that someone will ignore this warning, construct a trend line based on victimization data from both before and after the implementation of the redesign in 1992, and conclude that there was a "phenomenal" (or pick another superlative) increase in crime in the early 1990s.

Chapter 3

RACE, ETHNICITY, AND
CONTEMPORARY GANGS

Members of ethnic minority groups seem to be overrepresented in juvenile gangs (Miller 1975; Siegel and Senna 1988; Stafford 1984). For example, one police department study of New York gangs found that 54.7 percent of gang members were Hispanic, 35.7 percent were African American, and the remainder were European or Asian American (Collins 1979). In Klein, Maxson, and Miller's (1995) survey of research on contemporary street gangs, they conclude that about 85 percent of street gang membership is comprised of youth of color. The ethnic composition of gangs may be reflective of their inner-city location. Also reflecting their inner-city nature, gangs tend to be racially homogeneous: all African American (Miller 1962; Short and Strodtbeck 1965), all Hispanic, or more specifically, Puerto Rican, Cuban, or Mexican American (Erlanger 1979; Horowitz and Schwartz 1974; Moore 1978; Moore et al. 1983), all Vietnamese (Morganthau 1982), or all Chinese or Japanese American (Joe and Robinson 1980; Takagi and Platt 1978). Ethnically homogeneous gangs remain the most common pattern (Klein 1995a; Knox 1993). Summarizing previous gang research, Jackson (1989) concluded researchers should continue to look at the variations in gangs and gang behavior across ethnic lines because important differences exist among ethnic groups.

Increasingly more attention is being paid to the immigration of gangs to the United States. The press has been quick to pick up on the increased activities of the immigrant gangs to the United States (Leo et al. 1988). Some of this current attention to immigrant gangs parallels the concerns raised in the nineteenth century over southern European immigrants to the United States. A key question may be whether these gangs decline as the immigrant groups become acculturated, as the earlier southern European gangs did (Leo et al. 1988).

Classification and Typology Issues and Ethnicity

Chapter 7 reviews several typologies that could serve as a basis for conceptualizing and categorizing gangs. This chapter uses ethnicity as a basis for organizing information about gangs in contemporary American society. This is not the only way to understand gangs, but gangs are organized along ethnic lines, and it would be a mistake to ignore ethnicity as a variable that may affect the nature of juvenile gangs. Although gangs of mixed race and ethnicity exist, some researchers continue to find ethnicity and race useful in understanding gangs (see Johnson, Webster, and Connors 1995). Others, however, suggest that race and ethnicity may not be useful in understanding all gang phenomena. For example, Maxson and Klein (1994) found that ethnicity was not particularly useful in predicting the structure of street gangs.

How we should classify ethnic gangs becomes an important question. For example, scholars have used a variety of terms to refer to what we call Hispanic gangs, including Hispanic, Latino, Latin American, Spanish surname, and more specific terms such as Mexican American, Chicano (male) and Chicana (female), Barrio gangs, Cuban, and Puerto Rican gangs. The same issue arises for Asian American gan s which may be called Asian American, Oriental, Far Eastern, or more specifically Japanese, Chinese, Vietnamese, Filipino, Korean, etc. We have chosen to use the categories African American, Hispanic (including Mexican American, Cuban, and Puerto Rican), Asian American (including Japanese, Chinese, Korean, and other Asian ethnic gangs), and white ethnic (including non-English, non-Hispanic white ethnic gangs whose members are most often of European ancestry) to describe broad categories of gangs. Where it is appropriate, we have also used more specific designations, such as Chinese American or Mexican American gangs.

Ethnicity and the Evolution of the Underclass

The concept of the "underclass" has received much attention in recent years. As described by Wilson (1984; 1987), the idea of the underclass is that economic growth does not benefit everyone. Some people are excluded and effectively cut out of the mainstream of the economy. Moore (1989) defined the underclass as men and women "permanently excluded from participation in mainstream occupations." There is some debate about whether the underclass is exclusively African American, or whether other minority groups are included in the underclass (Duster 1987; Lehmann 1986a, 1986b; Moore 1989). Authors who argue for the existence of an underclass suggest that the underclass has been formed as a result of declines in low-skill jobs in parts of the United States.

Fagan (1989) and Hagedorn (1988) described the social isolation of gang members from legitimate economic opportunity and mainstream society. Fagan (1989:662) suggested that increased isolation may lead to an " ... ossification of gangs in a closed social system." Youths are socialized into a world in which gangs are taken for granted and assumed to be a natural feature of life. A matter-of-factness about their existence pervades youths' perceptions of their social world. Youths lose sight of mainstream norms and conventional morality. Gangs within this context assume more importance in shaping the outlook and activities of youths by providing an alternative to the unfamiliar and foreign mainstream society.

AFRICAN AMERICAN GANGS

African American street gangs have been a feature of major cities throughout the United States for many years (Drowns and Hess 1990). Early research on African American gangs included the work of the Chicago school, most notably Thrasher (1927). More recent research on African American gangs includes Hagedorn's (1988) study of African American gangs in Milwaukee, Labov's (1982) study of African American gang terminology and structure, Campbell's (1984b) study of New York gangs, Dawley's (1992) ethnographic description of the Vice Lords in Chicago, and Huff's (1989) work with African American gangs in Cleveland and Columbus. Perkins (1987) conducted a historical study of the evolution of African American gangs in Chicago. Reinhold (1988) studied the "Bloods" and the "Crips" across metropolitan areas. Brown (1977, 1978) studied African American female gangs in Philadelphia, and also studied gangs as extensions of the family. Keiser (1969) studied African American gangs in Chicago. Seeking to discover why youths joined gangs, Keiser traced the history of the "Vice Lords" to boyhood friendships. Short and Strodtbeck (1965) examined the relationship between African American and European American gang members and their respective communities. Johnstone (1981, 1983) also studied factors that influenced recruitment to predominantly African juvenile gangs in suburban Chicago. In spite of all of this and other research, some researchers suggest that we continue to know relatively little about African American gangs (Klein, Maxson, and Miller 1995).

African American Gangs and Political Action

More than any other ethnic group, the political motives and activities of African American gangs have drawn scholarly attention. This attention is partially due to the association between African American gangs and the civil rights movement of the 1960s and the 1970s. African American gangs in the late 1950s and early 1960s do not appear to have been oriented toward politics and social change. The civil rights movement apparently had little impact on most African American gangs (Short 1976).

During the later 1960s and the 1970s, some African American gangs worked toward consolidation and forming alliances in major cities. One example is the "Blackstone Rangers" in Chicago (Miller 1976). These efforts were short-lived and generally failed. Short (1976), based on his work in the 1960s, noted that he was impressed by the lack of political and social awareness of African American gangs at that time. During the 1960s there were a few attempts to politicize African American gangs. For example, the political potential of these gangs became evident in Chicago during Chicago's Freedom Movement in 1964. Gangs were recruited by community organizations with little success. The Black Panther party made efforts to politicize gangs in Chicago; however, it failed to make any serious inroads for a number of reasons (Perkins, 1987).

Dawley (1992) wrote an autobiographical account of Chicago's Vice Lords (Conservative Vice Lords). Dawley, a member himself, traced the creation and expansion of this large Chicago gang to a club formed by jailed youths. The initial club crystallized over time for protection from other gangs. The initial gang grew by expanding into other gangs' territories. During the 1960s and the years that followed, the Vice Lords would fight other gangs to break them up and claim their territories. Gang violence for this gang was very restrained compared to today's gangs. Gang violence during these gang wars was mostly limited to fistfights and sometimes the use of weapons. Status for gang members was largely based on their ability to fistfight. Gang leaders were typically the best fighters and the toughest. Gang members saw the need to use weapons as a sign of weakness. Homicide was not the intent of gang members but rather reputation of toughness on the street. Some defeated gang members would join the Vice Lords resulting in expansion of the gang. As the gang became more established, it embarked in a number of legitimate businesses designed to meet the needs of the African American community. The gang became a successful enterprise.

Other characteristics of the Vice Lords were that they wore their own identifying clothing that included capes, earrings, and black scarves. They had a female auxiliary, known as the Vice Ladies, that supported the Vice Lords. Females never had the same status as males but did contribute to gang activities. Gang members used alcohol but were not heavily involved in the use of illicit drugs. The Vice Lords were age graded into three levels, "peewees," "juniors," and "seniors." It is interesting that the age of associating with the gang for the peewees was between 8 to 9 years of age. This relatively young age compares closely to the very young ages that modern gang researchers report for gangs in the 1980s and 1990s.

Helmreich (1973) studied the rise and fall of one African American political gang, the "Crusaders," from 1968 to 1969. The Crusaders were more an adult gang than a juvenile gang, with members' ages ranging from 18 to 28. The 200 members tended to come from lower class backgrounds and single parent families. The gang had clearly defined leadership, and political and economic goals. It was highly organized along paramilitary lines with standard uniforms and hierarchical ranks. The gang was also age-graded and held fund raisers for its various projects. Although the gang accomplished some of its goals, it did not last long. Helmreich attributed the decline of the gang to (1) political opposition, (2) the role of the media in conveying a negative image of the gang, (3) community education about the role and goals of the gang, and (4) the lack of community support. The group had some confrontations with the police, but was essentially non-criminal.

The Bloods and the Crips

The Bloods and the Crips, two predominantly African American gangs, are the two most widely known juvenile gangs operating in the United States in the late 1980s and early 1990s. Both are really national confederations of local gangs,[1] and reportedly have members in Portland, Denver, Minneapolis, Akron, Cleveland, Omaha, and other cities outside their home base in Los Angeles. According to Sanders (1994), the

Crips were the first African American gang to emerge as a major force. The two gangs are identified by their respective colors. Bloods wear the color red and Crips wear the color blue in their hats, bandannas, and other clothing. Colors other than red and blue, such as green (in it for the money) or purple or have been adopted in some specific metropolitan areas. Each gang has its unique sign language, called *flashing*, which serves to reinforce gang identity. For example, Crips form the letter C and Bloods the letter B with their hands to indicate their affiliation. Bloods and Crips also use language (or argot) to reinforce their gang identities. For example, Crips greet each other with "cuzz" (cousin) and use the initials "BK" to mean Blood Killer. Crips will intentionally avoid using the letter B in writing and spoken language. Bloods use the term "Blood" (once a sort of generic greeting between African Americans, possibly derived from the term "blood brother" or suggesting "blood" kinship, that is, a common heritage or racial background) as a greeting and the initials "CK" to mean Crip Killer. They will avoid the letter C in writing or talking.

The Crips are also known for their intra-gang rivalries and violence. Fights between Crips factions were said to be responsible for up to one-half of all inter-gang fights in the Los Angeles area (Baker 1988). The Bloods were formed largely in response to the Crips. Violent encounters between the two groups are well documented, and has led to much of the public concern over the two gangs. The Los Angeles County Sheriff's Department observed that the Bloods fight the Crips and the Crips fight the Crips, but the Bloods do not typically fight other Blood gangs. The LASD (1985) estimated that in the state of California alone there were over 12,000 members of the Crips and the Bloods in California Youth Association facilities or on parole. Crip and Blood gangs have loose and informal structures. "Old Gangsters" (OGs) or "shot callers" sometimes assume leadership roles. Typically the gang member with the most money, women, drugs, and other desired objects receives the most respect from other gang members. Gang members with the most respect and power are said to have "juice." The size of the Crip and Blood gangs is estimated to vary from as low as 5 to as high as 1,000 members (Operation Safe Streets 1995).

Crips and Bloods refer to their gangs as *sets* and the neighborhoods they operate in as *'hoods*. Both gangs are territorial, but territory is linked more to drug distribution than to identification with particular neighborhoods. The Crips and Bloods in Los Angeles are reported to have direct contacts with major drug importers and use Southern California as a major cocaine and crack shipping center (Porché-Burke and Fulton 1992). Both groups mark territory with graffiti, which often has coded and violent messages. Morgenthau et al. (1988) provided an example: "Big Hawk 1987 BSVG ɇ 187," found on one Los Angeles wall. Big Hawk is the name of the gang member; BSVG stands for Blood Stone Villains Gang; the c is crossed out, which means that the writer kills Crips; and 187 is the California Code offense number for murder. Law enforcement agencies sometimes find that reading these codes is beneficial for knowing what is going on in gang areas, and gang units typically place some importance on interpreting gang graffiti.

Crips and Bloods draw their membership from African American "wannabes," grade school children, and adolescents. Reports of members as young as ages 8 and 9 exist. Although these gangs sometimes attract members from grade school-aged youth, some authorities have found that some gang members may continue their affiliation well into their forties (Operation Safe Streets 1995). Recently, the press has reported that affluent European American youths are also joining established African American gangs, including the Crips and the Bloods (Mydans 1990). The extent of this phenomenon is unknown. The reports suggest that gang life represents a romantic adventure for some European American youths. What is clear is that many youth have adopted Crip and Blood subcultures in terms of dress and identity, thus making the extent of true Crip and Blood activity in the United States impossible to accurately estimate. Many gangs spread out throughout the country attach Crip or Blood to their gang names and identities without any connection between their gangs and the larger Crips and Bloods confederations. This practice was found by Sanders (1992) in San Diego where Filipino gangs used African American gang names and colors with no connection. The senior author's contacts with gang members supports the conclusion that some youth believe that being labelled a Crip or Blood adds power and legitimacy to otherwise ordinary juvenile gangs. For example, in some small mountain towns in Colorado there are middle class white youth that call their gangs Crips or Bloods for effect.

People and Folks

Similar to the Bloods and the Crips has been the creation of two alliances of gangs in the Midwest known as People and Folks. During the mid-1980s, a Chicago gang known as the Latin Disciples, a racially-mixed gang allied with the Black Gangsters Disciple Nation (BGDN), a gang consisting mostly of African American males, formed the Folk alliance. Shortly thereafter, the Latin Kings, who were mostly Latino men, and the Vice Lords, who are almost all African American men, formed the People alliance (Block and Block, 1993). Other gangs belonging to the folk alliance include the Black Disciples, Blank Gangster Nation, Young Latins, Simon City Royals, Gangster Disciples, and others. Gangs belonging to the people alliance include Black P Stone Nation, Honky Heads, and Loco Boys, among others.

People and Folks in Hagedorn's Milwaukee Gangs

Hagedorn's (1988) study of African American gangs in Milwaukee, a city in the American Rustbelt (North Central and Northeastern states that traditionally had their economic base in manufacturing and heavy industry) has stirred a surprising amount of controversy. Hagedorn proposed that gangs in Milwaukee were a new phenomenon evolving from the growing African American underclass. Hagedorn explored the role the underclass plays in creating and perpetuating gangs. He found that there was continued adult involvement in Milwaukee gangs, in contrast to the more usual pattern of "maturing out" of gang involvement with age. Hagedorn suggested that adult participation in gangs in Milwaukee was a product of the evolution of the underclass: "It is the contention of our study that increased gang involvement by adults is largely due to the drastically changed economic conditions in poor minority neighborhoods" (Hagedorn 1988:111). Gang members participate in gangs longer, and fail to "mature out" in their early twenties, because there are so few good jobs and opportunities to provide alternatives to gang involvement. Gang leadership varied with the gang, and each age group had its own leaders, according to Hagedorn. Some gangs collected membership dues and had initiation rites. Only a small portion of time was devoted to criminal activities. Hagedorn noted that gang structures rarely resembled law enforcement images of gangs. He also found that fighting was an age-related phenomenon, decreasing as gang members got older.

Hagedorn addressed the question of how gangs formed in Milwaukee and suggested that street corner and break dancing groups crystallized into gangs as a result of intergroup conflict, followed by media accounts often highlighting racial tension as a source of conflict. Authorities such as the police provide an additional source of negative reaction, and help to promote the crystallization of the group into a gang. Hagedorn denied that expansion of larger gangs from nearby Chicago played a major role in the formation of Milwaukee gangs, although there was some evidence of imitation or mimicry of the larger Chicago gangs by the Milwaukee gangs.

Hagedorn described at length the changing relationship of gangs to their neighborhoods. According to Hagedorn, gangs have a lower sense of community than gangs in the past did. He proposed that "... a number of factors have more recently acted to weaken this tie between gang and neighborhood" (Hagedorn 1988:134). Hagedorn reported that gang members neither valued nor necessarily lived in their gang neighborhoods. They were alienated from their neighborhoods and from other members of their own ethnic groups.

The lack of community awareness and allegiance, according to Hagedorn, is partially a result of school integration policies that moved youths out of their home neighborhoods into schools across town. He later identified the desegregation of schools through busing as the true reason for reduced neighborhood loyalties on the part of gang members. This lack of neighborhood loyalties was further reinforced by the increased mobility afforded gang members by automobiles and mass transit systems.

Sampson (1990) has expressed concern about the methods and generalizations made by Hagedorn, but viewed the study as an important contribution to the field. In a critical review of Hagedorn's research, Miller (1989) noted that the emphasis on underclass membership as a contributing factor in gang membership made an assumption about the relationship between unemployment and the prevalence of gangs. "In fact, the city with the lowest Afro-American unemployment rate, Boston (4.5%) has both a sizable Afro-American ghetto and serious gang problem, with at least 10 gang-related homicides in 1988, a homicide rate close to that of Chicago (unemployment 24.5%)" (Miller 1989:786). Thus, according to Miller, Hagedorn's emphasis on unemployment is not supported by his own data. Miller also challenged the idea that if we get rid of the underclass we might get rid of gangs, since gangs existed prior to the growth of the underclass. Finally, Miller argued that Hagedorn failed to establish that the Milwaukee gangs Hagedorn studies were new and different from gangs in Milwaukee in the past.

This latter idea is critical, and raises an important point. Sociologists and criminologists have been aware for decades that economically depressed and socially disadvantaged groups have existed. They have also conducted many studies on the relationship of socioeconomic status and crime and delinquency. The idea that an underclass exists is not altogether new, but represents an outgrowth of the work of the Chicago School in sociology, as represented in the works of Thrasher (1927), Shaw and McKay (1942), and others. What may be new about the underclass as described by Wilson (1987), Hagedorn (1988), and other contemporary researchers is the sense of utter hopelessness and the nearly total isolation from mainstream economic institutions experienced by people in inner city minority (especially African American) neighborhoods.

Other Studies of African American Gangs

According to Brown (1978), the African American family plays a role in the formation of gangs. Gangs represent a strategy for survival for some inner-city youths. African American youths in poor, inner-city neighborhoods may have early exposure to street life, including crime and violence, and this may promote gang membership. The gang may supplant the family as the primary reference group for some youths because the gang, unlike the family, can be counted on when it is needed.

Johnstone's (1981) secondary analysis of juvenile gangs in the African American suburbs of Chicago provides another view of gangs. He found that the type of community influenced the prevalence of gangs. Gangs were more prevalent in areas with large concentrations of poor families, large numbers of youths, female-headed households, and lower incomes. Johnstone's description is consistent with earlier research by Shaw and McKay (1942), Thrasher (1927), and other researchers in the human ecological tradition of the Chicago school. Johnstone focused on racial tension among gangs, and found that the prevalence of conflict did not increase with racial tension, as some might expect. Poverty appeared to have more explanatory power in understanding gang involvement and conflict among African American and European American youths in the suburbs.

Huff (1989) viewed African American gangs as a product of the underclass in Cleveland and Columbus, Ohio. Gang members were economically and socially disadvantaged youths. Huff's research on predominantly African American gangs found that members were usually fourteen to twenty-four years old, with some gang members as young as ten or as old as thirty years old. Gangs were age-graded, and started through some of the same patterns (break dancing clubs or informal social groups) or were started by the movement of ex-members of gangs into communities. Huff reported that there were three different types of gangs: hedonistic, instrumental, and predatory. Drug use was common to all types of gangs, but the emphasis placed on drug use was different in different types. Predatory and instrumental gangs were involved in property crimes. Gang structure was typically loose.

Campbell (1984b) researched a New York City group labeled by police as a gang. The "Five Percent Nation" adopted Islam as a way of life, was predominantly African American, and had both political and religious goals. A second gang described by Campbell was the "Sex Boys," which included both African and Hispanic Americans. This gang engaged in turf wars with neighboring gangs and committed crimes such as robbery. The gang had a core group of about ten members and was estimated to have a total membership of about one hundred.

In a study of violent gangs in Chicago, Spergel (1984) reported that African American juvenile gangs were more homogeneous than gangs of other ethnic backgrounds. In Chicago, Curry and Spergel found that the number of homicides attributed to African American gangs rose from 61 in 1978–81 to 160 in 1982–85. Potential problems with such data are detailed in Chapter 2. It is possible, for instance, that more homicides are (correctly or incorrectly) being attributed to gangs, even though the rate of gang homicides has not changed. Curry and Spergel also found that African Americans contributed proportionally less to the gang homicide rate than did Hispanics. They attributed this finding to greater social disorganization among Hispanics, who were relatively recent immigrants to Chicago, in contrast to the African Americans who had resided in Chicago for a longer period. In the Los Angeles area, however, Spergel (1990) suggested that gang homicides were disproportionately committed by African Americans rather than Hispanics.

HISPANIC GANGS

We probably know more about Hispanic gangs than about most other American gangs, and they have received considerable attention from scholars in recent decades (Erlanger 1979; Harris 1988; Moore 1978; Moore 1991; Moore et al. 1983; Rodriquez 1993; Vigil 1983, 1988, 1990; Zatz 1985, 1987). Much of the focus on Hispanic gangs has been on the important role their cultural heritage plays in their lives, in and outside of gangs. It has been suggested (Operation Safe Streets 1995) that to some Hispanic adolescents and adults, the gangs are a way of life. Hispanic gangs include the "Mexican Mafia," "El Hoyo Maravilla," "Nuestra Familia," "White Fence," and "Mojados" in Southern California, and the "Savage Skulls," "Savage Nomads," "Dirty Ones," "Satan Souls," and "Sandmen" in New York City (Harris 1984; Rosario 1980). A new trend reported by Skolnick et al. (1990) among some Hispanic gangs is to adopt Crip or Blood names into their gang titles. Many, if not all, of these gangs have adult as well as juvenile members.

Hispanic gangs have existed in this country at least since the turn of the century, and may have become a way of life for some Hispanics (Heller 1966; Paz 1961). Harris (1988) found evidence of Hispanic gangs, whose members were called pachucos, in the "barrios" (neighborhoods) of Los Angeles going back more than sixty years (see also Vigil 1983 and 1988, and Chapter 5). An important feature of Hispanic gangs in southern California is that they have become institutionalized in the social fabric of the Hispanic barrio subculture (Vigil 1983). In other words, as Hagedorn suggested for the African American gangs of the Midwest, gang life is not a transient juvenile phase, but endures well into adulthood.

Moore et al. (1983) identified reasons why Hispanic gangs in Los Angeles are different from the gangs studied by Thrasher in the late 1920s. Specifically, these gangs are longer lasting and sometimes span several generations (Harris 1988; Moore 1991; Vigil 1983; 1988). Some of the gangs and gang members have not assimilated into the larger American culture, and maintain cultural characteristics that are distinctively Hispanic, usually Mexican American. In addition, some gang members stay in the gang until middle age, which until recently has not been typical of most participation in juvenile gangs.

Marginality and Hispanic Youths

An important focal point of gang researchers has been the question of the ability of Hispanic youths to obtain status from the larger society. Many of the studies on Hispanic gangs have concluded that Hispanic youths are marginal to the mainstream society and must find status through gang membership. This is not always true. Horowitz and Schwartz (1974) and Horowitz (1982) found Chicago Hispanic gang members to be adept at assuming socially desirable roles. These gang members could attain status and success in the larger society and had socially acceptable alternatives to gang membership, but they still participated in gangs. This suggests that marginal Hispanic youths could adapt quite well to the mainstream. Other studies by Harris (1988) and Vigil (1988), however, seem to underscore the importance of marginality in gang formation. One possible reason for the differences is that differences between different Hispanic groups (e.g., Mexican Americans as opposed to Cubans and Puerto Ricans) are being highlighted here, and that marginality is a more important explanation for gang membership among Mexican Americans because their marginality is more pronounced than that of other groups.

Gang Characteristics

The longevity of some Hispanic gangs is exceptional. The White Fence gang of southern California has existed for several generations. Some authors have suggested that Hispanic gangs may be a way of life in some barrios (Heller 1966; Paz 1961). Hispanic gang members and marginal Hispanic youths are sometimes referred to as Cholos (for males) or Cholas (for females) (Harris 1988; Vigil 1983). Contemporary Cholos and Cholas carry on the tradition of barrio gangs in southern California, but not all Cholos or Cholas are gang members. Gang members have a preferred style of dress that conveys gang membership. Popular among gang members are khaki pants and Pendleton® shirts. Pants are usually worn baggy and either "sagged" or high on the waist. Shirt collars are often buttoned-down. These styles change over time and are likely to be modified. The general adoption of this and other styles of gang attire by non-gang youth results in some individuals' being incorrectly identified as being in gangs. Klein (1995a) argues that this adoption of gang styles is problematic, beyond any confusion it may engender in identifying gang members, insofar as it positively reinforces gang culture in the larger society.

Vigil (1990) noted that there is a historical linkage between the term "Cholo" and the concept of marginalization. The essence of this is that Hispanics are not fully integrated into the mainstream socioeconomic and cultural system. They are marginal because of discrimination, prejudice, and differences in language and culture. Cholos have a distinctive style of dress which includes loose fitting khaki pants, coats, and bandannas. Some link the Cholo style to the zoot suit style of the 1930s and 1940s (see Chapter 5).

Territory and the Barrio

Controlling or protecting turf, specifically in the barrio, is a major concern of Hispanic gangs. Hispanic gangs claim to view themselves as protectors of the neighborhood from threats or aggressors, including government agencies, law enforcement officials, and rival gangs (Operation Safe Streets 1995). Moore (1978) found that Hispanic gangs emphasized protecting their neighborhood from outside gangs. Hispanic gangs are territorially based so that the word for the gang and for the neighborhood are the same (Moore 1978). Some gang members may live outside the barrio because they or their parents have moved, but they may still continue to be members of the gang in the old barrio (Moore et al. 1983). Residence, although important, is not a necessary or sufficient condition for barrio and gang membership.

The identification with territory finds expression in a number of ways. Graffiti and specifically "placas" or stylized gang signatures are common in Los Angeles and other Hispanic areas. Placas mark the boundaries of gang territories and warn other gangs to stay away. The importance of placas to gangs has been acknowledged for years, and at least one intervention program was based on this concern. By involving gang members in painting walls, specifically by mural painting in East Los Angeles, one program reported success in reducing gang tensions in the 1970s (Zucker 1978). The program used government funds to hire Hispanic youths to express their identity in sanctioned murals rather than gang-related graffiti. Teams of mural painters were made up of members of rival gangs in an attempt to promote cooperation and understanding.

Drug Use

Hispanic gangs, like other juvenile gangs, are involved in the use and sale of drugs. Harris (1978) found drug use to be very extensive in Hispanic gangs, with PCP, alcohol, and marijuana being the most prevalent drugs. PCP or "Angel Dust" preceded the present crack epidemic in the barrios (Rodriquez 1993). Drug use by Hispanic gangs has been attributed to alienation (Bullington 1977; Moore 1978). According to Moore (1978), drug and alcohol use enhance the youth's sense of belonging in the group. Heroin use has had a long history (since the 1950s) among southwestern Hispanic gangs (Moore 1991). Heroin use is more typical of older gang members (*veteranos*), while PCP is more often used by younger gang members (Operation Safe Streets 1995). Drug use among Hispanic gang members is very much a social activity. Vigil (1988) found that drug use served a variety of functions, including serving as a social lubricant.

Violence

Hispanic gangs have been characterized as being very violent and vengeful. Joan Moore (1978; 1991) has argued that all Hispanic gangs are fighting gangs. While much of the violence is between rival gangs, fights among gang members, whether they are male or female, sometimes occur within the gang. Gang rituals such as "walking the line," where a violator of a gang rule must run between two lines of gang members while they beat him or her with sticks, have also been reported (Horowitz 1982). Gang-related, drive-by shootings have been reported for over a decade by the press (Chavira 1980). Some of the reasons for gang violence include invasion of territory, rivalry over dating, sports, and gangs backing up individuals over personal matters (Moore 1991). Revenge has been identified as an important motive for Hispanic juvenile gangs. Gang wars between rival barrios have been known to persist for decades. When barrio gang members are attacked or killed, their gang usually tries to avenge the attack. Ruth Horowitz (1983) has proposed a basic thesis that gang violence is an attempt to resolve the ambiguity or conflict that develops between traditional family-oriented culture that revolves around "honor" and modern culture that emphasizes socioeconomic success (See Mirandé and López (1992).

As noted earlier, Curry and Spergel (1988) found that in Chicago, Hispanic gangs accounted for a disproportionate share of gang homicides. Spergel (1984) found that of 55 identified violent gangs, 33 (60 percent) were Hispanic, 15 African American, and 7 white ethnic. From 1978 to 1981, approximately 60 percent of gang homicide victims and perpetrators were Hispanic, and 30 percent were African American. Hispanic gang members were more likely to be involved in homicides with multiple victims; African Americans were more likely to be involved in homicides with a single victim. Similarly, Bobrowski (1988) reported that in Chicago the number of Hispanic gang members suspected in 82 gang-related homicides outnumbered African American gang members, even though African Americans comprised 41 percent of the city's population and Hispanics only 16 percent. As noted earlier, there is some regional variation in this pattern, and Spergel (1990) reported that in Los Angeles, homicides committed by African American teenage gangs far outnumbered homicides committed by Hispanic juvenile gangs.

It is important to note that Hispanic youths, particularly those living in the Los Angeles area, have also been interested and involved in essentially non-criminal activities such as car clubs (Schwendinger and Schwendinger 1985). These clubs can sometimes resemble gangs. Although car clubs occasionally get involved in violent conflicts with other car clubs, members do not consider themselves to be gangs, and work against having the gang image applied to themselves (Holtz 1975; Schwendinger and Schwendinger 1985).

Machismo

One characteristic of Hispanic gangs which has received considerable attention is the role and importance machismo plays in the gang and the larger community. Definitions of machismo differ, as does the importance researchers have attached to it (Harris 1988). One of the basic assumptions of machismo is that its emphasis on masculinity and violence helps explain why Hispanic gangs are violent, male, and involved in displays of masculine prowess. Erlanger (1979:235) reported that while there is a Hispanic subculture which differs from the dominant American culture, it does not " . . . require or condone violence." Rather, Erlanger concludes, it is not so much Hispanic values, but social structural factors and estrangement from larger society that contribute to violence. In this context, research results presented in Chapter 6 suggest that Latin American gangs have historically been *less* violent than their North American counterparts, but may be in the process of becoming more violent and more similar to Hispanic gangs in the United States.

Horowitz (1987) examined the attitudes and responses of Hispanic adults toward the violence of Hispanic adolescents. She wanted to know how the adult population dealt with acts of violence, including homicide. Her research revealed that nongang individuals of all ages basically tolerated the violence, not because they thought it was desirable, but because they understood it as an expression of a man's honor. According to Horowitz, Hispanic communities understand how important it is for Hispanic adolescent males to be tough and macho, and are willing to tolerate expressions of violence out of respect for cultural traditions that call for males to be courageous.

Structure

Some authors suggest that Hispanic gangs differ from other gangs in many respects, including their emphasis on machismo and the importance of identity with the barrio. In addition, Hispanic gangs tend to be modeled after the extended family. They have a sense of *carnalismo*, or brotherhood, among members (Moore 1978; Vigil 1990). Hispanic gangs have been characterized as highly cohesive with members having strong loyalties to the gang. Mirandé and López (1992:25), noting that Hispanic gangs are very cohesive, commented, "What made them different is not that they were "foreign," more violent, or innately criminal but that they were more cohesive and such cohesion was intensified by the fact that Mexican youth existed in a hostile environment."

Hispanic gangs are predominantly male, although there are female gangs and mixed gender gangs. Most research suggests that gender segregation among gangs is the most common pattern. Male gangs will often have female auxiliaries, who frequently take their titles from the male gangs. The age at which youths join Hispanic gangs has been placed as low as eight or ten years old (Horowitz 1982), or eleven and twelve years old (Chavira 1980). Some Hispanic gangs begin recruiting members from grade schools. Most Hispanic gangs consist of teenagers, but gang membership is known to last well beyond age twenty for some members. Gang membership is divided about every two years into age-grades, cohorts, cliques, or "klikas." As children get older, they pass with their age cohort from younger to older klikas of the gang (Harris 1988; Horowitz 1982; Moore et al. 1983; Vigil 1983). Moore (1991:45) noted that each clique forms while its predecessor is active and visible on the streets." She then added, "It forms, generally, with the sense that it can match or outdo its predecessor." Leadership within the klikas is informal, loosely organized, and lacks a clear, solid chain of command. Moore (1978) places much importance on the role of age in defining Hispanic gang structure. The klikas remain important throughout the lifetime of many, but not all, gang members (Moore 1978).

Hispanic gangs have a variety of rituals associated with entry and exit from the gang. Initiation rites often include attacks on the individual. These rites are called "courting in" or "jumping in." The degree of violence of the initiation may differ according to the residence of the initiate, with non-barrio individuals being subjected to more violent initiations (Moore et al. 1983). Gang tattoos are also viewed as part of the initiation into some Hispanic gangs, as are the wearing of gang colors (Horowitz 1982). The tattoos usually identify the individual's barrio and gang membership. Tattoos also represent a sign of the individual's toughness and commitment to the gang. Another measure of commitment to the gang is the individual's willingness to back up or fight for other gang members. Members not willing to support other gang members during fights or respond to outside threats to the gang are viewed as disloyal.

As the gang member participates in gang activities, there is an internalization of values, which evolves into a shared sense of common destiny. This latter appears to be more characteristic of Hispanic gangs than other gangs. Hispanic gang membership is more often linked to the larger Hispanic subculture than other types of contemporary gangs are linked to their ethnic subcultures. The gang provides a sense of belonging and a sense of identity. This identity is sometimes expressed in the notion of *La Vida Loca* (The Crazy Life). The crazy life is what we call the barrio gang experience. It is a lifestyle born out of the pachuco gangs of the 1930s and 1940s and the cholos. Although meanings differ, it is often meant to convey a sense of a life out of control and fatalistic. It is frequently symbolized in a triangular tattoo of three small dots usually located on the gang members hand. Each dot represent one of the words in the *La Vida Loca* phrase.

The social nature and functions of Hispanic gangs are well documented in the literature on Hispanic gangs (Harris 1988; Horowitz 1982; Horowitz and Schwartz 1974; Moore 1991). Extensive exchanges and mutual obligations reflect gang cohesion and longevity of relationships (Horowitz 1982). These ties of trust and mutual support may help explain why Hispanic gangs tend to endure longer than other gangs. It should be noted that even though Hispanic gangs do tend to endure longer than other ethnic gangs, gang relationships change over time, as gang members marry, raise children, and find work (Horowitz 1982). The adult gang member may maintain a dual commitment to the gang and to the conventional world.

Vigil's Barrio Gangs

Vigil (1988) studied juvenile gangs in southern California. Having been raised in the barrio, Vigil had personal knowledge of the barrio gangs, and like other researchers (Hagedorn 1988; Moore 1978) he incorporated gang members into his research team. Vigil traced the historical development of gangs in southern California to the turn of the century, and noted that Mexican-American juvenile gangs have remarkable longevity. He concluded that the historical roles of migration and discrimination against Mexican Americans, dynamics which may be found in contemporary American society, were important factors in the evolution of juvenile gangs.

Vigil used the concept of "multiple marginality" to explain the existence and persistence of Mexican American gangs. He proposed "The multiple marginality framework better allows for descriptions and interpretations of particular (and perhaps peculiar) facts of people, time, and place" (Vigil 1988:10). The multiple marginality approach stresses historical-structural and cultural-ecological criteria influencing the formation and nature of gangs. The recognition of the marginality of the population from which gangs are drawn is critical to understanding gangs. Vigil concluded by noting that the multiple marginality approach to gangs is capable of incorporating many other theoretical explanations for gangs. Vigil viewed previous gang theories as failing to consider the historical development of gangs.

Vigil recognized and stressed the community context of the barrio in the emergence and persistence of gangs. The barrio, in Vigil's view, separates Mexican American youths from mainstream society. There is also a strong sense of identity in the barrio. Vigil (1988:91) noted that the barrio and "familia" (family) are sometimes used interchangeably by youths. This sense of barrio or territory is highly refined in the minds of youths, and at times promotes violence between rival barrio gangs. The continued importance of the barrio in Vigil's gangs stands in marked contrast to the deemphasis of the importance of the neighborhood by Hagedorn's gangs.

Discrimination in schools, family difficulties, a poor labor market, poverty, gang subculture, and Cholo subculture are factors viewed by Vigil as contributing to the formation of juvenile gangs. Vigil observed that gang youths, more frequently than other youths in the barrio, find themselves in problematic situations in the home (e.g., disruptive families) and school (e.g., school failure). The gang fills the voids created by disruptive families, poor schools, and a hostile mainstream society (Vigil 1988:35). Also, Vigil found that male family gang members had more influence than peers on the decision of youths to join gangs. Instead of being a reinforcer of conventional morality and norms, the family could thus be a source of pressure for gang membership.

Padilla's Working Gangs

Padilla (1993, 1995) conducted a study of a Puerto Rican gang, the Diamonds, that was involved in drug sales in Chicago. Padilla found that members were involved in street level dealing as part of the gang and also as individuals acting independently of the gang. The gang started out as a violent gang but over the years became more involved in the sale of drugs. Youths turned to the gang searching for employment that paid better than the legitimate jobs available to them. They believed that they could not make enough money working in conventional jobs to pay for the material things they wanted. They also did not believe that education would help them. Members in this gang, and others as well, perceived the gang as a business enterprise, and in that context attached importance to ethnic and group solidarity. Padilla concluded that street dealing did not really pay the members much better than conventional jobs, because few members actually made much money from their dealing. Padilla's description of the working gang is an example of how gangs may evolve from one type of gang to another, a topic to be discussed in more detail in Chapter 7.

WHITE ETHNIC GANGS

We know relatively little about white ethnic gangs other than what the mass media have provided or what has been provided by somewhat dated studies. Historically, this is ironic given that many of the first gangs in the United States were mostly white ethnic youths from European countries. The Irish, Polish, Italian, and other European countries all found representation in nineteenth century American gangs (Asbury 1926; Thrasher 1927). As these immigrant groups assimilated into the American culture, the number involved in gangs declined. One frequently cited study of gangs in New York City estimated that European Americans represented only about 9.3 percent of gang members (Collins

1979). Klein's (1995a) study of cities reporting the existence of gangs found only 10 percent of the cities reported the presence of predominantly white ethnic gangs. The relative absence of white ethnic gangs in official studies may be a product of a number of factors including the difficulty in identifying them (Friedman et al. 1976) and biases in reporting and public perception (Chambliss 1973). The absence in some urban areas, such as San Diego, of an identifiable ideology or cultural history may help explain why white ethnic gangs are absent or rare (see Sanders 1994).

Recently, the media and researchers have reported the existence of a variety of suburban white ethnic gangs including "Stoners," "Satanics," "Punks," and white supremacist gangs (Dolan and Finney 1984; Wooden, 1995). The variety of white ethnic gangs may be partially attributed to their broad range of organizing foci such as racism, drugs, satanism, neo-facist ideology, fighting, and motorcycles (Goldstein and Glick 1994). In addition, since the mid-1980s, there have been reported increases in white ethnic middle class gang activities in suburban Los Angeles (Conklin 1989), some of which are white supremacists and others of which are satanist gangs. A common thread running through the descriptions of these different gangs is a general rebellion against adults and conventional society. Alienation from and rejection of mainstream society are common themes in much of the research on White ethnic gangs. This pattern is not new; Short and Strodtbeck (1965) noted that white ethnic juvenile gangs were more rebellious, sexually delinquent, and involved in drug use than African American gangs in Chicago.

Skinhead Gangs

One type of white ethnic gang that has received attention recently in the press is the "Skinhead" gang. Relatively little is known about the nature and prevalence of skinhead gangs. Some researchers have raised the issue of whether skinhead gangs are really gangs or are simply members of a neo-facist youth subculture (Hamm, 1993). What is most likely is that some skinheads are members of law violating youth groups, other gangs, and others only identify with skinhead subculture. What all experts agree on is that race and ethnic issues seem to be at the core of skinhead groups. Either skinheads are racist or they make a special point of declaring they are non-racist. We know that they have been reported in several cities with names such as the "Confederate Hammer" in

Dallas, "DASH" (Detroit Area Skinheads) in Detroit, and "CASH" (Chicago Area Skinheads) and "Romantic Violence" in Chicago. Other American cities including Denver, Portland, Los Angeles, Orlando, Tampa, Tulsa, Cincinnati, San Francisco, and Atlanta have also reported skinhead activity. Other major regional skinhead confederations of gangs include the "Western Hammer Skins," "American Front," "National White Resistance," and "Old Glory Skins."

Different estimates of the number of skinhead gangs and gang members vary widely (Reed 1989; Moore 1993; Mydans 1990a) because there are no reliable data from which to estimate skinhead gang membership. Most authorities agree that the numbers of youths joining skinhead gangs is growing but the absolute number remains small in the United States. The numbers of skinheads are low enough in most cities and areas that they do not have sufficient numbers to stake claim to territories. Rather, as Moore (1993) noted, they tend to float from city to city, as is the case in Florida where skinhead gang members have migrated between Tampa and Orlando. Skinhead gangs usually consist of European American youths who are non-Hispanic, non-Jewish, Protestant, working class, low income, clean shaven, and militantly racist and white supremacist. Skinheads are often motivated by changes in racial diversity occurring in their communities and the attention they receive by the media (Wooden, 1995).

Most authors trace the evolution of the skinheads as a subculture to the 1970s and the working class in Great Britain (see Chapter 6). The roots of the skinhead movement in England can be traced to the 1950s and the teddy boys who wore Edwardian coats and tight pants. An interesting twist is that the original skinhead look can be traced back to Jamaican immigrants to England who wore their hair very short and played their own type of music. Known as Rude Boys, their hairstyle and music would eventually be adopted by white working class youth (Wooden, 1995). The basic values of the original skinheads were those of the British working class (Taylor 1976). The British working class was very concerned about the invasion of foreign immigrants to England. Immigrants were seen as destroying British society and taking needed jobs from citizens. The skinhead subculture expanded to the United States during the late 1970s and early 1980s (Moore 1993).

Skinheads typically attack immigrants, gay men, and women, and other groups judged to be weaker. Such attacks were viewed by some skinhead, white supremacist, and Neo-Nazi groups as a form of initiation of members into the gang. In the United States, increased skinhead violence in recent years, much of it anti-Semitic, has been reported in Portland, Tampa, San Diego, Hartford, and other cities (Sears 1989). The violence ranges from beatings and abduction to murder. Skinhead violence has been a common theme in reports about skinheads (Came et al. 1989a, 1989b; Coplon 1988).

Skinheads may be identified by their physical appearance, which typically includes shaved heads, Nazi insignia, heavy jeans that are rolled up over the boots, heavy steel tipped boots (Doc Martens), suspenders, and leather clothing which is often marked with racist and white supremacist slogans. Some youth will have tattoos of swastikas, a circled letter "A," and "666," the satanic mark of the beast. Skinheads use their suspenders to convey meaning. Suspenders worn down mean the wearer is ready to fight. The color of the suspender may also mean what group the wearer is against. For example, yellow suspenders may mean the wearer is against the police or the color green against people who are gay. Similar to other gangs, youth are often jumped in to the gang. White shoe laces may represent white pride, red laces white power, and yellow the wearer hates police. Membership in skinhead gangs ranges in age from sixteen to the early twenties. Members frequently come from working class broken homes, but some skinheads are from middle class backgrounds. Moore (1993) suggests that skinheads from working and middle class backgrounds want and need a firm identity and a sense of belonging to something similar to an extended family. Some skinheads overtly reject the upper class and material wealth, and appear to believe that opportunities for them to attain wealth and status are closed. Some research has identified being labeled a "bully" as one of the most common predictors of youth belong to racist skinhead groups (Wooden, 1995).

Links have been suggested between the skinheads and the Neo-Nazi movement, including the Aryan Brotherhood, Aryan Youth Movement, and White Aryan Resistance (WAR). An early sign of skinhead activity in a community is Nazi and anti-Semitic graffiti. Not all skinheads believe that they are racist, however, and some reject the Nazi movement (Reed 1989). Some skinhead groups such as "Skinheads Against Racial Prejudice" (SHARP), "Skinheads for Racial Justice" "SAR" (Skinheads Against Racism), and "SHAFT" (Skinheads Against Fascist Tendencies) suggest that there is a broad range of political and racial orientations among skinhead groups (Sears 1989). Nevertheless, most skinhead gangs have racist, white supremacist values at their core.

In addition to racism, at the core of skinhead gangs is violence. Skinheads vent their anger toward people or groups they judge to be different and in some way a threat to their way of life. Their victims, as noted by Wooden (1995), are typically, defenseless, outnumbered, and unarmed. According to some research, skinhead and hate gangs have lower reported rates of involvement in drug trafficking (Johnson, Webster, and Connors 1995) than other ethnic gangs. Some skinhead gangs are loosely organized and lack formal structures. Others are organized with formal structures. The more organized gangs select leaders, hold regular meetings, collect dues, distribute propaganda, and attend rallies (Levin and McDevitt 1993).

Stoner Gangs

"Stoner" gangs are another type of white ethnic gang. The term "stoner" has long been associated with America's drug subculture. When first used, it was directed toward long-haired youth involved in heavy drug use during the 1960s and 1970s. The term was expanded during the 1980s when the "stoner" subculture became collectively identified as a group. According to Spergel (1990), stoner gangs are characterized by their heavy use of drugs and anti-social behavior while under the influence. Drug use relative to stoners has been thought of as a form of retreatism. This has not changed but some research indicates that while they continue to be retreatist and they also have become more violent in orientation (Wooden, 1995). Although Stoner gangs are predominantly white, they can include members from other ethnic backgrounds, and sometimes reflect the ethnic composition of their neighborhoods (Operation Safe Streets 1995).

Stoner gangs represent a relatively rare form of juvenile gang. Stoner gang members represent only 3 percent of all white males in the custody of the California Youth Authority institutions (see Wooden, 1995). According to Wooden (1995), stoner gangs vary from 10 to 40 members, ranging from 13 to 20 years of age. According to Trostle (1992), there are four levels of involvement in stoner gangs. Similar to other gangs, there are "wannabes" (want-to-bes), gang members, hard core gang members, and satanic hard core members. The latter two types of members are most likely to be involved in crimes against others.

Stoner gangs tend to congregate at fixed locations, such as shopping malls. They are not territorial in the same sense as other gangs, but they do have specific areas where they hang out and abuse victims (Trostle, 1986; 1992). Typically stoner gangs do not engage in turf battles with rival gangs and can be found operating within the territories of other gangs. Jackson and McBride (1985:45) wrote:

> To date, there is little evidence of open conflict with established street gangs except for occasional flare-ups. On the contrary, what has happened is that many stoner groups have formed in areas inhabited by established gangs have allied themselves with the gang. In some cases, they have actually been accepted into the gang en masse as a separate clique.

Other gangs do not usually view them as a threat, but rather as strange and "wimps." Members of stoner gangs frequently associate with heavy metal music and may have preference for specific bands, which some will identify on their T-shirts (Jackson and McBride 1985; Trostle 1992). Stoner gang members often wear drug and satanic paraphernalia, such as pentagrams, roach clips, Converse® tennis shoes (because the trademark star represents a pentagram to them), zodiacs, and other items.

Stoner gangs are characterized by their anti-social and non-conventional behavior. They are anti-authority and view their purpose to destroy rather than protect. For example, some stoner gangs, especially those with a satanic outlook, have been found desecrating cemeteries, grave robbing, and vandalizing churches. When they create graffiti, it is usually full of satanic messages and symbols. There is a mysticism and secretiveness to their graffiti. They sometimes write messages backwards. Besides the use and sales of illegal substances, stoner gangs commit other criminal offenses, such as burglary, assault, and vandalism. Wooden's (1995) study of youth in the custody of the California Youth Authority found that 70 percent of the youth identified as stoner gang members were committed with burglary as their main offense. Regardless of offense, illegal drug use and abuse runs at the core of all stoner gangs. Wooden (1995) found that for those stoner youth in institutional settings, 94 percent were polydrug users and many reported early drug use in their lives.

Some stoner gangs are heavily involved with satanic rituals and are fascinated with the occult. Trostle (1992) contends that an understanding of satanism is critical to understanding stoner gangs. A key difference between the basic stoner gang and those with satanic orientations is the latter are more engaged in ritualistic activities (Wooden, 1995). Youth who tend toward the satanic rituals tend to be drawn from higher socioeconomic backgrounds than youth involved in other forms of street gangs (Wooden, 1995). It has been proposed by Wooden (1995) that youth involvement in satanism may be a dramatic attempt to reject the conventional values, beliefs, and religion of parents. These youth have a distinctive style of dress and tend to be more territorial than their stoner counterparts. They make a conscientious effort to be secretive about their rituals.

Other White Ethnic Gangs

Studies of white ethnic gangs other than skinheads include Whyte's (1943) study of European American working class youths, and Myerhoff and Myerhoff's (1964) study of European American middle class gangs. These gangs were delinquent at times, but most of their activities were non-delinquent. The gangs studied by Myerhoff and Myerhoff had all the trappings of the middle class, including good clothes and cars, yet chose to participate in gangs. Automobiles were a central concern for these youths. They did not consider themselves to be delinquent. They also were unconcerned about upward mobility, and seemed to be generally assured of some degree of success in life by virtue of their middle class backgrounds. These gangs, in Myerhoff and Myerhoff's view, approximated Yablonsky's near groups because they lacked organizational structure, were not cohesive, and had unstable memberships.

Lowney (1984) conducted an ethnographic study of middle class European American youths in California. He found the "Wall Gang" to be loosely organized, composed of youths from middle class backgrounds, and involved in drugs and alcohol. The gang had twenty-three members, who were seventeen to nineteen years old. The gang had unclear roles, and peripheral members participated sporadically in the gang. Youths' needs for companionship with other youths with similar backgrounds seemed to be the main reason for gang involvement. Crime and delinquency were not major pursuits of the gang. In the final analysis, the "gang" described by Lowney seems to be more of a social club than a true gang.

ASIAN AMERICAN GANGS

There are a variety of Asian American gangs including Korean, Chinese, Hmong, Taiwanese, Pacific Islander (Fijian, Samoan, Tongan), Thai, Laotian, Cambodian, Vietnamese, Filipino, and Japanese gangs (Sanders 1994). The role national histories has played in influencing the formation and characteristics of Asian American gangs is an important theme in much of the research and literature (Klein, Maxson, and Miller 1995). The national and ethnic differences between these gangs are important and should be kept in mind when considering Asian American gangs. It is also important to note that crime and delinquency rates historically have been low in Chinese American communities (Chin 1990), and that we have not been aware of much juvenile gang activity in these communities until relatively recently. Adult triads and tongs (see Chapter 6), however, have had a long history of activity in Chinese American communities. Asian gangs are found primarily in coastal cities such as New York City, San Francisco, and Portland, which have large Asian immigrant populations. Duran (1987) reported that Asian gangs outnumbered white ethnic gangs by a margin of two to one.

Asian American gangs have been of particular concern in San Francisco, New York, and Boston. Chinese American gangs have been the subject of considerable research (Chin 1986; Joe 1994; Joe and Robinson 1980; Rice 1977; Takagi and Platt 1978). There is some evidence that these gangs have been increasing in size and activity. Some authors attribute the rise of Asian American gangs to the increase in immigration of Hong Kong Chinese during the 1970s (Miller 1977). Hong Kong gangs are thought to be more organized than other Asian American gangs. More recently, southeast Asian gangs have also been increasingly prevalent and active.

According to Klein (1995b), Asian American gangs have a wide variety of structures and tend to be less street-oriented than other gangs. In addition, these gangs tend to be less territorial, specialize on certain types of crime, and practice instrumental as opposed to expressive forms of violence. Violence for Asian American gangs is usually seen as a means to an end. Official estimates of the age of Asian American gang members range from 10 to 40 years old (Operation Safe Streets 1995). They may use tattoos to symbolize power or indicate membership, but graffiti is of little importance.

Asian American juvenile gangs have a history of violence. This has been particularly true for Chinese gangs, whose American roots stem back to the early 1900s and the "Tongs," secret fraternal organizations out of which emerged the more youthful Wah Chings (Youth of China). The Wah Chings were first formed to protect foreign-born Chinese from American-born Chinese. Over time the Wah Chings became increasingly predatory and started to victimize Chinese people in their communities (Chin 1990a). The Wah Ching became so violent that the Chinese community eventually opposed them. From the Wah Chings came other juvenile gang organizations, the "Yu Li," "Bamboo United," "Young Suey Sing," "The Four Seas," and "Joe Fong Boys" organizations. The development of tongs in the United States was fueled by the Chinese Exclusion Act of 1882 which prohibited Asian Americans (Chinese) from obtaining good jobs in mainstream society. This forced Chinese men to turn inward to their communities for employment which in turn provided fertile ground for the development of Tongs (see English 1995). The violence of Asian gangs appears to be linked to issues of territoriality, links with organized crime, and protection of markets for illegal services (Campbell 1984; Chin 1986; Chin 1990, 1990a; Posner, 1991).

Chinese American Gangs

Joe and Robinson (1980) studied Chinese American juvenile gangs in the San Francisco area. They found that gang members tended to be male, 13 to 19 years old, recent immigrants, and had school problems and difficulties in learning English. The gangs had fairly high turnover rates, and consisted of between 10 and 20 members. Characteristic of the gangs was the practice of "ah fai," a form of antisocial behavior. A common "ah fai" was public display of martial arts, which also helped create the warrior image of the gangs.

Key to the gangs studied by Joe and Robinson was the relationship between the larger host society and the gangs. The youths in the gangs were for the most part alienated from the larger society. They perceived themselves as lacking access to socially desired roles in the larger society. This perception of blocked opportunities, Joe and Robinson suggested, perpetuated the Chinese American juvenile gangs. The absence of good jobs, the existence of job discrimination, and the poor quality of education and housing have also been identified by Rice (1977) as contributing to participation in gangs by Asian youths.

The importance of Asian cultures in contrast to the larger American host culture seems to be another theme in much of the research on Asian American gangs. Rice (1977) studied Chinese American gangs in New York. Some of the gangs he identified as operating in New York were the "Black Eagles," "Ghost Shadows," "White Eagles," and "Flying Dragons." Rice linked the prevalence of gangs to the breakdown of the traditional Chinese family and its values. The flood of immigrants from Hong Kong has exacerbated problems for the Chinese American communities, as the teenage population in these communities has increased. Rice argues that these immigrants have prior experience with gangs in Hong Kong, and this facilitates their involvement in gangs in the United States. Their criminal activities, according to Rice, include robbery, drug sales, burglary, theft, muggings, gambling, and gang warfare. Extortion and loan sharking have also been used as sources of income by Chinese American gangs (Chaze 1984).

According to Rice, the Chinese American juvenile gangs were all male, with about a dozen members who were 13 to 20 years old. Rice characterized the gangs as more organized than other types of juvenile gangs. Like Joe and Robinson (1980), Rice (1977) provided some information on community responses to Chinese American gangs in New York. According to Rice, Chinese Americans of New York City were generally unwilling to talk with outsiders about juvenile gangs. Older Chinese Americans were fearful of gangs, and criminal activity by gangs was seldom reported to the police. Citizens feared reprisal by the gangs. In addition, the communities did not want the negative publicity associated with gang activity. The gangs usually did not assault tourists in the area, but rather selected other Asian Americans as their victims.

Takagi and Platt (1978) studied Chinese American juvenile gangs in San Francisco's Chinatown. They contended that youth groups are incorrectly labeled as gangs by the mass media and the criminal justice system. Groups of youths were identified as being criminal, and this was used as evidence of gang behavior.

Chinese American Gangs in the 1980s and 1990s

Chin (1986, 1990, 1990a) provided more recent studies of Chinese American gangs in New York City and elsewhere in the United States. These gangs were actively involved in drug sales and specialized in the distribution and sale of heroin. The gangs had strict norms against drug use by gang members because it interfered with the business operations of the gang. It was assumed by the gang that heroin addicts were not dependable. According to Chin (1990), most Chinese American gang members were males. Females hang out and perform limited functions but are not initiated into the gangs (Chin 1990a). Gang members are 13 to 37 years old, with an average age of 22.7. This range takes us out of the domain of juvenile gangs into gangs that are clearly adult gangs, but which include juvenile members. The gangs studied by Chin were ethnically homogeneous, predominantly comprised of Hong Kong, Vietnamese-Chinese, and Taiwanese immigrants, and ranged from 20 to 50 members.

In keeping with most of the research on Asian gangs, Chin found a fairly rigid hierarchical organizational structure with well-defined norms which were enforced by severe physical sanctions. The gangs had several levels of command, and specialized roles such as shooters and streeters (those who directed members at the street level). In addition, a core, inactive, and peripheral membership structure was also identified. This pattern is again typical of Asian gangs (see Chapter 6). Chin reported that direct links between juvenile gangs and adult triads and tongs were common. Some of the gangs had branches in other cities. Chin's (1986, 1990; 1990a) gangs used violence to control territory and to coerce the Chinese American community. Even though territories were clearly defined, Chinese American gangs were less oriented toward protecting territory than other ethnic gangs, unless their economic interests were threatened.

The relationships and differences between tongs and youth gangs are not always understood by outsiders, and specifically law enforcement. Tongs and tong members sometimes hire youth gangs to help control the street and carry out criminal activities. Tongs do not tend to view juvenile gangs as part of their structures (English 1995). To the outsider the tong and the gang are one in the same but in the view of the tong they are not. The gang is simply a hired gun for the tong and nothing more. Rights and privileges of membership are not extended to the gangs by the tong. Joe (1994) reported that gang links to the tongs of San Francisco were tenuous at best (only the older gang members knew much about the tongs) and were more a matter of personal than collective linkages. The gang members she interviewed (half of whom were Chinese, with others of Chinese-Vietnamese, Vietnamese, Cambodian, and other Asian origins) appeared to be largely ignorant of the triads in the San Francisco area.

Chin (1990a) reported that Chinese American gangs often had codes of ethics that was rigidly adhered to by members. For example, one code prohibited members from burglary (seen as a less honorable crime), victimizing the poor, harming rival gangs' families, and hurting or cooperating with the police. Chin (1990) also summarized other characteristics of Chinese American gangs which, in his view, made them different from other gangs. Chin argued that culturally bound concepts used to explain other gangs may not be useful in understanding Chinese American gangs. Briefly, Chinese American gangs associate with powerful community organizations, conduct legitimate business in addition to their illegal activity, form networks (national and international), are influenced by traditional Chinese criminal organizations such as tongs and triads, are systematic in their victimization of businesses, and are motivated primarily by economic gain.

Another study of Chinese American gangs was conducted by Mano (1986). Mano's interviews with Chinatown residents revealed that non-English speaking youthful immigrants from Hong Kong had increased the numbers of gang members. Youths in these gangs were sometimes sponsored by adult criminal organizations. These gangs were actively involved in drug sales, extortion, and gambling. Difficulties experienced by youths in assimilating into American culture and learning the English language, as well as dropping out of school, were identified as influencing the youths to join gangs.

Campbell (1984b) noted that Asian American gangs may be small in numbers, but they tend to have high homicide rates, possibly because of their links to organized crime. Most Chinese American gangs are motivated by profit and have clearly defined economic objectives. Chin (1990), summarizing the research on Chinese American gangs, suggested that they could become a major organized crime problem in the United States in the 1990s, as they become dominant in heroin and other racketeering activities (see also U.S. Department of Justice 1988a, 1989). Their links with adult Chinese American crime organizations may facilitate this evolution.

Other Asian American Gangs

The existence of other Asian American juvenile gangs is well documented (Vigil and Yun 1990). Indochinese gangs of Cambodian, Laotian, Thai, Hmong, and Vietnamese youth have reportedly been actively involved in extortion, welfare fraud, auto theft, and commercial burglary in the United States (Operation Safe Streets 1995). Recently, there has been a notable increase in the number of Southeast Asian gangs in the United States (Klein, 1995b; Operation Safe Streets 1995). Part of this increase can be attributed to the reluctance of communities and people to report to authorities or outsiders the extent of gang crime or activity (Klein, 1995b; Vigil and Yun, 1990). San Francisco has Vietnamese American gangs including the Paratroopers, Hopsing Boys, Black Eels, and Frogmen, and Los Angeles has the Viet Ching, V–Boyz, and Pomona Boyz. Vietnamese American gangs in California communities have been covered by the press, investigated by congress, and examined by scholarly researchers (English 1995; Morganthau 1982; Willoughby, 1991; Senate Subcommittee on Juvenile Justice 1983; Vigil and Yun 1990).

Some Vietnamese American gang members may dress distinctively, but they avoid gang insignia and other gang trappings in order to avoid being identified as gang members by authorities. Vietnamese, as is typically the case with other Asian American gangs, are difficult groups for outsiders to penetrate. When coupled with the fact that most Asian American gangs, including the Vietnamese, victimize people from their own communities, it is easy to understand why so little is known about these gangs.

Without adequate social controls, such as law enforcement, community rejection, and culture sensitive education, these gangs have been able to proliferate without much social resistance. It has been suggested that as refugees, many of these youth are unfamiliar with American culture and social expectations. The breakdown of traditional family support created a void that gang membership seems to fill (Willoughby, 1991). There have been reports of Vietnamese gangs in many of the major cities such as New York; Washington, D.C.; Boston; Minneapolis; and Houston (English 1995; Willoughby, 1991).

Vigil and Yun (1990) described some of the experiences of Vietnamese youths immigrating to the United States, including discrimination, difficulties with culture and language, alienation, and the development of a subculture within American society. They characterized Vietnamese gangs as economically-oriented and pragmatic. Like other Asian American gangs, Vietnamese American gangs are most likely to victimize their own ethnic group, other Vietnamese Americans (See also Willoughby, 1991).

T.J. English (1995) conducted a detailed case study of one Vietnamese gang, the BTKs (Born to Kills) that operated in New York City. English found the gang to be mostly comprised of teenagers, but some older members of Vietnamese gangs could be in their mid-thirties. English found the gang to be extremely violent and engaged in criminal activities in the Chinatown district of the city. The gang limited its criminal activities to Asian Americans because members knew victims did not understand the criminal justice system and were unlikely to report crimes to law enforcement. The gang had a sense that Asian Americans were isolated from the mainstream and did not benefit from the criminal justice system. The most common criminal activities were extortion, drug sales, and robbery. Drug sales focused on heroin and crack, with members using crack and alcohol as their drugs of choice. One form of violent crime this gang and other Vietnamese gangs are known to practice was home invasion. Home invasions are robberies where the perpetrators plan the crime so that the family will be home. The advantage is that the family members can be bound up, tortured, terrorized, and made to reveal where the family hides its wealth. Part of the reason that this is effective is that many recent Asian immigrants, perhaps out of mistrust or uncertainty about American financial institutions, keep their money at home instead of in the bank, thus making them more vulnerable to such robberies.

Members of the gang were called *sai lows* (little brothers) and the leader the *Anh hai* (number two brother). The gang had no initiation rituals but had rules for getting out of the gang. Gang members routinely got tattoos to signify gang membership but the tattoos could be of anything they chose. Among Vietnamese gang members, tattoos of skulls, dragons, and knives are popular (Willoughby, 1991). The gang spelled out gang rules and loyalties on paper. The rules were: no betrayal of other gang members, no cooperation with the police, tattoos had to be removed when members left the gang, and criminal acts needed to be cleared with local gang members. Vietnamese American gangs are structured, but members are permitted to come and go as they please. The gangs are not oriented towards turf issues. There is little evidence of formal initiation rites, and membership is linked to preexisting personal relationships. The age of gang members reportedly ranges from age 11 to the mid-twenties (Willoughby, 1991). There is little or no role differentiation.

Vigil and Yun found that gang members fought rarely, usually as a last resort in resolving a dispute over money. Like Chinese American gangs,

Vietnamese gangs appear to have financial gain as their primary motivation. The crimes they are involved with include extortion, drug sales, bookmaking, armed robberies, auto theft, and kidnapping. Some juvenile gang members will occasionally work for adult Vietnamese gangs. If they have a purpose, most would say that it is survival. Unlike the Chinese American gangs, Vietnamese American gangs do not form ties with adult organizations in the community (Chin 1990a). Vietnamese gangs are difficult for authorities to track because when involved in crime sprees, they typically move from city to city unlike other Asian American gangs that tend to stay in the same area (Willoughby 1991). This mobility is facilitated by their adaptability to live out of cars, crash pads, or motels in a number of cities. They are sometimes referred to as "nomads," "casual," or "motel" gangs. They are also hard to track because Vietnamese gang members and gangs can easily blend into other gangs.

JAMAICAN POSSES

Jamaican youth gangs are relatively new to American society, and are primarily located in cities along the Eastern seaboard, but are also found in cities such as Seattle and Anchorage (Drowns and Hess 1990). Known as the Jamaican Posses, Jamaican gangs have been connected with cocaine trafficking and the violence that goes along with it. Ironically, some of the most violent examples of Posse activities have occurred in the small (population 13,000) community of Martinsburg, West Virginia. Originally the Jamaicans arrived in Martinsburg as migrant farm workers, and it is believed that many entered the United States illegally. In recent years, bolstered by criminal contacts in their native Jamaica, some of the Jamaican settlers in Martinsburg became involved in dealing cocaine on the streets in plain view for all to see. From 1986 to 1988, 20 homicides were reported in Martinsburg, all related to the illegal drug trade. In a normal year, Martinsburg would have only one or two homicides. The drug trafficking and its associated violence had so occupied the community that residents, once able to leave their houses unlocked and free to walk the streets without fear of personal injury, could hardly go outside their homes without being offered cocaine in their driveways (Newsweek 1988).

Laurie Gunst's (1995) 10-year ethnographic study of Jamaican posses in Jamaica and the United States depicts posses as having youth but also adult members. She does not elaborate on the ages or other characteristics of the posse members operating in the United States. Youth belonging to posses migrate to the United States, frequently New York and Miami, to sell drugs. She describes Jamaican posses as being violent with a fatalistic attitude and outlook on life. Violence is used by the posses to control territory for the drug trade. The dangerous life on the streets of America's cities is viewed by posse members as a better alternative to life in the slums of Jamaica (see also Chapter 6).

CONCLUSION

Ethnic gangs in the United States represent unique blends of cultures of origin and the American host culture. In the case of African American gangs, little appears to remain of the African culture, largely lost through the centuries of slavery. Even African gangs with an Islamic orientation reflect not African culture, but the experience of African slaves and their descendants in the United States. Exceptions to these generalizations may be Jamaican, Haitian, and other Caribbean gangs, which come from areas in which African culture was not so thoroughly suppressed as it was in the United States during the period when slavery was legal.

Hispanic gangs may have concerns (brotherhood, machismo, loyalty to the barrio) similar to those of gangs in Latin American countries, but those concerns may be expressed differently in the cultural context of the United States. Machismo in Latin America, for example, may be more often expressed in sexual prowess and the ability to father children, especially sons (Thomlinson 1976:178). Hispanic gangs in the United States, in contrast, seem more likely than their Latin American counterparts to express machismo by engaging in violent behavior.

Asian American gangs appear to most closely resemble the gangs in their cultures of origin. Unlike African American, Hispanic, and white ethnic gangs, Asian American gangs appear to be highly organized and pragmatic. Profit is the principal motive. Asian American gangs tend to focus more on predatory property crime than other ethnic gangs, and violence is typically avoided except as a last resort. When Asian American gangs think of territory, they tend to be flexible, and think of turf boundaries as representing populations of potential victims. Asian American and Hispanic gangs share one important characteristic, the linguistic barrier that exists between them and the host culture, a barrier less evident for African American and most contemporary white ethnic gangs.

White ethnic gangs, common in the nineteenth and early twentieth centuries, appear to be much less prevalent and active in the last third of the twentieth century. One interesting perspective on this is provided by an African American female gang member, who, when asked why there were so few white gangs, responded, "Are you kidding? They got the two biggest gangs in this country—the KKK and the cops."[2] Recent (as of this writing) events involving police brutality toward nonwhite Americans, including a videotaped police beating of an African American suspect in Los Angeles, plus the existence of skinhead gangs and white supremacist organizations, can only fuel this perception that the difference between European American gangs and minority group gangs may be a matter of technical legal status, not behavior.

In a racially and ethnically divided society, the existence of gangs organized along racial and ethnic lines may be inevitable. Gangs appear to evolve out of primary friendship groups, and to the extent that segregation in our neighborhoods and schools leads to racially and ethnically homogeneous friendship groups, we may also expect it to lead to racially and ethnically homogeneous gangs. This is especially true when, in addition to skin color or country of origin, we add the language barrier experienced most acutely by Hispanic and Asian American communities with continuously high rates of immigration (and thus high prevalence of individuals who do not speak English). Eliminating racial, ethnic, and linguistic segregation would not, in all likelihood, eliminate gangs, but it would probably eliminate race, ethnicity, and language as criteria for gang membership, and result in more racially and ethnically heterogeneous juvenile gangs.

CHAPTER NOTES

[1]"Confederation" is a term that may give us some problems here. Malcolm Klein, in a personal communication, disagrees that the Bloods and Crips are a national confederation, and suggests that the Bloods and the Crips are not really confederations even in Los Angeles. (He also cautions that recruitment from among grade school children is rare.) As noted later in the chapter, there is a fair amount of imitation going on, with gangs using the "Crip" or "Blood" label to try to enhance their status. Similar appropriation of gang names to enhance gang status occurs in prison gangs (Fong et al. 1996). Also as noted in the chapter, the confederation (if it exists) of these gangs is a loose one, and rivalries and violence may arise between gangs that are nominally

members of the same confederation (more so for Crips than for Bloods). Whether one calls them a confederation or uses some other term (we are open to suggestions), it remains the case that there are gangs who call themselves Bloods or Crips in several American cities, that this identification may reflect actual rivalries between groups of gangs, and that even if the gangs are linked by no more than name, the "Crip" or "Blood" label appears to be an important element of their gang identity both to the members and to law enforcement officials and the larger community.

[2]Ice T (1994) takes this even farther: "The United States Army is one big gang. The cops are a gang. When they come, they come in units. . . . The Mafia uses the same tactics. Any organization—the FBI, the CIA—is a club, and if you [expletive deleted] with one member, they'll call for backup."

Chapter 4

FEMALE GANG MEMBERS AND FEMALE GANGS

One of the most consistent predictors of illegal behavior is gender (Elliott et al. 1989; Gold and Reimer 1975; Kercher 1988). Whether official statistics on arrest or self-report data on behavior are used, males have a higher prevalence and frequency of delinquent behavior than females. Some estimates of the extent of female participation in gangs are low. This finding is especially true for more serious offenses. Males also have higher rates of alcohol, marijuana, and other illicit drug use. These differences are so pronounced that they have led some researchers— mistakenly, we believe—to exclude female delinquency from consideration, and to exclude female subjects from their research designs.

Attempts have been made to construct separate explanations of male and female delinquency. Earlier efforts at explaining female delinquency focused on the presumed biological and psychological inferiority of women, or personal maladjustment (Giordano 1978; Rosenbaum 1991: 505–513; Shoemaker 1990:248–252). Later theories blamed female criminality on the women's liberation movement (Rosenbaum 1991:517–521; Shoemaker 1990:225–257). More recently, feminist theory has been applied to female delinquency (Chesney-Lind 1989; Rosenbaum 1991: 521–524).

A recurrent theme in both research and theory has been that female delinquency is quantitatively and perhaps qualitatively different from male delinquency. It should come as little surprise, then, that female gang participation differs substantially from male gang involvement, in a pattern that mirrors male-female differences in delinquent behavior more generally.

Gang research has consistently found that although females join juvenile gangs, they do not do so to the degree that males do (Miller 1975, 1977; Short 1968). Although historical evidence documents female participation in gangs since their inception, female participation in gangs has been relatively rare and minor compared to male involvement. Thrasher (1927) found only a half-dozen female gangs among the 1,313 gangs he studied, and he only considered two of them to be true gangs. He characterized female gangs as being immoral rather than criminal, and noted that illicit sex and occasional muggings were the typical gang activities. He suggested that the lack of female participation in gangs was a result of females' being more closely supervised by adults, and also a result of the influence of strong social traditions that dictated that "proper" female behavior was inconsistent with gang behavior.

Asbury (1926) reported historical evidence which indicated that females participated in gangs throughout the last 75 years of the nineteenth century. Asbury found that women assumed many active roles within the gangs of New York, and were not always auxiliaries. They also had gang leaders and full gang membership. Additional evidence of continued female involvement in gangs during later decades exists. For example, female gangs such as the Black Widows and the Slick Chicks were formed to support male zoot-suiters in the 1940s. Bernard (1949) found female gangs with names such as the "Robinettes" and "Chandeliers" were present in New York. Females being initiated into these gangs were expected to have sexual relations with male gang members, and were affiliated with male gangs.

Although historical evidence indicates female involvement in gangs, their participation rates have been low. Miller (1975) reported that no more than 10 percent of gang membership in major American cities was female. Conklin's (1989) summary of research on gangs estimated that males outnumbered females as gang members by a ratio of twenty to one. Gang researcher Anne Campbell is cited by Mydans (1990) as estimating about 10 percent of gang membership is usually female (see also Campbell 1991). These low estimates of female participation have been supported by other research (Campbell 1984b; Short and Strodtbeck 1965). A self-report study by Giordano (1978), however, found higher levels of female gang involvement, at least among hardcore delinquents. Esbensen, Huizinga, and Weiher (1993) found females represent about 20 to 46 percent of gang members in a Denver sample. Bjerregaard and Smith (1993) found female gang members constituted 22 percent of gang members in Rochester, New York, and Fagan (1990) found that 33 percent of gang members were female. Criminal justice data on offenses committed by gang members supports the low level of participation of females in gangs and gang delinquency. Esbensen and Huizinga (1993) reported that female gang members were likely to report lower levels of delinquent activity than males. Arrest statistics consistently indicate lower arrest rates for females than males in gangs (Spergel 1986). Goldstein and Glick (1994:9) conclude that males continue to outnumber females at a ratio of 20 to 1. Other estimates indicate a higher ratio of females to males. Summarizing much of the contemporary research on street gangs, Klein, Maxson, and Miller (1995) note the ratio of females to males can range from one female for every male to one for every ten males. A confounding factor in all of these estimates is that there is evidence that females may claim to be in gangs and dress like gang members, even when they are not really members. The Los Angeles Sheriff's Department found that in some of the most hard core gang areas, females will wear gang colors and claim they are gang members when in fact evidence shows that they are not (Operation Safe Streets 1995).

The low levels of female participation make those females involved in gangs particularly interesting because they are so exceptional in terms of their behavior, compared to other females. Female gang membership has been documented in Boston (Morash 1983; see also Giordano 1978), Philadelphia (Brown 1977), New York (Campbell 1984b; Hanson 1964), Los Angeles (Bowker et al. 1980; Bowker and Klein 1983; Harris 1988; Murphy 1978), and other cities (Miller 1973; Rice 1963; Quicker 1974). As Campbell (1987) noted, much of the research on female gangs and gang membership has a journalistic rather than a scientific focus. Campbell (1987, 1990) expressed a concern over the lack of scientific research on female gangs and females participating in gangs (see also Harris 1988; Hopper and Moore 1990). Bowker et al. (1980) also noted the relative dearth of scholarly research on female delinquent gangs of female participation in delinquent incidents with male gang members.

STUDIES OF FEMALE GANGS

Hanson (1964) provided a journalistic account of what female gangs were like in her study of a New York gang, the "Dagger Debs." She found that female gangs were affiliated with male gangs, but often functioned independently of the males. The gang she studied had twelve members and discernible leaders and members who played special roles within the gang, such as war counselor. Females had lower statuses than male gang members, and the male gang members placed considerable emphasis on the role of female gang members as sex objects. Within the gang, females' statuses depended on their fighting prowess. Gang members expressed a sense of territory and of control over that territory. The

Dagger Debs were violent, and participated in fights with other female and male gangs. Campbell (1990) observed that Hanson's emphasis was on the sexuality of the gang members, an emphasis typical in early female gang research.

At about the same time, Rice (1963) studied a female gang in New York, the "Persian Queens," who associated with members of the "Mohawks," a male gang. Female gang members lacked a sense of power and status within the community, and had low self-esteem. Rice concluded that there was little a female could do within the gang to achieve a sense of power. Although fighting among females occurred, it was not respected by males. At the same time, gang members who behaved in stereotypically feminine ways were open to sexual exploitation. Thus neither fighting prowess nor more conventional behavior served as avenues for status attainment for the females in the gang.

Miller (1973) studied the "Molls," an all white, female, Roman Catholic gang, and the "Queens," an African American, female gang. The Molls were 13 to 16 years old, and were involved with truancy, theft, non-marital sex, vandalism, and assault. Truancy and theft were the most common offenses. Like many female gangs, the Molls were affiliated with a male gang, the "Hoods," which provided them with approval and leadership. The Molls were viewed in their neighborhood as "bad girls," and they attempted to emulate and find favor with their male gang counterparts. Again like many other gangs, the Molls had more active and less active members. Only 20 percent of the Molls finished high school.

The Queens were lower class African American females, affiliated with the "Kings," a male gang. The Queens, in contrast to the Molls, were largely noncriminal, with the exception of assaults. During Miller's study, the Queens bested a male gang in numbers of assaults. The Queens were less cohesive than the Molls, and most (80%) finished high school and were upwardly socially mobile.

Brown (1977) described an all female, African American gang with 20 to 30 members. The gang was located in Philadelphia, and was unusual because it was a fully autonomous female gang. Gang members were in their early teens to twenties. Members were initiated into the gang by demonstrating fighting prowess. Violence and conflict were part of the gang's activities, and members worked to build reputations as fighters.

Brown concluded that females shared some parallel experiences with their male gang counterparts, but were different in some important respects. Compared to males, females had stronger family obligations, different exposure to mainstream society, and more powerful peer pressures. The reasons for female gang membership were basically social, including desires for popularity and excitement.

Harris' (1988) study of Chola (Hispanic female) gangs in southern California found a Hispanic subculture with mixed American and Hispanic influences. The subculture, in turn, affected gang participation. High dropout rates, low aspirations, lack of commitment to achievement and success norms, and an orientation to the present rather than to the future all contributed to the development of a Hispanic delinquent subculture, which in turn helped to lead to the formation of gangs. Moore's (1978) study of Hispanic female gangs in southern California found them to be territorial, age-graded, combative, and involved in drug use. Affiliations with male gangs were common.

Campbell (1984b) studied individuals from three different female gangs in New York City: the "Sandman Ladies," who identified themselves as a biker gang, although motorcycles were uncommon to the gang; the "Five Percent Nation"; and the "Sex Girls." The Sandman Ladies, a predominantly Puerto Rican gang, wore all of the trappings of an outlaw biker gang, including Nazi and satanic symbols. Some of the members of the gang had children, and looked upon themselves as good mothers, despite their gang activity. [Horowitz (1983) found a similar orientation among Hispanic female gang members, who went to great lengths to ensure that their children were taken care of, well dressed, and loved.] The Sandman Ladies were involved in drugs and conflict with other gangs, and were affiliated with a male gang.

The Sex Girls were formerly auxiliaries of a former male gang which at the time of the study had almost disintegrated. The Sex Girls were mixed Hispanic and African American, and were involved in robbery, burglary, and drug dealing. The Five Percent Nation were African American, organized around an unorthodox religion, and incidentally but frequently involved in crime.

Campbell noted that gangs tended to be local and isolated, not to know the names of gangs in other cities. Even when they were being sought by police, gang members were reluctant to leave their own turf. The gang structures imitated structures in conventional society: business, the military, the family. Crime was part of a lifestyle that often included relatively conservative values, but these values were applied at the primary group level, not universalistically. Gangs were viewed as a means of protection for families and neighborhoods. Like other researchers, Campbell noted that gangs tended to break up as members got older and were increasingly involved in heterosexual relationships. Again, like other researchers, Campbell found that the gang did little to improve the status of its female members.

Jack Moore's (1993) research on skinhead gangs noted that females joined skinhead gangs but not to the same extent as males. While they shared many of the views of the males, they typically did not engage in criminal behavior or decision making to the same extent as the males. Rather, they assumed secondary roles and statuses to male members. The males typically thought of themselves as superior to the females. Skinheads did not make leadership roles available to females. Moore (1993:80), commenting on their participation, concluded, "Women are definitely on the skinhead bus, though perhaps toward the back and rarely as drivers."

Carl S. Taylor (1993) conducted a recent study of Detroit's inner-city female gang members. African American females had been involved in gangs in Detroit for decades. He found the African American females joining gangs felt abandoned by African American leadership and society in general. He characterized them as being disenfranchised from society. Unlike much of the research on females and gangs, the gangs Taylor studied were much more than simple auxiliaries to male gangs. They acted quite independent of male gangs. Taylor concluded that there has been a major attitude shift among females. The nature of the gangs, as described by the women he interviewed, varied. Underground economy is a reality and the only avenue available for these women. The opportunity to make money in corporate or scavenger gangs was an attractive lure for African American females in Detroit. Taylor observed that African American female gang members were invisible to society and that gangs filled the void created by unemployment and homelessness. Taylor classified many of the females and the type of gangs they belonged to as scavenger gangs in that they do whatever they need to survive. Females in these scavenger gangs, like their male counterparts, may commit crimes as individuals or as members of the gang.

Goldstein and Glick (1994) provided brief descriptions of two female gangs that operated in the Brownsville (near Crown Heights) section of New York. The Deceptanets were formed in 1985. This gang consisted of about 50 members who pulled their hair back and wore worn jeans and Reebok® sneakers. They used needles, mace, and razors as weapons. They were known as a vicious gang whose members robbed other females of their jewelry and rode subways to victimize commuters. The Deceptanets were known to stick needles into their victims in order to distract them while they took their wallets. The gang recruited members from local high schools. The Brownsville Girls formed in 1991. There were about 25 members of this gang who ranged in age from 16 to 21. They dressed neatly, wearing slacks, Timberline® boots, and blouses. This gang formed to protect themselves from other female gangs, including the Deceptanets. They did not attend school, but did hang out in front of school to recruit new members. Goldstein and Glick noted that they used razors to protect themselves, but were not known as a violent gang except when trying to defend themselves.

THE NATURE OF FEMALE PARTICIPATION IN GANGS

Miller (1975) noted that women have traditionally been involved with gangs in three ways: as branches or auxiliaries of male gangs, as autonomous gangs, and as participants in mixed-sex gangs (see also Hardman 1969; Short 1968). The women's auxiliary, Miller (1972) found, was the most common form, but other authors have suggested that this form may be on the decline (Bowker 1978; Bowker and Klein 1983; Taylor 1993).

Females form auxiliaries to male gangs and not vice versa. A common practice is for a female gang to feminize the name of the male gang, such as the "Little Diablas" in Los Angeles (Bernard 1949; Hanson 1964; Harris 1988; New York City Youth Board 1960; Rice 1963; Taylor 1990). Bowker and Klein (1983) found that in the 1960s, female gangs were always affiliated with male gangs in east Los Angeles. Evidence exists that female auxiliaries are often important components of male gangs (Hanson 1964; Harris 1988). Harris concluded that there is usually a female component to male Hispanic gangs. There is some evidence, however, that all-female gangs that are not auxiliary to male gangs are becoming more common in larger cities (see also Taylor 1993). In addition, evidence on contemporary female gangs indicates that some female gangs and gang members resist and resent male intrusions into the affairs of the female gang (Campbell 1990).

Female Gang Members as Sex Objects

With few exceptions, researchers have portrayed female gang members as sex objects, at least in gangs of mixed gender (Bernard 1949; Hopper and Moore 1990; Rice 1963). The theme of women as sexually delinquent appeared in Cohen (1955), who suggested that female gang members expressed their strain between goals and achievement through female sexuality. This led some gang experts to conclude that the best way to curb female participation in gangs was to turn them from sex objects into "good wives." This was attempted by teaching them homemaking and cooking skills, how to wear makeup, and other stereotypically feminine activities (Campbell 1984) in the period following the publication of Cohen's (1955) theory.

Hanson (1964) concluded that females were sex objects within the gang context. She also reported that female sexuality was used to promote wars between gangs, and that females sometimes baited rival male gang members into conflicts. In a study of biker gangs, Hopper and Moore (1990) found that females were classified as "Mamas," who were expected to have sexual relations with any male gang member on demand; "Old Ladies," who occasionally faced similar expectations, but basically were linked to one male and were labeled as his property; and "Sheep," new recruits to the gang who were expected to have sex with all male gang members as an initiation rite. Some female gang members worked as strippers and prostitutes to make money to support the gang. The conclusion reached by Hopper and Moore was that females in these gangs were sexually abused and exploited. Their status was lower than the status of the males in the gang.

This pattern of females being sexual objects is not true for all females in gangs, particularly members of all-female gangs. Some female gang members actively avoid the label of being sexually loose. For example, Campbell (1984b, 1987) found that sexual promiscuity was frowned upon by members of female gangs. Female gang members did not want to be labeled whores by others in the gang.

Box 4.1: Male comments about female gang members in Denver

"If girls want to be in it [the gang], either they could have sex or be beat in, either way. Sometimes there are three guys with one girl, they take turns."

"There are a few girls in gangs. They're there to fill our needs."

Contemporary gang researchers question the emphasis placed on females as sex objects within the context of the gang. It is becoming increasingly clear that to reduce female participation to mere sex objects presents an incomplete picture of female gang activity. It remains the case, however, that female gang members, particularly in mixed-sex gangs, are not viewed as equals by their male counterparts. Mary Lou Salazar, a former high school counselor, has studied Hispanic gang members in Denver. Excerpts from her interviews are presented in Box 4.1. It is clear that the male gang members present the view that female members are not only treated as sex objects, but are also supposed to be subservient to the males. Moore (1991) cautions us that although some males do view females as sex objects, there is a wide range of attitudes held by males of females within Hispanic gangs. What is unclear is the extent to which this is merely posturing, and to what extent it accurately reflects the attitudes of the male gang members.

Crime and Delinquency

As noted previously, delinquent and criminal activities among female gangs are not as prevalent as in male gangs. Police records consistently have shown that female gang members are arrested less frequently and for less serious crimes than male gang members (Fagan 1990; Miller 1975, 1977). Fagan, however, notes that the delinquency of female gang members is substantially higher than the delinquency of nongang males or females (see also Bjerregaard and Smith 1993). Giordano (1978), using a self-report scale, found that females in gangs reported higher levels of delinquency than nongang females.

In mixed-sex gangs, males and females may have opposite effects on each other's delinquency. Female involvement with male gangs may have a dampening effect on male crime and violence (Bowker et al. 1980; Bowker and Klein 1983). Klein (1971) noted that female gang members were less likely to start gang violence and participate in gang violence than males. When females did participate in gang delinquency, they were more likely to participate in minor incidents rather than in more violent or serious events. Male gang members, on the other hand, appear to increase the delinquency rates of female gang members (Giordano 1978).

It is important to note that female involvement in delinquent and criminal activities as members of mixed-sex gangs may be encouraged by male gang members because females are less likely to be caught or to suffer legal consequences than males. Some male gangs use females to carry drugs and weapons because they believe that females are less likely to be searched by law enforcement officers, who are predominantly male (Campbell 1984b). It would be wrong to conclude that females perform such functions solely for the approval of males in the gang. Some evidence indicates that for female gang members, acceptance or approval by their female peers is more important than acceptance or approval from male gang members (Bowker and Klein 1983; Giordano 1978).

Some authors have lamented the growing number of violent female gangs as early as the 1960s (Hanson 1964). Hanson concluded that female gang leadership and status were based on fighting prowess and the degree of the gang member's participation in "Bopping" (gang warfare). Conflicts involving female gang members tend to be directed toward rival female gangs or toward other members within the same gang, in the latter case usually over boyfriends (Campbell 1984b; Harris 1988; Weisfeld and Feldman (1982). Moore's (1991) research on two Hispanic gangs in Los Angeles found that most female gang members reported that they dated males from other gangs. Females historically have been less likely than males to use guns, and tend to rely on fists and knives (Campbell 1984b). There is a possibility that this may be changing, however; Fishman (1995) suggests that as African American females face worsening conditions of racism, poverty, and fewer opportunities for legitimate employment, they may be more inclined to join criminal gangs for economic gain.

Female Status Within Mixed-Sex Gangs

Research on female participation in juvenile gangs has focused on the status of females within the gang structures and status relationships between male gangs and associated female gangs. Much of the research has found that females generally are treated as subordinates and assume inferior statuses compared to male gang members (Hopper and Moore 1990; Rice 1963; Short 1968). Typical is Miller's (1973) study of the female gang called the "Molls." Miller found that status for females was attained only through association with the males. Miller later reported (Miller 1975) that female roles had not changed, and that they continued to have secondary roles in the gang, such as decoy or weapons carrier. Bowker et al. (1980) reached a similar conclusion. They found that most females were excluded from planning and action phases of gang delinquency. They are treated as possessions of the gang rather than as participating members. This pattern is not always the case. Joan Moore (1991) found that almost two-thirds of Hispanic female gang members she questioned felt they were not treated like possessions by the male gang members. More of the males questioned, however, agreed that females were treated as possessions. In a summary of 30 years of experience in gang research, Klein (1995a) noted that females participate in some gang meetings, but are routinely excluded from more important meetings, partly out of chivalry and partly out of fear that they will reveal information to police, rival gang members, or others. In general, research suggests that females have not been successful in achieving high status, legitimate or illegitimate, through gang membership.

Socially, the hanging out behavior characteristic of male juvenile gangs is also typical for female gangs (Klein 1971). Campbell (1984b) found that hanging out was a main activity of female gangs. Similar patterns were observed by Miller (1973) and by Harris (1988). Much of the "effort" of hanging out is placed on street talk and developing reputations as being crazy, tough, and good fighters, all of which relate to the females' perceived status in the gang.

CHARACTERISTICS OF FEMALES IN GANGS

Female gang members, like their male counterparts, tend to come from impoverished backgrounds and dysfunctional families, and have histories of physical and sexual abuse (Campbell 1984; Harris 1988; Moore 1988). Dropping out of school, low academic achievement, and involvement in drugs and alcohol are also typical of females who join gangs. In addition to all of the disadvantages based on their social and economic background, they are also confronted with the additional influences of sexual discrimination and sexism. They have even fewer opportunities for success, such as employment in well paying jobs, than their low income male counterparts. Finally, females more than males suffer the consequences of teenage pregnancy, and the burden of raising children as single parents.

Ages of female gang members have been reported to range from 15 to 30 in New York (Campbell 1984b), 15 to 18 in Los Angeles and Watts (Mydans 1990), early teens to twenties in Philadelphia (Brown 1978), to mid-thirties in white biker gangs (Hopper and Moore 1990). Females tend to leave the gangs at earlier ages than males. For example, by the age of 18, many of the females in Hagedorn's 1988 study of Milwaukee gangs had left the gang.

Attention to ethnicity has been useful in understanding both male and female gangs. Female Hispanic gangs (Hanson 1964; Harris 1988; Murphy 1978; Mydans 1990) and African American gangs (Brown 1977; Campbell 1984) have been documented and studied by scholars and journalists. Asian American female gangs, by contrast, are conspicuously absent from the gang literature. From the studies of Asian American gangs, it appears that female participation with full membership is rare.

WHY DO FEMALES JOIN GANGS?

The traditional explanations for female involvement in crime and delinquency often rely on psychological adjustment and personal problems as explanatory factors (Bowker et al. 1983). For example, Short (1968) suggested that females associated with gangs because they were less socially adequate and less attractive. Other scholars have concluded that females in gangs are more likely than males to be placed on the "socially disabled" list (Giordano et al. 1986). The same view has generally been held by delinquency theorists, who assume that female delinquency is a result of maladjustment (Rosenbaum 1991).

This approach differs from the explanations for male involvement, which focus on social structural factors such as blocked opportunities, low socioeconomic status, and other social factors (Giordano 1978). Evidence suggests that females are also affected by social structural factors similar to those factors that affect males. In one study comparing psychological and social structural factors, Bowker et al. (1983) concluded that for African American females, racism, sexism, poverty, and limited opportunity structures were more likely to determine female involvement in gangs than psychological adjustment factors, personality problems, sexual adjustment difficulties, or other problems of maladjustment. Similarly, Bjerregaard and Smith (1993) found that delinquency, drug abuse, peer delinquency, and early adolescent sexual activity were related to female participation in gangs, but low self-esteem, family processes, poverty, and social disorganization were not. In short, it appears that the explanations for female gang membership are not unique, but parallel the explanations for male gang membership.

Women's Liberation and Female Gang Members

One of the more controversial topics regarding female delinquency involves the role of the feminist movement. Adler (1975) suggested that females, in part as a result of the women's liberation movement, were becoming more assertive and were increasingly involved in traditionally male-dominated forms of crime and deviance. Adler hypothesized that there is a direct link between sex role changes occurring in society and increased female delinquency and crime. According to Rosenbaum (1991), UCR statistics for 1971 to 1985 indicated that male arrests increased by 6 percent while female rates increased by 37 percent. This suggests that there is, in fact, a greater increase in female crime than in male crime, and that female crime rates are becoming more similar to male crime rates, as Adler (1975) suggested.

Relative to gangs, if Adler's hypothesis is correct, then females may eventually catch up with males and participate in juvenile gangs in the same proportions as males. Adler and Adler (1979) concluded that females were becoming more involved in gang activity as they adopted male roles. Some of the change, however, may be a result not of changes in the behavior of females, but in the behavior of the criminal justice system toward females. Simon (1975) noted that statistics on female involvement in crime could have increased as a result of less favorable treatment by the criminal and juvenile justice systems.

Self-report data cast a different light on female crime and delinquency. Although males have higher rates of offending than females generally, this difference is more pronounced for serious offenses than for minor offenses (Elliott et al. 1983; Elliott et al. 1989). Canter (1982) found that females were not catching up with males in juvenile delinquency rates. Steffensmeier and Steffensmeier (1980) found that female involvement in minor offenses had increased, but that their involvement in major and violent offenses had not. Furthermore, totally autonomous female gangs remain relatively rare in American society (Giordano 1978).

Longitudinal data have not supported the thesis that the feminist movement has had any effect on the types of delinquency committed by females. Neither has any pattern of increase in levels of female criminal or delinquent activity been discovered (Steffensmeier and Steffensmeier 1980). Gold and Reimer (1975) found that both male and female delinquency tended to remain stable over time, with the exception of increased female substance use (mostly marijuana use) in the late 1960s. Large scale studies of juvenile gangs have also found little change in the extent of female participation in gang delinquency (Klein 1971; Miller 1975). Overall, the evidence suggests that female crime, delinquency, and gang activity, although more evident in official records now than in previous decades, has probably not changed substantially relative to male crime, delinquency, and gang activity, in terms of actual behavior.

FEMALE GANG STRUCTURE AND PROCESSES

Campbell (1984b) and Hanson (1964) found that female gangs have a discernible structure, with initiation rites, meetings, and other characteristics of formal organization. She also found that female gangs had a sense of "sisterhood" perhaps parallel to the "carnalismo" (brotherhood) found in male Hispanic gangs. According to some authors (Brown 1977; Campbell 1984b, 1990; Harris 1988), a strong sense of belonging to and identification with the gang is typical of female gangs, and expressions such as "sisters," "home girls," and "family" are common (Campbell 1990).

Moore (1988) and Harris (1988) found that females are not actively recruited into gangs, but join on the basis of friendship and family relationships and contacts. Initiation rites for female gangs in Los Angeles (Harris 1988; Mydans 1990), sometimes referred to as "court ins" or "jump ins," may involve physical violence. The prospective member ("wannabe") is attacked by female members of the gang to determine her sincerity in wanting to join the gang and to determine how tough she really is. On occasion a "fair fight" is held between a single gang member and the inductee. Winning or losing these fights is less important than demonstrating that the inductee has "heart" or courage. Other gangs simply allow new members to "walk in" without any initiation rite. While in the gang, however, the member typically must show toughness and courage in support of the gang. Otherwise she may be "courted out" or "jumped out," a ritual that may involve a mild to severe beating, depending on the circumstances surrounding the departure. Jumping out may be voluntary, as when a member leaves the gang because of marriage. Generally, the literature suggests that females are allowed to join and leave gangs more easily than males (Spergel 1990).

Research evidence indicates that while female gangs can have unique features, they are structured and have processes similar to if not exactly the same as those in male gangs. For example, they have a sense of territory, have leadership, hang out, occasionally commit illegal acts, are age graded (as in the case of Hispanic klikas), have more or less formal structures, act in concert, and otherwise operate in ways similar to male gangs. In some respects, female gang members may be more adept at forming close relationships with their peers than males (Campbell 1990).

CONCLUSION

A theme common to many of the studies of females in gangs is that they often live in contradictory worlds. They participate in theft and gang violence, but also hold more conventional values and aspire to conventional roles, such as being married, having a family, and caring for their children. (In this regard, they parallel some male Hispanic gang members.) They see the gangs as a way to be protected, to achieve some status, but membership in gangs leaves them vulnerable to sexual exploitation by male gang members and violent attacks by rival gangs. Females tend to join gangs later in life but also leave earlier. The latter tendency may be a result of a number of factors such as their having children, assuming parental responsibility, their aging out earlier than males, and other gender-related factors.

Differences between male and female gangs and gang members reflect differences between males and females more generally. Male gangs and gang members are more violent, more heavily involved in illegal activity and drug use, and more likely to be accorded status, respect, or approval for their violent behavior. Still, female gang members may be more involved in violent and illegal behavior than males who are not gang members. Female gang members face the same disadvantages as their male counterparts, and also the added dimensions of sexual discrimination and lack of opportunity, both in conventional and subterranean society. Campbell (1990:266) wrote of the experience of female gang members: "But in the end, gang or no gang, the girls remained alone with their children, still trapped in poverty and in a cultural dictate of womanhood from which there was no escape."

Chapter 5

GANGS IN WESTERN HISTORY

The previous chapters have provided a description of contemporary gangs in the United States. In this chapter and the next chapter, we broaden our focus, first in time and then across national boundaries, to try to put contemporary American gangs in a broader historical and comparative context. If we are to develop an adequate understanding of juvenile gangs, it is essential that we know not only what exists here and now, but how present-day American gangs differ from gangs in other times and places.

What we know about gangs in history is dependent on the amount of attention historians in different periods have paid to gangs. Nineteenth century American and British gangs have received considerable attention, but there is relatively little material on juvenile gangs in prior centuries. We cannot tell whether the lack of information about juvenile gangs in earlier centuries is attributable to scholarly neglect or to their relative scarcity. Taylor (1990) suggested that the origins of serious juvenile gang activity were tied to the shift from agrarian to industrial society. If so, then we would expect little juvenile gang activity prior to the eighteenth century. Still, by examining the historical evidence we can try to trace the evolution of juvenile gangs over long periods, and view the general social conditions associated with gang activity.

In spite of the value of the longitudinal view that the historical perspective offers, this perspective has important limitations for studying juvenile gangs. Definitions of gangs have varied over time and within historical contexts, just as they may vary from one jurisdiction to another today (see Chapter 1). Measures of crime and delinquency, insofar as they are available, have also varied, and have been if anything more limited in scope and reliability than contemporary measures. Information may be lost or biased by the writers and keepers of historical records. Another common pitfall is the projection of characteristics of contemporary society to the past by contemporary historians. Bearing in mind all of these qualifications, it remains the case that historical research has the potential for broadening our perspective on juvenile gangs, and helping us to discern the unique features of contemporary gangs from features that have characterized gangs across time.

GANGS AND PROTOTYPE GANGS PRIOR TO THE NINETEENTH CENTURY

Gangs or prototypes of gangs have probably been around much longer than most people would believe. For example, more than 1,600 years ago, Saint Augustine (A.D. 354–430) makes references to perhaps a type of adolescent gang in his *Confessions* (St. Augustine 1949). Saint Augustine describes his own involvement in criminal activities as a member of a group of youths. Morales (1992) notes that Saint Augustine believed that crimes committed as a party to a group seemed more rewarding. During the Middle Ages, youth groups sometimes formed and engaged in delinquent acts. Some of these youth groups only hint at being gangs (Capp 1977), while others clearly were gangs as defined in Chapter 1 (Bellamy 1973; Hanawalt 1979; McCall 1979). Chaucer used the term gang in his writing as early as 1390 (Klein 1995a). Historians generally agree that gangs were common during the fourteenth and fifteenth centuries, but the extent of youth involvement in these gangs is not always clear. Juvenile crime is relatively obscure during the Middle Ages because of the different practices of classifying offenders. Offenders were sometimes treated without respect to age by the criminal justice system (Hanawalt 1979). In fourteenth century England, Hanawalt found that criminals and criminal gangs were often sadistic and violent. These gangs stole livestock, committed robbery, extortion, rape, and numerous other offenses. Material gain was a clear motive for gangs in the Middle Ages (Bellamy 1973; Hanawalt 1979; McCall 1979).

In the fourteenth century, some of the gangs studied by Bellamy (1973) averaged about six members, came from all walks of society including the gentry, had internal organization, defined leadership, a hierarchical structure, and specialization of roles. Members were often related. Bellamy cites the example of the Coterel gang, whose core was comprised of James Coterel and his brothers. Membership in these gangs was interlocking. Gang members moved from gang to gang, and gangs sometimes cooperated on larger criminal endeavors. It is evident from the historical record that gangs of the Middle Ages were every bit as violent as contemporary gangs. The principal difference is that gang homicides in the Middle Ages were more physically direct and personal than today's drive-by shootings.

Not all medieval youth groups operated entirely outside the law. Youth groups known as "Abbeys of Misrule" because they drew their membership from abbey or trade schools existed in medieval France. These groups participated in violent football games, fights, and socially condoned activities. There is evidence of similar youth groups in England, but with less organization than those in France (Capp 1977). Germany and Switzerland also had similar groups (Willis 1974). Often these youth groups viewed their role as being the guardians of social morality; they performed social control functions and had the moral support of the community.

One practice of these groups was the *charivari*. Charivaris were mob-like demonstrations usually directed toward deaths, scolds, cuckolds, and upcoming marriages between mismatched couples (Davis 1971). They enforced the social order, but could also be part of religious, political, and economic protests (Shorter 1977; Thompson 1984). The principal motive of charivaris was to disrupt the community and harass the victims until they paid a bribe to quiet the commotion. The charivaris were similar to gangs in the respect that youths were identified with a specific group, performed delinquent acts, and acted in unity as a gang would. English church and court records indicate that while many of the activities of these youth groups were condoned by adults, some acts were clearly criminal (Capp 1977). The records show that gangs of youths rioted and battled with rival gangs from other schools and abbeys until as late as the seventeenth century.

During the 1600s English gangs with names such as the Hectors, Bugles, and Dead Boys fought each other and damaged property (Pearson 1983; Spergel 1995). These gangs wore colored ribbons to identify themselves. In Germany during the seventeenth and eighteenth centuries, bandits did not operate exclusively on their own, but were typically members of gangs, or at least of delinquent or criminal groups. Gang activity usually involved four to six members, with no criminal court records indicating more than twelve members involved in a single gang incident (Danker 1988). The groups were organized for crime and had specialists in certain areas, but lacked well-defined leadership, had no induction ceremonies, and had no fixed leadership.

The Industrial Revolution had an effect on juvenile gangs in England and other countries. The slums spawned by the Industrial Revolution were known to harbor gangs such as the "Redskins," the "Black Hand," and the "Beehives" in England (Fyvel 1961). Other nineteenth century English gangs included the "Gonophs," "Fagins," and the "Swell Mob" (Whitfield 1982).

There is some evidence that juvenile gangs existed in colonial America (Fox 1985). During the seventeenth and eighteenth centuries, there is substantial evidence of group or gang delinquency in New England (Beales 1975; Hiner 1975; Thompson 1984). One account in *Dunlop's American Daily Advertiser* complained about groups of juvenile boys creating problems for the citizens of Philadelphia (Sanders 1970). Stover (1986) reported that the citizens of Philadelphia met in 1791 to address the problem of bands of youth hooligans. Common activities of these youth groups included drinking, fighting, reading sexually-oriented material, sexual experimentation, and theft. These groups, however, were transitory, lacked group cohesion, and lacked other characteristics we would associate with contemporary juvenile gangs.

THE NINETEENTH CENTURY AND THE EVOLUTION OF THE TRUE JUVENILE GANG

The nineteenth century is regarded by many scholars as the century in which true juvenile gangs first appeared in the United States (Inciardi 1978). Asbury (1927) traced the appearance of gangs in the United States to the early 1800s in Chicago and New York. According to Asbury, the first gang may have been the "Forty Thieves," which operated out of New York. During the 1820s, the Forty Thieves, an Irish American immigrant gang, had a sub-gang of younger members called the Forty Little Thieves (Asbury 1927). The colorful names of these gangs give us a hint of their character. Early gangs included the "Pug Uglies," named after their pug hats, the "Shirt Tails," so named because they wore their shirt tails out of their pants, the "Bowery Boys," "Kerryonians," "Roach Guards," and "Dead Rabbits." These gangs operated out of the Five Points, Hell's Kitchen, and Bowery sections of New York City. The early gangs were in conflict with one another and had gang wars among themselves. Often they were associated with the underworld and local bars and gambling establishments. Street brawls, theft, gambling, robbery, and other crimes were typical. Gangs were also known to have operated in Philadelphia by the 1840s (Davis and Haller 1973). The extent of youth involvement in these early nineteenth century gangs is unknown, but there is evidence of participation by juveniles.

In England, true juvenile gangs probably started in the nineteenth century as well. Burt (1925) reported that during the first quarter of the nineteenth century, dangerous delinquent gangs were present in England. The nineteenth century was the Victorian age, and the period of Charles Dickens, an astute observer of nineteenth century British society and street life. Dickens provides a plausible account of what juvenile gangs of the Victorian period may have been like in his book *Oliver Twist*. The gang portrayed by Dickens consisted of a loosely organized group of youths who were led by an adult. The members specialized in different street crimes, such as picking pockets and other forms of theft, to support the gang. The gang's main purpose was to provide a collective way to cope and survive in Victorian society.

Later in the nineteenth century, juvenile gang conflicts occurred in New York City during the Civil War over control of turf. These conflicts were so violent that the police refused to intervene until the violence had subsided (Asbury 1927). During the 1870s, the inhabitants and press of New York City were concerned with prowling juvenile gangs that terrorized citizens and committed crimes. These juvenile gangs included the "Nineteenth Street Gang" and the "Short Boys" among others (Hawes 1971). These gangs were often affiliated with saloons and political parties. The gangs would drive the competition from the neighborhood and help ensure that elections had the "correct" outcome by using strong-arm tactics. In return, gangs either were paid or were guaranteed protection from public officials, including the police. These juvenile gangs were often led by adults.

Women also participated in these gangs. Asbury (1927:29) describing gang wars of the period, wrote, "On the outskirts of the struggling mob of thugs ranged the women, their arms filled with reserve ammunition, their keen eyes watching for a break in the enemy's defense, and always ready to lend a hand or a tooth in the fray." One female gang member, called "Hell Cat Maggie," was a legendary gang fighter. Asbury also described. Chinese immigrant gangs, called *tongs*, that operated in Chinatown. The tongs were linked to gambling interests and the opium trade. Tong wars over territory were often violent and lasted for years.

The concentration of Italians, Jews, Irish, and other immigrant groups in New York and Chicago promoted the rise of ethnic juvenile gangs. Thrasher (1927) noted that gangs provided economic and political career opportunities for immigrant youths. In addition, juvenile gangs were involved in other activities. The Civil War draft riots in New York City were thought to have been instigated by juvenile gangs (Asbury 1926; Spergel 1990). Riis (1894), a social reformer and friend of Theodore Roosevelt, believed that gangs provided a natural channel for youthful tendencies. Gangs, according to Riis, were also a product of the city's inability to provide adequate services to children. Children therefore turned to the streets. The urban gang, Riis thought, responded to the needs of the child's instinctive nature.

Many of these early gangs were organized along racial and ethnic lines (Inciardi 1978). For example, there were several gangs of Italian and Irish youths in New York in the nineteenth century. In the first annual report of the New York Children's Aid Society in 1854, we find suggestions of juvenile delinquent gangs thriving in the streets of New York:

> Crime among boys and girls has become organized, as it never was previously. The police state that picking pockets is now a profession among a certain class of boys. They have their haunts, their "flash" language, their "decoys," and "coverers," as they are called, or persons who will entice others where they can be plundered, and protect the thieves if they are caught. (Cited by Bremner 1970:420–421)

A popular view held in the nineteenth century was the assumption that there existed a *criminal class,* people including juveniles who were more likely to commit crime and delinquency. Typifying this view, one London citizen wrote in 1851, "The existence and numbers of the criminal class is a great evil, and, it may be, a great and grave error of society at large" (Sanders 1972:225). Moralists and scholars lamented the presence of "street Arabs" in American cities (Pickett 1969). There may have been a moral panic created by the press, police, and welfare organizations (Humphries 1981) concerned with the lawlessness and violence of gangs. As a result, attempts were made to curb juvenile delinquency and juvenile gangs. These attempts included the Boys Clubs of America, founded in the 1870s to help "pavement children" (Vigil 1988) and the Children's Aid Society.

In England, according to some historical evidence (Sanders 1970; Tobias 1967), groups of boys lived independently of their parents, sometimes in settings not unlike those portrayed by Dickens in the novel *Oliver Twist.* Roaming the streets during the day and staying in dirty lodges with prostitutes, drunkards, and adult criminals may have been common. Some youths teamed up with adult leaders who provided shelter and food in return for a share of the earnings.

Other youths formed casual partnerships with other boys in non-hierarchical and temporary groups (Tobias 1967). Picking pockets, theft, burglary, and begging were often used to support these groups. Members usually specialized in specific types of delinquent and criminal behavior, such as cutpursing (cutting money pouches loose from people's belts) or picking pockets. These groups were relatively small, typically ranging from two to five members (Sanders 1970).

Some gangs were highly territorial, well organized, with regular meeting places, age-graded, hostile to outsiders, and took on neighborhood names and occasionally had female satellites (Willis 1974), much like contemporary juvenile gangs. Also similar to contemporary gangs, immigrant groups and other minorities were sometimes the targets of nineteenth century English gangs (Humphries 1981). These characteristics, plus the extensive involvement of gangs in illegal activity, particularly violence and theft, persisted in gangs of the twentieth century.

TWENTIETH CENTURY GANGS

Some of today's juvenile gangs can trace their origins to the turn of the century. For example, Perkins (1987) indicated that some of Chicago's modern African American gangs can be linked to the race riots of 1919. According to Perkins (1987), African American gangs operating in Chicago between 1900 and 1920 were rare compared to white ethnic gangs, were small, were not predominantly delinquent, had loose structures, had members aged between 16 to 20, and had limited territory. We know that gangs were sufficient in number the first two decades of the twentieth century to warrant public concern and research. Early gang studies provide a glimpse of what juvenile gangs were like in the first part of the twentieth century. Puffer (1912) studied 66 juvenile gangs and concluded that most were predatory, that is, they committed criminal acts for gain. He also found that gangs existed in middle class areas and that these gangs were shorter lived than gangs from lower class areas (Hardman 1967; Puffer 1912). Puffer found that the age of gang members ranged from ten to sixteen years. The gangs he studied were ethnically mixed, locally based, had members that came from poor backgrounds, were loosely knit, but had rules and initiation rites. Puffer concluded that gangs, similar to other aspects of adolescence, represented a manifestation of more primitive behavior. Like nineteenth century writers, Puffer thought that gangs were a product of unsupervised immigrant youths.

The 1920s and 1930s

Interest in juvenile gangs continued in the 1920s. This was the decade when Thrasher (1927) wrote his influential book, *The Gang,* a study which has had an enduring influence on gang research. Thrasher identified and studied 1,313 gangs. Of these, he thought 530 were delinquent, 609 were dubious, and 52 were non-delinquent. Thrasher observed that most of the African American gangs were involved in crap shooting and minor theft. In contrast, some of the white gangs during this period had notorious reputations for extortion, murder, and bootlegging. Thrasher found that most gangs were structured into three subgroups: the core (with a leader and his lieutenants), the rank and file, and marginal members. Thrasher concluded that the gangs he studied were not permanent but transitory in nature. Gangs were a transitory phenomenon that reflected the neighborhoods going through transition (change). Membership changed over time, and marriage was the main reason for members' leaving the gang. To Thrasher gangs, along with other social problems such as mental illness and poverty, were the product of weakening social controls, especially among the newly arriving immigrants. Conflict integrated the gang into a more cohesive unit. One of Thrasher's major premises was that gangs were a natural and normal adaptation to the urban slums. He also concluded that gangs took a wide variety of forms.

Furfey (1926) reported findings similar to those of Thrasher with respect to gang characteristics. He also concluded that lower class gangs were better integrated than other gangs, and that gangs that were better integrated lasted longer, a finding consistent with Puffer's (1912) finding, noted above, that gangs in lower class areas lasted longer than gangs in middle class areas. Furfey's gangs consisted of youths 10 to 14 years old, were age-graded, were locally based, and were loosely organized most of the time but could be well organized in some cases. Furfey concluded that the reason poor youths joined together in gangs was economic, to obtain money.

The juvenile gangs of the 1920s and 1930s drew their memberships mostly from the children of recent immigrants, and ethnicity was an important factor in the composition of gangs. Taylor (1990) described the rise of a major Jewish gang in Detroit from a protective Jewish youth group called the "Sugar House Gang," which formed in the 1920s to protect Jewish merchants. Taylor also (1993) described another Jewish gang that operated in Detroit during the 1920s and 1930s known as the Purple gang. The Purple gang was one of the earliest corporate gangs in the United States. It was actively involved in illegal alcohol sales. During the latter years of the Great Depression a few prominent African American gangs emerged in Chicago, such as the Four Corners, but they were the exception rather than the rule (Perkins 1987). Bogardus (1943) studied Mexican immigrants to southern California, the development of the *barrios* or ethnic neighborhoods of Los Angeles in the 1920s, and the sources of barrio gang formation. He attributed barrio gang formation to a combination of culture, language problems, poverty, discrimination, and school dropout. Despite these problems, according to Bogardus, few youths actually joined gangs. These southern California gangs, according to Tuck (1943) and Mirandé and López (1992), were generally not seen as a threat or social problem before World War II.

The 1940s

By the 1940s, Americans had become convinced that juvenile crime was increasing (Binder et al. 1988). With the increase in concern about juvenile crime, increasing attention was given to juvenile gangs. Some of this concern was warranted. For example, in Detroit during the 1940s, gangs of Jews, Irish, Italians, Sicilians, Hungarians, and African Americans roamed the streets (Taylor, 1993). An assumption held by the public and by scholars at the time was that basic changes in the family contributed to the rise of gangs in the 1940s and later in the 1950s. Some scholars identified parental neglect, parental immorality, and parental absence as factors giving rise to juvenile gangs (Hardman 1967). Himber (1941) proposed that broken homes and weak religious ties contributed to gang formation. Other factors including racial tension and political and socioeconomic frustrations were also identified as leading to gang involvement (Dumpson 1949).

During the early 1940s, Whyte (1943) reinforced Thrasher's proposition that gang members' movement to more serious criminal activity occurred gradually. Members of the "Norton Street Gang" sought social support, prestige, and reassurance from the gang because the future held limited employment opportunities for the gang members. The gang, according to Whyte, offered rewards to members that they could not obtain in the larger society. Whyte found that the gang members were older than members of most juvenile gangs, that the structure was more formal, and that the gang continued to function as a gang after the members had married. Gang leadership was important for the gang, because the leader set the tone for the gang's activities. Hanging around and participating in social activities made up the bulk of the gang members' time together. Whyte found that juvenile gangs were less violent and more conforming than most outsiders would have believed.

The 1940s also saw the emergence of the "zoot suit" fad among minority youths. Zoot suits were characterized by their baggy pants, stiff and broad-shouldered jackets, long chains, and wide-brimmed hats. They were dramatically different from other styles of dress, and drew much public attention and ridicule (Vigil 1990), especially along the coast of California where many military personnel were stationed. Zoot suits became particularly popular among Hispanic youths, and became a symbol of ethnic identity for them (Cosgrove 1984). Zoot suiters used alcohol and marijuana (Moore 1978; Vigil 1988), occasionally fought among themselves, and in the Mexican American population, came to be identified as *pachucos,* a general term for Mexican Americans who wore zoot suits and affected a hip street style (Vigil 1990).

Police and military personnel viewed zoot suits as deviant and a waste of cloth in a time of war rationing, and they harassed Hispanic and African American zoot suiters. In California, rumors of Hispanic zoot suiters attacking white girls fueled hatred of the zoot suiters and led to police arrests and attacks on Hispanic youths. Joan Moore (1991) suggested that the zoot-suit panic had little to do with the criminality of young Hispanic men but a lot to do with how Anglos saw them in Los Angeles. According to Mirandé and López (1992) a combination of negative media portrayals, xenophobic attitudes, and law enforcement attitudes and practices also created an image of zoot-suiters as dangerous gangsters. This in turn led to riots and helped crystallize youths into gangs for mutual support and protection against attacks (Moore 1978). The Zoot Suit Riots may have been the turning point that led to the development of the serious gang problem that characterizes Hispanic barrios in the Pacific southwest today (Vigil 1990). Mirandé and López (1992) concluded that the "zoot-suit riots" did much to support the view that violent Mexican youth gangs were a serious social problem.

In the period after World War II, juvenile gangs or youth subcultures were present in England and other European countries (Campbell et al. 1982; Cavan and Cavan 1968; Fyvel 1961). In countries devastated by war, such as France, Germany, and Belgium, juvenile gangs flourished. Statistics are unreliable for this period, but it appears that World War II had major effects on rates of delinquency and gang activity in European countries (Cavan and Cavan 1968; Louwage 1951). Groups of youths pillaged, worked in the black market, and became involved in prostitution, theft, and vagrancy. Economically motivated delinquent acts were a method of surviving for groups of youths who had lost their homes, lost one or both parents, and lost their means of support (Cavan and Cavan 1968; Fyvel 1961). Similarly, Jungk (1959) found orphaned and abandoned children joining gangs for survival in the chaotic post-atomic environment of Hiroshima.

Robison et al. (1946) characterized gangs in Harlem in the mid-1940s as violent, hostile toward non-members, with only a core of members involved in delinquency. Members were 10 to 18 years old, with leaders a little older, between 15 and 20. The size of the gang averaged about twenty members, with affiliated groups of younger boys. These juvenile gangs were sometimes connected with adult gangs that drew their members from the ranks of the juvenile gangs. The gangs were formal in the sense that they had agreed upon meeting places and there were specific roles within the gangs. Gangs fought each other, and the most aggressive members were viewed as heroes. Cliques existed within the gangs, and members exhibited a strong sense of loyalty to one another. The gangs committed crimes such as theft, mugging, and extortion for financial support.

Dumpson (1949) characterized gangs in Harlem as loosely structured face-to-face groups. According to Dumpson, the largest of the gangs had about one hundred members. Bernard (1949), who also studied gangs in Harlem, concluded that gangs ranged from 25 to 200 members, were age-graded, and had both core and peripheral members. Gang members performed specialized roles, carried weapons, and participated in gang warfare, but most of their time was spent "hanging out" rather than engaging in violent or criminal activities. According to Bernard, gangs were limited to a single ethnic group: Irish, African American, Puerto Rican, or Jewish. In addition, gangs were characterized by their distinctive dress and were occasionally tied to adult gangs, a characteristic also noted by Robison et al. (1946).

Perkin's (1987) review of the history of African American gangs in Chicago covered gangs during the 1940s. During the 1940s African American gangs in Chicago such as the Deacons were primarily fighting gangs. These gangs had formal and hierarchical structures with well-defined roles and statuses including presidents, vice presidents, war counselors. The Deacons held regular meetings and had a female auxiliary known as the Deaconettes. The Deaconettes paralleled the male Deacons in structure. The focus of these gangs was fighting rival gangs rather than criminal or delinquent activities. These gangs and others did not pose any real criminal threat to the neighborhood. Since the 1940s, Perkins proposed that these self-contained neighborhood gangs became preoccupied with crime, drug sales, and expansion.

Harding's (1952) study of gangs in the 1940s also found that gangs tended to be homogeneous. Gang members were predominantly lower class, from broken homes, and oriented toward fighting. Harding concluded that some gang members went on to adult criminal careers, but others simply left the gang when they began to participate in adult activities such as work. Gangs often disintegrated as gang members matured.

Wattenberg and Balistrieri (1950) also suggested that poorly supervised homes contributed to gang involvement. The underlying assumption of many gang researchers in the 1940s and later in the 1950s was that broken homes and environmental factors contributed to delinquency and gang participation. Wattenberg and Balistrieri concluded that broken homes alone did not lead to gang involvement. Instead, they concluded that the lack of home supervision in the youth's life was what really mattered.

The 1950s

Many of the most popular images of gangs developed in the 1950s. This was the period of gang movies such as *The Wild Ones, The Blackboard Jungle,* and *Rebel Without a Cause.* Some of the images provided by these movies remain popular today and serve as models for juvenile gangs outside the United States (see the next chapter). The black leather jacketed, chain-carrying, conflict oriented gangs owe their image and origin to the 1950s.

In the United States, the 1950s were characterized as a period of high gang activity or at least increased public awareness of gangs (Siegel and Senna 1988). During the 1950s and through the 1960s, as Siegel (1989) observes, "the threat of gangs and gang violence swept the public consciousness." This was the period when some of the large "supergangs" such as the Blackstone Rangers of Chicago and the Latin Kings started smaller gangs in other Midwestern cities (Hagedorn 1988). Some question whether these supergangs were really single gangs, and suggest that they were really confederations of smaller gangs (Campbell 1984b). These supergangs continue to exist in the present, although their nature has changed.

Concern over "turf" (territory under the gang's control) and demonstration of "heart" (courage) became more important during this period (Campbell et al. 1982). Demonstrations of masculinity and fighting prowess were important as well. The image of the gang fight or "rumble" with scores of youths becoming involved in the brawl was popular. In a rumble, according to Gardner (1983:23):

> Times, places, and uses of weapons were agreed upon in advance by the war council or leadership of the two warring gangs. Usually, the location chosen would be a deserted area of the city, where police were not likely to discover them. In those days, gangs fought each other with bats, bricks, clubs, and chains.

In addition, gang loyalties started to carry over into the correctional system during the 1950s (Moore 1978). The 1950s also witnessed the increased use of heroin in some gangs.

In the late 1950s, the New York City Youth Board (1960) conducted a comprehensive study of the city's gangs. The Board concluded that there were a variety of youth groups, including street clubs, groups, and gangs with different structures and activities. The Board, paralleling earlier research, found that gangs had core members, "floaters," and peripheral members. Gang members were 12 to 22 years old, and usually had conflict-ridden relationships with the communities in which they lived. Gangs maintained control of members by using sanctions which they levied against members who broke gang rules. Most of their time was spent hanging out. Gangs developed their own argot and customs. The Board concluded that detached street workers were the best way to curb the negative aspects of juvenile gangs. This conclusion had a lasting influence on how gang interventions were conducted in later decades (see Chapter 10).

The 1960s to the Present

Delinquency prevention became a national priority in the 1960s (Piven and Cloward 1971). As so often has been the case, part of this public consciousness of delinquency and gangs was fueled by the mass media. The press took great interest in reporting gang-related activities. During the 1960s, large inner-city gangs such as the "Blackstone Rangers," the "Devil's Disciples," and the "Vice Lords" received considerable attention from the mass media and consequently from the general public.

This was the period of the civil rights and anti-war movements, a period when youths protested against violence in its various forms. From World War II until the 1960s, gangs were not politically active (Miller 1974; Short and Moland 1976). In the 1960s, however, many of the gangs became more politically active. The Vietnam War had an impact on many youths in the ages typical of gang members, and by drawing away some of the more positive male role models may have fueled the evolution of barrio gangs (Vigil 1990). The war may also have focused attention away from domestic concerns.

According to some authors, there was a lack of gang activity during the late 1960s (Haskell and Yablonsky 1978; Miller 1975). No one knows for sure why this was the case, but the aforementioned increase in political awareness and political activity may have been part of the explanation. People expected youths who were drawn from the same strata (oppressed, minority, lower class youths) as gang members to be involved in social reform and civil rights movements. The political awareness of youths during this period may have focused activity on constructive social movements rather than gang behavior.

During the late 1960s, juvenile gangs and gangs that included both youths and adults sometimes became active in the civil rights movement. Historically, gangs had been used as tools for entrenched politicians, as noted earlier in this chapter. In the 1960s, some politicians and social activists thought that gang energies and resources could be channeled into activism and constructive social change. Gangs such as the "Vice Lords," the "Black Panthers," the "Young Lords," and the "Black Liberation Army" provided politically conscious alternatives to traditional gang activity. The degree of these gangs' commitments to civil rights objectives varied, and the gangs ranged from tacit support to active militancy in the degree to which they supported the goals of the civil rights movement.

Much has been written about the politicization of these large gangs (Dawley 1973; Fry 1973; Perkins 1987; Short 1974b; Short and Moland 1976). Short and Moland found that politicization among the two groups they studied differed between communities and their associated gangs. Varying degrees of support for civil rights and militant groups existed among the gangs. Some gang members viewed violence as a method for political change, but others preferred more conventional, peaceful approaches to change.

Alternatively, the decline in gang activity in the 1960s may have been associated with increased drug use—a loose and diffuse form of the retreatist gang (Cloward and Ohlin 1960) on a massive scale—or the effectiveness of intervention programs that operated in the 1960s, or the effectiveness of gang control tactics used by the police (Siegel 1989). Others have suggested that the perceived decline in gang activity may be related to definitional issues as much as to actual declines in gang activity (Johnstone 1981).

By the 1970s, there was a resurgence of juvenile gangs and juvenile gang activity (Miller 1975). Relatively little attention, however, was paid to gangs by the mass media or by public officials (Horowitz 1990). Gangs of the early 1970s, unlike their counterparts immediately following World War II, were more likely to have economic motives for their illegal activities. Campbell (1984b) commented that male gang members turned away from ritualistic gang wars to more predatory crime. Violence increasingly became a mechanism for gaining control not only of turf but also of markets for illegal services. The high unemployment of the 1970s has been suggested as one factor which may have contributed to the increase in gang activity (Collins 1979).

In the 1980s and early 1990s, popular impressions of gangs included a shift to more lethal forms of violence, drive-by shootings, and increased involvement in the drug trade. Juvenile gangs have once again become a national priority. The Office of Juvenile Justice and Delinquency Prevention has funded or intends to fund a National Youth Gang Suppression and Intervention Project, Youth Gang Intervention Training, and an Impact Evaluation of Youth Gang Intervention Training, in addition to broader programs with gang intervention and prevention components. New ethnographic studies of gangs (Campbell 1984b and 1991; Hagedorn 1988; Vigil 1988) have been undertaken to provide information on contemporary gangs. After a hiatus in concern with juvenile gangs during the 1970s, juvenile gangs once again occupy a prominent place in the research and public policy agendas of the United States.

CONCLUSION

Most experts trace the evolution of juvenile gangs to the early nineteenth century, but there is some evidence that youths have participated in group delinquency and juvenile gangs, or at least prototypical gangs, for centuries (Hardman 1967). Contemporary gangs differ from gangs in the past in some important respects. Alcohol use and abuse appears to have been part of the juvenile gang experience throughout Western history, but we lack sufficient information to know its prevalence among gang members and the rest of society to determine whether it was more characteristic of gang members than of society more generally. Drug use was not common in juvenile gangs until the twentieth century, particularly from the 1970s to the present. The same is true of society generally, and this reflects the technological changes that have made psychoactive drugs less expensive and more readily available to the general public. Presently available evidence suggests that drug use is more prevalent among gang members than among individuals who are not members of gangs (Fagan 1990).

Gang violence has been characteristic of gangs throughout history. Gang violence has ranged from bludgeoning one's victim to death in a face-to-face encounter from the Medieval period to the mid-twentieth century, to the quick, impersonal, drive-by shooting of the 1980s and 1990s. Theft, extortion, and other property crimes have generally been the most frequently committed crimes by juvenile gang members. With the possible exception of some of the gangs of the Middle Ages, though, criminal activity among gangs has occupied a relatively small proportion of gang members' time.

Gangs have drawn their membership primarily from the urban lower class. Urbanization has been particularly important in gang development because urban centers provided both a large population base from which to draw gang members and a large wealth base from which to select victims of predatory property crimes. In addition, gangs seem most likely to flourish in times of rapid social change (Spergel 1990:171). Gang members have historically distinguished themselves from non-members by distinctive styles of speech and dress. Finally, explanations for gang membership and gang delinquency have, since the nineteenth century, focused on problems in the environments of lower class youths.

Age, sex, ethnicity, and social class repeatedly appear as criteria for gang membership. Gang activity is most frequent in adolescence, but adult gangs exist and sometimes recruit members from juvenile gangs (Asbury 1927; Thrasher 1927; Sullivan 1989). Gangs have always been primarily a male phenomenon. Females have participated in gangs, but not to the same extent that males have participated, and female participation has often been in the form of auxiliaries to male gangs (Asbury 1927; Bernard 1949; Campbell 1984b; Thrasher 1927). Although there are and have been ethnically mixed gangs, most gangs are and have been ethnically homogeneous. In the United States, the predominant ethnicity of gang members often has reflected the ethnicity of the most recent immigrant groups: Irish, Italian, Jewish, and German gangs in the nineteenth century, Caribbean, Mexican, and Asian groups toward the end of the twentieth century. In this respect, African Americans represent a special case of a minority ethnic group that never truly assimilated into mainstream American society.

Mutual protection and economic gain are recurrent themes in the explanation of gang formation and gang activity throughout history. Political activity by gangs has varied considerably over time, from the apolitical gangs of the 1950s in the United States, to the use of gangs as tools of establishment politicians in the nineteenth century and the politically aware and sometimes politically active gangs of the 1960s. Gangs appear to have grown in size over time, perhaps partly as a result of technologies of transportation and communication which permit the confederation of smaller gangs which are geographically separate from one another. This conclusion must be tempered by acknowledging that the size of gangs is inferred from the mass media and from official agency reports, and may reflect definitional issues as well as actually gang membership (Maxson and Klein 1990).

Chapter 6

COMPARATIVE PERSPECTIVES
ON JUVENILE GANGS

When American scholars think about gangs, there is a subtle tendency to view them as principally an American phenomenon. Campbell and Muncer (1989) characterize American gang research as taking a parochial view of gangs. Juvenile gangs, however, are a transcultural phenomenon with different manifestations in a diverse range of countries (Spergel 1990). Unfortunately, the research that has been translated into English about gangs in other countries is limited and sometimes dated. Consequently, it is easy for Americans to conclude that juvenile gangs are nonexistent or are effectively controlled in other societies. It also seems to follow that the United States must be different from other countries because of its relative abundance of juvenile gangs. Compared to some societies, this certainly appears to be the case. For example, the Eskimos of North America make little or no reference to juvenile delinquency, let alone juvenile gangs (Cavan and Cavan 1968).

There are several reasons why we should be interested in gangs in other countries. First, making cross-cultural comparisons has theoretical value. In order to assess whether explanations based on American gangs apply to gangs in other countries, we must first determine whether the patterns of gang activity in other countries parallel patterns of gang activity in the United States. Another value of international gang research is that through the study of gangs in different countries, we gain an understanding of the role played by cultural factors in shaping the nature of gangs. If it is true that culture matters, then we would expect to see differences between American gangs and gangs in other countries. It is important to understand the limits of generalizations about gangs based on the American experience, and to consider how those generalizations need to be modified by considering evidence from other countries (DeFleur 1967; Campbell and Muncer 1989).

Evidence exists that some juvenile gangs are internationally mobile, for example, Jamaican gangs immigrating to the United States. Even when the gangs themselves do not move across national boundaries, gang members in one country who immigrate to another may be more likely to join or form new gangs when they reach their country of destination. For example, youths belonging to gangs in Hong Kong may immigrate to the United States and join gangs in New York's Chinatown (Rice 1977). There is rising concern that Asian gangs may be a major problem, as southeast Asian and Hong Kong youths immigrate to the United States (see Chapter 3). It is also true, however, as Campbell (1984b) and Klein (1995a) have noted, that the United States may be exporting gangs to other countries.

How important is the host culture to gangs and gang activities? How violent are gangs in other countries? Does the process of acculturation eventually result in the disappearance of ethnic gangs? What gangs are most likely to become transnational? What aspects of gang behavior, organization, and membership patterns transcend national boundaries? To what extent can an understanding of gangs in other countries help us to understand similar gangs in our own (for example, Skinheads in England and the United States)? What roles do industrialization and urbanization play in the emergence of gangs in modern societies? Answers to these and similar questions may help us obtain a broader understanding of the gang phenomenon, and can only be obtained through cross-cultural comparisons.

METHODOLOGICAL PROBLEMS OF COMPARATIVE STUDIES

The study of juvenile gangs in different countries poses a complex set of methodological considerations for the researcher. Problems exist in the equivalence of measurement, definitions, sampling variation, and the validity of data, as well as problems in the conceptualization and operationalization of gangs and the measurement of gang activity. For example, different countries sometimes define adult and juvenile status differently, so that a juvenile in one country is an adult in another. Adolescence is not universally recognized as a stage in the life cycle (Cavan and Cavan 1968). Gangs may be defined differently in different countries, as Clinard (1960) observed when he attempted to study gangs in Sweden. Researchers and journalists frequently use inconsistent definitions of gangs, which adds to the confusion. In developing countries, what we have called law-violating youth groups may be called gangs. Klein (1995a) uses the term "gang-like" to describe some of these groups.

Vaz (1962), who conducted a study of Parisian gangs in the 1960s, concluded that relying on official delinquency and gang statistics is risky across national boundaries. Some countries may suppress information about juvenile gangs. Before the 1980s, the Soviet Union officially failed to recognize the existence juvenile gangs and youth subcultures. Until recently, therefore, statistics on juvenile gangs in the Soviet Union have been rare or nonexistent. In other countries, the quality and quantity of law enforcement data on gangs vary over time. The definition of what constitutes a gang, or gang behavior, varies (Cavan and Cavan 1968). According to Klein (1995a:214), commingling of terms such as gangs, peer groups, delinquent youth groups, street gangs, youth gangs, and so forth, presents another problem for researchers. Also, just as scholarly and public interest in gangs in the United States has fluctuated over the decades, it has fluctuated in other countries as well.

For English-speaking audiences, an added problem is the language barrier. Relatively little of the international research on gangs has been translated into English (and English speakers, especially Americans, are notoriously parochial when it comes to knowledge of languages other than their own). As a result, some of the references used in this chapter are limited and sometimes dated. Still, the value of studying gangs in different countries and in different periods should not be ignored, and rather than ignore this area altogether, we have attempted to bring together sufficient resources on gang activity in other countries to at least provide a useful context for the study of juvenile gangs in the United States.

CULTURES, SUBCULTURES, AND GANGS IN OTHER COUNTRIES

Certain themes recur in the work of researchers on juvenile gangs in other countries. One key concept is the role of the host culture in determining the nature of gangs and group delinquency. An operating assumption of many researchers is that culture influences the structure and nature of youth subcultures, group delinquency, and gangs, and that gangs should be expected to differ across national and cultural boundaries. Similarly, youth subcultures are often regarded as important influences on youths. In some of the cross-national research, what is described is as likely to be a youth subculture as a gang.

Another theme in the literature on juvenile gangs is the role of immigration in contributing to the formation of gangs. Immigrating youths are commonly thought to find it difficult to integrate into the host society because of differences between their cultural backgrounds and the culture of the host society. Consequently, youths may join gangs as an alternative to assimilation into the host culture. Immigrant language and cultural differences may fuel the need for youths to join gangs, particularly if they are beset by problems of discrimination and rejection. There is clearly a parallel here to the American experience, and the formation of new ethnic gangs corresponding to new waves of immigration (see Chapter 1).

The role of urbanization and modernization in generating a cultural milieu for juvenile gangs has received substantial attention from international gang researchers. Urban areas appear to be generally more supportive environments for juvenile gangs, regardless of country. It may be, as we suggest elsewhere in this book, that a critical population mass is a necessary (but not sufficient) condition for the formation of juvenile gangs.

Another theme that recurs in the cross-national literature on gangs is that key historical events, such as wars, have major impacts on juvenile delinquency, subcultures, and the nature and formation of juvenile gangs. For example, World War II appears to have had major effects on group delinquency in Europe. Some European youths lost one or both parents to prison or death during the war, and found it necessary to band together to survive (Cavan and Cavan 1968). World War II not only affected delinquency rates, but also increased the extent of group and gang delinquency in Europe (Fyvel 1961).

An assumption underlying the work of some international gang researchers is that rapid social change, resulting from urbanization, industrialization, and the modernization of nations, undercuts the existing social order and leads to increased social problems such as poverty and crime. This orientation may be traced to Durkheim (1947) and other scholars and social critics who viewed rapid social change as a source of social problems and deviant behavior (Merton 1957; Parsons 1951, 1977). From this perspective, we would expect to find higher levels of juvenile gang activity in the more industrialized and urbanized countries. An alternative explanation for the discrepancy, however, could be that the more urbanized and industrialized countries have more extensive and better developed record-keeping systems, which only make it appear that there is more juvenile gang activity.

In the remainder of this chapter, examples of juvenile gang studies from different parts of the world will be described. Because each study focuses on different aspects of gangs in different countries, comparisons are sometimes difficult. Still, by reviewing these studies, it may be possible to obtain some sense of how gangs operate in different countries, and of the role that culture plays in shaping gangs in different societies.

THE EXTENT OF GANG ACTIVITY IN OTHER COUNTRIES

We know that juvenile gangs have been identified in many countries outside the United States, especially in European countries. In some areas, however, juvenile gang activity is not as extensive as it is in the United States (Mayo 1969). Hood and Sparks (1970) concluded that gangs appear to be more prevalent in the United States than elsewhere.

African Gangs

The biggest gap in our information concerns gangs in Africa. Clinard and Abbott (1973) cite a few studies of gangs in Africa, but on the whole, research has been limited. Short and Strodtbeck (1974) mentioned the Tso Tsio of South Africa, and juvenile group delinquency has been reported in Ghana by Weinberg (1964). Weinberg found gang fights and battles over turf, but such violence was infrequent compared to similar violence in the United States. Weinberg also reported that cohesive relationships existed in organized juvenile gangs whose members were required to abide by the gang's rules, and whose predatory orientations and techniques were taught to members of the gang.

More recently, Ledochowski (1991) provides a brief description of youth gangs in the townships of South Africa. Nothing the collapse of community support and control structures and the cultural traditions that supported them, he contends that township youth band together in gangs to form identities and to earn livings. The gangs, referred to as *skollie* (ruffian) gangs, are organized along military lines with hierarchical structures. Youth are often pressured into joining the gangs for protection. Gang members have tattoos that signify membership in the gang. The tattoos limit their employability in legitimate jobs while they are in the gang and when they decide to leave. The gangs are involved in illegal drug and liquor sales. A primary purpose for the gangs is predatory (property) crime that provides an income for survival. He believes gang members are largely influenced by American media images of gangs and gang styles and the years of oppression living under an apartheid system. Insofar as we have evidence on African gangs, there appear to be some marked similarities to American gangs, but less violent activity.

Latin American and Caribbean Gangs

Juvenile gangs exist or have existed in Mexico (Collins 1979), Puerto Rico (Ferracuti et al. 1975), Argentina (DeFleur 1967), Brazil (Came et al. 1989b), El Salvador (Munoz 1996), Jamaica (Gunst 1989; 1995), Colombia, and elsewhere in South and Central America and the Caribbean. Some of these gangs, however, appear to differ substantially in some ways from their northern neighbors. There is also considerable variety in Latin American and Caribbean gangs. Cavan and Cavan (1968) reported that urban fighting gangs were largely absent in Mexico City, but did exist in rural areas of Mexico. More recently, however, Klein (1995a) reports the existence of street gangs similar to the Chicano street gangs found in the United States.

One possible reason for the convergence in American and Mexican gangs is imitation of American gangs by Mexican gangs. Another possibility is return migration of Mexicans or immigration of Mexican Americans who were gang members in the United States. Munoz (1996) described the involuntary repatriation of Salvadoran refugees, including individuals who had become gang members in the United States, to El Salvador. According to Salvadoran officials, this has either created a gang problem in El Salvador, or perhaps exacerbated an existing problem, with the introduction of drug trafficking as part of the criminal repertoire of Salvadoran gangs or gang members. Regardless of whether the problem is home grown or made in the U.S.A., Munoz's description of Salvadoran gangs suggests parallels with American drug dealing gangs, with the important difference that the Salvadoran gangs attempt to keep a lower profile (in this respect, more like Asian than Hispanic gangs in the United States) for fear of assassination by Salvadoran "death squads."

Laurie Gunst (1995) has conducted a ethnographic study of Jamaican "posses" in Jamaica and the United States. The Jamaican posses (Gunst 1989, 1995) appear to be political, violent, and involved with illegal drug sales. Members of the posses include youth but also adults in their fifties. The posses in Jamaica have a long history of being associated with political parties and have had unofficial ties with elected officials. Posses would work for politicians by using violence to control the polls during elections and intimidate or murder political rivals. Over the course of recent years, political change has occurred in Jamaica and the posses have become less political and more drug sales oriented. Jamaican politicians exercise less control of the posses than they had in the past, and the posses act fairly autonomously.

Gunst (1995) does not elaborate on the characteristics of the posse members other than they tend to have a fatalistic outlook on life and come from very extreme poverty. Youth belonging to posses migrate to the United States, frequently New York and Miami to make their fortunes selling drugs, specifically crack. She describes Jamaican posses as being violent and capable of torturing victims to gain control over drug sales. Violence is instrumental in gaining control of territory for the drug trafficking. Gunst reported that members of posses operating in the United States often send money back to their families from the United States. The life of the posses is seen by some Jamaican youth as an attractive alternative to the slums of Jamaica.

DeFleur (1967) studied juvenile gangs in the slums of Cordoba, Argentina. She found these gangs to be small, with about eight members of similar ages, and comprised entirely of males. Organizational structures varied from gang to gang. Some Cordoban gangs had strong and stable leaders, while others did not. There were no initiation rites, and there was no evidence of age-grading, but gang members tended to be comparable in age. These gangs appeared to be very hedonistic, with a "live for today" attitude. The gangs had their own argot. Although drugs were used, they were too expensive at that time for widespread use among gang members, except for alcohol. Illegal activities of the gangs included robbery and theft. There was little fighting, and vandalism was uncommon. Gangs were aware of territory, and fighting sometimes occurred among rival "barras," but territoriality and gang fighting appeared to be less important for Argentine gangs than it is for gangs in North America.

Ferracuti et al.'s (1975) study of Puerto Rican gangs also found that violence seemed to be much less prevalent among gangs in Puerto Rico than among Puerto Rican or other gangs on the U.S. mainland. Gang members were typically 11 to 17 years old. Gang fights, gang identification symbols, and other features of gangs thought to provoke violence were absent. The gangs were viewed by the members as means of coping or survival. Both the study by Ferracuti et al. and the study by DeFleur seem to emphasize that cultural differences between Anglo and Latin America are so great that generalizations from one culture to the other, with respect to juvenile gangs, may be inappropriate.

In Sao Paulo, Brazil, juvenile gangs known as "Trombadinhas" (little crunchers) commit robberies of unsuspecting adults. Dimenstein (1991) provides one description of the treatment of Brazil's street children that refers briefly to juvenile gangs. Dimenstein reports that the lure of the streets can be an attractive option for children growing up in the slums of Brazil. According Dimenstein, gangs recruit children because the criminal justice system does not hold children responsible for criminal acts. Most of the crime committed by Brazilian adolescents was property crime. Most of the children on the streets were males. Dimenstein notes that girls not able to cope with prostitution sometimes turn to gangs to support themselves. Youth may also join gangs during their stays in institutions. Dimenstein (1993) also refers to gangs of youth called *galeras* in the city of Manaus that have taken over control of neighborhoods. Juveniles in gangs and alone on the streets face the constant threat of being murdered by the police, rival youths, rival gangs, or death squads hired by business people and middle class to control crime on the streets. They are judged to be expendable because they have no futures.

Sociologist Alonzo Salazar (1992) interviewed adolescent gang members in Medellin, Colombia. Salazar describes the gangs as being extremely violent and comprised of youth ranging from the age of 12 to the early 20s. He found the average age of gang members to be 16. The gangs were age graded with the two to three older and tougher youth assuming leadership roles. Youth joined the gangs for socialization and identification, but mostly because they faced blocked opportunities to the good life they desired. The youth joining the gangs were from the poorest areas of the city. Regarding violence and gang structure, Salazar (1993:9) states, "At the bottom of the hierarchy of violence are the *pelados*, the kids, who are already learning the craft at the ages of 12 or 13, secure in the knowledge that few crimes are punished." The structure of the gangs is also influenced by whether the gang specializes in certain types of crime. Specialist gangs tend to be comprised of more successful gang members.

The gangs participate in a number of predatory crimes such as extortion (taxes), burglary, robbery, theft, drug sales, and murder. To gain membership in some gangs, youth had to commit a crime (do a job) and or go through an initiation ritual. The gangs form spontaneously from groups of friends and within neighborhoods. Similar to gangs in the United States, gang cohesion is fueled by external threats to the group.

Violent crime is a preoccupation with the gang members as well as the acquisition of the material things in life. According to Salazar, gang youth progress from crude to more sophisticated and expensive weapons as they age. A motorbike and gun, he states, are viewed as tickets to the good life. Murder for hire is characterized as one crime common to these gangs. Salazar (1993:4) writes, "Murder is the greatest cause of death among young males in this home to teenage gangs of *sicarios* (hired killers) and their paymasters, the infamous Medellin cartel." Salazar notes that the gangs are not the product of the drug trade in Colombia, as they existed before it became a growth industry. The gang members do not limit their employers to the cartel and freely work for whomever will pay them. They also kill to protect territory or carry-out vendettas. Territory is defended to exercise power and for self-defense. Neighborhoods tend to tolerate the gangs and may benefit, as petty external thieves are typically expelled by gangs from home neighborhoods. Gangs that are unsuccessful in their criminal ventures (they do not pull any lucrative big jobs) will turn on their host neighborhoods. This typically draws a negative response and erosion of support from the community.

Salazar makes several references to the cultural factors and socioeconomic conditions under which these gangs exist. Some cultural traditions in this region of Colombia that he considers deeply rooted in the gangs include the desire for money (material things), a religious sentiment (God, and in particular the Virgin Mary, forgive them for all the bad things they do), and the law of vengeance. Violence is very much a fact of life for these youth. Ever since the colonization of Colombia, and more recently the since the period known as *La Violenca* where as many as 200,000 rural people were killed by conflicting political factions, violence is a fact of life. Unlike adult professional gang members, such as those in the cartel, these youth gangs and gang members want to be noticed for their criminal accomplishments. They want to be openly feared and admired.

Canadian, Australian, and English Gangs

Canadian Gangs

Canada, like the United States, has had a history of juvenile gangs. One of the earliest studies on juvenile gangs in Canada was conducted by West and Elkin (1951). They studied juvenile gangs in an upper class suburb of Montreal. They found that gang members were conformists, and had a basically positive social outlook because they knew that they would be successful regardless of their gang activities.

In the late 1980s, Canadian juvenile gangs started to receive increased attention from the mass media, parallel to the increased interest in gangs in the United States (Came et al. 1989a, 1989b). Canadian media described the immigration of juvenile gangs such as the "Red Eagles," "Viet Ching," and "Lotus" to Canadian cities from Asia. The rise of juvenile gangs is viewed as a product of the failure of Vietnamese, Laotian, Cambodian, and other Asian immigrants to adjust to Canadian culture. Similar to immigrant youths in other countries, failure to adapt to the host culture and limited opportunities for them in Canadian society may be forces that contribute to the formation of gangs by Asian immigrants to Canada. These gangs are characterized as being violent and having economic motives (Bruman 1983; English 1995). Their principal criminal activities appear to be extortion, drugs, and gambling. The ages of gang members range from 14 to 25 years old (Banks 1985).

Ethnic differences serve as a key factor in gang membership in Canada. Gangs generally segregate along ethnic lines, and ethnic differences help account for the wide variation in the form and nature of Canadian gangs. Non-Asian gangs, such as Montreal's Haitian street gang, "Public Enemy Number One," and Toronto's "Untouchables," "Goofs," and "Jungle Posse" have received attention from the press. Violent skinhead gangs can also be found in major Canadian cities (Came et al. 1989a, 1989b), as can Jamaican gangs. Canadian skinhead gangs reportedly have been known to "swarm" victims by surrounding and then assaulting them. How often this activity occurs is unknown and may be exaggerated by accounts in the mass media. Some of these gangs parallel the skinhead gangs found in Great Britain (to be discussed below) and the United States.

A study by Le Blanc and Lanctôt (1994) interviewed 506 adjudicated gang members and non-gang members in Montreal. The study compared gang and non-gang delinquent youth on a number of dimensions.

The results found little difference between gang and non-gang members regarding age, family, and social status. Both groups came from disadvantaged backgrounds and disorganized families. However, Le Blanc and Lanctôt found significant differences between the groups on social control and deviant behaviors. Non-gang members reported less deviant attitudes, less stress in school, better parental supervision, and fewer opportunities for deviance. Non-members were more likely to adhere to conventional norms compared to gang members. In contrast, gang members were more socially and emotionally troubled.

Le Blanc and Lanctôt (1994) also included questions on the nature of the gang. They found that most youth described their gangs has having defined structures, that is they had characteristics such as leadership, territory, continual association, name, and identity. Other gang members reported their gangs had only a few of the structural characteristics of organized gangs. The study looked at other dimensions of gangs such as those associated with the "Punk" subculture, skins, and structured criminal gangs. The results suggest the retreatist Punk gangs have more family and drug problems. The criminal gangs recruited more often from immigrants to Canada and the violent (skins) had parents with more deviant attitudes.

Final comparisons were made by Le Blanc and Lanctôt (1994) between Haitian and white French Canadian gang members. They found that Haitian gang members were younger, more likely to have divorced parents, come from larger families, and have fewer contacts with social service agencies. The Haitian gang members did stay in school longer and favored delinquent rather than a mix of delinquent and general problem behaviors when compared to their white French Canadian gang counterparts. Le Blanc and Lanctôt (1994) argue that their results suggest that delinquent youth with lower self and social control join gangs that then activate offending patterns. They believe that the Canadian gang members are significantly different from non-gang members on a number of factors but not in terms of characteristics of their gangs, such as the degree of structure or subcultural orientation.

Australian Gangs

Bodgies and Widgies were terms used to identify juvenile gangs in Australia (Fyvel 1961; Short and Strodtbeck 1974). Although juvenile gangs exist in Australia, they do not appear to be as prevalent as in other countries. According to some researchers, highly structured juvenile gangs are not common in Australia (Braithwaite 1977; Daniels 1977). Daniels notes that much of the juvenile delinquency in Australia is not gang-based, but is simply group delinquency. Klein (1995a) cites data provided by Kenneth Polk of the University of Melbourne that also suggests that the problem in Australia is one of loosely structured groups with little or no organization or permanence of membership. These groups use public transportation, congregate in and move through public spaces, and seek low-cost or no-cost entertainment. Typically lower or working class and male, they sometimes engage in fistfights and knife fights, typically associated with alcohol use.

English Gangs

Numerous studies have been conducted on juvenile delinquency and juvenile gangs in Great Britain (Downes 1966; Hagan 1975; Patrick 1973; Scott 1956; Willis 1973). Labels attached to British juvenile gangs included "Teddy Boys" (Short and Strodtbeck 1974), "Skinheads" (Knight 1982; West and Farrington 1977), "Mods," "Punks," "Rude Boys," and "Rockers" (Whitfield 1982). Some writers have suggested that these groups represent subcultures rather than true gangs (Campbell et al. 1982; Campbell and Muncer 1989; Short 1968). Others believe that juvenile gangs are very much a part of the British scene (Whitfield 1982).

Social class differences are pronounced and acknowledged in Great Britain, and class differences are a source of identity. A working class solidarity appears to exist in Great Britain to a greater degree than in the United States. This observation has led to the suggestion that these clearly defined class differences affect the nature of juvenile gangs, a point which has served as a key question for researchers studying British gangs. It has been suggested that British youths differ from youths in other countries in their aspirations for success. Working class youths, it is argued, have no hope of upward mobility in British society, and accept their plight. Since opportunities for upward mobility are rare, British youths are thought to be less likely to be frustrated by blocked opportunities than their American counterparts. If this is true, then blocked opportunities, a proposed explanation for American gang involvement (Cloward and Ohlin 1960; Cohen 1955; Merton 1957) may not be an explanation for why British working class youths participate in gangs (Campbell et al. 1982).

As early as the late 1950s, British "Teddy Boy" gangs were active in racially motivated attacks on West Indian immigrants (Fyvel 1961). The "Teddy Boys," along with the "Mods" and "Rockers" continued to be active in the 1960s and 1970s. The Mod subculture was primarily interested in music, appearance, alcohol, and drugs. The Rockers were more interested in motorcycles, leather clothing, and had more in common with the American motorcycle gangs of the 1950s. It has been suggested that the Mods and the Rockers crystallized into well-defined subcultures with corresponding gangs partly in reaction accounts published in the British press (Cohen 1973). Representative gangs from the two subcultures occasionally fought each other in well publicized fights along the southeastern coast of England (Cohen 1972; Knight 1982; Moore 1993). The Mods eventually broke down into "Hard Mods" and "Smooth Mods." The former adopted wearing heavy boots and short hair and evolved as a precursor to the skinheads (Moore, 1993). In the mid-1960s and 1970s, Rastafarian youth groups linked to West Indies culture, and called "Rudies," "Rude Boys," also emerged and were influential in shaping skinhead subculture (Knight 1982). These gangs were identified by their short hair and style of dress, which includes heavy black boots, leather and denim clothing, and an overall air of toughness.

The "Skinhead" gangs observed throughout the West are thought to have originated in Great Britain in the 1970s (Clarke 1976). In England and other European countries there is a strong association between skinheads and football (soccer) teams. The skinheads have emerged in a climate of increasing prices, unemployment, and an increasing minority and immigrant population. Skinheads are characterized by their shaven heads (cropped hair), from which they derive their name and their distinctive style of dress. The short hair was thought to offer an advantage in fighting (nothing to grab). The characteristic skinhead uniform includes black leather clothing, hobnailed boots (Doc Martens), army greens, Ben Sherman shirts, chains, swastikas, braces (suspenders), and tattoos (Knight 1982). Unlike most American skinhead youth who have grown up under relatively comfortable economic conditions, the English skinhead youth have had years of experience living in an economy that has been on a steady decline. Because so many English youth have been affected by the lack of opportunity and declining economy, significant numbers of skinhead youth are present in England. In addition, these youth are able to form a critical mass much easier than their counterparts in the United States, where skinhead youth are more dispersed across the country (Moore 1993).

The skinheads are a violent subculture which, like their American skinhead counterparts, express racist attitudes and hostility toward the middle class and toward established political authority. They draw their membership from Britain's working class youths whose opportunities to work their way up the social scale are severely limited. Skinheads generally believe that minority groups and immigrants are taking over Great Britain. These targeted groups are seen as taking jobs away from the British working class and, correspondingly, from skinhead youths. Skinheads engage in "paki-bashing" (attacks on Pakistani and other nonwhite immigrants), and are also known to be aggressive toward youths from other British subcultures, for example, the punks (Campbell et al. 1982; Knight 1982). Possible links between the National Front, a neo-facist organization, and skinhead youth have been suggested by some research (Buford, 1990).

Gangs in Great Britain have been found to be more loosely organized and unstructured than American gangs (Campbell 1991; Cohen 1980; Downes 1966; Morash 1983; Scott 1956; Spencer 1964), with the possible exception of some Scottish gangs (Patrick 1973; O'Hagan 1976). Although some gangs have a sense of territory (Wilmott 1966), formal leadership may be absent, and some gangs do not identify themselves as being gangs (Downes 1966; Scott 1956). Again, some of the Scottish gangs may be the exception (O'Hagan 1976). The Scottish gang described by Campbell (1991) partially based membership, as did other gangs in Glasgow, on whether individuals were Catholic or Protestant. The gangs tend to be small; Cavan and Cavan (1968) estimated the typical size of British juvenile gangs to be three or four members. Age-grading appears to be present in some gangs, but not in others. Membership is typically drawn from lower or working class backgrounds (Campbell 1991; Knight 1982). There is disagreement on the extent to which subcultures are well developed, and to which gangs are able to flourish, in British as opposed to American society (West 1967; Campbell and Muncer 1989). The diversity of reported findings about British gangs suggests considerable variation in the size, degree of organization, cohesiveness, and structure of British gangs.

Gang membership appears to have little effect on delinquency in London (Downes 1966). Cavan and Cavan (1968) reported that about 11 percent of the offenses in London's courts were gang-related. Like gangs in other countries, British gangs' primary activities are not delinquent in nature, but consist of hanging out and socializing (Patrick 1973; Willmott 1966). When crimes are committed by gang members, they are usually attributed to small cliques within the gang (Downes 1966). Although British gangs have "punch-ups" or gang fights, the violence does not generally reach the severity found in contemporary American gangs. More recently, Sanders (1994) noted the lack of gang violence in London.

Some attention has been paid to the British youth subculture associated with European football (soccer). This subculture has been typically characterized by ethnographic based research as being violent, racist at times, ethnocentric, nationalistic, substance abusing, and more mob-like in nature than being similar to true gangs (See Buford, 1990). Campbell's (1991) personal account of his membership in a Scottish gang underscores the importance of alliance to soccer teams to some gangs. In addition, Klein (1995a) reports the existence of Chinese drug gangs with ties to the Chinese triads (see below), Jamaican drug gangs involved in hashish and heroin sales, plus some Indian and Pakistani conflict gangs in rivalry with one another, in London. Manchester has a similar pattern, with considerable violence associated with the drug trade.

European Gangs

It is clear that juvenile gangs have been common throughout much of Europe, especially since the Industrial Revolution (see Chapter 5). Gangs have been reported in Spain, where they are responsible for a large share of the criminal offenses (Hotyst 1982). The Netherlands had gangs called the Nozems in the late 1960s (Baur 1964) and skinhead gangs in the 1980s (Came et al. 1989b). Criminal juvenile gangs were reported to exist in Belgium in the 1960s, and in the late 1950s, the "Skinnknutte" operated in Scandinavia (Fyvel 1961). In the 1950s, teenage gangs were present in major Italian cities (Cavan and Cavan 1968). Short and Strodtbeck noted the existence of the "Vitelloni" in Italy and the "Tap-Karoschi" in Yugoslavia. Gypsy youth gangs are thought to operate throughout major European cities such as Paris and Rome. In general, gangs appear to be active throughout Europe.

French Gangs

Juvenile gangs in France are relatively rare compared to the United States. Like Great Britain, France has had juvenile gangs that take on a wide variety of forms and characteristics (Monsod 1967; Vaz 1962). According to Monsod, gang membership was drawn from the ranks of the unemployed. Gang members tended to have dropped out of school and had lower levels of educational attainment than non-members, but Vaz (1962) and Monsod (1967) have observed that substantial differences may exist between upper and lower class gangs in France.

French gangs, like gangs elsewhere, developed their own argot and clothes to distinguish themselves from outsiders. Like British gangs, French gangs may be difficult to separate from French subcultures. The "Blousons Noirs" were characterized as a gang (Short and Strodtbeck 1974) and as a subculture rather than a gang (Campbell and Muncer 1989). These gangs, named for their black leather jackets (blousons noirs), modeled their attire after images of the American motorcycle gangs of the late 1950s and early 1960s.

Vaz reported the typical size of French gangs to be five to eight members, but as large as sixty members. Monsod (1967) placed the size of French gangs at fifteen to twenty members, with some gangs having as many as forty members. Few females were involved in French juvenile gangs, but some were members of male-dominated gangs. French gangs place less emphasis on age-grading than American gangs. Gang members ranged from their mid-teens to the early twenties (Monsod 1967; Vaz 1962).

In Paris, Monsod reported a strong sense of social and territorial identity among French gangs in the 1960s. Gangs socialized and identified with specific areas of the city. Specific parks and neighborhoods were used as common grounds for Parisian gangs, and some gangs were even named after particular areas, similar to gangs in Los Angeles in the United States. By contrast, Vaz, in an earlier study, reported no sense of territory for French gangs.

Criminal activities of French juvenile gangs included vandalism, theft, illicit sex, assault, and robbery (Monsod 1967). Although fights did occur, violence was reported to be rare with most Parisian gangs (Vaz 1962). Fyvel (1961), however, reported that violence was common with the Blousons Noirs. Alcohol use was also very high, and drug use was also reported by Monsod (1967).

Summarizing some of the research on French gangs up to the late 1960s, Cavan and Cavan (1968) reported that French gangs were primarily adolescent, with few members under age 12 or over age 18. These gangs occasionally had adult leaders. They were impermanent, with little formal organization and only weak cohesion. Vandalism and theft were the most frequent crimes, and violence was rare. Females in gangs were rare, and usually took secondary roles to the male gang members. Delinquent acts were spontaneous and hedonistic. Membership was transitory: gangs formed and dissolved quickly.

More recently, according to Klein (1995a), the Blousons Noirs of earlier years have disappeared and been replaced by American-style gang imitators called *casseurs* in Paris and Marseilles, black African gangs (*zoulous*) in Paris, and also Algerian gangs. Gangs define themselves by territory and ethnicity, wear characteristic clothing, listen to rap music, and are involved in aggression on public transportation (buses and subways).

German Gangs

We know that juvenile gangs operated in Germany following World War II and were motivated by survival. The existence of juvenile gangs called "Halbstarke" (half-strong) in Germany and Austria was noted by Short and Strodtbeck (1974), Fyvel (1961), and Cavan and Cavan (1968). In the 1950s there were several youth riots by marginal youths called "Gammler." These groups were loosely organized and were probably not gangs, according to the definition adopted in Chapter 1, but were instead law-violating youth groups. Group delinquency is common in Germany. Brunner (1974) found that group membership and processes played a central role in three types of juvenile crime in West Germany. In fact, it was estimated that 80 to 90 percent of all juvenile crime involved groups of youths.

Recently, West Germany has been experiencing increases in its rates of juvenile delinquency (Hotyst 1982). The recent reunification of East and West Germany has given rise to a fear of increased crime and delinquency, including illegal activity by juvenile gangs. Especially if observations linking industrialization and urbanization to gang delinquency are correct, the restructuring of the German economy, especially in former East Germany, is likely to generate pressures toward juvenile gang formation and juvenile gang delinquency.

Presently, skinhead gangs exist in Germany (Came et al. 1989b). In 1991, about 600 racist and neo-fascist skinheads were responsible for firebombing a home for foreign workers and assaults on Vietnamese and Mozambican workers (Levin and McDevitt 1993). Concern for German skinhead violence is well documented in the media. There is apprehension, according to the press, of skinhead gangs by East Germans. One *New York Times* story reported that East Germans were "startled" by the violence of West German skinheads (Binder 1990). As in other countries, the skinhead gangs typically draw their membership from the working class. The neo-fascist movement and corresponding values underpinning the skinhead gangs underscores the concern felt by some East Germans. Neo-fascist groups, some of them appropriately labeled gangs, have attacked Africans, Jews, and other "non-Aryans" in Germany.[1]

In response to the skinhead attacks, immigrant youths have formed gangs or groups for self-defense. These include Turkish, Kurdish, Yugoslav, Polish, Lebanese, and Palestinian ethnic gangs. In addition, in some cities, there are groups of law-violating youths similar to the pattern described earlier for Australia, and some soccer hooliganism. Reporting these patterns, Klein (1995a) chillingly notes the low level of community controls and the tendency of Germans not to intervene in what happens on the street, a pattern Klein finds reminiscent of the Kitty Genovese incident in the United States (in which a young woman was repeatedly attacked and eventually brutally murdered as onlookers did nothing, not even calling the police for help, for fear of "getting involved"). Even more darkly, this may remind some readers of an earlier period when "good Germans" avoided getting involved and failed to intervene to prevent the persecution of Jews and other ethnic minorities in Germany.

Soviet Gangs Since the Russian Revolution

The extent of juvenile delinquency and youth gangs in the Soviet Union is difficult to determine. As Binder et al. (1988) concluded, national data on delinquency are absent, and only recently have Soviet scholars been able to address these topics openly. It appears that youth gangs and subcultures have been present in the Soviet Union at least since the beginning of the twentieth century. Today in post-revolutionary Russia, they are known as *bezprisornye* (Klein 1995a).

In the period just before the Russian Revolution, the term "hooliganism" was used by the government to describe rowdy behavior by students and youth groups (Chalidze 1977). The Russian Revolution itself left many youths homeless:

> Large groups of Russian youths, finding themselves in a disorganized society and without adequate adult supervision because of the death of one or both parents or the dislocations of their families, formed marauding bands, housing themselves in

cellars and makeshift shelters near large urban centers. These youths were referred to as "Gezprizornye," or the "neglected" (Binder et al. 1988:396).

Following the Russian Revolution, Thrasher observed that Russian youths joined gangs for survival.

> Russia's 100,000 neglected children are said to travel in gangs, winning a precarious living by stealing and finding shelter in deserted buildings and in Moscow and other cities in the sewers and catacombs (Thrasher 1936:40).

Similar gangs formed in the aftermath of World War II.

After the revolution, the term "hooligan" was used in a broader sense that included subcultures, law-violating youth groups, true gangs, drifters, and other nonconformists. The term as used in the Soviet Union implies that any nonconformity is a product of Western influences, idleness, a lack of family life, and an uncontrolled desire to learn about the world outside the Soviet Union. Commenting on juvenile delinquency in the Soviet Union during the 1950s, Fyvel (1961) noted that delinquency and "hooliganism" were major headaches for Soviet authorities. At this time, the term "hooliganism" again had a broad meaning, encompassing subcultures, delinquent groups, and true gangs.

Like their counterparts in other countries, Soviet youths tend to commit offenses in groups. Connor (1972) estimated that as much as 95 percent of all offenses committed by Soviet youths are done in groups. Others estimate that 70 to 75 percent of Soviet juvenile delinquency is group delinquency (Binder et al. 1988; Zeldes 1981). Whether these groups represent gangs or law violating youth groups is uncertain. Connor (1972) observes that these groups do not resemble the 1950s style American gangs, and concludes that these groups are spontaneous and temporary. Zeldes (1981) also supports this view of Soviet youth groups.

The Soviet government has labeled youths with interests in Western dress and ideas "Stilyagi" (Cavan and Cavan 1968; Fyvel 1961). Whether these groups of nonconformist youths are subcultures or involve factions of juvenile gangs similar to American juvenile gangs is questionable. Cavan and Cavan (1968) noted that organized gangs similar to those found in the United States had not developed in the Soviet Union as late as the 1960s.

Beginning in the 1960s, a Soviet youth culture became more evident. "Khippi" (hippies) and "fanaty" (gangs of soccer fans) emerged, and Bushnell (1990) likened the "fanaty" to a cross between British soccer fans and American street gangs. The fanaty drew their membership primarily from the middle class, but increasingly have drawn more membership from the working class. The fanaty fought gangs from rival teams, developed gang graffiti, and adopted other gang behaviors similar to gangs in the United States. Officials estimated the fanaty membership associated with one team, the Spartak Team, to number as many as 100,000.

By the late 1980s, a broad spectrum of Soviet youth subcultures was in evidence. Gangs of "punks," "pacifics," and "metallisty" formed (Bushnell 1990). The "metallisty" were associated with heavy-metal music, and wore leather clothing decorated with metal studs and chains. Subgroups of metallisty may function as true gangs that commit criminal acts and otherwise behave as gangs would in other countries (Fain 1990).

At the time of the breakup of the Soviet Union in 1991, the variety of youth groups and subcultures was surprisingly diverse. It included break dancers, new-wavers, punks, rockers, and left-wing extremists (Fain 1990). The Soviet "punks" are similar to punks in Western countries, and attempt to shock and disgust Soviet citizens by their behavior and appearance. "Majors" or "pseudiuhniks" are known for their Western style of dress. Soviet "rockers," like their British counterparts, imitate the American motorcycle gangs of the 1950s.

Some Soviet youths have adopted Nazi clothing and culture, but not necessarily Nazi ideology. According to Fain (1990), they wear Nazi symbols to express their group identity, have complex initiation rites, and commit criminal acts. They have organized structures including fuhrers (fiurery), chiefs (shefy), and other specialized statuses. They distribute racist and anti-semitic literature, and seem most akin to the skinhead groups of Western countries.

Left-wing extremist groups are a reactionary response to the other youth groups. They view themselves as rejecting the liberalization and Westernization of Soviet society by other youth groups. Youths in these groups train and exercise for physical confrontations with youths from other groups. They have distinct leaders, a sense of territory, rituals, and other gang characteristics. They have been involved in street clashes and fights with other youth subcultures and gangs (Fain 1990). Like Los Angeles street gangs, they may be named after the locality in which they operate or from which they come.

Regardless of the group, it appears that youths join these groups between the ages of 13 and 16, and depart when the males join the military. Few men return to the groups after military service. Females leave the groups when they get married. Alcohol abuse is likely in these groups, but this appears to reflect its prevalence in the larger Soviet society.

It is difficult to be sure whether these youth groups are true gangs or more spontaneous gatherings of youth subcultures. Soviet research on youth subcultures and gangs is still relatively undeveloped, but if current trends continue, it is likely to grow in the future. One reason for its future growth may be the growth of gang activity in the Soviet republics. For example, the Soviet newspaper *Sovetskaya Rossiaya* reported in 1989 that juvenile gangs in the city of Kazan divided the city into "zones of influence" which were controlled by gang violence (Wilson-Smith 1989). Gang violence, including rape, robbery, and fighting, has been reported in Moscow and in smaller cities. This represents a dramatic change from the absence of gang activity and violence reported two decades earlier by Cavan and Cavan (1968). Dmitri Likhanov (1991) provides a journalistic look at gang activity in the two urban centers of Kazan and Tashkent. According to Likhanov in the city of Kazan, anti-gang officials indicated that gangs are formed along the same principles. Twelve to 14-year-old boys belong to what is known as the "husk." As they grow older they become "supers" and then "juveniles." By age 18, they are known as "elders." All gangs have leaders. Gangs fight with rival gangs and commit property offenses to make money. In Tashkent, the leader of one gang reported to Likhanov that his gang was involved in fighting business and government corruption. Klein (1995a) reports the existence of gangs similar to American gangs, plus a wide variety of informal youth groups, some highly cohesive and resistant to intervention.

Based on the above descriptions, it seems fair to conclude that gangs, some of them associated with distinct subcultures, appeared to exist in the Soviet Union at the time of its dissolution, and some persist to the present. What the future holds for gangs in the Soviet republics is a matter for speculation. One possibility is that preoccupation with the restructuring of Soviet society will draw attention away from gangs in subcultures, as the social movements in the United States in the 1960s appear to have done. Another possibility is that the rapid social change being experienced by the Soviet republics will give rise to increased gang activity. It is evident that enormous changes occurred between 1960 and 1990, mostly in the direction of more extensive and more clearly identifiable gang activity (Gallagher 1992). It remains to be seen whether the trend will continue, or will be reversed by the breakup of the Soviet Union.

Other European Gangs

Klein's (1995a) review of the gang situation in Europe and elsewhere suggests that American-style gangs, skinhead gangs, and law-violating youth groups maintain a stable and, in some countries, an expanding presence in the European countries. In Sweden, he reports episodic skinhead activity, plus what we (following Miller 1982) have called law-violating youth groups of second-generation Turks, Yugoslavs, Moroccans, and others (children of guest workers and asylum seekers) that may be evolving into gangs. Sweden has patterns similar to those described for Australia (loosely formed groups of wandering youths in public places) and American-style taggers. Slovenia also has small, loosely structured, law-violating youth groups. Spain has little more than sports hooliganism. Zurich, Switzerland, appears to follow a pattern similar to the German cities, with Turkish, Yugoslav, Albanian, Lebanese, and Chilean minorities forming ethnic gangs. In Brussels, Belgium, there appear to be some small criminal gangs primarily involved in thefts from automobiles. It appears that law violating youth groups, some evolving into gangs, are increasingly evident as a feature of European societies.

Asian Juvenile Gangs

Increases in juvenile delinquency have been reported in Asian countries such as Hong Kong, Ceylon, Indonesia, Malaysia, Nepal, Pakistan, Philippines, Singapore, Sri Lanka, Thailand, and India (Clinard and Abbott 1973; Francia 1991; Hotyst 1982). We know that juvenile gangs exist in these countries, but information on them is limited. Juvenile gangs have thrived in Hong Kong for years, and may have found their way to major United States cities (Rice 1977). In the 1960s, criminal youth gangs were a problem in Indonesia and Thailand, and more recently it has been suggested that they commit a large proportion of the criminal offenses committed in these countries (Hotyst 1982).

India in the 1950s

In a study of Bombay, India's gangs, Srivastava (1955) concluded that gang participation and membership was based on caste, with members only joining gangs within their caste. According to Srivastava, gang membership was very small. The gangs were loosely defined affiliations, sometimes headed by adults, which were temporary and arose spontaneously to commit criminal acts, mostly property crimes. Over time, these groups might evolve into more lasting gangs. The average age of members of the more transient gangs, which may have been nothing more than law-violating youth groups, was 14, but more permanent gang members averaged 16 years of age.

Clinard and Abbott (1973) citing existing research by Sheth (1961) and others reported that gangs in Benares India were transitory in nature. Gang members had weak loyalties to the gang and each other. The gangs did not form for long periods of time. These juvenile gangs were sometimes supported by organized adult criminals. Similar to juvenile gangs in other developing countries, gang youth performed criminal tasks for adult gangs and adult leaders. Clinard and Abbott stated that juvenile gangs were loosely organized and criminal in focus.

There were two types of membership and organization. Gangs with only juveniles lacked discipline, had no social hierarchy, loose structure, and acted impulsively. Gangs with members of mixed ages, including adults or older youths, had hierarchies, defined leadership based on ability, and strategies for recruitment to perpetuate the gang. These latter gangs committed shoplifting, sexual crimes, and smuggled drugs and alcohol into areas where they were prohibited. Bombay's gangs were viewed as substitutes for other social organizations, such as schools and family, which failed to meet the needs of youths (Srivastava 1955; Cavan and Cavan 1968).

Chinese Gangs

China has had a long history of secret societies, possibly dating back as far as 1500 B.C. (Matheron 1988). These societies have been principally composed of Chinese men, and are called "triads." Traditional Chinese triads include the "Yellow Turbans," "Green Gloves," "Copper Horses," and "Big Spears." The triad is a equilateral triangle symbolizing the three concepts of heaven, earth, and man. In the late seventeenth century Buddhist monks founded a triad as a nationalistic rather than criminal group (Posner 1991). These triads sought to overthrow the Manchus, who were viewed as barbarian and oppressive invaders of China. The triads represented pockets of resistance to the Manchus. Eventually, the triads became quasi-governmental organizations performing administrative functions for regions in China. In the mid-1800s triads made significant attempts at overthrowing the Manchus, such as the 17-year Taiping Rebellion and Boxer Rebellion. With the communist revolution, the triads became more criminal in orientation.

Triads have been romanticized by the Chinese for centuries, and provide a cultural role model for Chinese juvenile gangs. Chinese triads are not restricted to mainland China; triad members have been arrested in Hong Kong and the United States (Matheron 1988; *Far Eastern Economic Review* 1989; Posner 1991). Although triads are primarily adult organizations, the triads use juvenile gangs to recruit new members.

Until recently, juvenile delinquency was not considered to be a problem in mainland China by Chinese authorities. From 1978 to 1980, however, one source indicated that juvenile offenders accounted for 70 percent of the criminal population and that this increased to 72 percent in 1986 (Zu-Yuan 1988). Zu-Yuan asserted that gang crimes have become more prevalent in China. The Chinese government took strong action against criminal gangs in 1983, but has not eliminated them completely. The increase in juvenile delinquent gangs in China parallels other trends in China, including a decrease in the average of juvenile offenders, an increase in violent crimes, and increased female delinquency (Zu-Yuan 1988). Bear in mind that these apparent increases may reflect real changes in behavior, or nothing more than changes in record keeping or definitions of incidents.

Some of the juvenile gangs identify with the triads or with feudal trade associations. Such gangs are organized into strata with rules and well-defined leaders. Leaders of juvenile gangs may jointly belong to triads as well as their gangs. Triads often review the performance of juvenile gang members as a probationary period prior to full triad membership. Matheron (1988) states that this period is known as "hanging the blue lantern." Juvenile gang members may progress to regular "street gangs," which are more violent and have stronger ties to the triads. Gang fights, extortion, and other criminal activity are common within these gangs.

Hong Kong Gangs

Youth gangs are known to exist and thrive in Hong Kong. Authorities have known about the presence in Hong Kong of very large organized crime syndicates, known as triads, for decades. Some of these triads actively recruit juveniles to join or perform criminal activities. There may be as many as 50 triads operating in Hong Kong with an estimated 150,000 members (Posner 1991). The triads in Hong Kong are characterized by elaborate initiation rituals. Members are "chosen" as opposed to simply joining. While triads are composed of members of all ages, it is clear that youth are chosen to join in lower entry level roles. Members of the triads select members based on whether they will be loyal and capable of criminal acts. Youth are sometimes rented by adults in the triads. Stronger youth are selected to serve as couriers for drugs and gambling. Strength is measured by the youths' ability to endure pain. Youth are also involved in drug sales. The triads have secret rituals, passwords, and codes of conduct. Rituals are designed to weed out youth that cannot endure pain or will be disloyal to the triad. At some point, initiation rituals always include taking loyalty oaths. Some rituals sacrifice chickens and mix blood to symbolize strong blood ties within the triad. Initiation fees are sometimes paid by new members to join. The concept of "Face" (honor) is important to the Chinese community and triad members are no different. To be humiliated in the community is not taken well by triad members and violent reprisals are taken by triad members who feel they have lost "face" in their communities.

The highly organized triads of Hong Kong represent to many authorities a serious worldwide problem as Hong Kong Island returns to China in 1997. It is reported that the triads have already established outposts in Australia, the Philippines, Canada, and the United States. There is some limited evidence in the United States that triads from Hong Kong have already made serious inroads into the heroin trade in New York (Posner 1991).

Taiwanese Gangs circa 1970

Western images of gangs and gangsters have influenced Taiwan's juvenile gangs (Kuo 1973), identified as lui-mang, tai-pau (boy gang), and tai-mei (girl gang). According to one study, the tai-pau and tai-mei are drawn from the upper and middle classes of Taiwanese society (Kuo 1973). In the later stages of a gang's development, youths from other classes may be permitted to join. Juvenile gangs in Taiwan are age-graded, with older members assuming leadership roles. The structure of the gang is similar to the family and is hierarchical in form. Kuo placed the size of these gangs at five to nine members, and seldom over twenty. Gangs exceeding twenty members were referred to as "peng," or crowd. Gangs are predominantly male, but there are some female members, and some female gangs (tai-mei).

Gang subcultures are often in evidence, represented by distinctive styles of clothing, language, and group norms. The tai-pau are known for their assaults on people, fights with rival gangs, fights with the police, and other deviant acts. Sexual offenses by gangs and gang members, theft, and drunkenness are reportedly rare, but some theft and extortion do occur. Like other gangs, however, a major pastime for the tai-pau is simply hanging out.

Korean Shoe-shine Gangs

Kang and Kang (1978) studied members of a Korean shoe-shine gang. Shoe-shine gangs were organized into territories which were used for criminal and business purposes. The legitimate business of shining shoes was the reason for their name and was part of the gang's activities. Membership was exclusively male, and was drawn from urban, minority group, lower class Koreans with limited access to social and economic opportunities. The prejudice experienced by these youths appears to have strengthened the bonds among gang members.

Shoe-shine gangs were highly organized, with a well-defined hierarchy and strong leadership. Status was determined by one's location in the hierarchy. At the top were the "wang cho," followed by the "daejang" or generals, then the "hyung him" or elder brothers and "oaji" or fathers. Youths worked their way up the organizational ladder, which operated similarly to a crime syndicate. Relationships among the gang members were often paternal, and higher ranking members served as role models for lower ranking members.

Neighborhood territories were well defined, and violent disputes occurred between rival gangs over control of turf. Violence sometimes resulted from such territorial disputes, or the expansion of one gang into another gang's territory. Control over territory was important to the gang because control guaranteed a source of income. In a sense, the territories were considered franchises, and were organized mainly along business lines. In addition to shining shoes, the gang engaged in criminal and delinquent activity in the same territory where they shined shoes. The general impression conveyed by all of this is reminiscent of the pattern of organized adult criminal gangs or juvenile drug gangs in the United States.

Japanese Gangs

Juvenile gangs and subcultures also appear to be present in Japan. Historical evidence from Hiroshima after the atomic bomb was dropped there indicates that abandoned and orphaned youths banded together and formed gangs for survival (Jungk 1959). These groups of youths resorted to both legal means, such as gathering and selling firewood, and illegal means, such as theft, in order to obtain food. These gangs closely resemble postwar European gangs, and were formed in response to the same type of stresses that affected postwar European youths who had been orphaned or abandoned.

Western images of gangs from the 1950s were influential on later Japanese gangs and subcultures, such as the "Yakuza," "Bosozoku" (wild tribe), and "Taiyozoku" (children of the sun) (Fyvel 1961; Loftus 1977). According to Loftus, members of Japanese juvenile gangs come from two-parent families and from middle class backgrounds. They are predominantly male, and usually consist of members under 20 years old. Most gangs had about one hundred members, with some as large as one thousand.

The gangs have leaders and relatively loose organizational structures. Some gangs collect dues, but initiation rites are rare to nonexistent. Gangs use logos and symbols to convey membership, and hair and clothing styles are also used to identify gang membership and rebellion from mainstream society. As described by Loftus, the essential motivation of these gangs is social rebellion as opposed to violence or economic motives. Although the gangs have been involved in violence with the police and with other gangs, criminal activity is relatively rare. Since the 1970s, however, juvenile delinquency, possibly associated with increased drug use, has reportedly increased in Japan (Hotyst 1982), and gangs may account for some of this increase.

Philippine Slum Gangs

One recent journalistic account provides descriptive and interview information about youth gangs in the Philippines. Luis Francia (1991), relying on observation and limited interviews, found barrio youth gangs. According to Francia, these gangs were comprised of teenagers and young adults aged to their early twenties. The gangs were fighting gangs organized around the protection of territory. The lack of official response to local neighborhood disputes by local police and corrupt officials gave rise to youth gangs that filled the need for social control. Francia found numerous types of gangs were present including *istambays* that were composed of unemployed "toughs," district gangs that covered several neighborhoods, *barkadas* that were harmless "social" gangs, specialized criminal gangs, and gangs based on region. The gang focused on by Francia was a fighting gang that drew its membership from youth seeking protection. Many of these youth were high school and college students from the area. The gang had hand signals, and fought with other gangs under agreed upon sets of rules. The gang was criminal but crime was not the central purpose or focus of the gang. The gang had an elaborate initiation ritual that involved blindfolds, various degrees of questioning, and striking with sticks or paddles. Gang members used drugs, such as glue and crack, but drug use was not encouraged. The gang had a formal leader but not an elaborate organizational structure. The gang leader had a person called an *aladay* that can best be described as a "gofer" and "groupie." The *aladay*, in return for service to the gang and leader, was protected. Gang members sometimes worked for adults who belonged to adult criminal gangs. Gang members either aged out or were recruited into adult criminal gangs operating in the barrio.

CONCLUSION: A COMPARATIVE PERSPECTIVE ON JUVENILE GANGS

Juvenile gangs are a worldwide phenomenon, but gangs exist to different degrees and take different forms in different countries. The studies reviewed in this chapter raise the question of whether American concepts and theories about gangs are useful in understanding gangs, law-violating youth groups, and youth subcultures in other countries. There are substantial differences among gangs in different countries at different times, but there is also evidence that the American youth subculture of the 1950s made a lasting impression on European and Asian youth subcultures and gangs, at least in terms of overt characteristics such as appearance and style of dress. The United States and other countries have also been influenced by British gangs, most notably the skinhead gangs. In some areas, however, the gang phenomenon appears to spring from independent cultural influences, as exemplified by the relatively nonviolent Argentine and Puerto Rican gangs of the 1960s and 1970s, and by the Chinese gangs modeled after the Chinese triads.

Allowing for these cultural variations, we may make the following generalizations about juvenile gangs, based on the cross-national and historical evidence presented in this and the previous chapter.

1. *Urbanization and Industrialization:* Juvenile gangs are more prevalent in urban than in rural settings, and appear to be more preva-

lent in more developed, industrialized countries than in less developed, nonindustrial countries (Friday and Stewart 1977).

2. *Gender:* Juvenile gangs in all countries are predominantly male enterprises. Female participation may be fairly substantial to nonexistent, but it is always less than the participation of males.

3. *Age:* Individuals tend to join gangs in early to middle adolescence, and to leave their respective gangs early in their twenties (if not earlier). Also, in more hierarchically-organized gangs, age-grading is common, with older youths having higher status in the gang. Juvenile gangs in less developed countries often work with adults and adult gangs to commit crimes (see also Clinard and Abbott 1973).

4. *Socioeconomic status and social class:* Although gangs are not uniformly drawn from lower, working, or middle classes in different countries, gangs do appear to reflect socioeconomic status or social class divisions in society. Where there are ethnic or caste divisions, these too tend to be reflected in gang membership.

5. *Structure:* With the exception of the far east, gang structures appear to be loose, non-hierarchical, and leadership is not always well defined. In part, this may reflect the absence of clear distinctions in the research between law-violating youth groups, subcultures, and gangs. Where there is strong evidence of gangs, as defined in Chapter 1, there tends also to be evidence of more structured, hierarchical organization.

6. *Activities:* The most common activities of juvenile gangs are noncriminal, and involve "hanging out" and socializing. Increasingly, however, violence and drug dealing appear to be characteristic of gang activity in other countries as well as the United States.

7. *Crime:* The most common criminal acts committed by juvenile gangs appear to be property offenses. A common pattern is for juvenile gangs to commit crimes to acquire Western items, such as clothes, appliances, and vehicles, that poor youth would otherwise not be able to afford. Moreover, if economic gain is the principal reason for the gang's existence, then the gang, regardless of country, tends to be more formally structured and hierarchical.

8. *Social disorganization:* There is evidence that in times of crisis, orphaned and abandoned youths have banded together in gangs in order to survive. Whether this represents a distinct type of gang activity, or whether gang behavior in inner city impoverished areas is a reflection of the same concerns as those experienced by children in the aftermath of

World War II in Japan and Europe, raises an interesting question about the origins and formation of juvenile gangs.

9. ***Crossing national boundaries:*** Larger youth subcultures, such as American motorcycle gangs in the 1950s and British skinhead gangs in the 1970s, may transcend national boundaries and influence the nature of gangs in different countries. Also, juvenile gangs as well as gang members may migrate across national boundaries, as the Hong Kong and Jamaican gangs have migrated to the United States.

10. ***Etiology:*** Despite variations in gang structure and activity, there may be common elements in the explanation of the existence of juvenile gangs. Summarizing the literature on European juvenile gangs, Cavan and Cavan (1968) noted the following patterns: broken families, school difficulties, employment problems, and low social status (but not frustration over socioeconomic status, as has been suggested by gang theorists of the 1950s and 1960s; see Chapter 8). Weinberg (1964) found similar factors as influences on gang formation and gang behavior in Ghana.

American gangs seem to place more stress on controlling territory than the gangs of other countries. This may be indicative of cultural differences in either (a) the concerns of gangs, or (b) the extent to which true gangs, as defined in Chapter 1, exist in the United States as opposed to other countries. There seems to be a consensus among researchers that American gangs appear to be more violent than gangs in other countries (Baur 1964). In addition, class consciousness is less evident in the United States than in other countries (1984), but despite the apparent absence of overt class consciousness, gangs, as noted above, tend to be organized along class lines.

CHAPTER NOTES

[1]In the late months of 1991, reports from Germany indicate that immigrant "guest workers" from Mozambique and Vietnam have repeatedly been attacked by neo-Nazi and skinhead gangs in Dresden and other areas in what used to be East Germany. The attacks appeared to be motivated at least in part by the social turbulence and economic instability brought about by the unification of East and West Germany (Levin and McDevitt 1993).

Chapter 7

TYPOLOGIES OF JUVENILE GANGS

For years, scientists and social scientists have attempted to develop schematas that would represent the ways that they perceive phenomena of interest to them. These schematas have gone by various labels and have been referred to as paradigms (Martindale 1960, 1979; Kuhn 1962; Sorokin 1964; Friedrichs 1970; Eisenstadt 1976; Ritzer 1980, 1981), ideal types (Weber 1949), and typologies (Tonnies 1963; Durkheim 1951; Gibbons and Garrity 1959). The common thread tying the above notions together has been their orientation toward making sense out of complex phenomena, thereby lending direction to empirical analysis aimed at their verification.

A typology is "a collection of types that catalogues the various ways in which a given complex of characteristics can be arranged to explain the behavior of acting units or individuals" (Ferdinand 1966:44). More simply stated, a typology is a set of rules used to classify cases or objects of study (people, cities, nations) into more or less homogeneous groups, in the belief that knowing the group to which a case belongs may help us understand or predict its behavior.

Typologies may be theoretical or empirical. In a theoretical typology, cases are grouped or classified based on a set of criteria that are set up before any measurement is performed on the cases being studied. An example of a theoretical typology is Merton's (1938) description of the modes of adaptation an individual may select in response to strain, the perception that he or she lacks access to legitimate means of attaining socially approved goals. Merton's typology is based on two variables: (1) whether the individual continues to aspire to the socially approved goal, and (2) whether the individual accepts or rejects the societal constraints that permit the use of some methods (legitimate means, such as working hard and saving money) but prohibit the use of others (illegitimate means, such as robbery and embezzlement). Merton's typology of responses to strain is diagrammed in Figure 7.1

According to Merton, there are five possible responses to strain: (1)

Modes of Adaptation	Cultural Goals	Institutional Means
I. Conformity	+	+
II. Innovation	+	−
III. Ritualism	−	+
IV. Retreatism	−	−
V. Rebellion	±	±

FIGURE 7.1: MERTON'S MODES OF ADAPTATION

Conformity, in which both the socially approved goals and the restrictions on means of achieving those goals are accepted; (2) Innovation, in which the goals are accepted, but constraints on the means of achieving them are not; (3) Ritualism, in which the goals are abandoned, but constraints on the acceptable means for achieving goals are still accepted; (4) Retreatism, in which both approved goals and means are rejected; and (5) Rebellion, in which the socially approved goals and means are rejected, but new goals and new means are advocated in a challenge to conventional society. In Figure 7.1, a "+" represents acceptance, a "−" indicates rejection, and a "±" indicates the combination of rejection of the old plus advocacy of new goals and means.

The different categories (conformity, innovation, ritualism, retreatism, and rebellion) in Merton's typology are *ideal types* (Weber 1949). These types are ideal not in the sense of being desirable, but in the sense of being extreme or pure types that real-life individuals may approximate, but never fit perfectly. Total acceptance or rejection of cultural goals or institutionally approved means is rare, perhaps nonexistent. Instead, individuals have a weaker or stronger commitment to the goals, a more or less frequent use of illegitimate means to achieve goals. One of the five types may be better than the others for describing a particular individual, but the individual may not fit that type perfectly. Just as a map represents a simplification of the surface of the earth, with some features (such as political boundaries) emphasized and other features (such as linguistic or religious boundaries) ignored, a typology represents a simplification of the characteristics of individuals, communities, nations, or other units of analysis.

Merton's typology is theoretical, based not on empirical research but on logical inference from a broader theoretical framework. An alternative approach is to construct empirical typologies. Empirical typologies begin with data collection. In the simplest form of an empirical typology, individuals may be asked to classify other individuals. For example, in prison studies, inmates may classify other inmates as "right guys" (inmates who do not report other inmates' infractions to the prison authorities, who may engage in illegal behavior within the prison, and who generally fit in well with other inmates), "square Johns" (inmates who do not fit in well with other inmates and who may have relatively limited criminal experience), "dings," "outlaws," and "politicians" (Schrag 1961).

A more technically sophisticated approach to the construction of empirical typologies involves the use of cluster analysis, factor analysis, or principal components analysis to detect groups of variables that tend to covary, or groups of individuals that tend to have similar values on a set of variables. An example of the use of this type of empirical typology is factorial ecology, which is used to classify different areas of cities into a small, manageable number of social area types (Abrahamson 1980:165–184; Palen 1987:102–105). Based on factor analysis, for example, social areas in cities appear to be distinguished primarily on the basis of socioeconomic rank, family status, and ethnicity.

A typology may be one element of a theory. It is not an end in itself. Once a typology has been constructed, the next step is to use the typology to predict or explain behavior. According to Merton (1938), we may expect the lowest rates of illegal behavior from Conformists and Ritualists. Retreatists should have the highest rates of alcoholism and drug abuse, but Innovators should have the highest rates of other types of crime, especially property crime. Similarly, urban areas characterized by low socioeconomic rank, family disruption, high residential density (including multiple-family rental properties) and high proportions of ethnic minorities are the areas predicted to have the highest rates of crime and involvement in gang activity (Shaw and McKay 1942). A well-constructed typology, then, may help us arrive at a clearer, more parsimonious understanding of, and ability to predict, behavior.

TYPOLOGIES OF CRIMINALS AND CRIMES

Typologies have existed in the criminological literature since the middle of the nineteenth century. The earliest typologies were proposed by the Italian positivist school of criminology in the work of Cesare Lombroso and his successors, notably Enrico Ferri and Raffaele Garofalo. Ferdinand (1966) has reviewed the use of typologies for juvenile delinquency, and Gibbons (1985) has reviewed typologies related to adult crime and criminals. Gibbons observed that typologies may focus on the type of crime or the type of criminal. Although the distinction between the two is not always clear in the work of authors who have attempted to construct typologies, it does seem evident that specific types of crime (for example, burglary) need not be committed solely or even primarily by a specific type of criminal (for example, burglars). The earliest typologies, Gibbons indicated, were person-centered. In the twentieth century, the focus has shifted from types of criminals to types of crime, but both types of typologies exist in the current criminological literature.

The Italian Positivists

Three scholars are generally recognized as comprising the Italian School of Criminology: Cesare Lombroso, Enrico Ferri, and Raffaele Garofalo. The typology that emerged from the investigations undertaken by Lombroso reflected his training as a medical doctor and psychiatrist. Lombroso's earliest observations of criminals were based on autopsies that he had performed on bandits, as well as physicals administered to law violating Italian soldiers (who differed from conforming troops because they wore tattoos).

Lombroso (1972) is best known for one of his criminal types, the "born criminal" or atavistic man. For Lombroso, the atavistic man was a born criminal, one whose primitive and savage composition made him incapable of abiding by the laws of his culture. Lombroso later modified his thinking to include two additional categories of offenders: criminaloids and insane criminals. Criminaloids were law violating males who were prone to a variety of criminal acts, given certain conditions. This class of criminals represented in excess of half of all offenders in Lombroso's schemata. Insane criminals included a wide variety of individuals with mental disorders, including idiots, imbeciles, epileptics, alcoholics, hysterical people, and the depressed.

Ferri (1909) developed a typology of criminals similar to Lombroso's. Included were insane offenders, born criminals, occasional offenders, and criminals by passion. Ferri argued for three determinants of criminality. These he identified as the physical, anthropological, and social influences on crime. Physical causes of criminality included race, climate, geographical location, temperature, and the effects of the seasons. Variables such as age, sex, and psychological criteria constituted the anthropological determinants of criminal behaviors. Finally, the social influences on criminality included a number of factors, most notably population density and customs. Ferri's socialistic leanings are important to his crime theory, for he believed that social, economic, and political factors interacted with one another to influence criminality. The occasional offender and criminals by passion were, therefore, products of their milieus.

Garofalo, the last of the Italian positivists, was a Darwinian who concentrated much of his writings on the punishment of offenders. Through his "law of adaptation" Garofalo (1914) detailed the conditions under which offenders were to be eliminated from and reintegrated with society (1914:217–269). In the tradition of Lombroso and Ferri, Garofalo proposed a typology of criminals. Garofalo theorized that criminals are deficient in probity (the ability to realize that their actions are wrong) or pity (the ability to empathize with the victims of their crimes). He described four types of offenders: murderers who kill for enjoyment; other types of violent offenders; sociopathic oriented criminals; and sexual offenders. The end product of Garofalo's thinking was that by eliminating criminals and their offspring from society, only citizens of superior constitution would be left, making social progress more feasible.

Stature and Physiological Types

The efforts of the Italian positivists drew attention from scholars with similar interests in both Europe and in America. In England, Charles Goring (1972) undertook a major comparison of convicted felons with noncriminals, and was unable to support the majority of Lombroso's claims concerning body type and criminality. However, Goring did conclude that when controlling for occupation, criminals were smaller in physical stature than non-criminals (his comparison group consisted of subjects from the Royal Engineers).

Goring's findings were questioned by the American anthropologist, E.A. Hooton (1939), who re-examined Goring's data and concluded criminals are innately inferior to non-criminals. As a general rule, Hooton's findings were supportive of the stigmata reported by Lombroso nearly 65 years earlier. On the basis of a sample of over 17,000 felons and noncriminals, Hooton was able to differentiate between several categories of offenders (1939:376–378). Hooton's categorization distinguished different types of offenders primarily on the basis of stature.

First, tall, thin men were reported to be violent. Second, tall, heavy set men were also violent, but also committed property offenses such as forgery. Third, men of smaller stature were reported to be thieves, and finally, shorter, heavy set males were found to have a greater likelihood of committing sex offenses. Hooton discovered that his typology failed to classify some offenders, and proceeded to identify one additional type of offender, men of mediocre stature. These he reported to be individuals who committed a wide diversity of offenses.

Sheldon (1949) attempted to link body type with personality. Based on a sample of 200 male youths who had been referred to a rehabilitation home by the courts and social agencies, Sheldon was able to derive three body types and their respective personality traits (1950:14–30). *Endomorphs* were fat youngsters who were submissive and who demonstrated little interest in physical activity. *Mesomorphs* were muscular youths who were physically active and who frequently engaged in daring behaviors. *Ectomorphs* were thin and fragile in stature, and tended to be introverted and inhibited. Sheldon reported that 60 percent of 200 males were mesomorphic, and concluded that muscularity, coupled with physical daringness was likely to be associated with delinquent behavior.

Sheldon and Eleanor Glueck (1950) also gave support to the mesomorphy hypothesis, reporting that slightly over 60 percent of delinquents were characterized by muscularity, while approximately 31 percent of non-delinquents were of the mesomorphic body structure. However, the Gluecks elaborated in more detail on the link between delinquency and mesomorphy. For the Gluecks, the mesomorph was a man of action, one who would act on impulse, especially in situations when his behavior had been labeled as antisocial. In their later work, Glueck and Glueck (1956) attempted to account for a multiplicity of factors that would interact with physical stature to affect the delinquent response, including valuables such as health, emotional stability, and poverty.

The studies by Sheldon and by the Gluecks were criticized for methodological flaws. In an attempt to address these criticisms, Cortes (1972) attempted to replicate their results on a sample of 100 convicted delinquents and a control sample of 100 private high school seniors. He also included a sample of 20 institutionalized adult felons. In general, Cortes' results supported those of Sheldon and of Glueck and Glueck.

Criticisms of Biological Typologies

Biological typologies have been extensively criticized in the criminological literature; for a review see Vold and Bernard (1986). We briefly review some of the criticisms here. First, biological typologies have had limited generalizability (if any at all) because of the peculiarity of the samples upon which they have been based. Lombroso based many of his characteristics of the atavistic man on his observations of Sicilian prisoners, and even the recent sociobiological works undertaken in Europe by Mednick and Volavka (1982), and Christiansen (1977) on twins and crime suffer from non-scientific samples. Similar conclusions have been reached on adoption studies (Hutchings and Mednick 1977; Gabrielli and Mednick 1984), and on studies on neurological dysfunctions and crime (Monroe 1978; Williams 1969).

Second, related to the problem of sampling, most biological studies have relied on comparisons of officially adjudicated delinquents and individuals who had not been adjudicated delinquent. Self-report data indicate that many, indeed *most* individuals who have no criminal record have engaged in behavior for which they could have been adjudicated delinquent (Elliott et al. 1983; O'Brien 1985). Even though some correlates of illegal behavior appear similar for official delinquency and properly designed self-report studies (Elliott and Ageton 1980), there are indications that official data may be biased with respect to some correlates of crime (Elliott et al. 1989; Huizinga and Elliott 1987).

Third, treatments based on biological typologies have typically not proven effective in reducing illegal behavior. The results of studies of biologically-based treatment are generally mixed and inconclusive (Vold and Bernard 1986). There also seems to be a logical flaw in the suggestion that there is a biological basis to specifically *illegal* behavior. Although it is plausible that individuals have biological predispositions to certain types of behavior, such as aggressiveness, it seems likely that social influences will channel that behavior into specifically legal (football, the legal profession, the military, selling used cars) or illegal (robbery, homicide) behaviors. In other words, biology may produce dispositions to broad classes of behavior, some of them legal and others illegal; but biology and legal codes are sufficiently unrelated to make a direct link between the two, unmediated by social influences, implausible.

Social and Behavioral Typologies

Merton's (1938) typology, discussed earlier in this chapter, is unusual as a criminological typology because it includes both criminal and noncriminal (Ritualist and Conformist) types. Although formulated in 1938, Merton's typology was not tested until recently. Menard (1991) found that Retreatists had higher frequencies of marijuana and other illicit drug use than other types, that Innovators had higher frequencies of minor and serious offending, and that Conformists and Ritualists had the lowest rates of illegal behavior, all as predicted by Merton. Other elements of Merton's theory were also supported; this is discussed in more detail in the next chapter.

Another typology that includes both offenders and nonoffenders is the typology proposed by Dunford and Elliott (1984). This typology includes both nonoffenders and very low frequency offenders (0–3 minor offenses, no serious offenses) in one category, then constructs three additional categories (exploratory offenders, patterned nonserious offenders, and serious offenders) based on the frequency of serious and minor offenses obtained by self-reports from respondents. This empirical typology also appears to have some utility in predicting crime, delinquency, and other problem behaviors, for example, predicting levels of drug use from crime patterns, and predicting crime patterns and mental health problems from types of drug use. (Dunford and Elliott 1984; Elliott et al. 1989; Huizinga et al. 1989).

Other criminological typologies have focused exclusively on types of crimes or types of criminals. Clinard and Quinney (1973) enumerated nine criminal behavior systems defined in terms of five dimensions: legal aspects of offenses, group support of criminal behavior, correspondence between criminal and legitimate behavior, societal reaction and legal processing, and criminal career of the offender. As Gibbons (1985) noted, the last dimension reflects a concern with kinds of criminals rather than with kinds of criminal activity. The nine types identified by Clinard and Quinney were (1) violent personal crime, (2) occasional property crime, (3) public order crime, (4) conventional crime, (5) political crime, (6) occupational crime, (7) corporate crime, (8) organized crime, and (9) professional crime.

Glaser (1972) identified ten types of adult offenders: (1) adolescent recapitulators, (2) subcultural assaulters, (3) addiction-supporting predators, (4) vocational predators, (5) organized illegal drug sellers, (6) avocational predators, (7) crisis-vacillation predators, (8) quasi-insane assaulters, (9) addicted performers, and (10) private illegal consumers. Gibbons (1965) developed a set of "role-career" typologies of criminal behavior. Gibbons' types were (1) professional thief, (2) professional "heavy" criminal, (3) semiprofessional property criminal, (4) property offender, "one-time loser," (5) automobile thief—"joyrider," (6) naive check forger, (7) white-collar criminal, (8) professional "fringe" violator, (9) embezzler, (10) personal offender—"one-time loser," (11) "psychopathic" assaultist, (12) violent sex offender, (13) nonviolent sex offender, "rapo," (14) nonviolent sex offender, statutory rape, and (15) narcotic addict—heroin.

Chaiken and Chaiken (1982) developed a typology of offenders based on an incarcerated sample of convicted felons. Their types were (1) violent predators [robber-assaulter-dealers], (2) robber-assaulters, (3) robber-dealers, (4) low-level robbers, (5) mere assaulters, (6) burglar-dealers, (7) low-level burglars, (8) property and drug offenders, (9) low-level property offenders, and (10) drug dealers. An interesting feature of this typology is that types ranked higher in the hierarchy (for example, violent predators or robber-assaulters as opposed to burglar-dealers or low-level burglars) committed more offenses of every kind than offenders ranked lower in the hierarchy. That is, the inmates classified as violent predators and robber-assaulters had typically committed more burglaries than the offenders classified as burglar-dealers or low-level burglars. What emerges from the typology constructed by Chaiken and Chaiken is evidence that individuals specialize in different types of crime primarily in the sense of limiting themselves to a certain level of seriousness. Individuals who commit the most serious crimes also commit the greatest variety of crimes, and have the highest individual rates of offending.

Box 7.1: Gibbons' Evaluation of Criminal/Crime Typologies

The typological idea is a fairly simple and straightforward one that has superficial plausibility, but it is also an idea whose time has probably gone. Many of the typological systems that have been suggested by criminologists, particularly those that assign criminal or delinquent persons to a relatively small number of distinct types, are fuzzy and ambiguous, making it difficult if not impossible to scrutinize them through research efforts. . . . In my own case, I have devoted about a quarter of a century to work of one kind or another on offender typologies. . . . But the research

> evidence we have examined here indicates that I have been engaged in a
> relatively fruitless endeavor, as have other architects of comprehensive
> typologies. The degree of patterning of offense behavior and other dimen-
> sions assumed in existing typologies is much greater than that which
> exists in the real world of lawbreaking. (Gibbons 1985:170–171)

The typologies of Clinard and Quinney, Glaser, and Gibbons are all
mixtures of offense and offender characteristics. All exclude nonoffenders
as a category. All, according to Gibbons (1985), are fairly useless.
Gibbons' assessment of criminal typologies is presented in Box 7.1.
Altogether, the evidence on individual-level typologies seems to indicate
that individuals tend not to specialize in certain types of crime. Instead,
the dimensions of variety, seriousness, and frequency appear to vary
together, such that an individual who ranks highly on one of these
dimensions will usually rank highly on the other two as well. Relatively
simple typologies, such as the theoretical typology of Merton (1938) and
the empirical typology of Dunford and Elliott (1984), both of which
include non-offenders as well as offenders, have proven useful in predicting
and understanding illegal behavior. More elaborate typologies, by contrast,
do not appear to be as useful.

One reason for this may be that the different types of illegal behavior,
with the possible exception of illicit substance use, have a common
etiology (Elliott et al. 1989); that is, the same causal influences operate
on minor forms of theft as on serious forms of assault. The difference lies
in the degree to which different causal influences are present for a
particular group or individual. The causes of illegal behavior, especially
as they apply to offenses committed by juvenile gang members, will be
considered in more detail in the next chapter. Now, however, we move
from individual-level typologies to a consideration of typologies of juvenile gangs.

JUVENILE GANG TYPOLOGIES

Different typologies of juvenile gangs or subcultures (sometimes with
no clear distinction between the two) have been suggested by Cloward
and Ohlin (1960), Fagan (1989), Feldman et al. (1985), Miller (1980),
Savitz et al. (1977), Schwendinger and Schwendinger (1985), Short and
Strodtbeck (1965), Spergel (1961; 1964), Taylor (1990), and Yablonsky
(1970). Cloward and Ohlin (1960) described three types of subcultures

and their associated gangs: Retreatist, Criminal, and Conflict. Retreatist gangs, parallel to Merton's Retreatist mode of adaptation, were gangs oriented primarily around illicit substance use. According to Cloward and Ohlin, Retreatist gangs should form in lower class areas in which there is little access to illegitimate opportunity (for example, through contact with adult criminal gangs) and in which community organization is sufficiently strong to suppress gang violence. Retreatist gangs may, in Cloward and Ohlin's view, have members who are "double failures," successful in neither legitimate nor criminal pursuits.

Criminal gangs correspond to Merton's Innovator mode of adaptation. According to Cloward and Ohlin's description, criminal gangs are most likely to arise in lower class areas in which there are well-organized adult criminal gangs, who may draw recruits from the most successful juvenile criminal gangs. Conflict gangs do not correspond directly to any of Merton's modes of adaptation (they could, arguably, parallel Merton's Rebels), and tend to arise in communities with few opportunities for financial gain from criminal activity, and inadequate social control to prevent violent gang behavior.

The typologies of Short and Strodtbeck (1965) and Spergel (1961; 1964) are derived from Cloward and Ohlin. Spergel (1961) described four types of gangs or subcultures: racket, theft, conflict, and addict. The racket and theft gangs are both variants of Cloward and Ohlin's criminal gangs, with more organization in the former than the latter. The conflict subculture or gang paralleled Cloward and Ohlin's conflict gangs. The retreatist pattern was also found but

> The patterns of retreatists, or drug users, have not been regarded as sufficiently distinct to comprise a special delinquent subculture. The delinquent behavior, norms, and values of drug addicts were found to be more like than unlike the respective modes of the delinquents in each of the three types of lower class neighborhoods. Therefore, the drug-use delinquent pattern is viewed as a variant or subcategory of each of the three forms of delinquent subcultures. It was observed to be primarily a late-teenage and young adult phenomenon. (Spergel 1964:xii–xiii)

In his earlier work, Spergel (1961) had considered the addict or retreatist subculture as a separate subculture, one that cut across different types of neighborhoods, and incorporated elements of the subcultures of those neighborhoods (racket, theft, and conflict), but which was characteristic of older, post-adolescent period in the life cycle. Importantly, the addicts had lower levels of income aspirations than other delinquents, a finding consistent with Cloward and Ohlin's description of the retreatist subculture.

Short and Strodtbeck deliberately set out to find gangs in Chicago that fit Cloward and Ohlin's typology. They succeeded in finding conflict gangs, had great difficulty in locating a retreatist gang, and were unsuccessful in locating a fully developed criminal gang. Based on a factor analysis of the behaviors of gang members, however, they identified five types of gang activity: stable corner-boy activities (including sports, social activities, and minor delinquency), conflict (serious assaults and other crimes), retreatism (including illicit drug and alcohol use, and also deviant sexual behavior), a pattern they referred to as stable sex (primarily sexual activity, but also alcohol use and work experience), and a pattern they called authority protest (a combination of auto theft, joyriding, runaway, truancy, public nuisance, and alcohol use). Their conflict and retreatist gangs parallel those of Cloward and Ohlin. The stable sex and authority protest patterns seem to be elements of gang activity, but not features around which gangs are organized.

Yablonsky (1970) described three types of gangs: social, delinquent, and violent. Social gangs appear similar to the stable corner-boy pattern found by Short and Strodtbeck. They are relatively permanent, centered around a permanent location, cohesive, often have clearly identifiable membership and leadership, and are relatively nondelinquent. Gang members tend to be emotionally stable, and to share the values and norms of the larger society. Delinquent gangs appear to parallel the criminal gangs of Cloward and Ohlin. They are organized primarily to carry out illegal acts for profit, and tend to be small, cohesive, exclusive (limited number of members, exclusion of nonmembers from gang activity), well-organized (including well-defined leadership and deliberate recruitment to perpetuate the gang), and to engage in violence and social activity as secondary and subordinate elements to their principal goal, illegal profits. According to Yablonsky, members of delinquent gangs have often been socialized to accept or tolerate illegal behavior. Violent gangs appear similar to Cloward and Ohlin's conflict gangs, and are organized around violent activity, which is performed for the emotional gratification of the gang members. Membership and leadership are nebulous, and members, especially core members, tend to be emotionally disturbed young adults. Gang organization is loose, and characterized by Yablonsky as a "near group," highly unstable and marked by a lack of cohesion or emotional ties among members.

Feldman et al. (1985) described three "styles" among Latino gangs and street corner groups in San Francisco. The "fighting" style involved violent defense of turf and violence in many contexts, including but not limited to drug use and drug dealing. Violence was part of the social process that promoted solidarity within the gang. The "entrepreneurial" style focused on attaining social status through money and the consumption of commodities money could buy. The entrepreneurial style was active in drug sales, and involved in situational violence motivated by money or commodities. The third style described by Feldman et al. was primarily social and recreational, with relatively little fighting or violence. These types appear to parallel Yablonsky's violent, delinquent, and social gangs, respectively.

Taylor (1990) described three types of gangs: scavenger (which he likened to Yablonsky's social and violent gangs), territorial gangs (organized around defending a particular territory or turf), and corporate gangs (similar to Cloward and Ohlin's criminal gangs). Taylor suggested that more successful scavenger gangs, which were characterized by petty and violent (often non-instrumental) criminal activity, could evolve into corporate gangs (e.g., through success in the drug trade), possibly with territorial gang organization as an intermediate step. Actually, Taylor's scavenger gangs sound more like law-violating youth groups than gangs. It is not until they evolve into territorial gangs (with a specific claim on "turf") that these groups become true gangs, which may parallel Yablonsky's violent or social gangs. Corporate gangs do appear to parallel Yablonsky's delinquent gangs and Cloward and Ohlin's criminal gangs.

Fagan (1989) described four types of gangs, which he labeled "Type 1" to "Type 4." Type 1, which included 28 percent of the gangs studied, was characterized by low rates of illegal behavior and drug use. According to Fagan (1989:649), "This is basically a social group whose patterns of use reflect general adolescent experimentation in drug use and delinquency. This type of gang appears to be a 'social gang.' " Type 2 (7% of the gangs studied) was characterized by low rates of illegal behavior other than vandalism, drug use, and drug sales. The drug sales appear to have been to support their own drug use, and Fagan characterized Type 2 as "party gangs."

Type 3 gangs (37% of the total) were heavily involved in most forms of illegal behavior, but only moderately involved in hard drug use and drug sales. Fagan described Type 3 as "serious delinquent" gangs. Type 4 gangs (28% of the total) were heavily involved in all forms of illegal behavior, including hard drug use and drug sales, and appeared to be highly cohesive and organized. Fagan described Type 4 gangs as "an incipient or nascent 'organization.'" Comparing Fagan's gangs to the gangs described by Cloward and Ohlin (1960) and Yablonsky (Yablonsky and Haskell 1988), Type 1 appears to correspond to Yablonsky's social gang, Type 2 to Cloward and Ohlin's retreatist gang (with its central focus on drugs), Type 3 to conflict or violent gangs, and Type 4 to criminal or delinquent gangs.

Schwendinger and Schwendinger (1985) described no fewer than seven subcultures, some of which overlapped with others: intellectuals (any social class, focus on doing well in school), socialites (usually upper or middle class, focus on parties and social activities), street corner boys or "greasers" (usually lower or working class, focus on parties and social activities), athletes (any social class, generally with dual affiliations, e.g., socialite athletes or greaser athletes), surfers (sometimes mixed with other groups), and hot rodders. Not all of these subcultures produced groups that could be regarded as gangs in terms of Miller's (1982) definition of gangs, but all formed groups or cliques, and most (the notable exception being the intellectuals) occasionally ran afoul of the law. Serious illegal behavior, particularly violence, appears to have been characteristic primarily of some of the corner boy groups.

Klein et al. (1991) did not examine gang types, but did suggest that the extent to which traditional street gangs were involved in the drug trade and in violence associated with drug distribution had been overstated by the mass media and by official sources. They suggested that there were specialized gangs whose activities centered on drug dealing. If so, these gangs would seem to resemble the criminal or delinquent gangs of Cloward and Ohlin and others described above.

Box 7.2: Miller's (1980) types of law-violating groups

1. turf games
2. regularly-associating disruptive local groups/crowds
3. solidarity disruptive local cliques
4. casual disruptive local cliques
5. gain-oriented gangs/extended networks
6. looting groups/crowds
7. established gain-oriented cliques/limited networks

7.1 burglary rings
7.2 robbery bands
7.3 larceny cliques and networks
7.4 extortion cliques
7.5 drug dealing cliques and networks
7.6 fraudulent gain cliques
8. casual gain oriented cliques
9. fighting gangs
10. assaultive cliques and crowds
    10.1 assaultive affiliation cliques
    10.2 assaultive public-gathering crowds
11. recurrently active assaultive cliques
12. casual assaultive cliques

Miller (1980) constructed an extensive classification of law violating groups, including but not limited to gangs. This classification is presented in Box 7.2. Of the types described by Miller, three clearly qualify as gangs: turf gangs (1), gain-oriented gangs/extended networks (5), and fighting gangs (9). The gain-oriented gangs appear to resemble Cloward and Ohlin's criminal gangs, and the fighting gangs appear to correspond to Cloward and Ohlin's conflict gangs.

Unlike the disparate individual-level typologies reviewed by Gibbons (1985), gang typologies contain common elements. Four general types seem to emerge: social gangs, retreatist gangs, conflict gangs, and criminal gangs. These types are not only common to several of the authors who have attempted to describe gang typologies, but they also appear in subtle ways in the descriptions of authors who do not explicitly deal with gang typologies, or who may even deny the validity of the typological approach to juvenile gangs.

Social, street corner, or *turf gangs* are described by Yablonsky (1970), Fagan (1989), and Feldman et al. (1985) as social gangs; by Savitz et al. (1977) as functional gangs; by Short and Strodtbeck (1965) as gangs oriented toward stable corner boy activities; by Taylor (1990) as territorial gangs; and by Miller (1980) as turf gangs. Insofar as the association or identification with, and protection of, some territory or enterprise is an element of the definition of a juvenile gang (Miller 1982), social gangs must, at a minimum, qualify as turf gangs; otherwise, they may be law-violating youth groups, but not gangs. Social gangs are primarily concerned with social activities: hanging out, partying, having a good time. Although they do not focus on illegal activity, their members are often involved, sometimes collectively, in minor forms of illegal behavior.

These gangs fulfill the basic definition of juvenile gangs proposed by Miller (1980): some structure, action in cooperation with one another, association with or control over some territory with which the gang is identified, and some involvement in illegal behavior. Beyond these basic criteria, social gangs encompass a broad range of behaviors. This is probably the most common type of gang, and it may be reasonable to regard other types of gangs as more specialized derivatives of social gangs. According to Hagedorn's (1988) description of Milwaukee gangs, most gangs start as social gangs. If the subcultures of Schwendinger and Schwendinger (1985) produce gangs, those gangs may generally be regarded as social gangs, with variations in socioeconomic background (greasers as opposed to socialites) or in specific interests (surfing, cars, athletics). Similarly, Hardman's (1969) small town gangs, with their limited elements of delinquent, aggressive, and retreatist gangs, appear to have been social gangs. For these gangs, "turf" was not a specific neighborhood, but the entire towns from which they came.

Retreatist gangs or subcultures are described by Cloward and Ohlin (1960), Spergel (1961), and Short and Strodtbeck (1965). Fagan's (1989) "party gangs" appear to have much in common with retreatist gangs, and both their infrequency of occurrence and their patterns of illegal behavior (low except for drug-related offenses) fit well with the retreatist type. Retreatist gangs are characterized by heavy alcohol or illicit drug use. Although alcohol and drug use is common in other types of gangs as well, for retreatist gangs it becomes a focus of group activities, and individuals who do not participate may be excluded from the gang. A good example of this is provided by Schwendinger and Schwendinger (1985, Chapter 19). Although they deny the existence of retreatist gangs, Schwendinger and Schwendinger described the formation of a clique within a street corner gang in which marijuana smoking became a central activity of gang members, and marijuana non-smokers were eventually expelled or excluded from participation in the group's activities. In addition, based on the descriptions in Schwendinger and Schwendinger (1985) and Short and Strodtbeck (1965), retreatist gangs appear to try to avoid violent conflicts.

Spergel (1964) failed to find evidence of retreatist drug gangs, and Short and Strodtbeck (1965) were able to locate a retreatist gang only with great difficulty. The difficulty in finding retreatist gangs may stem from several sources. First, as predicted by Merton (1938) and substantiated by Menard (1991), the Retreatist mode of adaptation is the least frequently adopted mode of adaptation. Second, gangs whose focus is on drug use appear from the descriptions in Yablonsky and Haskell (1988:245), Short and Strodtbeck (1965), and Schwendinger and Schwendinger (1985) to be unstable, with a tendency to disintegrate after a relatively short period of time. This may be related to the age of the gang members. The drug user or addict pattern tends to be characteristic of older adolescents or post-adolescent young adults (Spergel 1961; Elliott et al. 1989), whose other illegal activities and involvement with gangs would be expected to decline independently of drug use (Briar and Piliavin 1965; Elliott et al. 1989; Huizinga et al. 1989; Reiss 1986; Vigil 1988). It is possible, as Spergel (1961) suggested, that retreatist or drug using gangs are simply subtypes or variants of other types of gangs.

Conflict gangs have been described by Cloward and Ohlin (1960), Short and Strodtbeck (1965), and Spergel (1961; 1964); by Miller (1980) and Feldman et al. (1985) as fighting gangs; by Fagan (1989) as serious delinquent gangs; by Savitz et al. (1977) as functional gangs; and by Yablonsky (1970) as violent gangs. Taylor (1990) indicates that his scavenger gangs may also fall into this category, but as noted above, Taylor's scavenger gangs may better be regarded as law-violating youth groups. Conflict gangs are much more involved in serious crime and violence, including assaults and homicides, than other types of gangs. To some extent, this may be situational. A conflict gang may be a social gang that finds itself compelled by rival gangs to defend its turf or its honor, or risk victimization by members of rival gangs. The gangs described by Moore (1978), which were heavily involved in both fighting and drug use, seem on balance to be conflict gangs.

Involvement in conflict-oriented gangs may also be a function of age. Hagedorn (1988), Schwendinger and Schwendinger (1985), and Sullivan (1989), none of whom espouse a typological approach to studying gangs, all noted that gang fighting appears to be most common among the youngest gang members, and tends to decline with age. Sullivan (1989) indicated that for older gang members, fighting tends to be replaced by various forms of theft, and this would also be consistent with Taylor's (1990) suggestion that scavenger gangs may evolve into corporate gangs. In their study of Chicago gangs, Short and Strodtbeck (1965) found that conflict gangs were the most easily located gang type. This may be a result of their relatively high visibility to the police and social agencies. Conflict gangs are also the gang type most often portrayed in the mass media.

Criminal gangs have been described by Cloward and Ohlin (1960), by Short and Strodtbeck (1965), by Miller (1980) as gain-oriented gangs/ extended networks, by Feldman et al. (1985) as entrepreneurial gangs, by Fagan (1989) as incipient or nascent organizations, and by Taylor (1990) as corporate gangs. Spergel's (1961) theft and racket gangs, especially the latter, also appear to be criminal gangs. Short and Strodtbeck (1965) were unable to find a fully developed criminal gang in their study of gangs in Chicago. This was at least in part because the most promising prospect for a criminal gang was suppressed as soon as it was discovered by the police and by social agencies. It may also be because criminal juvenile gangs are relatively rare, consistent with the predicted (Merton 1938) and observed (Menard 1991) relative frequency of Innovation as a mode of adaptation.

Another possible reason for Short and Strodtbeck's difficulty in finding fully developed juvenile criminal gangs may be that they were not looking in the right place at the right time. As described in Chapters 3 and 6 of this book, Asian-American and Asian gangs seem to fit the criminal gang pattern more frequently than their African American or Hispanic counterparts. Such gangs tend to have strong leadership, a strong profit motive, relatively strong discipline, and an aversion for drawing attention to themselves. This last characteristic contrasts with the pattern for conflict gangs, in which building a public reputation for toughness may be an important goal for the gang. As noted earlier, the specialized drug dealing gangs alluded to by Klein et al. (1991) sound very much like criminal gangs.

Criminal gangs may demonstrate more variation than conflict or retreatist gangs, both in terms of typical offenses (drug sales as opposed to extortion) and in terms of their success relative to one another. According to Taylor (1990), gang evolution from scavenger to corporate may be based on the degree of success in competition with other gangs, especially in the drug trade. The tighter discipline of corporate gangs may be both cause and effect of success: a cause, in increasing the probability of avoiding apprehension, and an effect, as an emergent pattern designed to consolidate and protect past successes. It is also worth noting that juvenile criminal gangs, as opposed to other types of gangs, are more likely to have contact or be associated with adult criminal gangs (Cloward and Ohlin 1960; Chin 1990; see also Chapters 3 and 6 regarding Asian and Asian-American gangs).

Box 7.3: Types of Juvenile Gangs			
	Level of Illegal Behavior	Typical Illegal Behavior	Prevalence of gang type
Social	low	petty property crime, public disorder	high
Retreatist	moderate	drug use, alcohol use	low
Conflict	high	assault, vandalism, non-utilitarian offenses, violent property crime	moderate
Criminal	very high	profitable property crime	low

The different types of gangs are summarized in Box 7.3. A review of previous chapters suggests that most of the gangs described historically and cross-nationally may be classified as social gangs. Latin American gangs appear to be predominantly social gangs, with some violent gangs. The British gangs that have received the most attention, especially the skinhead gangs (which have also appeared in Germany and other European countries), appear to be primarily violent gangs, and truly criminal gangs appear to be relatively rare. Criminal gang types are most evident in Asian, especially Chinese, gangs, but comparatively new drug dealing gangs are a form of criminal gang that appears to be increasingly widespread not only in Asia but now also in Europe and the United States. In addition to true gang activity, there appears to be considerable evidence of law-violating youth groups in many countries, as described in Chapter 6, congregating in public places, using public transportation, engaging in moderately violent behavior (fistfights and knife fights), not really gangs but possibly evolving into gangs.

In the United States, the full range of gang types appears to be represented. Type of gang may vary by ethnicity and gender. There appears to be ample evidence of social gangs for both males and females, and within all major ethnic groups. Criminal gangs, however, are relatively rare (compared to other types of gangs) except for Asian and especially Chinese ethnic groups. Conflict gangs, by contrast, are relatively rare among Asian ethnic groups, but common among African American and Hispanic Americans. This latter is particularly striking, given the predominantly social nature of Latin American gangs. There is also some evidence of criminal gangs, particularly associated with drug sales, among Hispanic and African American gangs, but the criminal gang type is rare compared to social and conflict gangs for these two ethnic groups. Female gangs appear to be primarily social, and relatively rarely conflict or criminal gangs. The retreatist gang type does not appear to be associated with any particular gender or ethnic group, and may, as suggested above, represent a relatively unstable adaptation.

Alternative Typologies

Goldstein (1991, Chapter 1) reviews typologies of delinquent gangs, arranged along several different dimensions: theme (heavy metal, punk rock, satanic, skinhead), demographic (gender, ethnicity, race, age), level of criminality (serious, mixed, sophisticated, versatile, occupational, unconventional, respectable), social adaptation (diffuse, solidified, conventionalized, criminal secret society), organization (traditional, cluster, spontaneous, self-contained, specialty clique, violent), and stage of development (early, marginal, well established), as well as typologies based on activity or purpose. The typologies based on activity or purpose are the most frequently used typologies, and correspond most closely with the typology we have suggested as being most appropriate for studying juvenile gan s. The activity and purpose typologies include the typologies, described above, of Cloward and Ohlin (1960), Spergel (1964), Miller (1982), and Taylor (1990). For some purposes, other typologies may be useful, but we regard them as variables on which different types of gangs may vary, rather than as separate types.

Special mention should also be made of Klein's (1995a) street gangs. In terms of the typology we have proposed, Klein's street gangs excludes some social gangs (not sufficiently involved in illegal behavior) and retreatist gangs (not necessarily on the street, too focused on drug use), includes most but not all conflict gangs (Klein excludes skinheads, as well as soccer hooligans) and some but not all criminal gangs (Asian gangs specializing in extortion are included, but Asian gangs specializing in drug dealing are not). As noted in Chapter 1, Klein's separation of street gangs from skinhead, motorcycle, drug dealing, and other types of gangs is partly a definitional issue and partly an issue of delimiting the types of gangs that are of interest to a particular researcher.

Social, retreatist, conflict, and criminal gangs may vary, within each type, on demographic composition and stage of development. We have considered demographic variability in gangs in Chapters 1 (age, gender, residence, socioeconomic status), 3 (race and ethnicity), and 4 (gender). Level of criminality and patterns of organization may vary more between types (with criminal gangs being the most heavily involved in illegal behavior and the most highly organized, and social gangs being the least criminal and the least organized of our proposed types). "Thematic" gangs are primarily variants of social or conflict gangs. Social adaptation overlaps in part with typologies based on purpose or activity, and in part (diffuse, solidified, conventionalized) reflects patterns on which different types of gangs may vary. Again, while these other patterns of variation in gangs may be of interest for some purposes, we regard the typology of social, retreatist, conflict, and criminal gangs, based on the activity and purpose of the gang, as the most useful for describing and understanding patterns of collective and individual behavior in the gang context.

EVOLUTION OF GANG TYPES

Cloward and Ohlin (1960) suggested that gangs, gang members, and individuals need not specialize in one mode of adaptation for their entire life course, but might move from one to another over a relatively short span of time. Retreatist gangs and retreatist individuals, in particular, were viewed as possibly being "double failures," individuals or groups who had met with failure both in conventional society and in criminal enterprises, and who turned to drugs or alcohol to relieve the strain of their failure in both worlds. Retreatism, then, may be viewed as the end of the line, the final stage of development in the abandonment of conventional goals and means of achieving those goals, according to Cloward and Ohlin.

According to Hagedorn (1988:106), gang formation involves passage through a series of stages. At the ages of thirteen to sixteen, the incipient gang may be no more than a network of friends. During this period, group conflict generates group identity and leadership based on fighting skills emerges. Conflict with the police, with schools, and with other authorities helps shape deviant identity about and within the group. Notice that all of this sounds like evolution from youth groups to social gangs to conflict gangs. As the group ages, according to Hagedorn, new, younger groups of friends emerge, and they identify with and emulate the older group. The older group, meanwhile, turns from constant fighting and getting arrested to more adult concerns with survival. Implicitly, this may involve getting out of gang activity altogether, or becoming involved in more rational, profitable forms of illegal activity. The pattern described by Hagedorn is similar to the patterns described earlier by Shaw and McKay (1942) and Tannenbaum (1939), in which gang activity began as play activity within the group, then graduated to more serious gang delinquency and crime.

Taylor is most explicit about the evolution of gangs from his scavenger gangs (probably law-violating youth groups, as noted above) to turf gangs (conflict gangs) to corporate gangs (criminal gangs). Not all gangs pass through all of these stages, but Taylor appears to suggest that the establishment of some turf and involvement in violent conflict to defend it should precede the formation of corporate, criminal gangs. Further support for this sequencing may be found in Sullivan (1989), who indicates that the earliest gang involvement typically involves street fighting, which rarely results in arrest. As gang members and other youths got older, however, they became more involved in economic crime, crime for profit, and arrest became more likely.

If there is a sequence among the different gang types, it appears that the sequence typically starts with the social gang as the first step in gang formation. Law-violating youth groups, perhaps as a result of outside pressures and conflicts, crystallize into social gangs. The evolution of the gang may end here, or may proceed to one of the other gang types. Whether the process continues, and to which of the other gang types the social gang evolves, all depends on the specific situation in which the gang finds itself. In a hostile environment, where there is conflict with other gangs or adult groups, a conflict gang may develop. Presented with lucrative criminal opportunities, the gang may proceed directly into the corporate gang stage from either the social or the conflict gang stage. Taylor (1990), as noted above, appears to suggest that the conflict stage typically comes first. The retreatist stage, if it occurs, could be entered from any of the other three stages, but it appears to be the final stage in gang evolution. Not only is it characteristic of older adolescents (Spergel 1961; see also Elliott et al. 1989), but the advent of a focus on drug use in the gang appears to be a factor in the dissolution of the gang (Schwendinger and Schwendinger 1985, Chapter 19; Yablonsky and Haskell 1988:245).

TYPES OF GANG MEMBERS

As noted in Chapter 1, there appears to be a broad consensus that there are different levels of gang membership. Spergel (1990) describes four types of gang members: core, associate, peripheral, and "floaters." Core members include the "inner clique" that runs the gang and is actively involved in the everyday functioning of the gang. Core members typically interact frequently with each other, make key decisions, and are responsible for the recruitment of new members into the gang. Associates and peripheral members may be regular followers or irregular participants in gang activities, and may be involved with the gang primarily on the basis of their relationship to particular core members. "Floaters," according to Spergel, may exist within and across gangs. They are a special kind of associate with high status, not clearly identified as gang members, but often brokers across gangs with access to special resources. In addition to these different types of gang members, there are also "wannabes" and recruits who aspire to be members of the gang, but are not yet recognized as full members.

Hardman (1969), in his description of small-town gangs, provides a similar description of different levels of gang membership. His types of gang members include the core leadership elite, responsible for gang discipline and recruitment of new members; regular or full-time members, not involved in leadership functions, but involved in gang activities on a regular basis; hangers-on, fringe, or peripheral members, who are only occasionally involved in gang activities; and some adult hangers-on, who occasionally dabbled in gang affairs and exploited them to their own advantage, but were not accepted as members. These individuals, from Hardman's description, appear to be mere peripheral members, rather than the "floaters" described by Spergel.

Other authors, although not precisely reproducing the types described by Spergel or Hardman, have concurred that there are different levels of involvement with the gang. According to Hagedorn (1988:90), each Milwaukee gang is an age-graded group consisting of a "main group" that includes the gang's leaders and "wannabes" who are not regarded as full members, but membership status may change quickly. Vigil (1988) classified gang participants as regular members, peripheral members, temporary members who join the gang later and are part of the gang for a shorter length of time than regular or peripheral members, and situational members who party with the gang but avoid the more violent gang activities if possible. Yablonsky (1962) classified gang members into core members (both leaders and regular gang members who knew each other through face-to-face interaction, and who regularly participated in gang activities) and several categories of marginal members (including some who were unaware of their membership in the gang!).

The different types of gang members proposed by different authors appear to be useful primarily insofar as they distinguish core from non-core members of juvenile gangs. Among non-core or peripheral members, there may be variations in the extent and frequency of gang participation, but it is the core of the gang that makes (or fails to make) the gang a viable enterprise. As opposed to the distinction between core and peripheral gang members, distinctions within the peripheral membership group appear to be more variable, to indicate different degrees rather than necessarily different kinds of gang participation, and to be less important than the core-peripheral distinction.

CONCLUSION

Hagedorn (1988) has argued that there are not gang "types," just concentration on different activities at different times. Some of the variation in the focus of gang activities appears to be age-related, as noted above: violence in earlier adolescence, followed by predatory, instrumental property crimes, and then in late adolescence and early adulthood, a shift from other forms of illegal behavior to illicit drug use. Although concurrence among many gang researchers on the existence of four broad categories of gangs does suggest that serious consideration should be given to gang typologies as a way to understand gangs, Hagedorn makes an important point by suggesting that the variability in gang activities may be situational, contingent on external events, rather than purposeful choice on the part of gang members.

Whether we accept the idea that there are qualitatively different types of gangs, or Hagedorn's contention that there is just variation in gang activity, it seems clear that at any given time there is likely to be a difference among gangs in the relative amount of time that they spend in illicit drug use, violent conflict, profit-motivated crime, other illegal activities (vandalism, public disorder), and legal activities (hanging out, partying). A fully developed theory of gangs should help us to understand these variations, whether in types of gangs or in patterns of activity. Additionally, if the typological approach to understanding gangs is to prove useful, it should inform a theory of gangs and enable it to more accurately and completely describe and predict juvenile gang behavior. The present typology has the advantages of consistency with past research, and simplicity (an advantage, as noted earlier, for typologies of illegal behavior). Its advantages in evaluating past theories and constructing a more comprehensive theory of juvenile gangs should become evident in the next two chapters.

Chapter 8

PIECES OF THE PUZZLE: CLASSICAL THEORIES OF JUVENILE GANGS

U nderstanding juvenile gangs requires not a single, isolated explanation, but a collection of related explanations. The best explanation of how and why juvenile gangs form may have little to do with why individuals join gangs, although one cannot occur without the other. Once formed, juvenile gangs may persist or disintegrate for reasons that may have little to do with why they formed in the first place. In addition, different aspects of juvenile gangs may require not only different explanations, but different *levels* of explanation. For example, why gangs initially form may best be explained at the social institutional level, but why some individuals (and not others) join gangs may best be explained at the individual or social psychological level. Theoretical explanations of juvenile gangs must also consider the broader context of group and individual illegal behavior in order to understand the illegal behavior committed by juvenile gang members.

Much of the descriptive work, particularly ethnographic work, on juvenile gangs has been stimulated by different theoretical perspectives. Observers of juvenile gangs have often applied their observations as evidence for or against a particular theoretical orientation. To our knowledge, however, no one has previously developed a broad, comprehensive theory of juvenile gang activity that (a) considers the different aspects of juvenile gang activity—formation, persistence, and disintegration of gangs, gang membership and recruitment, gang structure, and delinquent behavior by gang members; (b) uses multiple-level explanations of juvenile gangs, including influences at the community, organizational, small group, or individual level; and (c) attempts to reconcile divergent studies of gangs over time and across cultures. The closest approach to such a broad perspective on gangs was the work of the Chicago School of Sociology (Thrasher 1927; Shaw et al. 1929; Shaw and McKay 1942) and the later work of Cloward and Ohlin (1960).

In this chapter, we will review past attempts to explain juvenile gang behavior. Special attention will be given to (1) what it is about juvenile gangs that each theory is attempting to explain, (2) whether the explanation truly deals with juvenile gangs or with other units such as groups or subcultures, and (3) how available evidence on juvenile gangs is consistent or inconsistent with each explanation or theory of juvenile gangs. We regard past theories as pieces of a puzzle, elements of a broader set of assumptions and hypotheses which, if properly joined with each other and with other pieces of the puzzle, would permit a more thorough understanding of juvenile gangs. Different theories often do not clearly distinguish which aspects of gangs they purport to explain, so the review is presented in roughly chronological order of publication, rather than in any topical order.

SOCIAL ECOLOGY AND CRIME

The social ecological perspective on crime and delinquency traces its roots back to European scholars in the early nineteenth century. Guerry in France and Quetelet in Belgium noted the existence of higher official crime rates in wealthier areas. They attributed this differential to the greater opportunity to commit profitable crimes in wealthier areas, and perhaps to personal strains resulting from living both in poverty and in close proximity to wealth (Vold and Bernard 1986:131–132). Their use of maps to delineate areas with different crime rates, and their attribution of rates of illegal behavior to social environmental influences was later reflected in the work of sociologists at the University of Chicago, nearly a century later. Park and Burgess (Park 1925; Park 1936; Burgess 1928) likened the city to a biological super-organism, or as we would now describe it, a highly interdependent ecosystem. They drew an analogy between plant ecology and human ecology, and described the structure of the city in terms of "natural areas" and processes of change within the city—invasion, dominance, succession, and growth—processes commonly observed in plant communities.

Park and Burgess described the city of Chicago in terms of concentric circles or zones, the innermost of which was the central industrial and commercial core of the city, and the outermost of which included satellite cities and suburban areas. Moving inward toward the center of the center of the city from the suburbs, one encountered wealthier and then poorer residential areas. At the border between the residential areas and the central city was the "zone in transition," an interstitial zone between the well-organized central city and the well-organized residential neighborhoods. This transition zone was a deteriorating residential area into which the industrial and commercial center of the city was expanding. It was characterized by low rents and dilapidated housing units, in which landowners were often reluctant to invest in their property, and hoped to have it purchased by interests promoting the expansion of the central city outward. The transition zone was populated by poorer residents and welfare recipients who could not afford to move out to the better residential areas. Immigrants and ethnic minorities were disproportionately concentrated in this area.

This conception of the city influenced the work of other Chicago sociologists, including Thrasher (1927) and Shaw and McKay (1942; Shaw et al. 1929). Thrasher (1927) observed that the interstitial areas of the city were characterized by *poverty, weak family controls over children,* and a general *weakness or breakdown of conventional social institutions.* In these socially disorganized areas, normal play groups comprising normal children evolved into gangs. One reason for this evolution, according to Thrasher, lay in patterns of intergroup relationships. Cohesion and a sense of identity could form as a result of hostility from other play groups, gangs, the police, or other adults. A second reason for the evolution of the play group into a gang was that the gang was able to fulfill some of the individual needs of its members, needs which the weak or nonfunctional social institutions in the area were incapable of fulfilling. The gang was built up as a replacement structure to fulfill the needs of its members, and to provide a degree of control and predictability not available from the poorly functioning social institutional structures (family, school, etc.) in the socially disorganized area. Thrasher may reasonably be considered one of the first researchers to propose a theory of gang formation (Stafford 1984).

Shaw et al. (1929) followed the lead of Park and Burgess and the nineteenth century European cartographers by mapping the ecological areas of the city and their respective crime rates. Like Thrasher, Shaw and McKay (1942) proposed that high crime rates in some areas were not the result of racial inferiority, psychopathology, or some innate predisposition to crime. Instead they asserted that criminal behavior was a normal response of normal individuals to conditions of extreme social disorganization in inner-city neighborhoods. *Social disorganization was, for Shaw and McKay, the underlying phenomenon manifested in correlated symptoms of high residential mobility, dependency on public assistance, truancy, high rates of family dissolution, and high rates of physical and mental illness.* Gang and group delinquency were additional symptoms of the broader problem of social disorganization.

Box 8.1: Gangs and Delinquency (Shaw and McKay 1973:316)

Of particular importance is the child's intimate association with predatory gangs or other forms of delinquent and criminal association. Through his contacts with these groups and by virtue of his participation in their activities, he learns the techniques of stealing, becomes involved in binding relationships with companions in delinquency, and acquires the attitudes appropriate to his position in such groups. To use the words of Frank Tannenbaum: "It is the group that sets the pattern, provides the stimulus, gives the rewards in glory and companionship, offers the protection and loyalty, and, most of all, gives the criminal life its ethical content without which it cannot persist."

Shaw and McKay (1972:321) explicitly focused on collective, not individual, delinquency. Shaw's (1930; 1931; 1938) life histories of delinquents and criminals suggested that delinquency was transmitted to children from parents and older children, by example and instruction, often deliberately. The tradition of delinquent behavior was reinforced by the presence of opportunities for illegal behavior, particularly predatory property crime, in socially disorganized areas of the city. Shaw and McKay (1972), more than Thrasher, emphasized not only the role of social disorganization in the formation of gangs, but also the role of gangs in provoking, supporting, and perpetuating delinquent behavior. In this respect, Shaw and McKay may be viewed as advocating a subcultural or learning theory explanation of delinquency (Kornhauser 1978).

Evaluation of the Social Ecological Perspective

The social ecological perspective contributes four pieces to the puzzle of explaining juvenile gangs. First, it describes the macrosocial conditions in which juvenile gangs are most likely to form: socially disorganized, inner-city, low-income neighborhoods in which gangs are only one of many problems. Second, moving from a macrosocial to an intergroup level explanation, the social ecological perspective suggests that the transformation from play groups to gangs occurs as a consequence of intergroup conflict, hostility between the play group and other groups with which the play group interacts. Third, the social ecological perspective explains why individuals join gangs: because gangs fulfill normal needs and desires, such as the quest for excitement or new experience, a sense of belonging, or protection, which are not fulfilled by conventional social institutions in the neighborhood or community. Fourth and finally, gang delinquency is explained as the result of learning in interpersonal interaction. In this last respect, social ecological theory parallels the differential association perspective of another Chicago sociologist, Sutherland (1934; 1947). The importance of social learning, particularly learning from delinquent peers, as an influence on delinquent behavior is reflected also in contemporary integrated theories (Elliott et al. 1979; Hawkins and Weis 1985; Kaplan et al. 1987; Patterson and Dishion 1985; Thornberry 1987) and in research results that emphasize the importance of delinquent peer groups as influences on delinquent behavior (Elliott et al. 1985; Elliott et al. 1989; see also the review in Kercher 1988).

How useful are the pieces of the puzzle provided by the social ecological perspective? First, specific details of the theory have been questioned, such as the assertion that natural areas in the city take the form of concentric circles as opposed to localized clusters or radial development along major arteries of transportation (Gist and Fava 1974). Other researchers have questioned the precise location of the interstitial areas. In Latin American cities, for example, the wealthier areas tend to be near the city center, and city growth occurs more by accretion at the outer edges than by expansion from within (Abrahamson 1980). This in turn leads to higher rates of official delinquency in the outermost areas of the city (DeFleur 1967). Ebbe (1989) in Lagos, Nigeria and Johnstone (1978) in Chicago found that the highest rates of delinquency occurred among lower-status youths living in higher status neighborhoods. Shaw and McKay concluded that racial differences in delinquency were largely explained by social area location, but other researchers (Jonassen 1949; Curry and Spergel 1988) have debated this issue. Vigil (1988) indicates that invasion and succession processes have little to do with the formation or persistence of barrio gangs in southern California, where neighborhood ethnic composition tends to remain stable across generations of residents.

Practically speaking, it may not be possible to make a sharp distinction between social disorganization and urban poverty. Although Shaw and McKay regarded inner-city poverty as one symptom of social disorganization, one could also argue that poverty is the cause of the other symptoms, or perhaps the cause of social disorganization itself. Hagedorn (1988) and Campbell (1991) focused on economic conditions (poverty, unemployment) rather than on social disorganization more generally as explanations of gang activity. Social disorganization generally and poverty more specifically may have different effects on different outcomes; Curry and Spergel (1988) found that the distribution of gang homicide rates was most consistent with a social disorganization explanation, but that the distribution of arrests for serious delinquency (burglary-theft and violent offenses) was more consistent with poverty than with more general social disorganization. As noted in Chapter 1, however, arrests are not necessarily a good indicator of actual criminal behavior.

Even more broadly, poverty, unemployment, and inequality have been suggested as explanations for crime in general, not just for gang delinquency (Blau and Blau 1982; Currie 1985; Johnstone 1978; Patterson 1991; Sampson 1985). Vold and Bernard (1986:130–141) reviewed studies of poverty, inequality, and crime, and concluded that inequality, rather than poverty, may best explain crime. "These studies suggest that poor people have high crime rates when other people around them are wealthy and that they have low crime rates when other people around them are poor" (Vold and Bernard 1986:141). This suggests that *relative* deprivation (deprivation compared to others within some comparison group) or inequality may be more important than absolute deprivation (an objectively low standard of living) as a predictor of illegal behavior.

Elements of social ecological theory have been used by contemporary gang researchers to explain gang formation, membership, and delinquency. Chin (1990) attributed the increase in Chinese gang activity in the United States to increased immigration, which resulted in disruption in Chinese communities and difficulties encountered by conventional institutions in providing services. Vigil (1988; Vigil and Long 1990) described gang formation as a response to poverty, substandard housing, poor-paying jobs, low levels of education, estrangement between parents and their more acculturated children, and widespread discrimination. Vigil (1988) explicitly suggested that there is support for Shaw and McKay (1942) in the patterns observed in barrio gangs, although as noted above, he rejected the processes of invasion and succession as explanations for barrio gangs. Campbell (1991:33) noted that "Gangs have always sprung from conditions of poverty and alienation common to those at the lowest levels of urban life," and also noted that gangs are most prevalent among minority group members. Hagedorn (1988) attributed gang formation to neighborhood economic and employment conditions, and Short (1990) also incorporated urban poverty, single (usually female) parent family structures, and instability of population and social institutions at the community level into his explanation of contemporary juvenile gangs.

A dissenting perspective was advanced by Schwendinger and Schwendinger (1985), who indicated that social disorganization does not necessarily produce crime. Crime, they argued, may emerge in socially organized areas, or may precede or aggravate social disorganization. The points they make are correct, but do not directly challenge the social disorganization or social ecological perspective. As Miller (1980) suggested, most delinquency is committed by law-violating youth groups, which occur in communities of almost any size, rather than by gangs, which usually evolve only in major urban centers. Most of the groups described by Schwendinger and Schwendinger were law-violating youth groups embedded in different youth subcultures, not gangs. Specific to gangs, there seems to be a general consensus among past and present researchers that either social disorganization generally, or more specifically, severe urban poverty (implicitly coupled with the coexistence of substantial urban wealth), constitutes an important part of the explanation of juvenile gang activity.

Despite some limitations and questions about particular elements of the social ecological perspective, it remains viable as an explanation, albeit an incomplete one, of delinquent behavior (Shoemaker 1990; Vold and Bernard 1986). Ethnographic studies of juvenile gangs and law violating youth groups (Campbell 1984; Hagedorn 1988; Spergel 1990; Sullivan 1989; Vigil 1988) consistently found more gang activity in general and more gang delinquency in particular in poor (although not necessarily the absolutely poorest) neighborhoods which are characterized not only by gang delinquency but by other social problems as well. These studies also supported the contention that gangs emerge from play groups (Sullivan 1989), break dancing groups (Hagedorn 1988), or other informal groups, at least in part as a response to perceived external threats to individual gang members or, more generally, to people in the neighborhood where the gang members reside. These ethnographic studies are also consistent with the observation that gangs fulfill personal needs not fulfilled by conventional institutions in the socially disorganized neighborhoods, and with the suggestion that illegal behavior is learned in the group context. Specific to juvenile gangs, then, the social ecological perspective has much to contribute. More generally, this perspective has enjoyed increased attention in the past decade as an explanation for juvenile delinquency, not limited to gang delinquency (Brantingham and Brantingham 1981; Bursik 1984; Bursik 1988; Byrne and Sampson 1986; Sampson and Groves 1989).

ANOMIE, OPPORTUNITY, OR STRAIN THEORIES

Durkheim (1933, 1951; first published in 1893 and 1897, respectively) introduced the concept of *anomie* to explain deviant behavior, particularly suicide. Anomie, according to Durkheim, was a social structural condition in which peoples' aspirations exceeded their means to attain those aspirations because the norms regulating aspirations or desires had become unclear. Normally, individuals limit their aspirations in accordance with their social status. In times of rapid social change, however, opportunities may expand or contract, and what aspirations are "appropriate" change correspondingly. During the period of change and for some time thereafter, it is unclear what the "appropriate" level of aspiration should be, and aspirations may thus exceed opportunities. To the extent that aspirations are unrealistically high, failure to achieve them occurs and produces strain in the individual.

Merton (1938) revised Durkheim's anomie theory and applied it to the United States. According to Merton, aspirations for economic success in the United States are universally, or almost universally, high, regardless of social class status. Opportunities to realize those aspirations, however, vary by social class. The discrepancy between aspirations and socially approved means of realizing those aspirations is again described as a social structural condition of anomie, and again gives rise to strain or tension at the individual level.

Merton further elaborated his theory by asserting that there were several possible responses to the strain or tension generated by anomie. Most commonly, individuals continued to accept both the culturally prescribed goals of economic success and the normative restrictions on approved means of reaching that goal, an adaptation Merton called conformity. Retaining the goals but rejecting the normative constraints on means produced an adaptation Merton called innovation, the adaptation most likely to result in deviant and criminal behavior. Rejecting the goal, but accepting the normative constraints on means, produced ritualism, an adaptation characterized by overconformity. Rejecting norms regarding both goals and means could produce the adaptation of rebellion (if one sought to replace the rejected goals and means with new normative goals and means) or retreatism (if one made no attempt to institute alternative goals or means). These modes of adaptation constitute a typology (see Chapter 7) of responses to strain. Merton did not explain why individuals would choose one adaptation over another.

Cloward (1959) extended Merton's theory by introducing illegitimate means as one influence on the choice between deviant and non-deviant adaptations. According to Cloward, opportunities to commit illegal or deviant acts are not constant, but like legitimate opportunities, they vary in the social structure. Merton (1959) regarded this extension of his theory favorably. This thesis was further elaborated by Cloward and Ohlin (1960), who attempted to integrate the ecological perspective of Shaw and McKay (1942) with the differential association theory of Sutherland (1947) and with Merton's anomie theory. According to Cloward and Ohlin, the prevalence of different patterns of adaptation to anomie vary, depending on the subculture within which the actor is located. Subcultures in turn vary by residential location (community, neighborhood).

Some neighborhoods or communities are more tolerant of predatory property crime than others, and opportunities exist for juvenile law-breakers to become integrated into adult criminal networks. These neighborhoods give rise to *criminal* subcultures, in which the adaptation of innovation is highly prevalent. In other neighborhoods, criminal activity may be strongly suppressed, and access to both legitimate and illegitimate means of achieving goals may be limited. In these neighborhoods, *retreatist* subcultures and modes of adaptation may be more common. The retreatist adaptation may be characteristic of "double failures," individuals who have failed to achieve success through conventional means and who have also failed to achieve any success at illegal endeavors. The *conflict* subculture arises in neighborhoods where both legitimate and illegitimate opportunities are limited, but where social organization is so weak that the neighborhood or community is ineffective at suppressing violence and other illegal behavior. Conflict subcultures are characterized by crime that is "individualistic, unorganized, petty, poorly paid, and unprotected" (Cloward and Ohlin 1960:173). Cloward and Ohlin's typology of gangs or subcultures has been discussed in Chapter 7.

Evaluation of Anomie Theory

Collectively, the theories of Durkheim, Merton, and Cloward and Ohlin have been referred to as strain theories. The term anomie theory is usually reserved for Merton and Durkheim, and the term opportunity theory is typically used to characterize Cloward and Ohlin's theory. Tests of strain theory have generally focused on the relationship between stated goals and perceived access to means, or on the relationship between economic disadvantage and illegal behavior. As Bernard (1988, 1987) observes, these tests of strain theory have generally been inadequate. A more complete test of Merton's anomie theory (Menard 1995) and Cloward's opportunity theory (Menard 1992) indicated that the explanatory power of these theories is considerably higher when the theory is fully operationalized than in studies which fail to include the mode of adaptation and other intervening variables between lack of access to opportunity and illegal behavior.

Criticisms of anomie or opportunity theory include the suggestion that numerous factors in addition to differential opportunity help explain gang delinquency (Toby 1961); that blocked opportunity may be not only a cause but also a result of delinquency (Bordua 1961); that much gang delinquency is for the excitement and fun of the activity and not necessarily for economic gain (Bordua 1961; Cohen 1955; Briar and Piliavin 1965; Matza and Sykes 1961). Buerkle and Kleiner (1966) found that African American youths living in a completely closed opportunity system did not share the goals and aspirations of the larger society, and issues of success and failure were not major concerns, yet these youths reported high self-esteem. Short and Strodtbeck (1965) and Miller (1958) suggested that status in the larger society is less important for explaining gang behavior than status in the more immediate neighborhood group or subculture.

An important question raised in some of the criticisms of Cloward and Ohlin is whether their theory applies solely to lower class youths, or whether differential opportunity may affect delinquency for other social classes as well. Cloward and Ohlin (1960) cast their theory as a theory of lower class subcultural delinquency, and Bernard (1987) has argued that their theory should be evaluated on that basis. Some research, however, has suggested that differential opportunity may affect middle class adolescents as well (Elliott 1962). General support for strain theory is indicated in the work of Clark and Wenninger (1962), Short and Strodtbeck

(1965), and Vigil (1988). Vigil and Yun (1990) explained Vietnamese gang activity in the United States in terms of strain theory when they suggested that Vietnamese youth gangs provide their members with things they could not obtain from legitimate sources: money (from theft and extortion), recreation, autonomy, and a sense of family. Sullivan (1989) provided indirect support for Cloward and Ohlin (and also for social ecological theory) by observing that different types of neighborhoods were characterized by different types of crime, and by reporting that illegitimate opportunities, in the form of local markets for illegal goods and services, were a critical influence on the extent of crime in different neighborhoods.

Cloward and Ohlin clearly indicated that blocked opportunities were neither a necessary nor a sufficient condition for gang delinquency. Neither did they assert that all gang delinquency was economically motivated—quite the contrary, in retreatist and conflict subcultures. The evidence that exists on the relationship between juvenile gangs, delinquency, and blocked opportunities indicates that occupational opportunities were perceived as less available to gang members (Short et al. 1965) and delinquents (Elliott 1962). Short et al. (1965) found that perceptions of legitimate opportunities were more closely associated than perceptions of illegitimate opportunities with official rates of group delinquency. This finding is consistent with Cloward and Ohlin's theory, because illegitimate opportunities become important according to Cloward and Ohlin only in the absence of legitimate opportunities. Menard (1995) found that the goal of occupational success was nearly universal in early adolescence, and (consistent with anomie theory, regarding the adaptations of ritualism and retreatism) declined in prevalence in later adolescence, and that blocked opportunities were linked to illegal behavior via Merton's modes of adaptation.

Strain theory is complementary to ecological theory in the explanation of juvenile gangs. While ecological theory explains gang behavior in terms of location in the residential structure of the city (the zone of transition), strain theory explains gang behavior in terms of location in the culture and the social structure. While ecological theory explains why play groups become gangs, why individuals join gangs, and why gangs engage in illegal behavior, strain theory uses illegitimate opportunity structures and modes of adaptation to explain why some individuals do *not* join gangs (even though they may be located in areas where juvenile gang activity is extensive), and why different gangs are more or less likely to engage in particular types of illegal behavior. Much of this is evident in Cloward and Ohlin's (1960) integration of the ecological, learning, and anomie perspectives. The importance of Cloward and Ohlin's integration of these perspectives, however, has often been overlooked because of a preoccupation with the strain theory elements of their work (Cullen 1988).

SUBCULTURAL THEORIES

Cohen's Theory of Subculture Formation

Cohen (1955) proposed a theory to explain the emergence and persistence of a delinquent subculture among working class males. Briefly, according to Cohen, working class boys are more likely than middle class boys to experience problems of adjustment in school, because the norms enforced in school are those of the middle class, which may be in conflict with those of the working class, and to which working class boys may not have been adequately socialized. In response to school failure, working class boys react against the middle class norms, at first individually, and then, when they discover through interaction that they have a shared problem, in groups. The delinquent subculture emerges when working class boys evolve norms in opposition to the norms of the dominant middle class culture. These subcultural or contracultural norms include approval of illegal behavior. The delinquent subculture then persists as long as it continues to fulfill the needs of its members. Cohen (1955:25; italics in original) described the delinquent subculture as "*non-utilitarian, malicious,* and *negativistic.*" Delinquency was committed for fun, not for financial gain, and status within the subculture was attained by defying conventional authority and breaking the norms of the middle class culture.

More recently, Vigil and Long (1990) have described the Cholo subculture of Chicano gangs in terms similar to Cohen's. They describe, on the one hand, the Cholo subculture's high valuation of friendship and partying, and selected elements of machismo (including sexual prowess and fighting readiness and ability), and the low value placed on scholastic achievement and most work. On the other hand, they describe the Cholo subculture as rejecting traditional American *and* Mexican American models of success and replacing them with "an arena for status attainment and enhancement in which these youths are capable of functioning." Parallel to Cohen, they describe the positive value placed on *locura* (craziness, wildness), including apparently irrational acts of theft and violence. Campbell (1984) also notes the usefulness of the *appearance* of unrestrained craziness as a method of self-defense, but also comments that individuals who appear to be truly mentally disturbed are avoided by gang members and non-members alike.

Kitsuse and Dietrick (1959) suggested that gang activity was less malicious and more purposeful than Cohen suggested. Hardman (1969) found little supporting evidence for Cohen's theory. Reiss and Rhodes (1963) found that status frustration was not common among lower class boys, and Kitsuse and Dietrick (1959) suggested that lower class boys did not care enough about middle class values to experience status frustration or to rebel against those values. Gordon et al. (1963) and Short and Strodtbeck (1965) also found that gang members do not reject middle class norms, as Cohen suggested.

Cohen's theory, with its emphasis on failure (in status attainment) as a cause of illegal behavior, is often regarded as a variant of strain theory (Vold and Bernard 1986). In support of Cohen's theory, Bernard (1987) suggested that it, like Merton's anomie theory and Cloward and Ohlin's opportunity theory, had not been properly tested. Cohen did not set out to explain gang delinquency, but instead attempted to explain the emergence and, to a lesser extent, the persistence of a delinquent subculture. Viewed in this light, Cohen's theory of delinquent subcultures is relevant to explaining juvenile gangs only to the extent that juvenile gangs are embedded within a delinquent subculture. Also, Cohen limited his theory to explaining male, working class delinquent subcultures. Taken at face value, this means that Cohen's theory is inapplicable to middle class or female gangs. More reasonably, one may test whether Cohen's theory has broader applicability, but if it does not explain middle class or female gangs, that fact should be regarded as a limitation, not a falsification, of Cohen's theory.

Miller's Theory of Lower Class Culture and Gang Delinquency

Miller (1958:5) focused his theory on "law-violating acts committed by members of adolescent street corner groups in lower class communities." Miller explicitly rejected the idea of a delinquent subculture that arose in opposition to middle class culture. Instead, he argued, there is a distinctive lower class culture that emerges in response to the physical and social environment, the way of life, of lower class people. In this lower class culture, norms are organized around a set of *focal concerns*, among which Miller listed trouble, toughness, smartness, excitement, fate, and autonomy. These focal concerns emerge from the day-to-day experience of lower class culture, including low income and wealth, disproportionate prevalence of female-headed households, and a broadly defined desire to obtain a respected status *within the context of one's own subculture.* Illegal behavior, according to Miller, is rational within the context of lower class focal concerns. It is an attempt to achieve ends which are valued in that culture.

Cloward and Ohlin (1960:106) denied that lower class delinquency was a response to, and constituted conformity with, lower class cultural norms. Instead, they asserted that lower class delinquency resulted from modes of adaptation to structural strains and inconsistencies within the social order. Horowitz and Schwartz (1974) found that inner-city Chicano gangs in Chicago endorsed conventional social norms regarding success and family. They suggested that there might exist a situation of normative ambiguity in which both conventional and unconventional norms coexisted, but neither set of norms was strictly enforced. Bordua (1961) noted that focal concerns could be results rather than causes of gang delinquency.

Bloch and Niederhoffer: Rites of Passage and Delinquency

Bloch and Niederhoffer (1958) suggested that gang participation was part of the male adolescent process of growing up. According to Bloch and Niederhoffer, adolescent males strive to attain adult roles and statuses in all societies and cultures. Some societies help adolescents to make the transition from adolescence to adulthood by institutionalized, patterns, ceremonials, rites and rituals, and socially supported emotional and intellectual preparation. In the absence of such preparation, similar forms of behavior may arise spontaneously among adolescents, reinforced by their own group structure. When adult support for adolescent attempts at making the transition between adolescence and adulthood is absent, adolescents experience a form of strain between the roles they have and the roles to which they aspire. Gangs become a substitute for the rites of passage practiced by other cultures, and gang membership is viewed by Bloch and Niederhoffer as "satisfying deep-seated needs experienced by adolescents in all cultures" (Bloch and Niederhoffer 1958:17).

Some of Bloch and Niederhoffer's observations are consistent with later work on delinquency. For example, they argued that delinquency was diffuse, similar for middle and lower classes except that middle class gangs were less militaristic in organization and less warlike in behavior than lower class gangs. This is borne out both by studies of self-reported individual delinquency (Elliott et al. 1989; Elliott and Ageton 1980) and by ethnographic studies of juvenile gangs (Myerhoff and Myerhoff 1964; Sullivan 1989; Vaz 1967). Like Cohen (1955), they suggested that adolescent subculture is "one of negation in which the positive values of the prevailing culture are distorted and inverted for uses best suited to a philosophy of youthful dissidence and protest" (Bloch and Niederhoffer 1958:13). Like other strain theorists, and unlike Miller (1958) or Schwendinger and Schwendinger (1985), Bloch and Niederhoffer suggested that the lower class boy experiences strain as a result of initial internalization of middle class values, coupled with the experience of failure in attempts to attain those values. The result, according to Bloch and Niederhoffer, is two status problems: one with respect to middle class status (as suggested by other strain theorists), and one with respect to adult status.

Reuterman et al. (1973) tested six propositions derived from Bloch and Niederhoffer's theory, and found mixed results. Overall, there was no support for the propositions that gang membership reduces anxiety for adolescent boys, that gang membership reduces feelings of being in danger from others, or that gang members do not believe that hard work leads to success and happiness. Their results suggest that gang members may not reject middle class goals or *prescriptions* for behavior, but gang boys may be more permissive than nongang boys of violations of *proscriptions* against illegal behavior.

Neither Reuterman et al. nor other researchers have dealt directly with the question of whether gangs are a substitute for rites of passage to adulthood. It does seem that there are rites of passage in American society that mark gradual passage from adolescence to adulthood: obtaining a driver's license, reaching the legal age to smoke tobacco or drink alcohol, attaining the legal voting age, and for most adolescents, high school graduation. Moreover, delinquent behavior generally (Elliott et al. 1989) and gang membership in particular (see Chapter 1) typically occur long *before* these milestones are reached. Considering this, plus the mixed evidence regarding other elements of Bloch and Niederhoffer's theory, we are led to conclude that Bloch and Niederhoffer's theory appears to add little to other theoretical explanations of juvenile gang involvement and gang behavior. This may be why, as noted by Bartol and Bartol (1989:227), the work of Bloch and Niederhoffer "has had little impact on thinking about gang delinquency."

Schwendinger and Schwendinger's Adolescent Subcultures

Schwendinger and Schwendinger (1985) attempted to explain the existence of adolescent subcultures within the context of capitalist development. According to Schwendinger and Schwendinger, there was an "explosion" of delinquency with the rise of industrial capitalism. In part, this may have been a result of the failure of capitalist society to integrate youths into legitimate social roles, as they had been in preindustrial societies. This does not, however, translate into the strain theory formulations of Merton or Cloward and Ohlin. Instead, Schwendinger and Schwendinger found that most young adolescents did not seriously consider the matter of occupational careers before high school, and might not even seriously think about occupational careers until after they left school. This finding was echoed by Sullivan (1989), who found that serious concerns about employment and occupational status occurred only later in adolescence, and by Werthman (1967), who suggested that such concerns become more salient toward the end of the high school years. Like other subcultural theorists, Schwendinger and Schwendinger suggested that real differences in norms and values exist between members of different subcultures.

Schwendinger and Schwendinger were less concerned with explaining juvenile gangs than with explaining the emergence of distinctive adolescent subcultures. In this respect, their work parallels the work of Cohen (1955), but Schwendinger and Schwendinger provide a much broader and more detailed picture of the different subcultures: "socialites," typically involved in minor and prankish forms of delinquency; "intellectuals," the least delinquent adolescents, drawn from every social stratum; "streetcorner" youths, with limited opportunities and higher rates of delinquency, the traditional subject of much gang research; and specialized subcultures such as athletes, surfers, and hot-rodders, distinguished less by levels of delinquent behavior than by more substantive interests. In Miller's (1980) terms, Schwendinger and Schwendinger may have been describing nothing more than law violating (or in some cases, largely law-abiding) youth groups.

Evaluation of Subcultural Theories

Matza and Sykes (1961) suggested that subcultural approaches to the explanation of delinquency all suffered the same fundamental flaw: all assumed or asserted that lower class values were different from middle class values. Matza and Sykes suggested instead that middle, working, and lower class all shared a common set of values which emphasized the desirability of autonomy, leisure, excitement, cleverness, and masculinity. Werthman (1967) also suggested that gangs and delinquency are outlets for desires (autonomy, respect, reputation) characteristically satisfied by other means in adulthood. What differs between middle and lower classes is the way in which these values are expressed, and this difference in turn reflects differences in the immediate and more general situations in which members of different classes are likely to find themselves. Rich people may satisfy their desire for excitement by gambling legally (on the stock market, or by flying to Las Vegas or Monaco, where gambling is legal). People with fewer financial resources exhibit the same behavior, but lacking the resources to engage in the legal forms of gambling, gamble in ways that are defined by the law as criminal.

Even more importantly for the purposes of this book, the subcultural theories described above are typically one step removed from the explanation of juvenile gangs. Cohen explains the emergence and persistence of delinquent *subcultures*. Once the subculture is in place, it is not possible to distinguish gang delinquency from the delinquency of law-violating youth groups that do not meet Miller's (1980) definition of a gang. Gang or group delinquency is seen as a process of implementing negativistic values with the encouragement and support of the group or gang. Miller (1958) similarly describes the impact of lower class culture on *group* delinquency, including but not specifically limited to gang delinquency. Schwendinger and Schwendinger (1985) describe "stratified domains" that give rise to subcultures and subcultural groups, which may be more or less delinquent. By way of contrast, Bloch and Niederhoffer (1958) do offer a theory of why gangs emerge and persist, in the context of a youth subculture. Their explanation is a variant of strain theory.

Short and Strodtbeck (1965) found no support for Cohen's thesis that gang boys have values that are oppositional to the middle class culture. Instead, they found that the *prescriptions* (valued goals, "thou shalt") of middle class culture were accepted by gang boys, but that the *proscriptions* (approved means, "thou shalt not") were more weakly supported or not supported by gang boys. These findings by Short and Strodtbeck are also more consistent with the suggestions of Matza and Sykes (1961) than with the analysis of Miller (1958). Other research (e.g., Menard 1995; Reiss and Rhodes 1961; Reuterman et al. 1973) has produced similar findings. Success goals appear to be nearly universal in American society, and to cut across sex, race, and social class boundaries, at least in early to middle adolescence. If there is a subculture of delinquency, the evidence suggests that it varies from the larger culture more with respect to the acceptability of different means (including illegal means) to success than with respect to the goal of success itself. Bursik and Grasmick (1993) conclude that the bulk of contemporary research fails to present a convincing case for the existence of a unique, crime-based subculture in lower class neighborhoods that could explain either the patterns of gang behavior or the development of an ongoing criminal tradition within stable neighborhoods.

VIOLENT GANGS AS NEAR GROUPS

Yablonsky (1962; 1970; Yablonsky and Haskell 1988) proposed a theory of gang membership and gang behavior in violent gangs. According to Yablonsky, the popular view of gangs as well-organized, cohesive groups with strong leadership and in-group loyalty is inappropriate for the most violent urban gangs. Instead, these gangs are *near-groups,* which fall somewhere between well-organized groups and totally disorganized mobs or crowds in the degree to which they function as a cohesive unit. Near-groups, according to Yablonsky, are characterized by (1) diffuse role definition, (2) limited cohesion, (3) impermanence, (4) minimal consensus of norms, (5) shifting membership, (6) disturbed (emotionally and psychologically) leadership, and (7) limited definition of membership expectations. True groups, according to Yablonsky, may manifest some of these characteristics in response to stress, but these characteristics represent the "normal" structure for near groups.

The structure of the gang comprises three levels of membership, with some subdivisions possible. The core group within the gang consists of the most psychologically disturbed individuals, the leaders, who provide the gang's most cohesive force and who (Yablonsky 1962:113) "desperately need the gang in order to deal with their personal problems of inadequacy." At the second level are marginal members who claim membership in the gang, but who only participate in the gang on an unpredictable, situational basis. Whether they participate at a particular time depends on their emotional needs at that time. The third group consists of peripheral members who may join in gang activity occasionally, but who seldom identify themselves as members of the gang.

Different members of the gang typically, according to Yablonsky, give different reasons for participating in a particular fight, crime, or other event. Different members also describe the gang structure differently. There is little consensus on who is a member, who is a leader, or what roles different individuals play in the gang. Gangs serve different functions for different individuals, and there is no clear agreement on what the primary function of the gang is (protection, partying, profit). Such near-groups may become more cohesive in response to outside pressures, including well-meaning interventions by agents of conventional society, who begin with an assumption that the gang is a cohesive group and act, unwittingly, in ways that encourage the gang to become more cohesive. Yablonsky gives examples of a group of boys arrested at the scene of a gang fight who, when asked the name of their gang, made up a name (the Balkans) for what had previously been just an unnamed group of boys; and of the consolidation and greater organization of a group of boys into a gang when a detached gang worker offered to provide a service (a trip to the country) for the "gang" reputedly led by two boys.

Evaluation of Near-Group Theory

At a conceptual level, Yablonsky has been criticized by Pfautz (1961) for not considering the sociological literature on collective behavior before introducing the concept of a near-group. Pfautz argued that violent gangs could be viewed appropriately as expressive social movements, from the perspective of collective behavior, and thereby incorporate Yablonsky's description without resort to the new terminology and invidious comparison between "near-groups" and "true groups" espoused by Yablonsky.

Yablonsky's description of the violent gang has also been criticized by Horowitz (1990) as having no support in recent data. Hagedorn (1988) also concluded that Yablonsky's characterization of gangs was incorrect. Taylor (1990), however, suggested that Yablonsky was essentially correct in his characterization of different types of gangs. Takata and Zevitz (1990) found support for Yablonsky's characterization of gangs as near-groups, and also support for his finding that gangs tend to be perceived by adults as more cohesive and structured than they really are. Similar findings have been reported by Cohen and Short (1958), Klein and Crawford (1967), Myerhoff and Myerhoff (1964), and Short and Strodtbeck (1965).

Sanders (1981) suggested that some of the disagreement over Yablonsky's characterization of gangs as near groups reflects the different types of gangs studied by different researchers. This point is especially important in view of the question raised in the last chapter regarding the utility of typologies of juvenile gangs. If Yablonsky is correct, it is not only the type of activity (legal and illegal), but also the very structure of the gang, that varies across types.

Yablonsky's contribution to the theoretical puzzle of explaining juvenile gangs is to offer a theory of how different types of gangs are structured, why violent gangs have their characteristic near-group structure, and why individuals join violent gangs and participate in their violent illegal activity. Yablonsky's theory also has important implications for gang interventions at the microsocial level. In particular, if Yablonsky is correct, it is inappropriate to treat gangs as cohesive, organized groups unless there is evidence to support such a description. Otherwise, intervention may make the problem worse, or create a serious problem where none existed before. The intervention implications of Yablonsky's theory stand in sharp contrast to the more macrosocial and less immediate implications of other theories, implications that would involve social structural change (reduction of poverty and residential racial segregation, for example) rather than individual level intervention.

LEARNING, LABELING, SOCIAL CONTROL, AND DETERRENCE

Learning Theory

In ecological, anomie, and subcultural perspectives, learning illegal behavior plays an important part in gang delinquency. Cloward and Ohlin (1960) included learning structures and performance structures in their description of illegitimate opportunities. Learning structures may encompass the learning of techniques of committing crime, getting away with crime, and (by a slight extension of Cloward and Ohlin) finding out about opportunities for crime. This last element provides a transition from learning to opportunity structures. Sutherland (1947) considered the community as the place in which much learning and differential asso-

ciation occurred, and regarded criminal behavior as the result of greater
duration, priority, intensity, and frequency of associating with individuals
who provided reinforcement (definitions) favorable to violating the law.
In the more general literature on delinquent behavior, exposure to delinquent behavior by friends (and also by others, including parents) appears
to be one of the best and most consistent predictors of juvenile delinquency (Elliott et al. 1989; Kercher 1988; Sullivan 1989:120–122).

Jensen (1972) examined different approaches to learning theory, including Sutherland's differential association theory and Short and Strodtbeck's
group process perspective. Contrary to differential association theory,
but consistent with Short and Strodtbeck's group process perspective,
Jensen found that the effects of association with delinquent peers were
not entirely mediated by definitions favorable to the commission of
delinquency, as Sutherland had suggested. Instead, he found that association with delinquent peers and attitudes toward delinquency had separate,
independent effects on delinquent behavior. The finding that delinquent peers have an independent, direct effect on illegal behavior has
been found in other studies (Elliott et al. 1985; Elliott et al. 1989;
Kaplan et al. 1987; Kercher 1988). Jensen interpreted this to mean that
association with delinquent friends produces situations in which the
individual may engage in delinquency despite a general commitment to
conventional norms and values (see Box 8.2).

Box 8.2: Learning and Delinquency (Jensen 1972:564, 568)

One of the major implications of Short and Strodtbeck's group-processes
perspective on delinquency is that delinquent peers can influence involvement in delinquency independently of definitions favorable and unfavorable to the violation of the law. While such definitions are likely to be
related to delinquent behavior and to be, in part, a product of interaction
with delinquent friends, it can be hypothesized that the delinquent peer
group may be a source of "situationally induced motives" (Briar and
Piliavin, 1965, pp. 35–45) and that delinquent peers can thus provide the
impetus to deviate before one has come to accept unconventional definitions and quite often in spite of commitments to conventional normative
standards. . . . [A]s predicted on the basis of group-process and situational
inducement perspectives on delinquency, association with delinquents
and the definitions score are independently related to delinquency
involvement. . . . Together, these two variables differentiate adolescents in
terms of delinquency fairly well.

Schwendinger and Schwendinger (1985:159) found that "Among delinquent youth, the sentiments that support illegal acts can also be acquired in childhood or adolescence with peers, parents, or other adults." If children acquire a sense that the act is (from an egoistic or instrumental perspective) "right," no further justification for committing the act is necessary. They also noted that in an area where delinquent groups already exist, new groups are often formed by younger adolescents in imitation of older adolescents. Hagedorn (1988), in his discussion of the evolution of juvenile gangs, makes a similar point. Vigil (1988) found that delinquent and criminal activity was often modeled on older siblings and adult relatives. Sullivan (1989), consistent with the "learning structures" aspect of Cloward and Ohlin's opportunity theory, noted the importance of learning manual skills and social skills for different types of crime. Winfree, Vigil-Backstrom, and Mays (1994) and Winfree, Mays, and Vigil-Backstrom (1994) found support for social learning theory as an explanation of gang membership and gang delinquency, particularly for what they called "group context personal crimes" (fighting in groups and aggravated assault at the behest of someone else). Presently, a school-based intervention program, Gang Resistance Education and Training (GREAT) is being implemented and evaluated; social learning theory (Akers 1985) forms part of the theoretical basis for this program (Winfree, Esbensen, and Osgood 1995).

Labeling Theory

Labeling theory (Lemert 1967; Becker 1963) focuses on the reaction of society to illegal behavior, rather than the causes of illegal behavior. Labeling theorists have suggested that individuals from the lower class are more likely than individuals from middle and upper classes to be officially labeled delinquent. Support for this perspective comes from comparisons of official statistics and self-report data on crime and delinquency (Huizinga and Elliott 1987) and from observational studies of juvenile gangs (Chambliss 1973). In a similar vein, some conflict theorists as well as labeling theorists suggest that official responses to gang members reflect their minority status and the oppression of the lower class by the criminal justice system, which acts as a tool of the middle and upper classes (Chambliss 1973; Horowitz 1983; see also Platt 1977). Although the status of labeling theory as a theory of the causes of crime is weak (Shoemaker 1990; Tittle 1975), labeling theory may provide some insights into the interactions of gangs, especially gangs from different social strata, and the police and other agents of social control.

Social Control Theory

Social control theory (Briar and Piliavin 1965; Hirschi 1969; Nye 1958; Reiss 1951; Toby 1957) has typically not turned its attention specifically to gang behavior. In part, this may reflect a running battle with learning theory over the influence of delinquent peers on delinquent behavior. According to some versions of control theory, particularly that of Hirschi (1969), association or involvement with delinquent peers is a result, not a cause, of illegal behavior. From a control theory perspective, joining gangs would be viewed as a result of past delinquent behavior. Reinforcement of delinquent behavior by the gang would be a reason for joining the gang, not a reason for the delinquent behavior itself. According to control theory, delinquent and criminal behavior is intrinsically rewarding, and needs no explanation other than the intrinsic rewards it provides. There is, according to Hirschi and some other control theorists, a "natural motivation" to crime. What is problematic is not that individuals commit crime (they are naturally motivated to do so), but that they refrain from committing crime. What prevents most individuals from committing crime is the presence of internal or external social controls.

Hirschi (1987:198) asserted, "A major point of contention between control and learning theories is the causal ordering of delinquency and involvement with delinquent friends. Control theory says delinquency comes first." If so, then control theory is usually wrong, for according to Menard and Elliott (1990), exposure to delinquent friends usually occurs before the onset of delinquent or criminal behavior. Kornhauser (1978) suggested that control theory could be modified to include the influence of delinquent friends on delinquent behavior. Attempts at integrating theoretical perspectives (Cloward and Ohlin 1960; Elliott et al. 1979; Hawkins and Weis 1987; Thornberry 1987) have typically combined learning and control theories, but without the assumption of a natural motivation to crime. Peer influences are built into the integrated theoretical models, sometimes as influences on illegal behavior and sometimes as variables that both affect and are affected by illegal behavior.

Elements of control theory are incorporated into other perspectives, notably the ecological perspective. Shaw and McKay (1972) attributed high levels of delinquency in inner city zones of transition to the breakdown of social organization and the lack of effective social control. Cloward and Ohlin (1960) included elements of social control theory in their explanation of delinquency, especially for explaining the prevalence of different types of subcultures in different neighborhoods. For example, retreatist subcultures were most likely in neighborhoods where legitimate opportunities were scarce, where illegitimate opportunities were limited, and where the neighborhood or community was sufficiently organized to suppress conflict-oriented gangs. Although social control theory in its purest form, as elaborated by Hirschi, does not appear to be particularly useful for the study of juvenile gangs, elements of control theory, as integrated into ecological and other perspectives, appear to be fundamental to understanding the formation and illegal behavior of juvenile gangs.

Deterrence Theory

Deterrence theory may be regarded as a special form of social control theory, in which the one element of control is the fear of negative consequences of illegal behavior. In early formulations of control theory (Reiss 1951), deterrence was explicitly included as one element of social control, along with other elements including bonding to conventional social institutions and individuals, and internalized beliefs that it was wrong to commit crimes. Deterrence theory is derived from the classical theory of crime (Vold and Bernard 1986) and from behavioral psychology, both of which assume that individuals behave rationally to maximize pleasure and minimize pain. Although both formal and informal sources of punishment should be relevant to deterrence according to classical criminology and behaviorist psychology, only formal or official sources of punishment are commonly considered in criminological research on deterrence theory.

The effectiveness of official deterrence is generally hypothesized to depend on the certainty, swiftness, and severity of punishment. If punishment is certain (or at least highly probable), if it follows quickly after committing the offense, and if the severity of the punishment exceeds the rewards obtained from the illegal behavior, then the probability of the illegal behavior is reduced. In a review of the research on deterrence, Conklin (1989) suggested that (a) much of the research on deterrence is inconclusive; (b) it appears that instrumental crimes such as white collar crime and tax evasion are more responsive to deterrents than homicide, conventional crime (robbery, burglary, assault), or expressive crimes (vandalism, public disorder); and (c) to the extent that there is a deterrent effect, certainty of punishment may be more important than severity of punishment. Paternoster (1987) found that longitudinal, multivariate panel models typically find no support for the deterrent effects of certainty or severity of punishment.

Sullivan's (1989) ethnographic data provide another perspective on deterrence. According to Sullivan, arrest seems to deter some individuals from crime, or at least from specific types of crime. Arrest, violent confrontation, or sometimes even mere recognition as a perpetrator by victims or others are repeatedly mentioned as events which precipitated abandonment of illegal activity or a change in the type of crime being committed by adolescent boys. Sullivan's report also suggests that informal sanctions were as important as formal sanctions. Some individuals avoided dealing heroin not because of fear of official sanctions, but because the heroin trade was viewed as potentially violent and too risky for both customers and sellers.

CONCLUSION: THE STATUS
OF JUVENILE GANG THEORY

If one were to read reviews of theories of juvenile gangs written at the end of the last decade (for example, Binder et al. 1988:154–163; Kratcoski and Kratcoski 1990; Shoemaker 1990; Vold and Bernard 1986; Whitehead and Lab 1990; Stafford 1984), one might well be excused for thinking that theoretical developments on the topic of juvenile gangs stopped with the publication of *Group Processes and Gang Delinquency* (Short and Strodtbeck 1965), and that everything written on juvenile gang theory since then has been a test or commentary on theories produced before 1965. Cohen (1990) commented that "the state of theory—and correspondingly our ability to account for variation [in gangs]—is not that impressive. Particularly striking is the recurrent sameness of explanations but the differences among the *explicanda.*" By contrast, juvenile delinquency theory (exclusive of juvenile gang theory) has undergone substantial change, and arguably progress, with the integration of major theories of delinquency (Elliott et al. 1979; Hawkins and Weis 1987; Thornberry 1987) and the development of new perspectives such as the power-control theory of Hagan et al. (1985) and the routine activities theory of Felson and Cohen (1980). To some extent, this has found its way into gang research, for example, in Fagan's (1990) use of integrated theory. Klein (1995a) has proposed an integrated theory of gang onset and persistence (to be reviewed in the next chapter), and the theoretical basis of the GREAT program (Winfree et al. 1995) includes elements of both social learning (Akers 1985) and self-control (Gottfredson and Hirschi 1990) theories.

It is commonplace to assert that no one theory is adequate to explain juvenile gang activity, and that elements of several theories are useful in understanding juvenile gangs. Hardman (1969:256) made this statement over two decades ago, and Vigil (1988) has echoed it more recently. It is not enough, however, to say that the pieces of the puzzle (some of them, anyway) are on the table. It is time to try, once again, to put the whole puzzle together. In adopting this stance, we reject Hagedorn's (1990) suggestion that we lack sufficient knowledge to formulate a theory of juvenile gangs. Any theory we construct at present may be incomplete, just as theories of juvenile delinquency remain incomplete, but we believe that we have accumulated sufficient information, through ethnographic and comparative studies, through historical and survey research, that a new attempt at constructing a more comprehensive theory of juvenile gang behavior is warranted. In this chapter, we have surveyed some of the elements, the puzzle pieces, that we would like to fit into a theory of juvenile gangs. It is to this task that we turn in the next chapter.

Chapter 9

THEORETICAL PROPOSITIONS
ABOUT JUVENILE GANGS

A theory of juvenile gangs has much to explain. In the previous chapter, past theories of juvenile gangs were reviewed for the purpose of extracting elements of those theories that could be used to construct a more comprehensive theory of juvenile gangs. In this chapter, we attempt to account for a broad range of phenomena associated with juvenile gangs: gang formation, the persistence or disintegration of juvenile gangs, gang structure, illegal behavior by gangs and gang members, and the evolution of different types of juvenile gangs. In part, this project involves the incorporation of past theories of juvenile gangs into a broader framework. In addition, however, it involves the incorporation of other, sometimes newer, perspectives along with the older gang theories in order to achieve a broader understanding of juvenile gangs.

The theory outlined in this chapter is, if you will pardon the cliché, a theory of the forest (or better yet, the ecosystem), not the individual trees. Like any good ecological theory, however, it examines both macro- and micro-level processes in an attempt to understand and explain juvenile gangs. It also attempts to lay out a framework for predicting and understanding the likely consequences of different approaches to gang intervention, to be discussed in Chapters 10 and 11, and the prospects for improvement or deterioration in the problem of juvenile gangs, to be discussed in Chapter 12.

The project is admittedly ambitious, and we are unlikely to be completely successful in fully explaining juvenile gangs, perhaps in the same measure as contemporary theories of crime and delinquency are unsuccessful in explaining criminal and delinquent behavior. We hope, however, to provide a theory that, first of all, presents a more useful and more complete framework for understanding juvenile gangs than has previously been available, and secondly, a framework that may be modified, extended, or adapted by future research and theoretical development to

212

better explain, understand, and predict the behavior of juvenile gangs and their members. The theory is presented as a set of interrelated propositions, with relationships among different propositions indicated wherever appropriate.

GANG FORMATION

We begin our theory by considering how and why gangs form. From the historical, comparative, and contemporary literature on juvenile gangs, two elements appear to be necessary preconditions to the formation of true juvenile gangs, as opposed to mobs, tribes, subcultures, law-violating youth groups, and other collectivities: critical mass and social disorganization.

Critical Mass

Proposition 1: *In order for juvenile gangs to form, there must be an adequate number of potential gang members who are typically close enough to each other to engage in frequent face-to-face interaction and to operate as a collective unit, rather than as isolated individuals.* In other words, there must be a *critical mass* (Macy 1990; Oliver et al. 1985; Oliver and Marwell 1988; Marwell et al. 1988) of potential gang members within a limited area, within which they would ordinarily come into contact with one another.

The term "critical mass" comes from atomic physics, and describes the phenomenon that in order to have a self-sustaining atomic reaction, it is necessary to have some minimum amount (the critical mass) of plutonium or other radioactive material in one place. Even before the atomic age, however, the concept of a critical mass was implicit in research that indicated that juvenile gangs were primarily an urban phenomenon. From the Middle Ages to the present (see Chapter 5), in Western and non-Western societies (see Chapter 6), gangs appear to have been most prevalent in large urban centers. The increase in the prevalence of juvenile gangs that occurred with the industrial revolution may be explained indirectly in terms of technology, and more directly in terms of the concentration of populations in the massive labor pools that only urban centers could provide.

How many constitute an "adequate number," which individuals are "potential members" (or eligible for gang membership), and what constitutes "close enough" are the ambiguous parts of the first proposition, and precise definition of these terms will be possible, if at all, only through empirical research. Moreover, there may be variation over time and place in what constitutes an adequate number, eligible, or being close enough.

Three examples may help to illustrate this point. First, as noted in Chapter 1, the age range of gang members appears to have increased in the recent past. This suggests that individuals who would have been considered too old or too young for gang membership in the past are now becoming members, thus indicating that a change in membership criteria ("eligibility") may have occurred. Second, suppose that the probability of joining gangs increased (for eligible youths) from 5 to 10 percent. Whatever the reason for the increase (perceived need for protection, high profits from gang activity, etc.), as a result of the higher probability of joining a gang, the size of the "pool" from which eligible members could be drawn would only need to be half as large as before in order to sustain the same level of gang activity.

Third, what is "close enough" may be affected by technology and social policy. If "close enough" means, for example, that gang members or potential members need to be within 15 minutes travel time of one another in order to function adequately as a gang, then the distance represented by that time increases as gang members move from foot to bicycles to automobiles as the best available means of transportation. The trend to the use of automobiles and even more sophisticated methods of transportation, and the correspondingly greater mobility of gangs, has been described in Chapter 1. In addition, if Hagedorn (1988) is correct in suggesting that the spread of gangs is related to school desegregation, it may be a combination of wider exposure between gang members (a larger pool of potential gang members) plus a wider area from which a critical mass of gang members may be assembled.

Once one or two juvenile gangs exist in an area, especially if they have persisted for any length of time, they may reduce the critical mass necessary for the formation of new gangs by increasing the probability that law-violating youth groups will crystallize into gangs, either in emulation of the existing gangs or in defense against them. The existence of juvenile gangs also may increase the probability of youths' joining a gang (see "Gang Membership," below), so that the juvenile gang problem, once initiated, feeds upon itself, and escalates even without outside pressure to escalate. This variability in what constitutes a critical mass under different conditions necessitates the vagueness in the above proposition; a single number appropriate for one location or condition is unlikely to be valid for another.

Social Disorganization

Proposition 2: *In order for juvenile gangs to form, the neighborhood or community in which they form must be socially disorganized.* Social disorganization is used here in the same sense as the term was used by Shaw and McKay (1942), to refer to an underlying condition that typically manifested itself in symptoms such as welfare dependency, marital dissolution, and high residential mobility (see Chapter 8). According to this proposition, some minimal level of social disorganization is a necessary prerequisite to the formation of juvenile gangs in a neighborhood or community.

Neighborhood and Community

The terms "neighborhood" and "community" in the second proposition are intended to refer to two separate concepts. The neighborhood is a physical place with more or less identifiable boundaries within which an individual has her or his principal dwelling place. The size of the neighborhood may encompass a single block on a single street, or a much larger area, depending on subjective perceptions and the area in which the individual typically moves freely.

The community, following Wellman and Leighton (1979), is a network of interpersonal ties which provide sociability, support, sentiments of solidarity, and activities in common with other members of the community. In Wellman and Leighton's approach, the community may, but need not necessarily, be located within the neighborhood. Communities are relatively dense social networks that may be centered at school or at the workplace, or which may span several states. Communities, in other words, refer to patterns of interaction that may or may not be spatially specific; neighborhoods, on the other hand, are places within which there may or may not be extensive interaction. For most purposes, we shall use these terms interchangeably, but they may have different implciations for theory. Most importantly, the use of "neighborhood *or* community" recognizes that the conditions of social disorganization may prevail within an arena other than the neighborhood, and still have an effect on gang formation and other aspects of gang behavior.

Social Disorganization and the Underclass

Wilson (1987) suggested that in contemporary cities, there exists an urban underclass, consisting primarily of nonwhite, particularly African American men and women who live in areas characterized by many of the features characteristic of social disorganization (poverty, dependence on public assistance, family instability), but who were also characterized by a lack of connections with organizations and institutions in the larger society, particularly labor markets and educational institutions. Although it appears that this idea of the urban underclass is sometimes presented as a contrast to social disorganization, the urban underclass and social disorganization are conceptually complementary. Bursik and Grasmick (1993) describe this complementarity as a focus on public and parochial social networks in the urban underclass approach, and on private networks in the social disorganization approach. The integration of the two perspectives is even more evident in work by Wilson, Delbert S. Elliott, and others (Elliott et al. 1995 and forthcoming), in which the two perspectives are combined. Elliott et al. note that even in the face of severe disadvantage in the neighborhood context, as measured in terms of public and parochial as well as private support networks, most individuals succeed in making the transition to adulthood (social support networks of family or friends, successful transition to adult work at home or in the labor market, acceptance of fundamental societal norms and values, and absence of serious problem behavior), and they examine the factors that lead to the successful transition from adolescence to adulthood.

Social Disorganization as a Necessary
Condition for Gang Formation

It should be recognized that social disorganization is not a yes-or-no, present-or-absent variable. Different types and degrees of social disorganization may exist in different neighborhoods or communities (Cloward and Ohlin 1960; Esbensen and Huizinga 1990; Klein 1969b; Short 1989; Vigil 1988), and this may affect both the type and extent of juvenile gang formation in those neighborhoods. For example, Klein (1969b) suggested that there are two types of urban slums, "transitional" slums characterized by high residential mobility and loosely structured juvenile gangs, and "stable" slums in which population shifts are minimal, neighborhood traditions may form, and gangs may be larger and have more vertical structure. Short, similarly, distinguished between the "unstable poor" communities of the African American underclass and the "stable poor" communities of the European American lower working class.

According to Spergel (1990), juvenile gangs are located primarily in lower class slum, ghetto, or barrio neighborhoods. He suggested that race and ethnicity interact with neighborhood characteristics, such as poverty, social instability, and failures of interagency organization in those neighborhoods to produce juvenile gangs. Spergel also noted that gang problems are not necessarily most severe in the poorest urban neighborhoods, and that gang members are not necessarily the poorest youths or from the poorest families. This suggests that poverty, although one element in the explanation of the prevalence or formation of juvenile gangs, may not be the only aspect of social disorganization relevant to gang formation.

It is almost tautological to say that in social systems with strong social institutional or community social controls, gangs are unlikely to form. The existence of juvenile gangs may be viewed as one indicator of the underlying problem, social disorganization, that manifests itself in other ways (high residential mobility, dependency on public assistance, truancy, high rates of family dissolution, and high rates of physical and mental illness, high rates of juvenile delinquency other than gang delinquency). It is not tautological, however, insofar as we can deduce a corollary from this proposition, namely that *in the absence of these other manifestations of social disorganization, juvenile gang formation will not occur.*

A word may be in order here about the *concept* of social disorganization, as opposed to indicators or symptoms of social disorganization. Residential mobility is one, but only one, symptom of social disorganization. Family dissolution is likewise a single manifestation, not a defining characteristic, of social disorganization. It is entirely possible for gangs to form in neighborhoods where there are low rates of residential mobility or fairly stable family structures, if other manifestations of social disorganization are present. Other symptoms, particularly poverty and welfare dependency, may be more important indicators of the presence of social disorganization. Indeed, as noted in the previous chapter, it may not be possible to completely separate social disorganization from urban poverty. In the work of Shaw and McKay (1972), it was economic indicators that had the strongest relationships with illegal behavior at the neighborhood level.

When Vigil (1988) notes that invasion and succession processes have little to do with the formation or persistence of barrio gangs in southern

California, where neighborhood ethnic composition tends to remain stable across generations of residents, this observation is interesting in light of the social ecological tradition that forms the basis of social disorganization (or in Shaw and McKay's terms, differential social organization) theory, but it is nonetheless possible, even with stable ethnic composition, for a neighborhood to be disorganized, in the sense in which social disorganization is used by Shaw and McKay, and in the sense in which we have used it here. At a minimum, however, we would expect that at least *some* of the symptoms of social disorganization would appear in neighborhoods in which gangs form. It is also necessary to distinguish between the *formation* of gangs, for which social disorganization is a prerequisite, and the *persistence* of gangs, which may occur in the absence of social disorganization. As noted at the beginning of the previous chapter, once gangs exist, the removal of conditions that led to their formation does not necessarily result in their dissolution.

Levels of Social Disorganization and Gang Formation

Proposition 3: The probability of gang formation in a particular neighborhood or community is directly proportional to the social disorganization of that neighborhood or community. Total absence of any symptoms of social disorganization is unlikely in any neighborhood or community. For this reason, Proposition 3 may be more useful for the purposes of theory testing. Proposition 3 also is weaker than Proposition 2, insofar as it suggests a direct relationship between social disorganization and gang formation, but does not specify that social disorganization is a necessary condition for gang formation. A corollary derived from the Proposition 3 is that *the probability of gang formation will vary directly with rates of residential mobility, dependency on public assistance, family dissolution, and physical and mental illness.* In other words, the probability of gang formation should be positively related to other indicators of social disorganization. To the extent that this proposition receives empirical support, the general proposition that gang formation is influenced by social disorganization may be regarded as receiving empirical support.

In partial support of this proposition, we may note the relative scarcity of middle class gangs. The middle class "gangs" described by Myerhoff and Myerhoff (1964) appear to have been either law-violating youth groups or car clubs (not unlike the "hot-rodder" subculture described by Schwendinger and Schwendinger 1985) rather than true juvenile gangs. This is not to say that middle class gangs do not exist. For example,

Coleman (1970) described the formation of what appears to have been a true gang in a middle class suburb. It does appear, however, that gangs are relatively rare in residential neighborhoods characterized by low rates of welfare dependency (such as middle class neighborhoods) and other indicators of social disorganization.

Intergroup Conflict and Gang Formation

The demographic conditions for gang formation are the framework within which the process of gang formation takes place. The process itself, however, takes place on a microsocial level, and involves face to face interactions between individuals and groups of individuals. One stimulus to the process of gang formation, according to Thrasher (1927), is intergroup conflict.

Proposition 4: *Gang formation and particularly gang identity are facilitated by conflict between the law-violating youth group and other groups with which the law-violating youth group comes into contact.* The Circle (Coleman 1970) became a fully developed gang as a result of conflict with the police and (consequently) with adults that stemmed from an incident when the boys attempted to hide a runaway girl in their clubhouse. The Balkans (Yablonsky 1959), who may have been an unnamed gang or a law-violating youth group before getting into trouble with the police, first made up their name when they were asked by the police what their gang was called. The pattern of naming Hispanic gangs after *barrios* or neighborhoods may reflect little more than the recognition, when they first became gangs, of the neighborhood origins of the groups that evolved into gangs.

Klein's (1995) Model of Gang Formation

Klein (1995a) proposed a model of street gang formation or onset, and persistence or maintenance, which has a more limited scope but several common elements with the propositions presented in this chapter. Here, we review the part of his model that applies most directly to gang formation. Later in the chapter we will summarize and review the whole model. Based on Wilson's (1987) study of the urban minority underclass, Klein suggests that urban underclass conditions including shifts in the labor market (see also Proposition 9 below), failures in the educational system, minority segregation, and the out-migration of the middle class, particularly the minority middle class, from the core cities to the suburbs, lead to a set of conditions he describes in terms of *proximal gang onset variables.* The industrial shift plus educational failure result in an absence of jobs in the neighborhood. Minority segregation leads to concentration of minority populations. Out-migration of the middle class leads to an absence of acceptable alternative activities and to an absence of social control. In addition, if there are high crime rates in the neighborhood and a sufficient number of eligible youth (see also Proposition 1 above), gang formation is likely to occur.

Absence of jobs (unemployment), absence of acceptable alternative activities, high crime rates, and absence of social control in the neighborhood are all indicators consistent with the presence of social disorganization. Elliott et al. (1995 and forthcoming), working from a perspective based on social disorganization theory, use these variables as parts of their operational definitions of neighborhood social disadvantage and neighborhood organization. In this respect, Klein's model for gang onset is consistent with the first three propositions above. It departs somewhat from a social disorganization perspective insofar as Klein includes minority segregation and concentration of minority populations in his model. According to social disorganization theory, it is ethnic diversity in a neighborhood that tends to produce a lack of consensus on norms and values. This lack of consensus in turn results in weaker social controls, and weaker social controls lead to higher rates of crime. Evidence from Elliott et al. (Forthcoming) regarding youth development outcomes (including but not limited to illegal behavior) suggests that (a) where ethnic diversity is accompanied by a *lack* of normative consensus, rates of illegal behavior and other neighborhood outcomes tend to be worse; (b) where ethnic diversity is accompanied by the *presence* of normative consensus, ethnic diversity does not produce worse outcomes; (c) *all* ethnic groups appear to do well in predominantly (over 50%) white neighborhoods; (d) some ethnic groups may do well in neighborhoods whose predominant ethnic composition reflects their own ethnicity, for example, African Americans in predominantly African American neighborhoods, but for other ethnic groups (for example Hispanics), there is little advantage to being in an neighborhood that is predominantly of that ethnicity; and (e) all ethnic groups appear to have the worst outcomes in neighborhoods where another minority ethnic group is dominant. Returning to Klein's point, if gang formation parallels youth development outcomes generally, ethnic concentration may not be the important variable. Instead, ethnic diversity, coupled with the level of normative consensus (as suggested by social disorganization theory, and thus included in Propositions 1 and 2 above) may be the ethnically-related variables that matter for gang formation (and see also Proposition 26 below). This is an issue that can only be resolved through careful empirical research.

GANG EVOLUTION

Proposition 5: *Gang formation is a gradual process which begins with informal groups such as play groups or groups with a common interest (cars, surfing, break dancing), which next become law-violating youth groups, then social gangs, then more specialized conflict/violent, criminal/corporate, or retreatist gangs. This evolutionary sequence is gradual rather than abrupt, and it may stop at any stage.* The play group or car club may never become involved in delinquency as a group, and members may commit no more than infrequent, relatively trivial or nonserious offenses. The social gang may never evolve into one of the more specialized gang types. It is probably necessary, however, in the process of gang formation, to pass through these successive stages in sequence. The most important point with respect to gang formation is that gangs typically evolve from informal play groups to law violating youth groups to social gangs, and the social gang is the first true gang in the evolutionary sequence (See Figure 9.1).

Play group → Law-violating youth group → Social gang → Other type of gang

---

FIGURE 9.1: Evolution of Juvenile Gangs

Proposition 6: *A group at an earlier stage in the evolutionary sequence (group, law-violating youth group, social gang, specialized gang) will tend to remain at that stage unless subjected to some external stimulus.* One stimulus for gang evolution, intergroup conflict, was suggested by Thrasher (1927), and has been incorporated into Proposition 4. Another possible stimulus, however, may have nothing to do with intergroup conflict: money. The lure of financial gain may lead a law-violating youth group or social gang to evolve into a corporate or criminal gang, as described by Taylor (1990). In addition to these general stimuli, it is possible that there may be situational stimuli that cannot easily be generalized, or other general stimuli not considered here, that lead to evolution from one type of gang to another.

Cloward and Ohlin (1960) suggested conditions under which different types of gangs might emerge in different communities or neighborhoods. Although the existence of these different types of gangs has been fairly well researched, the processes by which gangs develop into criminal, retreatist, or conflict gangs has not. It does appear that adult criminal gangs may be important in the emergence of criminal or delinquent or corporate gangs, as suggested by Cloward and Ohlin (1960) and supported by Thrasher (1927), Shaw and McKay (1942), and more recently for Chinese gangs by Chin (1990), but the role of adult gangs in the emergence of specialized drug dealing gangs (Klein et al. 1991) is presently unclear. Cloward and Ohlin suggested that retreatist gangs resulted from double failure, failure in both conventional and criminal activities, but evidence from Spergel (1961), Schwendinger and Schwendinger (1985), and Short and Strodtbeck (1965) suggests an alternative hypothesis. Instead of being double failures, retreatist gangs may emerge as part of a commonly observed shift in late adolescence from violent behavior and property crime to alcohol and drug use (Elliott et al. 1989; Sullivan 1989).

GANG MEMBERSHIP

Fagan (1989) has suggested that the decision to join a gang is a multifaceted process that involves opportunities more than actual recruitment by gangs. At a purely personal level, the reasons why individuals join gangs are varied, situational, sometimes unique. Examples of stated reasons for joining juvenile gangs are given in Box 9.1 for male and female gang members. These reasons and the language in which they are cast range from simple motives (revenge, protection) to more complex comparisons of the relationship between interactions in the family and in the gang. It would be naive to take these stated reasons for gang membership at face value (Miller 1974; Schwendinger and Schwendinger 1985). Johnstone (1983:296) emphasized that gang membership represents a combination of macrosocial and microsocial influences: "the opportunity to gang is established by the external social environment, but the decision to do so is governed by social and institutional attachments and by definitions of self." Simcha-Fagan and Schwartz (1986) also emphasized the importance of both community contextual factors and individual level variables as influences on gang membership. Hagedorn (1988) noted that the neighborhood is usually influential in gang formation. After the gang is formed, the neighborhood sometimes continues to be a basis for recruitment and organization, but in other instances the neighborhood may cease to be important.

Box 9.1: Reasons for joining gangs (Salazar 1991)

"Some kids join because they are afraid, they are followers, and they need the security of the gang. Others fear if they don't join the gang, they'll get them." (Female)

"To get a reputation. I want to kick with my group [be with my own kind], I like to trace signs." (Male)

"I think I got into the gang to get revenge on the other gang that killed my best friend." (Female)

"Protection, like whenever somebody wants to pick on me I have friends to turn to and they are easy to get along with." (Female)

"It depends a lot on the people themselves. Some Hispanics make money, use drugs, and get guns. Other gangs started out because they were always fighting. Some are not doing it for drugs or money, but if they mess with or get sweated on." (Male)

"There may be a lot of problems at home, poverty, dysfunctional relationships and roles, fear and security, yet the gang fosters interpersonal relationships, be it through fun, flirting, love, sex, drugs, and partying." (Female)

Macrosocial Influences on Gang Membership

Proposition 7: *At the community level, the probability of joining a gang increases as social disorganization of the neighborhood increases.* In Box 9.2, McKinney (1988) describes how the gang moves in to provide services and support to juveniles that the community and agencies such as the police, schools, families, and social welfare agencies fail to provide in socially disorganized areas. If the gangs are portrayed as cynically exploiting the needs of juveniles in Box 9.2, how should we characterize the community and the local agencies that failed to provide for those needs? Simply put, as gang researchers have long asserted, the gang fills a social void by performing functions that no other organization in the community performs. To the extent that neighborhood and community organizations fail to provide for food, clothing, shelter, protection from attack, and the emotional needs of juveniles, and to the extent that gangs are able to do so, the probability of joining juvenile gangs will increase.

Box 9.2: Social Disorganization and Gang Membership (McKinney 1988:5)

Reaching these youngsters before the gangs do is a challenge. "Chicago gangs have really analyzed the adolescent needs of youngsters on the street. They know how to push the right buttons," [Robert] Martin [Director, the Chicago Intervention Network] said. He cited an example of gang members who recently offered emotional support to a 13-year-old boy whose mother had died; they comforted him at the grave site, talking and grieving. It wasn't surprising that this youngster told Martin: "They're my family. They sat with me. I don't know where my father was, but they sat with me all week after the death of my mother." This young boy is now willing to do anything for his gang—his family.

Other gangs in Chicago have taken over vacant housing complexes, providing shelter and clothing for juveniles who are out on the streets. Such emotional hooks earn gangs the loyalty of juveniles who they ultimately use to commit crimes. One gang member told Martin: "We don't have to intimidate youngsters to recruit them. They want to be with us now. We know what they need."

Proposition 8: *The probability of joining a juvenile gang is proportional to the level of juvenile gang activity in the neighborhood or community.* Another macrosocial influence on the probability of joining juvenile gangs is the extent of gang activity in the neighborhood, community, school, or other area where youths are present. The activity may be legal (parties) or illegal (robberies), but to the extent that it makes youths aware of gang membership as an option, individuals will be more likely to join juvenile gangs. Support for this proposition may be found in Cloward and Ohlin (1960) at a theoretical level, and in Moore (1978) and Vigil (1988) at an empirical level. In principle, it is possible that gang activity may "turn off" neighborhood youths to the gangs, but there is little or no evidence of this in the literature on juvenile gangs. It is possible that heavy reliance on ethnographic studies of gang members may bias the findings to make gang membership look more attractive to youths than it really is; the anti-gang neighborhoods and nonmember youths may be largely ignored.

A third potential source of influence on gang membership at the macrosocial level has been identified by Jackson (1991). Jackson suggested that the movement of the United States economy toward post-industrial development has resulted in major dislocations in the inner cities, particularly losses of relatively unskilled jobs that could previously have been filled by more educationally disadvantaged minority group members. Hagedorn (1988) made a similar point, and emphasized the importance of economic conditions as an influence on gang membership among older adolescents and young adults. According to Hagedorn, changes in the economic structure have altered the maturing-out process and resulted in the institutionalization of gangs as coping mechanisms for the economic distress and social isolation of the urban minority underclass. It appears plausible therefore to advance **Proposition 9:** *Social changes in the labor market that reduce the availability of unskilled jobs, especially for educationally disadvantaged inner-city residents, increase the probability of juvenile gang membership, not only in terms of the probability of joining juvenile gangs, but also in terms of the probability of remaining a member in late adolescence and early adulthood.*

Microsocial Influences on Gang Membership

At the individual level, the influences on gang membership are similar to the influences on delinquency generally. Borrowing from the integrated theory of Elliott et al. (1979, 1985, 1989), we may advance a number of propositions.

Proposition 10: *The most important influence on the decision to join gangs is whether parents, siblings, and friends are or have been gang members. The more of one's parents, siblings, and friends are past or present gang members, the higher the probability of gang membership.* The most dramatic demonstration of this proposition may be found in the literature on Hispanic gangs in the United States, in which membership in a particular gang may be transmitted from one generation to the next, even when the family has moved away from the neighborhood in which the gang is active, as noted in Chapter 3. The emergence of gangs from informal friendship groups also lends support to this proposition, as do both older (Shaw and McKay 1942) and more recent (Moore 1978; Vigil 1988) studies in the social disorganization and subcultural traditions.

Proposition 11: *Strong attachments to and involvement in family, school, and other conventional institutions indirectly reduce the likelihood of gang membership by (a) reducing the probability that one's friends will be gang members and (b) reducing the acceptability of illegal gang activity to the* *individual.* Strong social bonds or internal social controls plus strong beliefs that it is wrong to violate the law lead to choosing friends who share strong proscriptions against illegal or deviant behavior, and who reinforce the strong proscriptions against illegal behavior. Elliott et al. (1989) and Menard and Elliott (1994), among others, have found that the influence of beliefs that it is wrong to violate the law appear to influence illegal behavior primarily through their influence on exposure to delinquent peers. Winfree and Mays (1996) found a direct effect of attitudes toward illegal behavior or gang membership, but little direct effect of family context variables, on illegal behavior. Their findings would also be consistent with the presence of an indirect effect of family variables through delinquent peer groups on illegal behavior. By extension of these findings, we propose that belief and other indicators of social bonding also affect the choice of whether to join a juvenile gang primarily indirectly, through choice of friends. There may also be a weak direct effect, consistent with Menard and Elliott (1990; 1994) and Menard and Huizinga (1994).

Proposition 12: As suggested by Cohen (1955), Cloward and Ohlin (1960), Short and Strodtbeck (1965), and by contemporary gang researchers (Vigil 1988; Hagedorn 1988), *blocked social and economic opportunities result in an increased probability of membership in juvenile gangs.* In early adolescence, the influence of blocked social and economic opportunities appears to be indirect, operating through its effects on bonding to the conventional social order and exposure to others who are members of gangs. In later adolescence and early adulthood, however, the impact of blocked access to social and economic opportunities appear to become more salient to the individual (Menard 1995; Schwendinger and Schwendinger 1985; Sullivan 1989), and may have a stronger, perhaps a more direct effect on whether an individual who is already a gang member remains a gang member.

At a microsocial level, the effects of economic opportunities may reflect or be influenced by the macrosocial conditions described in Propositions 7 and 9. As suggested in the integrated theories of Cloward and Ohlin (1960) and Elliott et al. (1985; 1989), and in the ethnographic studies by Sullivan (1989) and Hagedorn (1988), neighborhood characteristics may be important influences on both actual and perceived economic opportunities. Consistent with Sullivan (1989) and Schwendinger and Schwendinger (1985), we would expect economic opportunities to have the greatest indirect (and perhaps even direct) influence on gang membership in later adolescence, when economic and employment concerns become more important for youths.

Proposition 13: *The probability that an individual will join a gang increases as (a) the threat associated with joining the gang decreases, (b) the threat associated with NOT joining the gang increases, and (c) the anticipated benefits of joining the gang (status attainment within the neighborhood, community, or gang; excitement and fun of participating in gang activities) increase.* In some cases, individuals may be coerced into joining gangs or into remaining members, either directly (Johnstone 1983; Shaw and McKay 1973:178; Spergel 1990; Vigil and Long 1990) or indirectly, through fear of other gangs (Friedman et al. 1976). Protection is often mentioned as a reason for joining the gang (Miller 1974). The avoidance of negative consequences, however, is not the only attraction to gang membership. Gang membership may provide comradeship (Tannenbaum 1939; Whyte 1955), a sense of honor (Horowitz 1983), self-esteem (Cartwright et al. 1975), status within one's group (Kratcoski and Kratcoski 1990; Miller 1958; Short 1989), excitement (Miller 1958), and just plain fun (Bordua 1961), benefits that are sometimes overlooked by theorists who emphasize the grimmer influences leading individuals to join gangs. At a microsocial level, this proposition reflects the macrosocial influence suggested in Proposition 7. Gangs serve important functions for their members, especially in environments where conventional social institutions fail to serve these functions.

This proposition may be viewed as consistent with social control theory (Briar and Piliavin 1965; Hirschi 1969; Nye 1958; Reiss 1951), classical deterrence theory (Vold and Bernard 1986), and rational choice theory (Cornish and Clarke 1986). Insofar as it is consistent with control theory, this proposition is consistent with integrated theories that incorporate elements of control theory, and is therefore included among the propositions derived from integrated theories.

Proposition 14: *Prior involvement in illegal behavior increases the likelihood of joining a juvenile gang.* Gang members have generally been found to be more highly delinquent than nonmembers (a) before they join the gang (Esbensen and Huizinga 1991; see Box 9.3), (b) while the gang members are in the gang (Esbensen and Huizinga 1991; Fagan 1990; Friedman et al. 1975; Short and Strodtbeck 1965; Wolfgang et al. 1972), and (c) after they leave the gang (Tracy 1987). For present purposes, delinquency before joining the gang is most important. Esbensen and Huizinga (1991) reported that most gang members did not join juvenile gangs until their teen years, after (Elliott et al. 1989) the typical age of initiation for illegal behavior. Prior delinquent behavior has been included as an influence on illegal behavior in later versions of the integrated theory of Elliott et al. (1985:66).

Box 9.3: Results from the Denver Youth Survey (Esbensen and Huizinga 1991)

The Denver Youth Survey (DYS) is a prospective longitudinal study of urban youth with samples selected to include youths at "high risk" for involvement in delinquent behavior and drug use. The DYS collected self-report data on gang membership and delinquency, including data designed to distinguish gangs from other types of youth groups. Among the initial findings from the DYS are the following:

(1) Gang membership is transient; few (about 5% in Denver) join to begin with, and most of those who claim gang membership do so for no more than one year.

(2) Individuals who were *ever* (during the period of the study) gang members had higher rates of involvement than individuals who were *never* (during the period of the study) gang members in a wide range of offenses, including more and less serious offenses, drug use, and drug sales.

(3) Individuals who were *ever* gang members had their highest rates of "street delinquency" (serious assault, gang fights, serious theft, burglary, robbery, drug sales) *while they were members;* that is, their rates of "street delinquency" were much higher while they were in the gang than before they joined or after they left.

(4) Although individual gang members engaged in drug sales, not all gang members were involved in this activity, and for none of the gangs was drug sales an exclusive focus of gang activity.

Social Disability

As noted in Chapter 1, some authors (Short and Strodtbeck 1965; Yablonsky 1962) have noted the apparent incompetence in interpersonal and social skills demonstrated by gang members, and have suggested (Yablonsky 1962) that this social incompetence relegates those individuals to gang membership, which is perceived as less appealing than the groups to which nonmembers of gangs belong (Short and Strodtbeck

1965). The proposition that one would derive from this research, then, is
Proposition 15: *Social incompetence or social disability increases the probability of gang membership on the individual level.*

Box 9.4: Long-Term Adaptive Consequences of Gang Membership

"The youth gang is highly adaptive. It provides psychological, social, cultural, economic, and even political benefits when other institutions such as family, school, and employment fail. The individual grows and develops and learns to survive through his gang experience. But the gang serves the youth poorly, as a rule, in preparing him for a legitimate career and for a personally satisfying long-term life experience." (Spergel 1990: 222)

"Participation in the gang does little to prepare young people for conventional adult roles. Being 'streetwise' is not an asset in most available low-level jobs. Toughness and physical and verbal aggression are often counterproductive on the job, as is the casual attitude toward time displayed in hanging activities. Demands for punctuality, perseverance, and quality performance are likewise alien to gang culture. As a socializing context, the gang runs counter to many requirements of modern civilization." (Short 1989:253)

Alternatively, social disability may be no more than a manifestation of poverty, lack of education, and other personal attributes which may lead to both social disability and gang membership. In other words, the relationship between social disability and gang membership may well be spurious. A third possibility is that some gang leaders and members deliberately attempt to appear sociopathic or "crazy" in order to help them maintain control over the gangs (Hood and Sparks 1970) or in self-defense, to establish a reputation that will forestall others from challenging them (Campbell 1984b). Yet another possibility is that social disability is one of the long-term consequences of gang membership. Box 9.4 presents the assessments of Short (1989) and Spergel (1990) regarding the long-term effects of participation in the gang on the ability to cope with the demands of conventional society. Although Spergel reiterates the point that gangs serve functions for their members, both authors indicate that the gang may have harmful long-term effects on the individual's adaptation to life after the gang.

Level of Commitment and Stability in Gang Membership

Gang membership, as noted in Chapters 1 and 7, is a nebulous status. "Members" may be part of the small core of a gang, individuals who are continually active in gang activities and from whom gang leaders are selected, or they may be peripheral members, individuals who participate in gang activities on an irregular and infrequent basis. Membership in gangs is often transient, temporary. A youth who claims to be a member of a gang one week may not admit to being a member the next, and a youth who is a peripheral member one week may be a core member the next (Hagedorn 1988:88–90; Reiss 1986; Stafford 1984:173). According to Stafford, even in the case of relatively permanent membership, members may spend little time with one another.

According to Reiss (1986:130), "The stability of territorially based groups is threatened by three major contingencies: transiency, incarceration of members, and shifts to conventional careers." With the possible exception of criminal/corporate gangs, transiency seems to be characteristic of juvenile gangs. Some members may join tentatively, then decide to leave. Others may join with the intention of staying, but leave when they and their family move to a different location. Gangs may lose members not only to incarceration, but also to death in conflicts between gangs.

The most common reason for leaving the gang is "maturing out," moving into adult roles such as marriage and the acquisition of a steady job (Campbell 1991; Hagedorn 1988; Miller 1990; Vigil 1988). As Vigil (1988:99) illustrated, for core gang members, entry into the gang typically occurs at an earlier age, and maturing out at a later age, than for peripheral gang members. Departure may also be more difficult for core members; Spergel (1990) cited evidence that the departure of core members might be met with resistance, even murder, and other researchers (Campbell 1991; Vigil 1988) have indicated that for some members, leaving the gang may involve a violent "jumping out" or "beating out" ritual. Other gang members (particularly marginal members, whose membership status may have been unclear to begin with) may suspend their gang activities, either gradually or abruptly, with no adverse consequences (Campbell 1991; Hagedorn 1988; Spergel 1990; Vigil 1988).

Proposition 16: *The probability of leaving the gang or of reducing involvement in the gang increases at the individual level with the age-related* *acquisition of adult statuses and roles, particularly marriage, parenthood, and steady employment.* Marriage, parenthood, steady employment, and other aspects of adulthood do not come to individuals automatically with age, but as individuals leave adolescence and the high school years to enter young adulthood, their concern with adult roles and statuses increases (Schwendinger and Schwendinger 1985; Sullivan 1989). Although the temporary and part-time employment of adolescence may have little impact on behavior, steady employment after adolescence has been cited as an important influence on gang membership and illegal behavior by Hagedorn (1988), Vigil (1988), and Sullivan (1989). Departure from the gang may be abrupt, or it may involve a gradual decline from core to peripheral to nonmember status.

Proposition 17: *Acquisition of adult roles such as marriage and steady employment will be more difficult in more socially disorganized neighborhoods and communities than in less socially disorganized areas.* With this proposition, we return to the macrosocial influence on gang membership, this time as it affects departure from the gang. In socially disorganized areas, especially those inhabited by the urban underclass (Wilson 1987), there are fewer employment opportunities, both in terms of opportunities that are located physically close to the neighborhood and in terms of linkages to employers through informal social networks (Hagedorn 1988; Sullivan 1989). This acts indirectly, through the process described in Proposition 16, to postpone "maturing out" of the gang.

Psychological Variables and Gang Membership

Klein (1995a) suggested several psychological factors which might lead individuals to become involved in gangs, including social disability (see Proposition 15) and needs for status, identity, and affiliation. Goldstein (1991) examines delinquent gangs, primarily from a psychological perspective. Vigil (1994) chided us for not including more on psychological and personality variables in our earlier edition of this book. It seems necessary, in light of all this, to carefully consider and clarify our perspective on the psychological factors that contribute to gang membership and gang crime and delinquency.

We regard the social psychological process of learning norms, values, and patterns of behavior in the social context as the most important of all the variables, not just variables at the psychological level, for explaining gang membership and gang delinquency and crime. This is reflected in

Propositions 8 (learning by observing gang activity in the neighborhood is one way adolescents may be drawn into gangs), 10 and 18 (learning from the behavior, attitudes, and experiences of parents, siblings, and friends), and 14 and 21 (learning from one's own experience). Sentiments or feelings of attachment to conventional social institutions, organizations, and the individuals in them (Propositions 11 and 19) are also important. With some hesitation, we also consider the possibility that social disability (Proposition 15) is a risk factor for gang membership.

With the possible exception of social disability, none of these psychological variables should be considered an aspect of within-the-individual personality. Instead, all of them, arguably including social disability, represent a dynamic interaction between the individual and the (potentially ever-changing) social context in which the individual lives. Does personality also play a role in the choice to become a gang member and to be involved in gang-related illegal behavior? In our view, probably not. Instead, it appears to us, based both on the gang literature and on the extensive history of theory and research on illegal behavior and personality (see for example Vold and Bernard 1986 or Shoemaker 1990 for reviews) that gang membership and gang-related illegal behavior are *spuriously* related to such personality characteristics as needs for affiliation, identity, and status, "sociopathic" personalities, and other personality disorders. In other words, the personality characteristics that are associated with gang membership and gang crime (and with crime more generally) are *effects* of the same influences or risk factors that lead to gang membership and gang-related illegal behavior, *not causes* of joining gangs or breaking the law.

This position will no doubt raise some objections among researchers who believe that personality must strongly influence behavior, but based on our own examination of the social psychological and criminological literature, we are led to doubt that relatively static personality characteristics are useful explanations of gang membership or gang crime. Instead, it is the dynamic aspects of the person-environment interaction, where both person and environment may be changing over time, that show the most promise for understanding gang membership and illegal behavior. In contrast to personality theories of illegal behavior, theories involving the social learning process and, to a lesser extent, social bonding, have strong empirical support, as noted in the discussions of Propositions 10, 11, 18, and 19.

Conclusion: Gang Membership

All of the above propositions are cast in probabilistic terms. They attempt to identify patterns of influences on gang membership at the macrosocial and microsocial levels. Taken together, however, they do not and cannot present a complete explanation for gang membership. At the individual, psychological level, there will be unique reasons and combinations of reasons for joining or not joining juvenile gangs. Specific incidents or life events, attention from a particular teacher or adult friend, and other variables unique to the individual may combine to generate an outcome other than that predicted by our theory for a specific case.

As stated earlier, however, our theory is about the larger patterns of gang membership, not about individual cases. Exceptions notwithstanding, we expect that predictions of gang membership that incorporate (1) the level of social disorganization in the neighborhood; (2) the level of gang activity in the neighborhood and school; (3) the influence of gang involvement by relatives and friends; (4) bonding to conventional social institutions; (5) blocked opportunities for achievement of education, income, and high occupational status; (6) the perceived rewards and liabilities of gang membership; (7) prior involvement in illegal behavior; and (8) age-related involvement in adult statuses and roles will explain much, though not all, of the variation in gang membership. Ethnicity and gender, discussed below, may also influence gang membership. Independent of these influences, we suspect that social disability, as described by Yablonsky (1962) and Short and Strodtbeck (1965) will have a limited impact on gang membership.

GANG DELINQUENCY

The proposed reasons for gang delinquency closely parallel the reasons for gang membership. One difference between the two is that macrosocial influences are hypothesized to be weaker and more indirect for illegal behavior than for gang membership. Gang membership itself is one variable that may be used to explain prevalence, frequency, and types of illegal behavior. The propositions outlined below refer, unless otherwise noted, to both prevalence and frequency of illegal behavior. They also refer to individual offending rates (Blumstein et al. 1986). Whether different indices of illegal behavior require different theoretical explanations is, at present, an issue in criminology whose resolution depends on further empirical research.

| Social ecology | → | Strain | → | Learning | → | Subculture |

FIGURE 9.2: VIGIL'S PERSPECTIVE ON GANG BEHAVIOR

The propositions are derived from integrated theory, particularly the theory of Elliott et al. (1979; 1985; 1989). Elliott et al. incorporate elements of strain, social control, learning, and social ecological theories into their explanations of illegal behavior. Sullivan (1989) has suggested that integrated theories are better suited to explaining illegal behavior than the older theories from which they are constructed. Fagan (1990) has incorporated theoretical integration into his research on gang delinquency and substance abuse. Vigil (1988) has argued in a similar vein for either theoretical eclecticism or theoretical integration, and suggested that no single theory adequately explains barrio gangs. His description of the influences on juvenile gangs and delinquent subcultures, as diagrammed in Figure 9.2 and described in Box 9.5, has much in common with the integrated theoretical perspective of Elliott et al. (1979; 1985; 1989).

Box 9.5: Vigil's (1988:xii–xiv) Perspective on Gang Behavior

A historical and structural interpretation suggests that residence in isolated and physically distinct barrio enclaves and a low-income life, especially for the most impoverished underclass members, makes for particularly troublesome ecological and economic problems. Repercussions from such conditions, in turn, generate social and cultural strains and stresses that make the youth within this segment more at risk to an orientation to street life. In fact, when home life becomes overly problematic, it is the streets that become the main socialization agent in their lives.

Much of the gang patterns and behaviors can largely be attributed to the realities of the streets. Ways of acting and thinking are fashioned to aid coping with the streets. . . . In short, the creation and perpetuation of a Chicano gang subculture is the end product of various interrelated influences that give rise to, and provide a means for dealing with, specific problems of identity in certain youths.

Microsocial Influences on Gang Delinquency

Proposition 18: *The most important influence on gang delinquency is the delinquency of parents, siblings, and friends, including other gang members.* This proposition, derived from social learning theory, has the strongest support of any proposed explanation of delinquent behavior (see Chapter 8). As indicated in Box 9.4, results from the Denver Youth Survey (Esbensen and Huizinga 1991) indicate that rates of illegal behavior are highest during the period when individuals are members of gangs; this, in turn, suggests that gang involvement increases already high rates of illegal behavior beyond what they would otherwise have been. This may be especially true for juvenile gangs with connections to adult criminal gangs, as suggested by Thrasher (1927) and Cloward and Ohlin (1960); see also Chin (1990) and Spergel (1990). Social learning theory is explicitly included as part of the theoretical base for one of the newer gang intervention efforts, the school-based Gang Resistance Education and Training (GREAT) program (Winfree et al. 1995).

There appears to be a clear sequence of behaviors in the lives of most adolescents, whether gang members or not. Just as gangs may evolve from one type to another (see Chapter 7), individual adolescents typically pursue a gradual, evolutionary path from less serious to more serious illegal behavior. The usual sequence (Elliott et al. 1989; Menard and Elliott 1990; Menard and Huizinga 1994) is exposure to delinquent friends, followed by weakening of beliefs and involvement in minor offending. This in turn is followed by escalation in the delinquency of the peer group, further weakening of beliefs, and more serious offending. Individuals may stop at any stage in this progression. Although offending is typically initiated *after* exposure to delinquent friends and weakening of beliefs that it is wrong to violate the law, continued exposure to friends who are involved in illegal behavior may prolong involvement in illegal behavior. Gang involvement tends to come at the end of this sequence. As indicated by Esbensen and Huizinga (1991) and also by Thornberry et al. (1993), gang involvement tends to occur *after* the individual is already heavily involved in illegal behavior, and gang membership appears to increase the frequency of illegal behavior, beyond what would be expected on the basis of past behavior alone. The decline in illegal behavior after leaving the gang, found by these authors, provides further evidence of the crime-amplifying effect of the gang.

Proposition 19: *Strong attachments to and involvement in family, school, and other conventional institutions indirectly reduce gang delinquency by (a) reducing the probability that one's friends, including other gang members, will be involved in delinquency and (b) reducing the acceptability of illegal activity to the individual.* Again, strong social bonds or internal social controls plus strong beliefs that it is wrong to violate the law lead to choosing friends who share strong proscriptions against illegal or deviant behavior, and who reinforce the strong proscriptions against illegal behavior. If the individual is a gang member, conventional social bonds will affect the degree to which the individual is willing to participate in gang activities that involve illegal behavior. If there is a choice between membership in different types of gangs, conventional bonding influences that choice in favor of the less delinquent (social as opposed to conflict, retreatist, or criminal) types of gangs. As with gang membership, the effects of social bonding are likely to be indirect, or weak and direct. Winfree and Mays (1996) and Winfree, Mays, and Vigil-Backstrom (1994) found attitudes toward or beliefs about illegal behavior or gang membership may have some direct effect on gang membership or illegal behavior, but family context influences had little or no direct effect. This would be consistent with an indirect effect of family context variables on illegal behavior, as suggested by Elliott et al. (1989).

Proposition 20: *Blocked social and economic opportunities result in an increased probability of gang delinquency.* The impact of blocked social and economic opportunities will be mediated by the delinquency of one's parents, siblings, and friends (Proposition 18); by conventional social bonding (Proposition 19); and by the social organization of the neighborhood, which may influence the type of gang that arises in the neighborhood, as suggested by Cloward and Ohlin. In part, this will be reflected in social controls and the delinquency of other gang members, but it leads to a separate proposition (Proposition 24) regarding the influence of neighborhood and community social disorganization on delinquency.

Proposition 21: *At any given time, rates of gang delinquency will be higher for individuals who previously had higher rates of delinquency.* In other words, past delinquency influences present delinquency. Absent any external reason for changes in behavior, behavior tends to remain the same. This corresponds to the concepts of inertia or momentum in the physical sciences.

Sanctions, Deterrence, and Maturation

Proposition 22: *Formal sanctions by police and other official agencies will have little impact on gang delinquency. Informal negative sanctions by parents, siblings, spouses, friends, lovers, and neighborhood residents, however, will lead to lower levels of gang delinquency.* From all of the literature on gangs, the basic response to the police is one of hostility and defiance in all but the least delinquent social gangs (Campbell 1991; Hardman 1969; Hagedorn 1988; Vigil 1988). Community and family support, on the other hand, appear to be important in shaping individual and gang behavior (Sullivan 1989), perhaps most notably in Hispanic barrios, where gang membership may be transmitted from one generation to another (Moore 1978; Vigil 1988). The presence of negative sanctions for illegal behavior in the family and community may be related to, but is not entirely determined by, the level of social disorganization in the community.

Proposition 23: *The effects of age and of adult social roles and statuses on delinquency are indirect, mediated by levels of exposure to delinquent friends and family members.* Menard (1992) and Elliott et al. (1989) have presented evidence that the effects of age on illegal behavior may be mediated by exposure to delinquent friends, or delinquent peer group bonding. This proposition asserts that individuals who get married, acquire a steady job, and otherwise make the transition into adulthood, but who still associate with others who are heavily involved in illegal behavior, will themselves continue to be involved in illegal behavior. Some evidence of this may be found in Campbell (1991) and in studies of Chinese (Chin 1990) and Hispanic gangs (Moore 1978; Vigil 1988), in which adult involvement in or support of the gang appears to be more evident than in other ethnic gangs.

Macrosocial Influences: Social Disorganization

Proposition 24: *Neighborhood or community social disorganization will influence gang delinquency indirectly, by influencing social and economic opportunity, conventional social bonding, exposure to delinquent peers, and the types of gangs that are more or less prevalent in the neighborhood or community.* The indirect influence of social disorganization on delinquency is an integral part of the integrated theory of Elliott et al. (1985:66; 1989:138), and is also consistent with the perspective advanced by Vigil (1988). The indirect influences of social disorganization on gang delinquency here closely parallel the hypothesized influences of social disorganization on gang membership.

Social Class and Types of Illegal Behavior

Propositions 18–24 apply primarily to rates of illegal behavior. Different individuals and gangs may also be involved in different types of illegal behavior (physical assaults, property crime for profit, property crime for fun, illicit substance use, public nuisance or disorder). The following proposition focuses on anticipated variations in the social class distributions of different types of offenses.

Proposition 25: *Middle class gangs will be disproportionately less involved than working class or lower class gangs in violent offending, and more involved in minor offending and drug use.* Chambliss (1973) noted that the lower status "Roughnecks" were more involved in violent offenses than the higher status "Saints." Myerhoff and Myerhoff (1964) characterized the offenses committed by their middle class gangs (which may really have been law-violating youth groups) as generally non-violent, analogous to adult "white-collar" crime. Schwendinger and Schwendinger (1985) indicated that the lower status "Greasers" were much more likely to engage in violence than the upper status "Soc" boys, and to define their status in terms of violence, apparently because violence was one arena in which the Greasers could beat the Socs. Elliott and Ageton (1980) confirmed that violent crime was class-related, and Elliott et al. (1989) found that social class status was significantly correlated with the most serious assaultive offenses, felony assaults.

Consistent with other research, Elliott et al. (1989) also found higher rates of public disorder and substance use offenses among middle class youths than among lower class youths. One possible reason for this is that middle class adolescents have more ready access to the money to purchase drugs and alcohol than lower class youths. The implications of this proposition, and of the findings that support it, are that insofar as middle class gangs exist, we should expect to see more social and retreatist gangs, and fewer conflict and criminal gangs, among the middle class than among working or lower class youths; and that, correspondingly, rates of violent gang delinquency should be lower, and rates of illicit drug use higher, for middle class than for lower or working class gangs.

Summary: Gang Delinquency

Gang delinquency is just like non-gang delinquency; there is just more of it. The same causes that produce nongang delinquency operate to produce gang delinquency. The important difference lies in the association with friends who express approval or toleration of illegal behavior.

Breznitz (1975) found support for Matza's "pluralistic ignorance" hypothesis; delinquents asserted that their friends were more committed to delinquency than they themselves were. Hagedorn (1988) and Schwendinger (1985) found that gang members in the presence of other gang members tend to express nonmoralistic, pragmatic sentiments toward illegal behavior. Short and Strodtbeck (1965) found that when asked about sexual behavior, (a) individually, boys expressed approval of conventional views, but (b) in the group setting, the same boys derided conventional views.

There may be no real contradiction between expressing more conventional values or norms individually, and expressing less conventional values or norms in the presence of other gang or group members. According to Briar and Piliavin (1965), (1) delinquent behavior is characteristically episodic, purposive, and confined to certain situations, and (2) motives for delinquent behavior are correspondingly episodic, oriented to short-term goals, and confined to certain situations. Thus, adolescents who express one set of attitudes or beliefs in one setting and another set of attitudes or beliefs in another setting may be telling the truth both times. Attitudes and values may be relatively weakly held, and expressions of attitudes and beliefs may be strongly influenced by the group context in adolescence.

The group context itself may be subject to influences of conventional bonding and, more indirectly, blocked opportunities, adult statuses and roles, and neighborhood or community social disorganization. These, in turn, may be influenced by socioeconomic status. With the exception of illegal behavior on the part of family and friends, the relationships between gang delinquency and the predictors outlined here may be weak and indirect. The individual decision to break the law is complex and, especially in adolescence, situational.

In general, the predictors of gang delinquency are no different from the predictors of nongang delinquency. Members of juvenile gangs are simply, by virtue of their gang membership, more at risk of illegal behavior based on a wide range of predictors than are nonmembers. Although our focus has been on gang delinquency, it is worth remembering that most delinquency is not committed by gangs, but by members of gangs and law-violating youth groups, acting in small groups of two or three, independently of the gang (Reiss 1986). It is entirely possible that gang membership itself has little influence on delinquency, net of the level of exposure to illegal behavior on the part of friends and family.

RACE, ETHNICITY, GENDER, AND JUVENILE GANGS

Ethnicity is undeniably linked to the phenomena of gang formation, gang membership, and to the structure and types of juvenile gangs. Gangs are usually racially homogeneous (see Chapter 3), and much of the violence that occurs between gangs in intra-ethnic (Spergel 1990). Racial hostility, in fact, seems to play a limited part in the ethnographic descriptions of gangs we have reviewed, and where it does exist, it appears to be directed at the non-Hispanic, European majority as much on the basis of socioeconomic status and power as on the basis of race. Hardman's (1969) small-town gangs were ethnically segregated, but not, according to Hardman, racist. Instead, Hardman contended, there existed a mutual respect between the African and European American gangs. Frictions seem as likely to exist within broad ethnic categories—between Puerto Ricans and Mexicans (Hagedorn 1988) or Chicanos and Mexicans (Vigil 1988)—as between various ethnic groups.

Racial differences in the frequency of gang formation such as the relative scarcity of non-Hispanic, white, ethnic gangs (Campbell 1984) may be explainable in terms of the smaller proportion of the non-Hispanic European American population that live in neighborhoods characterized by high rates of poverty, welfare dependency, single-parent households, and the other symptoms that characterize social disorganization (Sullivan 1989; Wilson 1987). Once again, this is not to deny the existence of non-Hispanic European-American gangs, of which the skinhead gangs are one example. Our intention is instead to recognize that Hispanic, African, and Asian American ethnic minorities are proportionally more likely than non-Hispanic European Americans to be located in poor inner city areas (Farley 1982), and to suggest that ethnic differences in gang membership may be at least in part a result of their living in socially disorganized, often racially or ethnically segregated neighborhoods.

Possible alternatives to social disorganization as the variable that influences gang formation include urban poverty (absolute or relative) and social inequality, as noted in the last chapter. Gang formation may arguably be traced to the existence of an impoverished, isolated, inner-city underclass of African Americans (Hagedorn 1989; Short 1990; Wilson 1984; Wilson 1987) or, in other locations, Hispanic Americans (Moore 1989). As noted above, however, the relationship between neighborhood poverty and the presence of juvenile gangs may be nonlinear in form, with some more impoverished neighborhoods having less of a gang problem than some less impoverished neighborhoods. Whether social disorganization generally, or some specific aspect of social disorganization proves to be the more important influence on gang formation, there is great consistency historically and cross-nationally that gang formation occurs primarily in the less advantaged strata of large urban population centers, and social disorganization theory is a good place to start to understand why this is so.

Ethnic differences may exist in the extent to which different gangs are identified with their neighborhoods. Hagedorn (1988) found that African American gangs were less closely identified with their neighborhoods than Hispanic and non-Hispanic, European American gangs. Different types of gangs appear to be prevalent within different ethnic groups. This, in turn, is reflected in the different types and frequency of crime committed by gangs from different ethnic backgrounds.

We suspect that ethnicity or race, in and of itself, has little to offer as an explanation of gang formation, persistence, membership, or delinquent behavior. We would contend that youths do not form ethnically homogeneous groups entirely voluntarily. Instead, such groups result from racial, ethnic, and social class segregation, especially residential segregation, among adults, and from the resultant segregation of children in the schools.

Proposition 26: *The ethnic composition of gangs in the United States simply reflects the ethnic composition of primary friendship groups, and of the neighborhood and school groups on which they are based.* Where there is residential segregation by race and ethnicity, and where schools are (*de facto* or *de jure*) segregated by race and ethnicity, gangs will tend to be racially and ethnically homogeneous. Where schools and neighborhoods are racially and ethnically mixed, gangs will tend to be racially and ethnically mixed.

Gender

Proposition 27: *Net of all other influences, females are less likely to join and quicker to leave juvenile gangs than are males. In addition, net of all other influences, females have lower rates of gang delinquency, especially violent offenses, than males.* It is possible that the propositions regarding gang membership generally would be adequate to explain female gang membership, but past research indicates that theories of delinquency have failed to fully explain differences between male and female illegal behavior more generally (Chesney-Lind 1989; Rosenbaum 1991), although some promising steps in that directly have been taken (Hagan et al. 1985; Morash and Chesney-Lind 1991). Even controlling for delinquent peer group bonding, bonding to conventional social institutions, and strain, Elliott et al. (1989) still found that gender was predictive of minor and serious delinquency. Elliott et al. (1985) found that their integrated theory produced similar results for males and females, but Morash and Chesney-Lind (1991) found different results for males and females in their test of power-control theory, and Fagan (1990) found evidence of different etiologies for male and female gang involvement. Until we have a fully-developed, adequate explanation for male-female differences in illegal behavior, those differences must be explicitly recognized in any theory of illegal behavior.

GANG STRUCTURE, SOCIAL ECOLOGY, AND GANG LONGEVITY

Gang structures vary considerably. In most social, retreatist, and conflict gangs, the structure tends to be nebulous, with no clear leadership roles or leaders and no hierarchy. This may change for conflict gangs during times when the gang is actually involved in conflict, at which time a quasi-military structure may emerge, only to recede once the conflict is ended. In female gangs (Campbell 1984b), the structure resembles that of the family, with some individuals taking "maternal" or "parental" roles, and other individuals taking the roles of big or little sisters. Interestingly, these roles appear similar to some of the roles taken by women in women's prisons (Giallombardo 1974). Criminal or delinquent gangs appear to be more formally structured than other types of gangs, with a hierarchy resembling a military or business organization. Retreatist gangs appear to have the least formal structure.

Gang structure reflects the intragroup relationships among the individuals in the gang, and also the environmental pressures experienced by the gang. According to Reiss (1986:131), "The more formally organized a group and the more provision it makes for the replacement of members, the more likely it is to survive, as studies of Chicago's black conflict gangs demonstrate." Formality of organization may take the form of hierarchical structure with clearly specified statuses akin to family, military, or business positions. Alternatively, it may take the form of age-grading, as suggested by Hagedorn (1988) and by studies of Hispanic gangs.

From the literature on complex organizations, we may infer that different organizational structures may be better suited to different environments and different goals or processes (Hall 1987; Hannan and Freeman 1977; Woodward 1958). Formal structure is likely to be more important for gangs that are in conflict or competition with other gangs or groups: violent gangs in active and recurrent conflict with other violent gangs, or corporate gangs competing for drug markets or other lucrative enterprises. In these situations, the more formally organized gangs are better able to mobilize personnel and other resources, and therefore better able to survive. This leads us to **Proposition 28:** *Gangs that have more formal, hierarchical structure, whether based on statuses within the gang or age-grading, will have greater longevity than gangs with less formal structure and less stable pools of eligible gang members.*

In addition to structure, success in recruiting new gang members is essential for gang survival. The longevity of Hispanic gangs appears to be attributable not only to the age-graded *klika* structure, but also to the relative stability of the barrio. Different generations of a family may pass through the same sequence of gang membership, and barrio loyalties tend to be strong. By contrast, African American gangs appear to flourish in the most unstable, socially disorganized environments. Among African American gangs, it appears to be less a matter of the survival of specific gangs than the survival of the gang phenomenon. Gangs that were dominant one or two decades ago (the Vice Lords and the Blackstone P. Rangers) have given way to new gangs and coalitions of gangs (Bloods, Crips, Folks, People).

Proposition 29: *To the extent that social disorganization persists in a neighborhood or community, the existence of gangs in that community will also persist. Furthermore, to the extent that the population of that community is stable within that community (that is, the same families remain in the* *community), not only the existence of gangs, but the same gangs or gangs directly derived from them, will tend to persist.* As suggested earlier, certain social conditions spawn gangs, and these same conditions are favorable for the recruitment of new gang members. The combination of these conditions with a relatively stable residential population may additionally lead to reduced turnover (formation of new gangs, disintegration of old gangs) in gangs by providing continuity of membership that would otherwise be impossible. Another element in the stability of the Hispanic barrio populations may be the comparative linguistic isolation of the Hispanic population within a largely English-speaking society, coupled with high rates of Latin American immigration.

As noted by Vigil (1988), Hispanic barrios do not appear to experience the pattern of invasion and succession experienced by other groups. In part, this may reflect the size of the Hispanic population in the United States, which makes it comparatively easier to preserve their language, as compared with the more rapid linguistic assimilation of other ethnic groups with smaller populations in the United States. It may also be the case that other ethnic groups experienced a similar pattern at the height of their immigration into the United States, and that the situation will change only if Latin migration to the United States undergoes a substantial decline.

What emerges from all this is not a choice between a persistent gang problem and the elimination of the gang problem, but a choice between two different types of a persistent juvenile gang problem, as long as conditions of social disorganization, urban poverty, and the economic and social isolation of a minority-group urban underclass prevail. Reduction of Hispanic immigration or increased residential mobility out of the barrios would not, in all likelihood, result in the elimination or reduction of the gang phenomenon in those neighborhoods. Instead, the intergenerational stability of the Hispanic gangs would probably be replaced by the African American pattern of stability in the gang phenomenon, but relatively greater instability with respect to the survival of particular gangs.

Proposition 30: *Intergroup conflict has a nonlinear effect on the longevity or persistence of gangs. At low to moderate levels of intergroup conflict, gang persistence may increase, but at very high levels of intergroup conflict, gangs tend to disintegrate.* Low to moderate levels of conflict with other gangs, the police, or other groups, may contribute to gang formation (see Proposition 6), to individual decisions to join the gang (see Proposition

13), and to continuity of gang membership and thus continuity of the gang's existence. Klein (1995a) lists oppositional structures (police, school officials, etc.), rival groups (usually gangs), and gang intervention programs as external pressures on the gang that may promote cohesiveness in the gang. Cohesiveness may in turn contribute to the recruitment of new members, the retention of old members, and higher rates of illegal behavior among gang members, according to Klein.

Up to a point, it is reasonable to believe that external stimuli may help bring the gang members together and keep them together. Beyond that point, however, external pressures, particularly intergroup conflict, may weaken or destroy the gang. Campbell (1984b) described the disintegration of one gang as a result of conflicts that led to the killing of some of the gang members. Helmreich (1973) described the fall of an African American politically-oriented gang as a result of bad press, political opposition, and lack of community support. Short and Strodtbeck (1965) reported that their inability to find a criminal gang for their study of gangs in Chicago was at least in part a result of the suppression of the most promising candidate gang by police and social agencies. High levels of intergroup conflict appear to be dysfunctional for gang cohesiveness and gang longevity, both in terms of physical threats of death, serious injury, or loss of freedom to gang members, and (see Proposition 13) in terms of the difficulty of retaining members in the face of increasing threats to their liberty and physical safety.

Theoretical Developments in the Study of Gangs: The 1990s

In the relatively brief time between the publication of the first and second editions of this book, there have been two developments related to juvenile/youth/street gang theory that we regard with special interest. One is the development of a model of street gang formation, persistence, and membership proposed by Klein (1995a). The other is the blending of social learning and self-control theories in the theoretical justification for a school-based intervention program, the Gang Resistance Education and Training (GREAT) program (Winfree et al. 1995), and in the theory testing work of Winfree and his colleagues (Winfree, Vigil-Backstrom, and Mays 1994; Winfree, Mays, and Vigil-Backstrom 1994; Winfree and Mays 1996). The GREAT program is reviewed in some detail in Chapter 10. Here we would note that insofar as it is explicitly based on theory (especially social learning theory, which is an important of our own explanation of gang membership and behavior, and which has such strong support as an explanation for crime in the more general literature on crime and delinquency), *and* insofar as the program is successfully implemented (in other words, to the extent that the practice is consistent with the theory), the GREAT program offers us an opportunity to see whether gang theory, properly applied, has some *practical* value in dealing with the juvenile gang problem in the United States.

The other theory testing work of Winfree et al. has been reviewed above. Briefly, the results appear to be consistent with other results regarding learning and control theories. Association with others who are involved in illegal behavior generally has the largest effect on gang membership and illegal behavior, with social control theory variables having a weaker direct effect (attitudes toward illegal behavior and gang membership) or no direct effect (family context variables). These results vary by the type of offense, and group-context offenses (group fighting, group-instigated assaults) are better explained by their models than drug-related offenses or thefts. An important aspect of this research is that it directly applies both strong, well-implemented theoretical frameworks, along with quantitative, multivariate methods of data analysis, directly to the problem of understanding gang membership and gang behavior.

Parts of Klein's (1995a) model have been described in the discussions of gang formation, gang delinquency, gang membership, and gang persistence or longevity. Box 9.6 summarizes the elements of Klein's model. The first class of variables, urban underclass variables, are variables which, according to Klein, have no direct influence on gang formation or persistence, but which affect other variables (the proximal gang onset variables and psychological factors that lead to gang membership) that *do* lead to the emergence of gangs. In our own propositions, we have focused on direct influences on gang formation and persistence. Klein's description of the shift from manufacturing to service jobs is parallel to our own concern with the shift in the labor market that has resulted in fewer opportunities for workers with limited skills (Proposition 9). We also note (Proposition 9) the problem of educational disadvantage, parallel but not identical to Klein's concern with educational system failure. Our reservations about minority segregation *per se* were noted above (see the discussion after Proposition 4). We would agree that there is evidence to suggest that out-migration of the middle class, especially the minority middle class, has contributed to social disorganization generally, including the absence of conventional activities and the absence of social control in poor inner-city neighborhoods.

Box 9.6: Klein's (1995a) Model of Gang Onset, Maintenance, and Membership

---

Urban Underclass Variables (influence proximal gang onset variables)

1. Out-migration of minority middle class
2. Shift in industrial modes from manufacturing to service
3. Segregation of minorities
4. Failure of educational system

Proximal Gang Onset Variables (affect onset of gangs)

1. Sufficient number of minority youth
2. Absence of appropriate jobs
3. Absence of acceptable alternative activities
4. Concentrated minority population
5. Comparatively high crime rate
6. Absence of community and informal controls

Proximal Maintenance Variables (affect maintenance or continuity of gangs)

1. Oppositional structures and institutions (police, school officials, etc.)
2. Rival groups (gangs, in most cases)
3. Shared perceptions of barriers to improvement
4. Gang intervention programs

Psychological Factors (affect gang membership)

1. Status needs
2. Identity and belonging (affiliation) needs
3. Social disabilities

Klein's proximal gang onset variables closely parallel our concerns with critical mass (sufficient number of youths) in Proposition 1, and social disorganization (absence of appropriate jobs, absence of acceptable alternative activities, absence of community and informal social controls, and corresponding high crime rates) in Propositions 2 and 3. We do have some concern with Klein's "concentrated minority populations," as described in the discussion following Proposition 4, and also with his specifying "sufficient number of *minority* youth." Cross-national data on gangs (even street gangs) suggest that they arise even in societies that are largely homogeneous with respect to ethnicity. The differential involvement in gangs by different ethnic groups in the United States reflects in some measure the average differences in social class or socioeconomic status (or social and economic disadvantage; see Propositions 12 and 20) of the different ethnic groups (see also Proposition

26). In our view, it is lower socioeconomic status, not ethnic minority status, that drives gang membership and gang formation.

Three of Klein's proximal maintenance variables, oppositional institutions, rivalries, and gang intervention programs, reflect our concerns with the influence of intergroup conflict on gang formation, membership, and persistence. Proposition 30, new to this edition, was in large measure stimulated by Klein's discussion of the importance of gang cohesion in gang formation, persistence, and illegal behavior. His fourth proximal maintenance variable, shared perceptions of barriers to improvements, parallels our concern with blocked social and economic opportunities (Propositions 12 and 20). Finally, as noted above, we have included one of Klein's psychological factors (social disability, Proposition 15) as a possible influence on gang membership, but we would argue that the other psychological factors are spurious correlates, not causes, of gang membership. In part, this is reflected in Klein's model, when he suggests that the causes of these psychological factors include three of his urban underclass variables (educational failure, minority segregation, and middle class out-migration), plus parental competence.

To the extent that Klein's model and our propositions attempt to explain the same things, it seems to us that our respective cups are three-fourths or so full of agreement. Klein puts more emphasis than we do on educational failure, and describes the industrial shift in somewhat different terms. He does not use the term "social disorganization," even though some of the variables he uses are consistent with the social disorganization perspective. These and several other differences strike us as differences more of emphasis than of substance or direction. Where we find ourselves most in disagreement with Klein's model is in the role of psychological factors in gang membership and the role of ethnicity in gang formation. To some extent the latter may also be more a matter of emphasis than substance, but our difference regarding psychological factors in gang membership is one that, in all likelihood, can only be settled with good empirical research on the subject, research that goes beyond correlations to examine the causal relationships between psychological or personality factors and gang involvement and behavior in detail.

CONCLUSION

In constructing our theory of juvenile gangs, we have used some of the building blocks described in Chapter 8, but not all of them. We have deliberately and consciously excluded the subcultural approaches of Cohen (1955), who also included elements of strain theory in his explanation of delinquency; Miller (1958); Bloch and Niederhoffer (1958), who, like Cohen, included elements of strain theory in their explanation of delinquency; and Schwendinger and Schwendinger (1985), who coupled their subcultural approach with an economically-based conflict theory. Although these theorists have informed other gang researchers—Vigil (1988; Vigil and Long 1990), in particular, appears to incorporate elements of Cohen's theory in his explanation of juvenile gangs—we do not find the concept of a subculture useful in explaining juvenile gangs. Instead, we agree with critics of the subcultural approach, that there exists a common set of cultural values in American society, but that those values are implemented in different ways by individuals and groups who confront different social conditions (Matza and Sykes 1961; Reiss and Rhodes 1961; Short and Strodtbeck 1965; Werthman 1967). In addition, we have some reservations about the social disability hypothesis (Short and Strodtbeck 1965; Yablonsky 1962), and like Shaw and McKay (1972), we question the utility of race or ethnicity, independent of other variables, for understanding juvenile gangs.

Social ecological theory is used to explain many of the macrosocial aspects of the gang phenomenon. Social disorganization increases the likelihood of gang formation, gang longevity, and gang membership, and leads to higher rates of illegal behavior, especially more serious illegal behavior. Its influence on gang formation appears to be direct, with little intervention at the microsocial level. Its influence on other aspects of the gang phenomenon is largely indirect. This is especially true for gang delinquency, which depends primarily on individual-level variables.

In addition to the social ecological perspective, an integrated theoretical perspective combining elements of strain, social control, and social learning theories was used to explain microsocial aspects of juvenile gangs. The theory also incorporates elements of the social ecological perspective, and the result is a theory that is integrated across as well as within levels of explanation (Short 1989). This integrated perspective was taken primarily from the work of Elliott et al. (1979; 1985; 1989), but could almost as easily have been taken from the theoretical work of Cloward and Ohlin (1960), who are too often recognized only as strain theorists, Shaw and McKay (1973), who are too often categorized only as social ecological theorists, Hawkins and Weis (1985), or Thornberry (1987). It could also have been extracted from the empirical, ethnographic work of Sullivan (1989) and Vigil (1988).

Fagan (1990) has applied an integrated theoretical perspective, a combination of social learning and control theories, to the explanation of gang delinquency. Our own application of integrated theory is broader than Fagan's, and includes gang formation, membership, longevity, and structure, in addition to gang delinquency. In laying out the propositions of our integrated theory, we have attempted to provide propositions that specify the relative strengths of the influences on gang phenomena, to integrate the theory both in terms of levels of explanation (macrosocial and microsocial) and proximity of explanation (direct and indirect effects), and to construct theoretical propositions that lend themselves readily to empirical testing. The time has clearly come to abandon adherence to one or the other of the older theories of juvenile gangs, and to incorporate integrated theoretical perspectives into the explanations of juvenile gang phenomena.

Chapter 10

LEGAL AND JUSTICE SYSTEM GANG INTERVENTIONS: INCAPACITATION AND DETERRENCE

Intervention means many things, including tough law enforcement strategies that emphasize punitive enforcement measures and strict sanctions, and rehabilitation strategies that stress the need for positive individual and group changes (Trojanowicz 1978; Carney et al. 1969). Here we consider as gang interventions any actions, official or unofficial, that are intended to change, redirect, or eliminate the behaviors and belief systems of juvenile gangs. By official intervention, we refer to actions by criminal justice and social service professionals. More narrowly, legal and justice system interventions refer to actions by the police, courts, and correctional officials, and the legislation that provides them with the authority to take action. Unofficial measures include steps taken by private groups or individuals to deal with juvenile gang problems, usually in their own neighborhoods and communities. There are some occasions when official organizations work in conjunction with the private sector to counteract juvenile gang activities.

In this chapter, we review some of the major attempts made by the legal, criminal justice, and juvenile justice systems to reduce gang membership and gang-related crime and delinquency. We focus on four areas: legislation, police enforcement, court procedures, and corrections. In the next chapter, community organization, social intervention, and opportunity programs are considered. Both classic and contemporary attempts at gang intervention are reviewed. Our intention is not to provide an exhaustive review of past or present gang intervention programs. Instead, we focus again on the forest rather than the trees, and offer a review of broad categories of programs, with specific illustrations presented in some detail. The examples we use are designed to illustrate the different types of gang intervention programs in some detail, and to evaluate the success of different types of programs in reducing gang delinquency and crime.

TYPES OF INTERVENTIONS

Trojanowicz (1978) classified intervention programs as pure prevention, rehabilitative, punitive, corrective, and mechanical programs. Pure prevention programs are aimed at stopping delinquency before it begins, and typically target adolescents who have not been adjudicated delinquent by the courts, but who may face higher probabilities of trouble with the law because they reside in socially disorganized communities or because of other problems, such as being in dysfunctional families. Rehabilitative strategies are concerned with changing delinquent behavior after it has occurred, and include counseling, therapy, probation, and other programs that are directly oriented toward changing antisocial behaviors. Punitive strategies deter delinquency through the use of threats of arrest or punishment directed at potential lawbreakers. Corrective measures target the presumed causes or motivations for delinquency, such as school failure or unemployment. Mechanical prevention involves stopping illegal behavior by more effective security systems, increased police patrols, and other measures that make committing illegal acts more difficult.

Spergel and Curry (1990) described four principal types of gang intervention strategies. Community organization includes programs intended to involve members of the neighborhood or community directly in delinquency prevention and anti-gang activities. Social intervention includes outreach programs and counseling programs designed to prevent gang delinquency, reduce gang membership, or rechannel gang activity into more constructive pursuits. Opportunity programs include job training, provision of employment, and education programs designed to attack the causes of gang involvement and delinquency. Suppression efforts include arrest, incarceration, and supervision of gang members in order to prevent delinquency. A fifth strategy, which may be supplementary or facilitative to the other four, is organizational development and change, designed to make law enforcement and social service agencies more effective in their respective tasks, and thereby to increase their effectiveness in dealing with the juvenile gang problem.

Other classifications have been proposed by Knox (1995) and Klein (1995a). Knox divided prevention into primary (before the individual has been exposed to gangs), secondary (after exposure but before there is a strong commitment to the gang), and tertiary (after the individual has joined the gang and become heavily involved in gang activities). Tertiary prevention is really rehabilitation. Klein's typology includes prevention, reform, and suppression. Prevention involves the identification of potential gang members and, like Knox's primary prevention, focuses on individuals before they have become gang members. Reform is aimed at directing gang members to more positive behaviors. Suppression involves attempts by the justice system to reduce gang activity and reduce gang-related illegal behavior through arrest, sentencing, and incarceration.

According to the National Youth Gang Survey, as reported by Spergel and Curry (1990), the most common strategies for dealing with juvenile gangs were suppression and social intervention. The strategies perceived as most effective by law enforcement, justice, and community agencies, however, were the strategies of providing opportunity (in cities with chronic gang problems) and community organization (both in cities with chronic gang problems, and in cities with emerging gang problems). Based on the National Youth Gang Survey, then, there appears to be a mismatch between the approaches perceived as most effective and the approaches most commonly implemented in response to problems with juvenile gangs.

Kleiman and Smith (1990) have suggested that the most effective way to deal with such drug-dealing supergangs as the Bloods and the Crips may be to treat them like organized criminal enterprises, and to hold them accountable for their illegal behavior. This orientation was echoed by the panel of experts on which McKinney (1988) reported. They recommended two steps to deal with the escalating violence of juvenile gangs: reform of the juvenile justice system so that it holds juvenile offenders more accountable for their illegal actions, and intensified efforts to keep youths from joining gangs. Increased enforcement efforts alone were not considered adequate to deal with the juvenile gang problem because "Although the police do a good job of apprehending and moving hardcore juvenile gang members off the street and into the judicial system, 'there are 10 other youngsters . . . just waiting to take their place' " (McKinney 1988:5).

Hagedorn's (1988) recommendations include deemphasizing the criminal justice system as a way of handling gang problems. Instead, he suggested providing full-time meaningful employment, improved education, and the involvement of gang members in a meaningful way in gang intervention programs as staff, consultants, and clients providing input into those programs. Hagedorn emphasized that programs would need to be tailored to specific times and places: what is good for Milwaukee in 1988 may not be what is good for Phoenix in 1988, or for Milwaukee in 1995. Hagedorn also emphasized the need for good research as a component in any intervention program.

In this chapter, we focus on what Trojanowicz calls punitive, mechanical, and (in one form, namely deterrence) pure prevention programs, what Knox calls tertiary prevention, and what Klein and Spergel and Curry call suppression efforts. Programs of this nature form the primary thrust of legal and justice system intervention strategies. We begin with a brief discussion of deterrence, incapacitation, and rehabilitation as justice system goals, then move to specific ways in which legislation plus police, court, and correctional policy are used to try to suppress and control gangs.

DETERRENCE, INCAPACITATION, AND REHABILITATION

The legal system, of which the criminal and juvenile justice systems are components, has several goals, and those goals are different for different components of the system. One goal is *incapacitation* of offenders, incarcerating them so they cannot commit additional crimes in the community. A second goal is *deterrence*, persuading potential or past offenders through the use of sanctions or punishments that they should not, for practical reasons, commit crimes in the present or future. Incapacitation and deterrence are sometimes confused in everyday speech, but the distinction is that with deterrence, the offender makes a choice; with incapacitation, the offender has no choice. A third goal of the criminal and juvenile justice systems is *rehabilitation*, persuading an individual not to commit crimes using means other than the threat of punishment. (Some researchers and practitioners object to the "re" in rehabilitation, suggesting that many offenders were never "habilitated" in the first place.) Methods used to achieve rehabilitation include group and individual counseling, programs designed to prevent alcohol and drug abuse, educational and job skills training programs, and other social service programs carried out within the context of probation, parole, community correction, or detention facilities.

Incapacitation as a goal tends to be favored by individuals who believe either (a) criminals deserve to be punished, and deprivation of liberty is an appropriate punishment for crime, or (b) deterrence and/or rehabilitation programs simply do not work, and the best we can do to protect innocent citizens from criminal victimization is to take the criminals out of circulation and keep them out of circulation for as long as possible. McKinney (1985), cited above, casts some doubt on this latter proposition with respect to juvenile gang members. Even if an individual offender is locked up, there may be others ready to take her or his place, with the result that citizens are at no less risk of victimization than they were before. More generally, the United States, with the highest incarceration rate of any major Western industrialized nation, including a higher rate of incarceration for African American males than South Africa's rate of incarceration for black African males (Allen 1995), has, by any reasonable measure, the highest rate of violent crime of any major Western industrial nation. As Allen notes, our rates of incarceration have increased dramatically since 1980, but as indicated in Figures 2.1 and 2.2 (Chapter 2), there has been no apparent decrease in rates of homicides, violent victimizations, or crimes known to the police.

Deterrence as a goal is more complex. Briefly, building on the general literature on deterrence (Gibbs 1975; Paternoster 1987; Tittle 1980), plus Klein's (1993) analysis of the application of deterrence principles to reducing gang activity, there are three elements commonly recognized as important to a theoretically appropriate deterrent strategy: *certainty* of punishment, *celerity* or *swiftness* of punishment, and *severity* of punishment. The more certain the punishment, the more likely it is to deter (as long as it is reasonably swift and severe); the less certain the punishment, the less likely it is to deter. From a learning theory perspective, based on evidence from behavioral psychology, the best way to extinguish a behavior is to punish the behavior every time it occurs. (The best way to encourage a behavior, in contrast, is to reward it occasionally and irregularly.)

Unfortunately, offenses are rarely known to the police, much less punished. Both victimization and self-report rates of offending are much higher than rates according to either crimes known to the police or arrests (Menard and Covey 1988; Menard 1987). Even of the crimes that are detected and result in arrest, few actually result in incarceration, although this varies by type of crime. Of offenses known to the police, less than one-half of the violent crimes and less than one-fifth of the property crimes are cleared by arrest (Maguire and Pastore 1994:408).

With victimization rates about four times as high as rates of crimes known to the police, and self-reported offending rates even higher, this translates into something like one out of every 15 or 20 violent crimes and one out of every 100 property crimes, *at best,* resulting in an arrest. At the federal level, only a little more than half of the cases referred to court result in prosecution (prosecution is declined in about one-third, and cases are referred elsewhere about 10% of the time), about five of six that are prosecuted result in a conviction, and about two-thirds of the convictions result in incarceration (Bureau of Justice Statistics 1993). Figures in local jurisdictions will vary from these figures and from one another, but appear to be similar for felony arrests (Walker 1994). Based on these data, a reasonable estimate of the probability of *any* punishment beyond arrest itself for any offense would be about 1–3 percent for violent offenses, and less than one-half of 1 percent for other offenses— hardly a high certainty of punishment. Given the low probability of punishment, coupled with the typically long period between commission of the offense and punishment (if any), the prospects for serious deterrence through criminal and juvenile justice system actions are bleak (see Proposition 22, Chapter 9). Even a very serious punishment, if a potential offender does not really expect it to occur, is unlikely to be effective.

The targets or objectives of deterrence vary. Deterrence may be aimed at preventing initiation of offending (primary deterrence) or repetition of offending, once initiation has already occurred (secondary deterrence). In the former case, deterrence is most often targeted at the general population (general deterrence), although some predelinquent intervention programs (Lundman 1984) may be aimed at specific individuals (specific deterrence). More usually, specific deterrence is a form of secondary deterrence targeted at known offenders to prevent them from further involvement in illegal behavior. General deterrence operates primarily vicariously, by example: see what happens to people if they break the law. Specific deterrence operates more by direct experience: see what happens to *you* if *you* break the law. Whether vicariously or experientially, deterrence depends on the individual's *perception* of the certainty, swiftness, and severity of punishment, presumably influenced by reality, but also, as noted by Klein (1993; 1995a) likely to be interpreted and mediated by one's primary group, particularly one's gang if one is a gang member.

On one level, deterrence is predicated on an individual's rational calculation of the costs and benefits of gang membership and gang-related illegal behavior. The attempt to make the costs outweigh the benefits of gang membership and crime focus on one element of the theoretical framework in the previous chapter, the costs and benefits associated with gang membership (Proposition 13). It is worth noting here that this is *not* the most important influence on gang membership or gang crime. Studies of deterrence have confirmed that delinquent friends and beliefs that certain acts are wrong are stronger influences on illegal behavior than certainty or severity of punishment, and in some instances researchers have found that deterrence has no effect above and beyond delinquent peer group bonding and moral beliefs (Alcorn 1978; Erickson and Gibbs, 1978; Meier et al. 1984; Silberman 1976). On a cruder, less rational level, deterrent policies seek to instill an aversion to committing crime because of fear of the consequences that will occur if one does commit a crime.

Different goals are emphasized by different components of the justice system. The police are to some extent limited to deterrence, preventing illegal behavior by the threat of apprehension (and implicitly punishment, but that function belongs to another component of the justice system). Police may, however, also participate in "softer" efforts at gang control through the strategy of "community policing" and through education and employment programs. Courts are, in principle, primarily concerned with due process and, in the case of juvenile courts, with finding the disposition that is best for the child. Their involvement in deterrence, incapacitation, or rehabilitation is largely embodied in their authority to sentence convicted offenders or adjudicated delinquents. Corrections attempts to incapacitate by keeping convicted offenders securely confined; to deter by using the threat of deprivation of liberty as a means of discouraging other potential offenders from violating the law (a function they share with the courts; the courts provide the initial sentence, but the parole board may recommend earlier or later release, and probation officers may revoke probation and recommend incarceration for violation of probation conditions); and attempt to rehabilitate through various programs within correctional facilities or connected to probation, parole, or community corrections. All of this depends on legislation, a function of the broader legal system, which defines offenses, the penalties for those offenses, and the degree of latitude or discretion available to justice system officials for dealing with suspected, accused, and convicted offenders.

LEGISLATIVE ATTEMPTS TO
CONTROL JUVENILE GANGS

Legislation is not a direct intervention but an indirect approach to prevention and control of juvenile gang delinquency and gang crime. Enabling legislation provides tools that can be used by police, prosecutors, and correctional officials in their attempts to control gang behavior. In most instances, the legislation centers on illegal behavior, regardless of whether it is gang-related. Exceptions to this are the federal Racketeering Influenced Corrupt Organization (RICO) statutes, originally designed to combat (adult) organized criminal enterprises but more recently applied to gang activity, and California's Street Terrorism Enforcement and Prevention (STEP) Act, which was specifically designed to control illegal behavior by street gangs.

RICO and Juvenile Gangs

The RICO statute is part of the 1970 Organized Crime Control Act. The RICO law provided law enforcement officials with greater legal powers in the war against organized crime by broadening the definition of racketeering. The RICO statute applies to any act or threat, including but not limited to any act or threat in violation of federal statutes, which is chargeable under state law and punishable by a prison sentence of more than one year. Included under the RICO statute are murder, kidnapping, gambling, bribery, extortion, and dealing in narcotics or other dangerous drugs. To expand the list of offenses defined as racketeering, the federal statutes covered by RICO included (1) Hobbs Act violations, which make it a federal crime to engage in behavior that interferes with interstate commerce; (2) bribery, including sports bribery; (3) counterfeiting; (4) embezzlement from union funds; (5) loan sharking; (6) mail fraud; (7) wire fraud; (8) obstruction of state or federal justice; (9) "white slavery" (transportation of individuals across state lines for purposes of engaging in prostitution); (10) bankruptcy fraud; and (11) drug law violations.

Eventually, as fears associated with juvenile gangs increased, the states began to consider the application of the RICO statutes beyond the adult criminal organizations that were their original target. By 1993, 14 states had passed their own anti-gang laws, and 31 other states had adopted RICO legislation that applies to juvenile gangs. Typically, this state-based RICO legislation is founded on two major criteria. First, gang membership in itself is grounds for criminal justice processing. Second, the conspiratorial nature of gang activity is reason for additional laws and sentences (Klein 1995a:177–178). Knox (1995:5) has also noted the existence of the RICO law at the state level as it applies to youth gangs. Spergel (1995:208) has observed that judges are increasingly willing to view juvenile gangs as dangerous to American society, as political pressures and public opinion have encouraged a more hard-line approach to gang intervention. As of this writing, however, the effectiveness of the RICO statutes in reducing gang activity is unknown. In practice, it may be unknowable because of the difficulty of separating the effects of RICO statutes from other intervention efforts.

STEP Legislation in California

California's STEP legislation represents one of the most controversial anti-gang laws adopted in the United States. Until STEP legislation was passed in California during the 1980s, offenses committed by street gangs were not singled out for special prosecution under the law (Cummings and Monti 1993:266). STEP laws define street gangs as

> any ongoing organization, association, or group of three or more persons, whether formal or informal, having as one of its primary activities the commission of one or more of the criminal acts enumerated, which has a common name or common identifying sign or symbol, whose members individually or collectively engage in or have engaged in a pattern of criminal activity (Cummings and Monti 1993:267).

Under the STEP act, participation of individuals in street gangs with knowledge that its members are or have been involved in a pattern of criminal activities, or providing assistance to or promoting the criminal activities of street gangs, is prohibited. According to STEP legislation, punishment may include imprisonment in the county jail for up to one year, or in the state prison for up to three years. Klein (1995a:181) notes that the STEP act has been copied and enacted in Florida, Georgia, Louisiana, and Illinois.

Operationally, the STEP act is legally in force when a gang member is notified that he or she is participating in a street gang. This is done by presenting the gang member with a letter, which names the gang and informs the member of the illegal activities of the gang. Once the individual has received the letter (or been "STEPped," in the language of the officials enforcing the program), he or she becomes subject to the increased penalties provided under the STEP law for criminal conspiracy, if he or she participates in or aids other gang members in illegal behavior. Klein (1995a:181–182) reports that gangs have changed their names (to invalidate the STEP order) and older gang members "make themselves scarce" (in order to avoid receiving the notification letter), suggesting that this individual-level deterrence approach may be taken seriously by gang members. He also mentions the risk that the STEP program, if misapplied, could reduce its credibility and effectiveness.

Use of Existing Laws to Suppress Gang Activity

Klein (1995a) cites the use of civil abatement laws and other laws to suppress gang activity. Civil abatement laws are used to limit such things as excessive noise, public eyesores (the accumulation of trash or junk in one's front yard), and violations of building safety codes. These laws have been used to arrest gang members and find them in contempt of court for such offenses as writing graffiti and blocking public areas, and to compel landlords to improve safety measures and remove graffiti from their buildings. Landlords can also be sued for allowing drug dealing or gang activity in their buildings. Other measures have included tougher laws against drive-by shootings, gang recruitment, drug dealing, weapons violations, and battery, such as those enacted in the state of Wisconsin, legislative decisions that have created "safe zones" around schools, legislation allowing the automatic transfer from juvenile to adult court of a minor accused of unlawful use of a handgun on school grounds (Spergel 1995:289–290), and closing public parks to reduce gang activity (Klein 1995a). As with other examples of using legislation to control gang activity, these measures have not been evaluated. As of this writing, there is no way of telling whether they have had any substantial effect on gang membership or the illegal behavior of gang members.

POLICE INTERVENTIONS

The police role in dealing with gangs can be split into two parts. One part is the law enforcement role: collecting information on gangs and their members, deterring gang activity by the physical presence of the police, and making arrests of gang members for illegal behavior. The second part of the police role is a social service role, participating in school-based educational gang prevention programs or in social service or employment programs that provide gang members with legitimate, alternative roles and opportunities. The latter role will be discussed in Chapter 11. Here we focus on the police role in gang suppression. Kratcoski and Kratcoski (1990) characterized gang suppression programs as the "isolation and destruction" approach. Gang suppression typically involves obtaining information useful to the police through gang intelligence units and the use of that information to secure arrests, prevent major outbreaks of gang violence, and to prevent recruitment of new members into the gangs. Relationships between police and gangs are typically hostile. One reason for this hostility is the accusation by gang members and others that police practice racism, brutality, and unfairness in the enforcement of the law.

Police Interactions with Adolescents

Research has frequently identified race, sex, and social class as the primary correlates of police interactions with adolescents. A number of studies have chronicled the differential treatment of young males as opposed to young women, a phenomenon referred to as "judicial paternalism" by Chesney-Lind (1973). Terry (1967) reported that females were more likely than males to be referred by the police to community agencies after apprehension. The implication is that because they are females, the police escort young women to environments where they are more likely to be protected from situations that could compromise their morality and personalities. Likewise, Dungworth (1977), Datesman and Scarpitti (1977), and Pope and Feyerherm (1982) all noted that young girls were more likely than males to be detained by the police for committing status offenses. In their research on criminal sanctions and the systems of justice, Nagel and Hagen (1982) have explained the differential treatment of males and females as a function of the preconceived notions of gender appropriate behavior that are held by law enforcement officials. Simply, in the eyes of the authorities, young women are not supposed to engage in behaviors that run counter to the law and to sex role definitions. As Chesney-Lind (1973:54) has written about young women "even minor deviance may be seen as a substantial challenge to the authority of the family, the viability of the double standard, and to the maintenance of the present system of sexual inequality."

Research on the relationship between race and police disposition of juvenile cases has received much attention, but produced inconclusive findings. Terry (1967) was unable to report any prejudice in his study of race and police dispositions. Instead, he found that seriousness of the offense was the primary determinant of how the police responded to young people. A similar finding was also reported by Black and Reiss (1970), Green (1970), Lundman et al. (1978), Pawlak (1977), and Weiner and Willie (1971). Some studies, however, have identified racial bias at the police discretionary level. For instance, Ferdinand and Luchterhand (1970), Hepburn (1978), and Dannefer and Schutt (1982) all reported that the race of the juvenile played a significant role in the actions of the police. A study by Fagan et al. (1987) found that the police had a higher likelihood of processing minority youths for nonviolent offenses. Rather interestingly, the authors noted that of those arrested, non-minority teenage males were more likely to be arrested for committing violent crimes than were minority youths.

The data on social class and police discretion have also resulted in inconsistent findings. Terry (1970) and Thornberry (1973) were unable to establish a clear pattern of bias by the police. According to Thornberry, however, a higher percentage of lower class youngsters had their cases referred to the juvenile court, apparently by probation officials. Other studies have echoed these same results. Research undertaken by Polk and his associates (1974) and by Williams and Gold (1972) were unable to discover systematic discrimination by the police against young minority teenagers.

The research that has reported bias by the police has identified variables such as police policies and attitudes as contributors to unjust law enforcement practices. Bittner (1970), Bouma (1969), and Garret and Short (1978) all reported bias at the police dispositional level, and basically came to the same conclusions. The authors all noted that law enforcement officers often have preconceived beliefs that slum areas are crime-infested, and consequently the youths who reside in them are more likely to violate the law. Furthermore, in her study of "Western City," Garret (1972) reported that the police tended to view lower class boys as more potentially recidivist, although her data were unable to support that assumption.

Police and Gangs

Understanding the nature of police relationships with young people, especially as this relates to minority populations, has implications for elaboration on the types of interaction that occurs between police and gangs. Delinquent gangs may be particularly hostile toward the police (Werthman and Piliavin 1967). Many of the most prominent studies on how law enforcement officials relate to adolescents have focused on the official response in minority and economically depressed areas. The most intensive police policies toward gangs have occurred in neighborhoods that were heavily minority or lower class.

Police actions with gangs can be dichotomized as follows: first, the police have adopted a strict law enforcement approach toward gangs, and second, the police have initiated gang intervention programs aimed at reducing antisocial gang activities. Some of the police efforts at intervention other than gang suppression are reviewed in the next chapter. The law enforcement approach involves police efforts at reducing illegal gang behaviors by arresting gang members and by patrolling areas where gang members reside. It is very difficult to assess just how effective this approach has been.

A study by Needle and Stapleton (1983) revealed three patterns of police-directed gang control activities: the Youth Service Program, reviewed in the next chapter; the gang detail; and the gang unit. The latter two programs are addressed together, since in actuality there appears to be little distinction between them. Both the gang unit and the gang detail are oriented toward the daily surveillance of gangs, with special emphasis on deterring the criminal activities engaged in by gang members. These two control-based responses differ in organization. The gang detail does not represent a specialized unit within a police department as such. Usually it entails no more than the assignment of two or more officers to gang control work. The officers can either be from the youth services division, or they can be detectives who have extensive training in investigative techniques. A major function of the gang detail is to gather intelligence on the activities of gangs and to use it for the purposes of making arrests and in order to better protect the community.

The gang unit is specially designed for the purposes of gang control. Its sole focus is on gang activities and how best to deter gang members from engaging in illegal behaviors. Unlike the youth service program, its strategies are more in line with the traditional role of the police. The gang unit makes arrests of gang members and spends a large amount of its time gathering intelligence on gang activities. Normally, the unit is limited to no more than a handful of officers.

In their survey of 27 police departments, Needle and Stapleton reported that only four had any written policies or procedures for dealing with gangs. The authors also noted that few if any of the departments surveyed offered any gang control training. The conclusion that they arrived at is that on a national basis there is a lack of consistency on the gang control policies of the police. Moreover, Needle and Stapleton argued that the gang control activities of the police are fragmented, thereby hampering any hopes of a nationwide coordination against juvenile gangs.

Jackson and McBride (1985; see Box 9.2) have commented on the limited ability of police to suppress juvenile gangs. They have also observed that juvenile gangs are unlikely to become violent with the police if they perceive that police officers are treating them justly. Since the peace officer is the primary authority figure juvenile gangs come into contact with, it is therefore very important that the police themselves show respect for the laws and the rights of others.

Box 10.1: The Limited Prospects for Gang Suppression (Jackson and McBride 1985)

"Even though a police officer may find a gang offensive to his or her sense of decency, the simple fact of the matter is that there is nothing illegal per se in belonging to a gang. Street gangs are not going to disappear just because society finds them repulsive. Furthermore, experience and studies have yet to show an instance in which a street gang was dissolved or put out of action solely because of suppressive police action. When police pressure is intensified on a street gang, its members typically go underground and become secretive, which may produce even greater problems. Therefore, start easy when working with a street gang."

CRASH, OSS, and Operation Hammer: Police Approaches to Gang Suppression

Police gang suppression activities may be more or less adversarial, and have higher or lower visibility in the community. Three examples may serve to illustrate this diversity: Community Resources Against Hoodlums (CRASH), Operation Safe Streets (OSS), and Operation Hammer. CRASH (Freed 1995; Klein 1993; Klein 1995a), a program of the Los Angeles Police Department (LAPD), involves "uniformed patrol officers, ... high visibility, street surveillance, pro-active suppression activities, and investigative follow-through on arrests (Klein 1993:100). Emphasis is on specific deterrence by increasing certainty and severity of sanctions. The basic orientation of CRASH officers toward gangs and gang members is described as hostile and adversarial; Klein (1995a:165) describes it as a "war mentality." CRASH also collects information on gang activities. Turnover among CRASH officers is high. One officer suggested that this was a good thing because it brought in "fresh blood and fresh ideas" and prevented officers in the program from sitting back and resting on their expertise. "You're gonna get all the [gang] expertise you need in six months anyway; anything else is gravy" (Freed 1995:291). CRASH officers received no special training in dealing with gangs. According to Freed, the mission of CRASH is "total suppression" of street gangs, implemented by "jamming" (harassing, making arrests for even minor infractions) gang members whenever and wherever possible.

OSS, a program of the Los Angeles Sheriff's Department (LASD), also has as its goal gang suppression, but its mission (Freed 1995) is "targeted suppression." OSS deputies work in plain clothes and unmarked cars, and try to become familiar with the community, the gangs, and the gang members in the area. OSS deputies also "jam" gangs, arresting targeted gang members for minor as well as serious offenses, but do not go out of their way to arrest non-targeted gang members for minor offenses. Gangs are "targeted" when they appear to pose a major crime problem. Once they are no longer considered a major crime problem, the OSS officers continue to gather information on them, but target their suppression activities at other gangs. Turnover in OSS is low, with officers typically staying with OSS for several years. In contrast to the lack of formal training received by CRASH officers, OSS officers spend 40 hours in class studying gangs and another 40 hours on techniques of investigating juvenile crimes.

Comparing the effectiveness of the two programs based on official statistics, Freed (1995) found that gang-related crime increased more within the jurisdiction of the LAPD than the LASD. Homicide data, probably the most valid of the official violent crime statistics, showed an increase for the LAPD, but remained fairly stable for the LASD. In addition, OSS appeared to have a better reputation than CRASH on the street (Freed 1995:290):

"The sheriff understands where you're coming from; he'll treat you like a man," said one gang leader from south Los Angeles. "They don't call you 'little punk' this and 'little punk' that, like the cops do. The sheriff'll kick your ass, but you gotta provoke him."

More recently, CRASH has moved closer to the LASD/OSS model for gang suppression (Klein 1995a).

Operation Hammer is described by Klein (1993; 1995a) as a street sweep program, with highly publicized street sweeps at irregular intervals, operated by the LAPD. Within a 2-day period, Operation Hammer sends hundreds of police officers (over one thousand in the first such sweep) into target areas. Armed with already existing arrest warrants, police picked up everyone they could on existing warrants, arrested others for all forms of illegal or criminal behavior, including minor offenses, and investigated any "suspicious" activity. In each sweep, hundreds of arrests were made, and because of the large volume of arrests, a mobile command post was set up to expedite the booking and release of offenders. In the first sweep, of 1,453 people arrested, 1,350 (93%) were released without charges; only about half of the arrestees were gang members; only 60 arrests were for felonies; and only 32 felony charges were filed (Klein 1995a:162). According to Klein, Operation Hammer represents an incredibly inefficient and probably counterproductive approach to dealing with gangs: inefficient because of the small number of serious charges from the huge number of arrests, and counterproductive because it may seriously damage the credibility of the police department as a deterrent, especially given the weakness of the sanctions. A 92 percent release rate may well send (or reinforce) the message that the police are impotent to impose any serious sanctions on the vast majority of criminal offenders. One officer described the probable effect of Operation Hammer on gang members as probably "good laughing material" (Klein 1995a:63).

COURTS AND GANG SUPPRESSION

Courts are involved in efforts at gang control primarily in two ways: through the establishment of case law precedent for the legality of different enforcement efforts, and through prosecutorial priorities and sentencing practices. Examples of the former include decisions affirming the legality of the definitions used in the STEP act as described above (Klein 1995a) and decisions affirming the rights of schools to impose dress codes to limit gang-related behavior in schools (Kodluboy and

Evenrud 1993). An example of the second approach, focusing on prosecution, is Operation Hardcore (Dahmann 1995; Klein 1993; Klein 1995a), a specialized prosecution program operated by the Los Angeles District Attorney's Office, and designed to improve the prosecution of violent gang offenses.

Operation Hardcore employs a strategy of low court caseloads and vertical prosecution for serious gang offenders. Vertical prosecution means that a single attorney or team of attorneys handles all phases of a case, from indictment through final disposition and sentencing. This permits the individual prosecutor a higher level of familiarity with the case and with the people involved in the case. The lower caseloads permit the prosecutor to focus time and attention on getting testimony from sometimes reluctant witnesses (other gang members, citizens who may fear gang retaliation) and holding them to their testimony later. Operation Hardcore has had a high conviction rate (Klein 1995a), but whether this has translated into a general deterrent effect is unknown.

CORRECTIONS AND GANG SUPPRESSION

Corrections, as noted earlier, has three goals: incapacitation, deterrence, and rehabilitation. The restrictive conditions of probation, parole, and community corrections, and the even more restrictive condition of being incarcerated, provide varying degrees of incapacitation. Rehabilitation is typically attempted through a variety of educational, job training, and group and individual counseling programs within correctional facilities and in community settings. Most of these programs are not specific to gangs, but examples of gang-specific programs do exist. The Gang Awareness Necessary for Growth in Society (GANGS) program reviewed by Duxbury (1993) focuses on increasing the incarcerated gang member's awareness of the negative impact of gangs on the offender himself, the offender's family, and the offender's community. The program also helps the offender work on positive strategies to maintain conventional, noncriminal behavior after release into the community. Self-respect, self-worth, personal responsibility, and the ability to make choices and take positive action are also emphasized. Except for the focus on gang involvement, these programs appear very similar to more general group and individual counseling programs in correctional settings.

As usual, evaluation research on these programs is sparse. General reviews of institutional rehabilitation programs (Gendreau and Ross

1983; Lipsey 1992; Tolan and Guerra 1994) suggest that institutional programs are less likely than community-based programs to have substantial, favorable effects on offenders, but also that multimodal approaches involving directed counseling and skills training (as in the GANGS program) have better results than less focused programs. Perhaps the best summary of results on institutionally-based intervention programs (with specific reference to violent behavior is provided by Tolan and Guerra (1994:41; italics added):

> Overall, although various methods appear to be effective in reducing antisocial behavior *within* the institutional setting, there is little evidence, to date, that institutional programs can affect adolescent antisocial or violent behavior after release. Documented effects seem to be temporary and limited to those exhibiting less serious behaviors. In fact, several recent meta-analyses suggest that institutional programs fare no better and sometimes fare worse than community-based programs in terms of their impact on subsequent antisocial behavior.

The implications for GANGS are mixed, and better evaluation research is needed to assess the worth of this and other institutionally-based programs for gangs.

In addition to incapacitation, the greater or lesser deprivation of liberty associated with incarceration, community corrections, probation, and parole are themselves supposed to act as a deterrent to illegal behavior. In addition, within the context of corrections, programs may attempt to deter or rehabilitate offenders, and there are a few examples of programs specifically aimed at gang members. The Los Angeles County Specialized Gang Suppression Program, or SGSP (Klein 1995a) focuses on gang members and potential gang members. Operating out of the Probation Department, it attempts to achieve gang suppression by monitoring probationers in the community and revoking probation and incarcerating probationers who commit new crimes or otherwise violate the conditions of their probation. Here again, evaluations are sparse, but the general literature on the effectiveness of intervention programs suggests that pure deterrence-oriented programs are the *least* effective of the intervention programs.

COORDINATED POLICE, COURT, AND CORRECTIONAL GANG SUPPRESSION

A San Diego program, Jurisdictions United for Drug Enforcement (JUDGE), incorporates elements similar to a combination of Operation

Hardcore and SGSP (Klein 1993; Klein 1995a). JUDGE is administered from the District Attorney's office, and includes prosecutors, police, and probation officers, each acting within their own legal sphere, but coordinating their efforts. Their target population includes street gang members who are on probation, plus other street gang members who are not on probation, but who are involved in drug use and drug dealing.

Prosecutors in the program are available on a 24-hour basis to assist with arrest warrants, search warrants, and legal advice. They also participate in training law enforcement officers and in sharing gang intelligence information. The prosecutors use vertical prosecution, as in Operation Hardcore, to deal with probation violations and new offenses. Police officers gather information on targeted offenders and supply profiles that include family history, gang identification, offense history, probation conditions, and involvement in narcotics use and sales for targeted offenders. This information is made available to the other JUDGE staff. Each law enforcement officer has a case load of about 30 targeted offenders. Using informants, undercover work, and drug testing, the officers seek to detect probation violations and new offenses. Probation officers in the program have case loads of about 20 probationers, and provide information about them to police and prosecutors. Probation officers also initiate revocation of probation for new crimes or violations of probation conditions. As with so many other gang suppression efforts, there is little evidence to indicate whether JUDGE is successful in deterring illegal behavior among gang members.

CONCLUSION: DETERRENCE AND GANG SUPPRESSION

Unless there are substantial increases in certainty (and perhaps—or perhaps not—swiftness and severity) of punishment, deterrence-oriented policies are unlikely to have a major impact on gang membership or behavior. Informal sanctions by relatives, friends, and neighborhood residents are more likely to have an impact on gang activity (see Proposition 22, Chapter 9). The principal payoff for a deterrent, "get tough" policy may instead be a matter of public relations, giving the impression of "doing something" about the gang problem. At worst, this illusion of doing something useful may backfire. Increased suppression by justice system and other agencies is a form of intergroup conflict (see Proposition 4), and may lead to increased solidarity within the gang (Klein 1995a). This increased solidarity, according to Klein, may in turn lead to the persistence of the gang as an entity, increased gang membership, and increased criminal behavior by the gang. If Klein is correct, this is a high price to pay for (temporarily) good public relations.

To the extent that legal and justice system interventions increase the perceived certainty or probability of punishment, they may increase the effectiveness of moderately or even mildly severe sanctions. If the expectation of an action is a net loss, even a small one, why bother taking the action? In this regard, Klein (1995a; 1993) suggests that better publicity about justice system successes (insofar as they exist) may help increase the deterrent value of the successes. From this perspective, the diffuse use of RICO and other laws may produce slight increases in severity, but probably no increase in certainty or swiftness of punishment, and may have little deterrent effect. By contrast, STEP legislation appears to increase the perceived probability of apprehension (you know we are watching *you*), and may have some promise as a deterrent strategy.

Operation Hammer, as noted by Klein, may have an effect opposite to the intended effect by trivializing the consequences of illegal behavior and arrest in the minds of gang members. CRASH, with its purely antagonistic approach to gangs, may promote a defiant attitude on the part of gang members. The importance of "respect" to inner city youth strikes us as important in understanding the character of contemporary gangs. Social commentators, journalists, researchers, and most importantly inner-city youth are becoming increasingly aware of the importance of respect to youth (See Anderson 1994; Perkins 1987; Prothrow-Stith 1991 and others). When you ask youth what is important to them, frequently they say respect. Many youth attach importance to being respected in their neighborhoods, sometimes for the wrong reasons. To be disrespected or "dised" by someone can result in violence and death. Today, youth in gangs must be careful on how they handle themselves in and outside of the gang. Likewise, youth in general must be careful not to disrespect the "wrong" person.

Respect, not of the gang but of the individual gang member, may also be an element of a successful gang suppression strategy. The differences in results between CRASH and OSS may be attributable to differences, not in deterrent effectiveness, but in the level of support and mutual respect between the officers and the community. Police can only act on the offenses they know about; courts can only prosecute the offenses brought to them by the police; and correctional programs can make serious attempts to help only individuals who come under their jurisdiction as a result of a conviction or guilty plea. To the extent that a more community-centered approach is more effective in uncovering illegal behavior and providing sufficient evidence for conviction, there may be a deterrent effect and the potential for other program effects to help reduce the gang problem.

All of this, of course, depends on the importance of deterrence and on the effectiveness of programs in deterring or otherwise persuading individuals to avoid illegal behavior. As noted earlier, deterrence does *not* address the most important influences on gang involvement and behavior. Programs that *do* attempt to address a wider range of causes of gang membership and illegal behavior, including some of the causes we believe are most important, include educational, employment, and other service programs reviewed in the next chapter.

Chapter 11

PREVENTION AND ASSISTANCE PROGRAMS: EDUCATION, EMPLOYMENT, OPPORTUNITY, AND EMPOWERMENT

In their general reviews of intervention programs, Gendreau and Ross (1983), Lipsey (1992), and Tolan and Guerra (1994) come to some similar conclusions about the characteristics of effective programs. One, as noted in the previous chapter, is the setting: community-based programs appear to have more favorable effects than institutionally-based programs. There are some exceptions to this pattern. For example, Lipsey (1992), in his meta-analysis of intervention programs, reported better success with institutionally-based than with community-based employment programs. This is the exception, however, not the rule. For most types of programs, non-institutional programs appear to have better results than institutionally-based programs.

The type of intervention also matters. Interventions based on social learning theory or Sutherland's differential association theory, programs that provide specific social and behavioral skills, family interventions, and especially multi-modal programs that combine elements of these and perhaps other types of interventions, tend to be more successful than psychotherapy, biomedical interventions, or counseling, especially in single treatment or unimodal interventions. Well-designed evaluations typically produce smaller estimates of program effects than evaluations that lack a comparison or control group, equivalence of experimental and control groups, and other elements of good research design, but as Reiss (1994) explains, it is just such effects, limited though they almost always are, that hold a realistic promise for progress in developing more successful interventions. Gendreau and Ross (1983) summarize the elements of effective programs as (1) clear explications of rules and formal sanctions, (2) anti-criminal modeling and reinforcement as suggested by social learning theory, (3) assistance in dealing with problems or difficulties by using prosocial coping strategies, (4) use of community resources,

272

and (5) empathy, trust, and open communications in relations with program staff.

In this chapter, we review programs designed primarily to prevent gang crime and delinquency by providing education, training, employment, counseling, and other assistance for individuals who are not under the supervision of the criminal justice system. In some instances, these programs are offered by the police or other agents of the criminal justice system. More often, they are offered in the context of public social service agencies, in the community or in the schools. Some are designed to address a broad range of social problems, or illegal behavior generally; others are specifically designed as gang interventions. We begin with community organization and intervention programs, then move to social intervention programs, which include direct interventions with gangs and school-based gang prevention programs, then consider opportunity and social change programs. We conclude with a brief discussion of multiple component programs that incorporate both the prevention and assistance components that are the focus of this chapter and justice system efforts at gang suppression like those discussed in the previous chapter.

COMMUNITY ORGANIZATION AND INTERVENTION PROGRAMS

The Chicago Area Project

The Chicago Area Project is one of the most significant and monumental social change programs undertaken by social scientists. It was an early attempt to apply sociological and social psychological perspectives to a major societal concern. The Chicago Area Project was founded by the University of Chicago sociologist Clifford R. Shaw. The Chicago Area Project was initiated in the 1930s and was based on major social ecological concepts of the "Chicago School" of Sociology. The Chicago School contributed to the study of the urban environment in an industrializing and urbanizing society. The concentric zone theory proposed by Burgess (1925) set the foundation for the analysis of the major social problems that were emerging in American cities early in this century. Shaw and McKay (1942) undertook extensive research on the correlation of poverty and arrest rates in parts of Chicago where immigration, instability, and youth gangs were most common and problematic. Their findings supported ecological theory predictions, that is that crime rates would be highest in areas marked by transience and poverty. The program that evolved from the theory and research embodied the major findings and perspectives of the Chicago School.

One goal of the Chicago Area Project was to reduce the high rates of juvenile delinquency and gang behavior in some of Chicago's most crime prone neighborhoods. A secondary goal of the project was to confront the problem of youth crime and gangs through a unified effort involving the residents from high delinquency areas. In this respect, the project aimed to convince these individuals that the problem of youth crime in their neighborhoods was as much their concern and responsibility as it was that of the police and social services agencies.

According to Kobrin (1969) there were two main strategies that characterized the Chicago Area Project. The first strategy was to enlist the support of local residents in order to lend credibility to the aims of the project. Local area leaders were identified and asked to assume influential roles in getting the citizens to cooperate and accept the program in their neighborhoods. Qualitative researchers have long recognized the advantages of utilizing respected individuals as a means of gaining access and entry into unfamiliar and perhaps unfriendly territories. The leaders also had one additional advantage. They were often acquainted with members of the target population—the delinquents themselves.

The second major strategy of the Chicago Area Project was to engender a sense of autonomy among the various groups, called local welfare organizations, so that the groups could proceed to resolve the problem of youth crime and gangs. Members of the local neighborhood groups were permitted to establish their own policies for dealing directly with crime and gang problems, even if these policies appeared unsound to the project personnel. This type of leeway and confidence shown in the local residents gave them precisely what the project coordinators wanted from the very beginning, the need for those directly affected by the crime and gang problems to assume responsibility for reducing their presence in their own neighborhoods.

Over the years a number of scholars have assessed the impact of the project on the incidence of juvenile delinquency and gangs in the communities where it was implemented (Kobrin 1969; Finestone 1976; Jensen and Rojek 1980; Empey 1982; Schlossman and Sedlak 1983). Most indications have been that the project had little, if any, effect on the reduction of crime rates and illegal gang behaviors. Kobrin (1969:320) observed that it is extremely difficult to obtain accurate measurements on field experiments such as the Chicago Area Project. The absence of a scientific control group in empirical research may limit the conclusions that can be drawn from such studies. In addition, Finestone (1976) reported that it was in the areas with the highest rates of delinquency and gangs that the Chicago Area Project was least efficient. Finestone attributed this result to the effects of excessive social disorganization on any attempts to intervene in the problem of delinquency.

There were additional problems with measuring the results of the project. The effort involved over twenty different strategies, including counseling services, recreational activities, and discussion groups. The multitude of reactive responses may have rendered exact measurement of project intervention meaningless, since it would have been necessary to analyze each specific service or activity in order to determine its contribution (if any) to the reduction in the incidence of crime.

The Chicago Area Project was not a complete failure. Kobrin (1969) concluded that the project demonstrated the importance of establishing youth welfare organizations in delinquency prone areas. The effect of this policy was that area residents came to believe that they could assume an important role in dealing with issues critical to their neighborhoods. In addition, Kobrin noted the significance of using workers to reach out to teenage gang members. The project pioneered this approach, later known as the detached worker strategy, an intervention technique that would be employed in future anti-gang programs. Finally, the project was successful in breaking down the impersonality found in the official response to the gang and delinquency problems. By their very nature, official organizations are bureaucratic and formal, and they discourage personal reactions to difficult situations. The Chicago Area Project found ways to involve the various primary groups (particularly family and peers) as important mechanisms for positive influences on youth and gang members.

It is also important to mention the contribution of social theory to the Chicago Area Project. The project was one of the earliest to apply concepts and theories from the social sciences to the problems of youth gangs and juvenile delinquency. Future programs, broader in scope, such as the war on poverty, which was based largely on differential opportunity theory (Cloward and Ohlin 1960), would also apply social scientific theories to the major social problems facing American society.

A number of other programs to be discussed in this chapter, such as the Mid-City Project, were also based on leading behavioral and social scientific theories.

The Mid-City Project

The Boston Mid-City Project, which operated between 1954 and 1957, represents the model anti-delinquency, anti-gang program of that decade. This project encompassed classic concepts from both sociological and psychodynamic theories. As such, it worked to bridge the gaps between individualistic and social orientations, both of which were critical to the project's intervention efforts. The primary objective of the Mid-City Project was to inhibit or to reduce the amount of gang behaviors and delinquency committed by adolescent residents of the targeted communities. In order to achieve this objective, project coordinators adopted a total community philosophy, which was undergirded by the belief that juvenile criminality is a consequence of environmental factors indigenous to the neighborhood of concern. This emphasis on the ecology of teenage crime and youth gangs had its origins in the Chicago Area Project.

According to Miller (1962), this project involved two major efforts, the first of which is reminiscent of the strategies of the earlier Chicago Area Project. The first major effort was to develop and to strengthen local citizen groups so that they could assume responsibility for and take direct action against delinquency in their areas. The second and perhaps the most important goal was to gain cooperation from organizations and individuals who had at least some direct relationship to the gang and delinquency problem. Settlement houses, churches, schools, mental health and medical clinics, elements of the criminal justice establishment (the police, courts, and probation personnel), and employment-oriented professionals were involved in the attempt to reduce youth gangs and delinquency.

Although juvenile delinquency in a general sense was the issue of concern, the Mid-City Project placed heavy emphasis on intervention with gangs. Intervention was accomplished by utilizing professionally trained human services workers to carry out direct change efforts with the gangs. Project officials decided to place a limit on the number of workers selected for gang intervention. Seven workers were assigned to over 400 teenagers, representing 21 corner gangs. Only one-half of these youths (N = 205, or seven gangs) were singled out for extensive treatment and attention by project officials. The case workers met with their respective gangs anywhere from three to six hours per week, with the contact period ranging from ten to thirty-four months. It should be noted that gang members were primarily of non-Hispanic European descent, and ranged from 12 to 21 years of age. The size of the gangs varied considerably, with the average estimated to be 30 for male gangs and nine for female gangs.

Miller identified three major phases of the Mid-City effort: the initial contact phase, the behavior modification phase, and the termination phase. The initial contact phase involved workers seeking out specific gangs and attempting to establish workable relationships with them. Critical to the success of this stage was the need for the workers to become familiar with and to understand the subcultures in which they were operating. On several occasions the workers were tested by gang members in order to determine how well they would adapt to the deviant activities of the teens. Some gang members would steal right in the view of the case workers thereby testing their sense of trust and friendship with gang participants. The importance of the first contact with the gangs cannot be underestimated, for the very success or failure of the project rested on the effectiveness of the initial relationships.

The second phase of the project, called "behavior modification via mutual activity involvement," encompassed the major change activities. In essence this phase involved attempts at changing the social structure and the ideologies of the targeted gangs. This phase was divided into three efforts: first, the workers attempted to organize the gangs in order to engage them in positive behaviors; second, the workers established themselves as intermediaries between gangs and adult institutions; and third, the project was geared toward personality change through direct influence techniques used by the workers themselves.

Organizing gang activities basically involved efforts at changing the infrastructure of the gangs from deviance-oriented to formal social organizations, such as clubs or athletic teams. Of course, a major reason for encouraging clubs was to teach the gang members how to operate under formal rules similar to those found in acceptable and respected social institutions. Program staff thought that this would promote open lines of communication between gang members and adult organizations. Eventually the gangs adopted their own constitutions, became involved in fund raising activities, and met on a regular basis (Miller 1962).

The intermediary emphasis of the behavior modification phase was a direct spinoff of the first phase, for it entailed the establishment of lines of communication with adult organizations, such as schools and employment agencies. Case workers met with officials, and acted as direct links between youths and individuals with the means to assist them. For example, when meeting with school personnel the workers would try to intervene in any problems with truancy, grades, behavior, or dropout experienced by gang members. In addition, the workers encouraged teachers and other school officials to become acquainted with the problems of corner gangs. Project officials drove gang members to job interviews after arranging appointments with employment agencies. They also counseled the youths on proper interview demeanor, and urged local businesses to hire them. The behavior modification phase also included worker contacts with the courts, lawyers, city authorities, and local businesses in order to broaden the range of alternatives that could be made available to gang members. Meetings between gangs and the police were arranged so that both might express their concerns and grievances. One of the objectives of the meetings with city officials was to make recreational activities and facilities more available to the youths. Discussions on raising funds for a baseball field and overall improvement of the local community were held.

The final part of the behavior modification phase included the direct influence methods by which the workers tried to modify the personalities of gang members through techniques such as direct suggestion, non-directive leadership, and collective reinforcement. In actuality, it was the presence of the workers themselves that appeared to have the most significant effect on the adolescents. The workers were educated and from middle class backgrounds. Exposure to these individuals, with their conventional normative orientations, was thought to be an important influence on any positive changes in the personalities of gang members (Miller 1962).

The final phase of the Mid-City Project was labeled termination and was characterized by a gradual withdrawal of the workers from their assigned gangs. The actual length of time each worker spent with a gang varied, and this made termination difficult for some of them. The rationale for ending worker-gang relationships gradually was to avoid any psychological feelings of loss that may have resulted from the abrupt departures of the case workers.

The Mid-City project was a major anti-gang, anti-delinquency effort that involved a significant amount of time, money, energy, and hope from diverse individuals, many of whom had a direct stake in the outcome of the project. Like the Chicago Area Project before it, the Boston program operated under the premise that the reduction of juvenile crime through self-help and determination was the key to any chances of success. However, the results from analyses of the effectiveness of the project produced very similar findings to those of the Chicago effort. Miller (1962) has undertaken perhaps the most in-depth examination of the Mid-City Project. He assessed its efficiency based on an analysis of arrest and court appearance data. From both sources, it appears that the Boston program had limited success.

Looking at the incidence of illegal or immoral behaviors committed by gang members from the initial through the final contact phases, Miller reported very little reduction in the quantity of such antisocial activities. For example, during the initial phase of the project, 49 percent of the behaviors engaged in by the targeted teens were identified as illegal. The figure was 45 percent at the final stage of the effort. By focusing his attention on court appearances, not only did Miller find little or no change, but his data strongly suggested an increase at various measurement periods of the project. Six months prior to the initial contact phase, gang members appeared in court 21 times, but approximately one year after termination of the project, the teenagers under analysis made 39 appearances before the juvenile courts (Miller 1962: 175–178). If the success of the Mid-City or similar projects is defined in terms of the reduction of crime rates and gang activities, then the results were disappointing. Miller (1962:187) concluded that there was no significant, measurable inhibition of law-violating behaviors as a result of the project.

Comparison of the Chicago Area Project and the Boston Mid-City Project

The Chicago Area and Mid-City projects became the standard by which other anti-gang efforts would be assessed and judged. Although it is clear that neither project met with the successes that were expected of them, the new ground that was broken in gang intervention methodology proved to be influential on gang intervention strategies for the next 40 years. The major difference between the two projects is found in the greater organizational complexity of the Mid-City program. The Mid-

City program was more specifically delineated in terms of project phases. The Chicago Area Project, while well conceptualized, was simpler in its organization and goals. In addition, the Boston program was broader in scope, extending its call for community involvement to a wider diversity of groups and individuals, such as mental health agencies and employment personnel.

One similarity between the two projects is their grounding in theories of the social and the behavioral sciences. Both programs had their origins in the urban-ecological approach of the Chicago School of Sociology. Second, both the Chicago Area and the Mid-City projects employed human services professionals as the main change agents for working with the gangs. These individuals were supposed to bridge the gap between theory and practice, and were charged with the difficult task of reducing gang delinquency while validating both the power and preciseness in which social and behavioral theories explained the nature and structure of youth gangs.

A third similarity between the two projects is found in their orientation toward community involvement in reducing gang activities. This philosophy can still be found in contemporary gang intervention projects (to be discussed later in the chapter) and is a logical extension of theory that is ecologically based. Finally, both efforts were geared toward the reduction of criminal gang behaviors. In this respect, neither program appears to have been successful.

Contemporary Community Organization: MAD DADS

Omaha, Nebraska, normally has had a low crime rate, especially a low rate of violent crimes. Since 1987, however, Omaha has experienced an increase in violent crimes committed by youth gangs. Additionally, the city has witnessed an increase in illegal drug trafficking engaged in by these gangs. Neither city officials, the police or the general public anticipated the emerging gang phenomenon and its consequent problems.

Official crime data, provided by the Omaha police department from the first nine months of 1990, will help to place the youth gang problem of Omaha in perspective. From January through September, 1990, youth gangs accounted for 39 felony assaults (assaults of a serious nature in which the victims required medical attention); nine misdemeanor assaults (the assaults were not serious and no medical attention was required); 17 drive-by shootings; two homicides; and 26 gang-related drug arrests. By contrast, just three years earlier, the Omaha police division was unable to report these kind of data for youth gangs. Omaha, while not immune to crime, has not experienced gang problems of this nature in years. Citizens of the city are not used to youth gangs who pose a threat to personal life or property.

According to Omaha Public Safety Director Pittman Foxall, the city of Omaha has had youth gangs for decades. The gangs have normally been linked to certain sections of the community, and have been territorial in nature. They have typically confined their activities to their own neighborhoods. On occasion, the gangs have been known to engage in violence, but their activities have usually been limited to offenses of a nonviolent nature, such as thefts, the use of alcohol and street drugs such as marijuana.

At some point in the late 1980s, elements of violent economic gangs from the Los Angeles area became situated in Omaha. The exact dates of the arrival of the Crips and Bloods is unknown, but by 1988 the city of Omaha had become aware of them through their participation in illegal activities, at first expressed by an increase in the prevalence of dangerous street drugs, such as crack cocaine. Since, as a general rule, citizens of the community were completely unfamiliar with these gangs, the city was unprepared for their potential effects on the crime rate, and how they could disrupt and threaten African American neighborhoods, as well as the feelings of security throughout the entire city.

By 1989, it was apparent that Omaha had been influenced by the Crips and the Bloods, since a number of African American male adolescents had begun to associate, join, and identify with them. Gang violence, especially in the African American community was on an increase, apparently associated with the marketing of drugs in African American neighborhoods and in the public schools. The concerns registered over the new drug threat and violence led individuals from the African American community to form MAD DADS, an organization dedicated to removing the Crips and the Bloods from Omaha.

MAD DADS, or Men Against Destruction—Defending Against Drugs and Social-Disorder, is comprised solely of adult male African Americans who are concerned about the effects of gangs on the African American community, especially as this relates to teenagers. The founders of this organization claimed that they could foresee the emergence of the youth gang problem before it became a reality in Omaha. It is not entirely clear what the basis for their claims was, but several of the founders of MAD DADS have traveled extensively around the nation and apparently became familiar with the threats and the techniques of the Crips and the Bloods, as well as other youth gangs, in other American cities. Their knowledge of the youth gang problem in other communities, especially in minority neighborhoods, made them concerned that this phenomenon would eventually find its way to Omaha.

The objectives of MAD DADS range from protecting African American teenage males from the negative influences of youth gangs to making a better life possible for the African American community as a whole. Their objectives are detailed in Box 10.1. MAD DADS perceives itself as an action-oriented unit. It feels that through action and not rhetoric that change is possible and without a unified effort to eradicate youth gangs from the city the gang problem will become far worse, eventually destroying the African American community.

Box 11:1: Objectives of MAD DADS

1. the visible presence of African American fathers throughout the African American community;
2. acting as surrogate fathers to young African American males;
3. counseling African American males on their personal problems and advising them on employment opportunities and techniques for securing employment;
4. working with law enforcement in identifying criminal influences in African American neighborhoods;
5. mobilizing residents of the African American community so that as many individuals as possible are active in the fight against youth gangs and drugs;
6. engaging in study of the efforts of organizations like MAD DADS nationally in order to become aware of similar programs;
7. relying on the use of the media in order to make the public more aware of the goals and the needs of MAD DADS;
8. promotion of African American unity and positive thinking;
9. demanding that all relevant officials will commit themselves to eliminating youth gangs from the city of Omaha; and
10. establishment of the following committees so that the efforts of MAD DADS are formalized and made to be more efficient:
    a. communication committee
    b. mobilization committee
    c. security committee
    d. administration committee.

As of the writing of this book, there is no empirical research on the effectiveness of MAD DADS. It is possible that this unofficial community program will have greater success than its predecessors, but past experience with community programs provides little reason for optimism.

SOCIAL INTERVENTION PROGRAMS

The city of Los Angeles, California, became active in gang intervention in the mid-1950s, and has had a leading role in such efforts since then. It is no accident that many of the gang suppression programs in the previous chapter were based on initiatives taken in southern California. Like the eastern seaboard states and cities such as Chicago, southern California rapidly urbanized and experienced heavy population growth, especially through immigration from other countries and in-migration from other states. The effects of such large scale change were followed by the advent of juvenile gangs in California's largest cities, especially Los Angeles.

Group Guidance: Early Research (Adams 1967)

According to Adams (1967), the city of Los Angeles was involved in anti-gang efforts as early as 1943. The probation department of Los Angeles County became involved with an intervention technique known as the group guidance method, which is very similar to the approaches used by the social workers in the two programs previously discussed. In essence, the group guidance method employed social workers as the primary contact and change personnel with juvenile gangs. The responsibilities of the workers included undertaking a study of the area to which they were assigned; establishing rapport with gang members; holding regular meetings with neighborhood gangs; engaging in intergang projects; and meeting with parents and other adults in order to open up lines of communication and to establish strong community relations.

Adams (1967) reported on a test of the cost efficiency of the group guidance method. The test involved three juvenile gangs in the Los Angeles area. Adams used two of the gangs as experimental units, and one of the gangs as the control group. The two experimental groups were Hispanic, and the lone control group was predominantly African American. The objective of the study was to ascertain whether the group guidance method was effective in reducing police and court contacts, thereby lowering the costs to the community of crimes committed by the gangs.

Although Adams' research design utilized two experimental groups, only one (the Spartans) received the full group guidance program. The other experimental subjects (the Gavilanes) were only partially exposed to the treatment conditions. Adams and his staff felt that the use of both a control group and a partially affected experimental group would help to amplify the affects of the group guidance technique more clearly than if they were to have remained with a traditional two comparison group strategy.

The work with the gangs, especially the Spartans, entailed intensive contact with gang members and leaders of the community. The workers operated within the social milieu where the gangs resided, thus enabling them to become more familiar with the values of both the gangs and community residents. By working directly with Spartan boys and literally "guiding" them to more productive lives, the workers played a very direct role in assisting the gang members to age-out of juvenile criminality.

The results of the research indicated that the Spartans had experienced a substantial reduction in rates of offending as a result of the group guidance method. The mean correctional cost per gang member also declined considerably. As expected, the Gavilanes were reported to have a reduction in both offenses and correctional expenses, but because they were only partially exposed to the treatment conditions, their decrease in both categories was less marked than the decrease for the Spartans. The African American juvenile gang, the Valiants, who were treated as the control group in the study, experienced a major increase in the mean correctional cost per gang member as well as in the incidence of juvenile criminality. Based on these findings, Adams concluded that the group guidance technique was an effective tool for working with juvenile gangs.

Adams' research was limited in several important respects. Adams employed noninferential statistical concepts that severely limited the power of his research conclusions. His statistical analysis was confined to the most elementary techniques such as presentation of arithmetic means and simple percentages. The research design was nonexperimental, and the use of an African American control group for Hispanic experimental groups is questionable. In addition, later research cast doubt on the effectiveness of the group guidance method.

Later Research on Group Guidance and Detached Workers

Klein (1967; 1968b; 1969a; Klein and Crawford 1967) examined the effects of detached worker programs with four clusters of juvenile gangs, all located in southern California. The detached worker program was subsumed under the group guidance project of the Los Angeles Department of Probation for a number of years. By definition, the detached worker concept simply means that a social worker is removed from the bureaucratic setting in which most social work is undertaken, and carries out her responsibilities in a social milieu to which he or she is assigned. The objective of the detached worker philosophy is to minimize the amount of paperwork that many human social professionals must face on a daily basis, and to maximize the time that she or he spends with clients in their areas of residence.

The activities reported by Klein that were included in the work with the juvenile gang clusters were: club meetings; special activities, such as youth sports events and dances; tutoring; a remedial reading project; community organization work; and intensive supervision of the delinquent gangs. The most important finding of the research is that the presence of the group worker had the effect of intensifying gang cohesiveness, thereby resulting in greater participation of gang members in juvenile criminality. The group guidance worker became a focal point of gang organization and belongingness, thus resulting in a greater feeling of "we-ness" among many gang members. This effect was totally unanticipated, but Yablonsky (1959) and Short and Strodtbeck (1965) have also reported that intervention efforts may increase gang cohesion and lead to increased illegal behavior. Another significant finding of the research was that there was no statistically difference concerning the effects of the project on core vs. fringe gang members. Involvement in juvenile delinquent activities was as common for the "wannabes" as it was for kids who were considered to be integral players in the juvenile gangs.

Klein's results, like those of Adams (1967), were non-experimental. In addition, it is unclear how Klein grouped gangs into clusters for purposes of comparison. The fact that the outreach program was part of the group guidance project, the methodological problems with the research of both Adams and Klein, and the different findings regarding the success of the program, prevent us from reaching a firm conclusion regarding the success of the detached worker or group guidance approaches to the reduction of gang delinquency. It may well be that the group guidance or detached worker approaches work better for some gang types than for others. The general impression based on the National Youth Gang Survey is that social interventions such as these are not especially effective in dealing with juvenile gangs.

The Ladino Hills Project: Success and Disappointment

Klein (1995a) described the Ladino Hills Project as a direct response to findings from earlier intervention efforts which suggested that group intervention programs led to increased group cohesiveness and increased gang crime. The project selected a highly delinquent gang with a thirty-year history of existence, and attempted to reduce gang cohesiveness by (a) reducing outside pressures on the gang and (b) selectively intervening with individuals rather than with the gang as a whole. Interventions included tutoring for gang members still in school, assistance with job placement and placement in training programs, and individual therapeutic interventions. Individuals were selected as targets for intervention based on the likelihood that they would reduce the cohesiveness of the gang.

In the short run, the program appears to have been a success. Klein reported a 40 percent reduction in group cohesiveness, a 35 percent reduction in arrests, and a gradual reduction in the size of the gang. The reductions in cohesiveness, gang recruitment, and delinquency lasted through the 18-month span of the project and continued 6 months beyond the end of the project. Several years later, however, the gang had regenerated itself. "In the absence of a sustained effort and in the context of a community that failed to follow up on the experimental interventions, a gang area continued to be a gang-producing area. We had affected the Latins, but we had not affected their community. The lesson is both obvious and important. Gangs are by-products of their communities: They cannot long be controlled by attacks on symptoms alone; community structure and capacity must also be targeted" (Klein 1995a:147).

Contemporary Social Intervention Programs

Other social outreach programs include youth service programs administered by police agencies and school based programs. McKinney (1988) listed several social intervention programs to deal with juvenile gangs. Operation Jeopardy, conducted by the Los Angeles Police, involves contacting parents of children identified as potential gang members to provide counseling and information about programs aimed at preventing their children from joining gangs. The Phoenix Police Activities League is a program in which police take young people on shopping trips; organize recreational, social, and educational programs; and arrange job opportunities. The Chicago Intervention Network involves counselors who work with youths, their families, and community groups. In addition, some drug prevention programs such as DARE (Drug Abuse Resistance Education) and SANE (Substance Abuse and Narcotics Education) are indirectly aimed at reducing gang problems by reducing one aspect of the juvenile gang problem, involvement in drug use and sales.

The Youth Service Program (Needle and Stapleton 1983) was developed as an alternative to arrest and surveillance of gang members, and is characterized by counseling and referral services, in which the police act as youth advocates. Troubled teens, who are often gang members, are given a lengthy lecture upon referral to the program, and if it is thought to be necessary, they are provided with counseling services. The objective of counseling is to improve upon the youth's interpersonal and learning skills. According to Collingwood et al. (1976) youths who went through the Youth Service Program in Dallas, Texas had lower rates of recidivism as compared to those teenagers who refused to participate in it. The authors also noted, however, that the youngsters who did not participate in the program may not have been comparable to those who did.

Drowns and Hess (1990) have reported on a number of school and community programs, including "Say Yes, Incorporated," which educates school staff members about neighborhood gangs, and how to deal with the problem of gang violence at school activities such as athletic events; and the "Gang Awareness Resource Program," a Los Angeles project aimed at placing one deputy sheriff on a full-time basis in the Los Angeles County School district as a resource person to answer questions about gangs and to provide orientation sessions about juvenile gangs to educators. One major shortcoming with these and other school anti-gang programs is that few have been rigorously evaluated (Spergel 1990), leaving us with a great deal of uncertainty about their impact, if any, on gang activity, membership, and gang-related crime. This does not mean that these programs do not work; it is simply an admission of ignorance.

Absent any scientifically rigorous evaluation, we simply do not know what does work and what does not.

Gang Resistance Education and Training (GREAT)

Gang Resistance Education and Training (GREAT) shares an acronym with another program, the Gang Reporting Evaluation and Tracking (another GREAT) program (Klein 1995a:190–193). The latter is basically an information gathering and storage system begun in Los Angeles, and spreading nationally. The former, the program with which we are concerned, is a school-based prevention program based on the Drug Abuse Resistance Education (DARE) program. The GREAT program had its origins in Phoenix, Arizona, in 1991 and has since expanded to 38 states, with over 950 police officers in 43 states having completed GREAT training (Esbensen 1996). The primary focus of GREAT is to discourage adolescents from gang involvement and violence.

The GREAT program is typically nine weeks in length, and the target student population is seventh graders. All teachers in GREAT are uniformed police officers, themselves trained and certified as GREAT teachers. In this and other respects, GREAT is modeled after DARE. The major characteristics and objectives of this antigang strategy are teaching students (1) conflict resolution skills, (2) cultural sensitivity, (3) the dangers and disadvantages of gang membership and involvement, (4) the importance of becoming responsible members of their communities, (5) personal goal setting, and (6) skills for resisting pressures to join gangs and to avoid involvement with other negative behaviors. GREAT is presently being evaluated in selected sites nationwide (Esbensen 1995).

In a study of the GREAT program in Torrance, California, a middle to upper middle income community of 137,000 predominantly white residents, Arboit (1995) found that 45 percent of seventh grade teachers surveyed believed that GREAT had deterred youth from gangs, but only 9 percent felt that it had reduced the gang problem in the community. Sixty percent of school officials and 83 percent of police surveyed reported that school safety had been improved as a result of GREAT. It should be noted that Torrance is virtually gang free, and this fact casts some doubt on the relevance of these findings. Is this a program that prevented the spread of gangs into a gang-free suburb, or a program that prevented something that would not have happened anyway? At worst, it appears that no harm was done; at best, it may have been helpful in preventing the spread of gang activity into Torrance.

Monnet (1995) has studied the implementation of the GREAT program in Las Cruces, New Mexico, a city in which Hispanic gangs predominate. The program was started in one middle school, and a second junior high school adopted the program in 1994. Monnet describes the pattern of gangs in Las Cruces as similar to the pattern described by Vigil (1988) in his study of barrio gangs: firearms, distinctive dress styles (now being downplayed in the face of strict enforcement against gang members), weapons being brought to school, and a handful of drive-by shootings. GREAT is not the only response to gang activity in Las Cruces. Gang suppression attempts have been made by the police, who make all possible charges for offenses involving apparent gang members, and suppression by the school in the form of dress codes, mediation programs, and suspension of rule breaking students. Gang members and gang leaders are confronted directly and informed about dress codes and expectations for behavior. The school also offers alternatives including support groups, counselors, social work interns, school activities, athletics, and academic competitions. Monnet indicates that gang problems seem to have been reduced somewhat, but it is difficult to tell at this stage whether GREAT, other efforts, or the combination have produced the results.

Other evaluations of GREAT (Arizona Prevention Resource Center 1994) suggest that in the short term, there is an increase in resistance skills, a reduction in the number of students wanting to be gang members, and fewer students getting into trouble after program participation. Students also retained the information they received in the program. The important reservations to these results are that they are only short term, they involve no comparison or control group, and the effects appear to be small.

OPPORTUNITY AND SOCIAL CHANGE

The classic gang intervention strategies of the 1950s and of the early 1960s were critical to the policies that would drive similar efforts in the next 25 years. Programs such as the Chicago Area Project and those in Los Angeles became the cornerstones upon which other projects would base their philosophies and actions. In addition to the models that preceded more recent anti-gang efforts, the decade of the 1960s was ripe for massive social and historical changes that would call for and receive the attention of the society at large.

American society was undergoing significant demographic, urban, technological, and value transformations that were not only affecting traditional social institutions, but were also challenging their credibilities in the eyes of the American citizenry. Cloward and Ohlin's (1960) differential opportunity theory integrated well with the turmoil that coincided with the social changes of the period. The theory itself became a foundation for social action and policy, most notably President Lyndon Johnson's "Great Society" programs, perhaps the most intensive anti-poverty strategies ever attempted by this nation. The Johnson presidency was marked by policies aimed at reducing crime and delinquency through the eradication of poverty. One such program, a direct descendent of differential opportunity theory was Mobilization for Youth.

Mobilization for Youth: 1963–1967

Mobilization for Youth was designed to deal with the problem of juvenile delinquency in general rather than with the specific problem of juvenile gangs. The objectives of the program were broad enough that the project officials included the targeting of juvenile gangs as part of their overall strategy (Bibb 1967). As a product of differential opportunity theory, the mobilization program was comprised of four parts that were all aimed at attacking the assumed sources of juvenile gang behavior, poverty, and social disorganization. The five services provided by the program were employment opportunities, educational opportunities, services to individuals and families, and group work and community organization work.

Differential opportunity theory was largely based on the belief that the lack of legitimate opportunities in society led some young people to choose less socially acceptable channels to recognition and prestige (Cloward and Ohlin 1960). In order to change this situation, Mobilization for Youth was heavily involved in employment alternatives for teenage males who were high-risk subjects for joining juvenile gangs. The program involved the creation of new jobs for lower class adolescents, educating them in the most acceptable ways to find and to secure employment, and informing the local public about existing job opportunities and the most effective methods for obtaining jobs.

The educationally-oriented policies included (1) increasing the school's responsiveness to lower class life, (2) reducing teacher turnover, (3) bringing parents into contact with the school so that educational efforts could be supported in the home, (4) developing curriculum material and methods consistent with lower class culture, and (5) providing extra tutorial help to grade school students in order to arrest the pattern of failure which starts in the primary grades. These elements were derived from sociological findings that supported education as the primary mechanism for upward social mobility. According to the proponents of differential opportunity theory, the slum child was inhibited from equal access to the legitimate means to success, and improvements in the relationships of poor teenagers to the educational systems were essential if the traditional cycle of failure was to be averted.

Mobilization for Youth targeted the conditions that were said to lead to membership in juvenile gangs as well as to juvenile criminality. All four of the elements employed in this national strategy had significance for gang intervention. Project officials attempted to reintegrate gang members with educational institutions and to make them more acceptable to potential employers. In many respects, Mobilization for Youth chose to treat its anti-delinquency efforts and gang programs as one and the same. It has therefore been difficult over the years to analyze the effects of this policy specifically on juvenile gangs.

Like so many of the programs before it, Mobilization for Youth met with limited success. Its problems were rooted in many issues that did not impact previous gang and delinquency oriented projects, such as replacement by broader based social policy (the "War on Poverty") and an alienating war in Indochina. By the time Mobilization for Youth began to have its effect, the Johnson administration had initiated a much more ambitious liberal policy aimed at reducing poverty on a large scale basis. Consequently, the more limited objectives of the "mobilization" program were sacrificed for a major national attack on poverty and its correlates, most notably crime (Empey 1982). It became practically impossible to measure the effects of the program on gangs and juvenile delinquency. By 1964 Mobilization for Youth had encountered criticisms and negative stereotyping that may have led to its premature termination. Marris and Rein (1973) have made the observation that political difficulties, resulting in funding problems, and the labeling of program officials as "commies," brought the kind of publicity that inevitably led to the program's demise.

The Legacy of Mobilization for Youth

A number of other programs grew out of Mobilization for Youth, including the Community Action Program (CAP) and the highly controversial Youth Organizations United (YOU). The Community Action Program was formed in cities across the nation and was based on the belief that the poor must help themselves if they were to improve their life chances and life styles. The thrust of this program was that in cooperation with the establishment, CAP could produce major changes in the conditions of poverty and crime. Like Mobilization for Youth before it, the Community Action Program encountered serious political difficulties that blocked its success (Empey 1982).

Youth Organizations United was designed to encourage juvenile gang leaders to play active roles in eradicating the horrid conditions that contributed to juvenile gang membership. At first glance, the program looked as if it could be a major success. The government was able to persuade potentially dangerous young males to assume a place of significance within their own communities. YOU quickly failed, however, primarily because of the lack of training provided to the gang leaders by project officials. The task to which they were assigned was far too complicated and demanding for untrained individuals to handle. Adding to the dilemmas and excessive expectations associated the program was the inability of the press and politicians to anticipate the impending problems. The political community and the media had overenthusiastically supported YOU, without sufficient information for doing so.

The Urban Leadership Training Program (ULT): 1967–1969

YOU was not the only intervention program designed to attack the gang phenomenon by addressing the issue of leadership. Thrasher (1927) had emphasized the relevance of the leader forty years earlier, by noting the leader's importance in the overall gang structure, in intergang warfare, and with violence in general. Thrasher had detailed the specific roles played by the leader as well as the ways in which the leader came to be selected in the gang. Thrasher reported that it was usually the toughest and the most violent male who rose to the status of gang leader.

Like Youth Organizations United, the Urban Leadership Training Program (ULT), founded on the east coast by academicians and African American community leaders, was designed to confront the problems of gangs by co-opting and intervening in gang leadership. The assumptions held by ULT officials were very similar to those of YOU. Both programs operated under the premise that the leader was important to other gang members and that to redirect his energies would result in the reduction in antisocial activities by gang members in general (Krisberg 1974).

The Urban Leadership Training program focused its efforts on 22 gang leaders, representing five local gangs. The 22 leaders had all encountered serious problems with the criminal justice system. Most had spent time in local and state correctional facilities; all had experienced unfavorable relationships with the schools; and all had unstable employment histories. The 22 gang leaders chosen for the program posed a substantial challenge to project officials. They were failures by the standards of success in American society, and ULT undertook a risk by securing them as its primary subjects. Yet it was exactly this type of delinquent/criminal that policy makers thought needed to be targeted for behavioral change. Their criminal pasts, coupled with the other indicators of maladjustment, made the leaders prime candidates for long-term incarceration.

The 22 gang leaders ranged in age from 18–23 years. They had established themselves as the older and experienced members of the gangs. ULT offered formal educational training for the leaders, and it was designed to have them network with the acceptable and successful residents of their neighborhoods. The formal education consisted of taking courses in the law, criminology, economics, community health, political science, sociology, communications, and black studies. All 22 "students" were African American, so the course in black studies was intended to educate them on the history of African Americans. The social science-oriented courses (political science and sociology) had the intention of sensitizing them to cultural diversity, and to the complexities of living in an industrial society. In particular, the course in political science played an instrumental role in helping the leaders to adapt to the nature of the community governmental structure.

Criminology and the study of the law served the purposes of familiarizing gang leaders with the causes and the consequences of criminal behavior. The study of the law gave the leaders a greater appreciation of the purposes and the functions of the legal system. The remaining course work in communications and community health educated the youths in the proper and the most effective techniques of interpersonal relationships and health care. For example, the importance of personal and communal health practices and standards were addressed in the health related course. The training received in communications skills was important for the relationships carried on with adults during most of the project. With some formal education and the ability to interact effectively and maturely with adults, it was hoped that they would learn how to become the future leaders of their respective communities.

In order to gain cooperation from the gang leaders, it was necessary from the beginning for project officials to promise them employment upon completion of the program's objectives. More than anything else, it was this commitment to long-term employability that attracted the gang leaders to the project. It was important for getting the gang leaders to listen and then to engage in the program, and it was also responsible for what appeared to be a high degree of emotional involvement with it.

Krisberg (1974) has reported that from its origins, ULT had every reason to expect success. Initially, the program was adequately funded, with over $500,000 allotted to it annually. The project also shared considerable support from the surrounding communities. Residents in the areas where the program was most intensely involved generally supported it and found it to be of benefit to their neighborhoods.

Although the Urban Leadership Training Program met with initial positive results and support, its funding was reduced and eventually eliminated. It is not entirely clear why this occurred, but ULT, as a "soft money" program, was by its very nature vulnerable to a reduction in financial support. Those closest to the program felt it to be on the right path to curbing juvenile gang criminality (Krisberg 1974). When one considers the broad approach taken by ULT project officials—placing emphasis on education as well as providing training in community relations—the possibilities for success appeared strong, if not for all 22 gang leaders, at least for some of them.

Unfortunately, the cynicism and doubts attached to efforts such as the Urban Leadership Training Program were not totally circumvented, particularly as they related to the promises of employment. When the program's funding was terminated, many of its participants became outraged, for they felt that they had been betrayed, especially after all of the work and hope they placed into it. After all, a primary reason for cooperating with it in the first place was to gain the skills and the contacts needed to find placement in a good paying job. For some of the gang leaders, this meant returning to participation in illegal activities. Others turned to heavy use of narcotics. The loss of funding, and particularly the inability to place the program participants in good jobs, was a failure of implementation from which the program participants were apparently unable to recover.

Grants to Gangs

During the late 1960s, federal funds were granted to gangs for community development in an effort to influence gang behavior. The assumption was that the leadership skills of gang leaders and the energies of their followers could be redirected into more constructive community service activities. Supergangs such as the Black P. Stone Nation and the Disciples received substantial grants, but the results were disastrous for several reasons (Short 1976a). Gang leaders lacked the organizational skills necessary to operate large scale programs. They also lacked the political sophistication to obtain community support to promote social change. Finally, there were instances of fraud and corruption in which the funds were misappropriated. The gangs were never effectively politicized, and they failed to develop viable social programs. The programs were poorly supervised and monitored, and official opposition, particularly by the police, undermined some of the programs. The result, according to Short (1976a), was an overwhelming failure.

The El Monte Police Department Gang Employment Program

El Monte, California, a community of nearly 80,000 citizens, is located on the east central side of Los Angeles. The city has had a significant gang problem, which has involved trafficking in heroin, violence (especially intergang fights), and gang graffiti. The gang phenomenon produced the normal citizen and police responses, ranging from extensive apprehension of gang members to social programs aimed at providing gang members with alternatives to their illegal activities. In the early 1980s, the police department of El Monte initiated a gang employment program, the objectives of which included (Willman and Snortum 1982) (1) obtaining information on job leads, (2) informing gang members about the possibilities of employment, (3) preparing gang members for job interviews through role playing situations, (4) instructing gang members on job application procedures, (5) arranging transportation for gang members to job interviews and to the first day of work, and (6) opening lines of communication with the proper police officials in order to discuss any problems arising from employment.

Initially, the gang employment program targeted gang leaders. Within the first few years, however, non-leaders became eligible for participation. Nearly three years into the program, the community relations office of the El Monte police department (the unit responsible for implementing and monitoring the program) undertook a follow-up analysis of the effects of the program and found that slightly over 50 percent of the participants were still employed, with only 9 percent having experienced additional troubles with the law. Although the data appeared encouraging, the department decided to take a more in-depth look at the effectiveness of the program. A scientifically-oriented study was commissioned.

A quasi-experimental research design was used to test for the effects of the program prior to and after involvement in it. Two comparison groups were established, an experimental group and a control group. Both groups were comprised of 100 subjects, matched on the basis of age, ethnicity, gang membership, and sex. The dependent variable of interest was detention. Willman and Snortum (1985) reported no significant differences between the post-detention rates of the experimental as compared to the control subjects. Gang members who went through the employment program were as likely to have encountered problems with the law as were those members who had no relationship to it. At all stages of the project, the experimental subjects were facing official contact with the police as frequently as the controls. These findings applied equally to property offenses as well as crimes committed against the person.

In their report on the effects of the gang employment program on criminal gang activities, Willman and Snortum failed to adequately address the reasons for its apparent ineffectiveness. Instead, they chose to discuss some plausible side benefits of the program on police-community relations. In this respect, the authors noted that as a result of the project, there was improved communication between the residents of the area and police officials. Still, we are left wondering why the program fell short of its goals. Since the gang employment program was not totally unlike other gang intervention strategies that also met with limited success, it is possible to speculate on why it did not achieve its objectives.

One possible interpretation is that the program itself lacked adequate human resources needed to constantly monitor the on-the-job as well as the nonworking hours behaviors of the experimental subjects. It is altogether possible that the gang members themselves gained very little of any direct positive value from their employment experiences. Just because a gang member gets a job doesn't mean that he or she will actually like it or gain anything of significance from it. Little was ever mentioned about the nature of the jobs offered to the gang members.

It is also unclear with whom the experimental subjects interacted after working hours. If they continued to mingle in their gang milieus and carry on friendships with past criminal associates, then any positive effects of their employment opportunities might have been negated by continuing their gang contacts. In addition, it is also possible that the youths might have spent their incomes on illegal drugs and on alcohol. Therefore, they may have used a positive benefit of the program to continue in their self-defeating behaviors. The problem is that, given the limited information provided by project officials, we may never know why the gang employment program failed to achieve its main objective.

MIXED OR MULTIMODAL APPROACHES

Based on limited successes from different single-mode interventions, it seems reasonable to consider whether a mixed approach may be appropriate. One example of this was discussed in connection with the GREAT program. As Monnet (1995) noted, the GREAT program in Las Cruces, New Mexico, operated in an environment that included gang suppression efforts and the provision of alternative, prosocial activities. Rather than focusing on an attempt to separate the effects of the different programs, it may be appropriate to consider whether a combined, multimodal approach may, by virtue of its inclusion of multiple modes of intervention, be more effective than a single-mode approach. This seems especially worth considering in light of the evidence, cited at the beginning of the chapter, that for individuals, multimodal strategies appear to work better than unimodal approaches.

Mobilization Against Youth Street Gangs in Portland, Oregon (National Conference on Juvenile Justice 1994), is one example of a mixed or multimodal approach to dealing with gangs. It possesses many characteristics of reaction or suppression programs, but also includes an effort to prevent gang behaviors before they begin, and incorporates a broad range of service providers and services. Citizens' groups; neighborhood associations; government entities; the school system; community-based programs; drug and alcohol programs; juvenile justice programs; the criminal justice system, including the police; residential treatment programs; and business and industry are all included under the umbrella of this program, all having a stake in the gang problem, and all brought together in an effort to form a cooperative, comprehensive approach to dealing with gangs.

With local, state, and federal dollars in short supply, the community has agreed to attack the youth gang problem as a unified whole. For example, the business community is attempting to create employment opportunities for Portland youths, with the objective of discouraging adolescents from future gang member or "wannabe" status. Youngsters who are perceived by the school system to be "at risk" and possible gangbangers are referred to appropriate resources, such as special education services, family counseling, and drug or alcohol education, in an effort to prevent their joining gangs and becoming involved in gang-related illegal behavior.

Integral to this model is the decision of Portland citizens that no group or organization working alone can solve the juvenile gang problem. In particular, claims of professional turf or territoriality, which may limit gang prevention or reaction efforts, are discouraged. Representatives from the different parts of the Portland program meet on a frequent basis to encourage cooperation among agencies and to evaluate their progress. Once again, however, it is necessary to repeat the litany: potentially promising, but not evaluated. Certainly the multimodal approach, which includes components that in the past have been slightly (counseling) to moderately (employment) successful elsewhere appears to be on the right track.

CONCLUSION

According to Lundman (1984) and to others, cited above, who have reviewed the community organization approach to gang intervention, there is no evidence that community organization works as a tactic to control gang activity, despite the impression by some officials (Spergel and Curry 1990) that it helps alleviate chronic gang problems. Attempts at social intervention may have the opposite of the intended effect. According to Miller (1976), attempts to channel gangs into conventional lines of action have just added to the behavioral repertoire of gangs. Klein and Crawford (1967) and Short and Strodtbeck (1965) indicated that disrupting the internal structure of gangs to diminish gang delinquency is unlikely to be successful, but instead tends to increase the cohesiveness of gangs and to increase gang delinquency. There is little indication that gang suppression, perhaps the most common response to gang delinquency and especially gang violence, is successful in reducing illegal behavior by gangs or gang members. The individuals who are incarcerated are simply replaced, and the illegal activity continues unabated.

Klein and Crawford (1967) suggested that reducing external sources of cohesiveness in gangs would be followed by dissolution of gangs and reductions in gang membership, but none of the programs reviewed here seem to be terribly successful in that area. Most promising, perhaps, have been the programs that focused on providing opportunities to gang members, but political opposition and lack of funding has often undercut such programs before they could be evaluated. Miller (1990) has suggested that the inability to form a national strategy, coupled with an unwillingness to face the problems of poverty and education that provide the context for gang life, and also a lack of theoretical basis or empirical evaluation for anti-gang programs, have resulted in a predictable failure to control juvenile gangs.

If the theoretical propositions set out in Chapter 9 are correct, ameliorating the juvenile gang problem can only be accomplished by a combination of macrosocial and microsocial intervention efforts. Suppression through police activity alone is unlikely to succeed, as is community organization without individual intervention. Because the social disorganization of the community provides the context within which the gang develops, and because social disorganization influences the microsocial causes of gang membership and gang delinquency, any successful strategy for controlling juvenile gangs must include a component aimed at reducing urban poverty and other elements of social disorganization. At the microsocial level, the most promising tactics would involve interventions to make schools and families more effective as social institutions, and to increase conventional bonding. This in turn would help reduce both gang membership and gang delinquency. Access to legitimate opportunities is also important, but this would presumably be a result of successful interventions to reduce social disorganization at the community and neighborhood level.

A potentially critical element in any gang intervention program is persistence. If we may use a medical analogy, the gang problem is a chronic disease, like a distended disc in the lower back, not an acute condition, like an infection. The cure is not a short term program that can be applied once and then forgotten, analogous to taking an antibiotic for a limited time, after which the disease will go away. Instead, given the persistent nature of the conditions that give rise to gangs, the appropriate course of action may be an ongoing program of enforcement (analogous to a pain reliever, reducing the symptoms) and provision of opportunities for employment, education, and alternatives to gang activity (analogous to daily stretching and strengthening exercises, preventing the symptoms from recurring), recognizing that the conditions, social disorganization and urban poverty (the distended disk) that produces the gangs and their illegal behavior (the pain in the lower back—an analogy sure to please some gang observers) is not likely to be cured. Instead, the focus may need to be on a long-term commitment to measures that minimize the adverse effects of those conditions on the body politic, multiple measures that deal with different aspects of the problem (relieving the pain, stretching and strengthening the back muscles).

In general, programs successful at reducing delinquency generally should be successful in reducing gang membership and gang delinquency, because the influences on delinquency are similar to the influences on gang membership and gang delinquency. As a start, Lundman (1984) provides a useful review of delinquency prevention and control programs, including some of the more important programs reviewed in this chapter. Given the absence of clear success in past attempts at juvenile gang intervention, the continuing spread of gang activity to previously unaffected cities, and the improbability of the massive social change that would be necessary to make major inroads against poverty, joblessness, and the lack of educational and other resources that characterize socially disorganized inner-city neighborhoods, the prospects for making serious progress in really solving the nation's gang problem appear to be bleak. If this conclusion appears too pessimistic, consider the fact that after over sixty years of gang intervention projects, beginning with the Chicago Area Project in 1932, we appear to have made little or no progress in ameliorating or controlling the juvenile gang problem.

Chapter Twelve

THE FUTURE OF JUVENILE GANGS

Toffler (1970) quotes a Chinese proverb, which supposedly says, "To prophesy is extremely difficult ... especially with respect to the future." That difficulty notwithstanding, we choose in this chapter to speculate about the future of juvenile gang theory, juvenile gang research, and juvenile gang policy. To some extent, especially with regard to juvenile gang policy, we do so in the spirit of Ray Bradbury, who is quoted by Clark (1984) as saying, "I don't try to predict the future—I try to prevent it." Judging from the past five decades of experience with juvenile gang policy, there is much worth preventing.

JUVENILE GANG THEORY

From 1965 to 1990, juvenile gang theory was largely stagnant. In part, this may be traced to the reduced attention paid to juvenile gangs in the 1970s and part of the 1980s. It is puzzling, however, that greater attention was not given to the use of new integrated theoretical perspectives to explain juvenile gang phenomena. For the future, two divergent and competing paths seem likely for juvenile gang theory. One is the use of old (Shaw and McKay 1942; Cloward and Ohlin 1960) or new (Elliott et al. 1979; Hawkins and Weis 1985; Thornberry 1987) integrated theoretical perspectives, quite possibly perspectives other than those cited here, to explain juvenile gang phenomena. More explicit recognition of the theoretical integration present in the older theories of Shaw and McKay and of Cloward and Ohlin may also be expected. The second path is the abandonment of theory in purely descriptive work, especially ethnographic work, on juvenile gangs. The latter path may yield rich descriptions and insights, but the former will become dominant in the study of juvenile gangs.

Predicting which theories will be included in integrated perspectives on juvenile gangs is a little more difficult. Clearly, social ecological and learning theories, elements of which are present in Shaw and McKay

301

(1942), Cloward and Ohlin (1960), and Elliott et al. (1979; 1985; 1989) should be included in any complete theory of juvenile gangs. Elements of control theory, common to all of both the older and newer integrated theories, should also be included. Arguments may be made for or against the inclusion of strain and subcultural theories, insofar as the former are separable from social disorganization (social ecology) and insofar as the latter are separable from social learning theories. Integrated theories of juvenile gangs may be further extended by the inclusion of elements of power control theory (Hagan et al. 1985), rational choice (Cornish and Clarke 1986), and routine activities (Felson and Cohen 1980) theories. Further empirical research may help clarify whether social disorganization generally, or poverty, or inequality more specifically, is most useful in explaining juvenile gang activity. There certainly remains ample room for theoretical development in the study of juvenile gangs.

JUVENILE GANG RESEARCH

Spergel (1990:177) noted, "Participant observation has been the favored mode of study, at times resulting in researcher overidentification with subjects. Insufficient use has been made of official statistics, systematic self-reports, or surveys of youths or adults in high-crime or gang-crime areas." Encouragingly, research of the kind suggested by Spergel has been undertaken, for example by Fagan (1989, 1990) and in the Denver Youth Survey (Esbensen and Huizinga 1990, 1991; see Chapter 9), and the results of the latter research are now becoming available.

Gangs appear to be more prevalent in the United States than elsewhere (Hood and Sparks 1970), even allowing for the demographic influence of the size of the urban adolescent population. Better comparative research on juvenile gangs may help us to understand why, and may inform our own policies with respect to juvenile gangs. There is also a critical need for good empirical theory testing research. Even more critical, perhaps, is the need for good program evaluation research. We need to know not only whether a particular program works but for whom the program works better or worse, so that the program may identify appropriate targets for intervention, and how well different programs are implemented in different settings. For example, if our theory is correct, employment programs should be targeted primarily at older adolescents, age 18 and over, and other interventions (particularly school-based interventions) should be used for youths in early and middle adolescence. The issue of the effectiveness of employment programs for reducing gang membership and gang delinquency is further addressed below.

JUVENILE GANG POLICY

Any program of intervention or change should be based on the answers to two questions about the phenomenon that is targeted for change. First, what are the causes of the phenomenon? Second, which of those causes are amenable or vulnerable to deliberate change? The first question identifies the things that need to be changed in order for the target phenomenon to be affected. The second question, as important as the first, identifies those points in the causal process at which deliberate, planned change is most likely to have some effect, the points for which manipulation based on policy is a practical option.

Community Organization and Area Projects

Evidence on the effectiveness of area projects such as the Chicago Area Project and the Boston Mid-City Project is mixed, at best. In some cases, the evaluation designs are such that it is nearly impossible to draw firm conclusions about the effects of the programs on juvenile gang delinquency or juvenile gang activity more generally (Lundman 1984). Although there is sometimes anecdotal evidence of success (Spergel and Curry 1990), the general conclusion appears to be that such projects have not provided any compelling evidence of success in dealing with the juvenile gang problem. National support for such programs therefore appears to be inadvisable. Local implementation of area projects may, however, be appropriate either to test the utility of an area program under certain specific local conditions, or to examine the impact of incorporating new elements into traditional area programs.

Community organization and social area programs may be expected to fail insofar as they fail to change the objective social conditions of poverty, single parenthood, transiency, and other elements of social disorganization within targeted neighborhoods. They are also likely to fail insofar as they fail to affect, directly or indirectly, the patterns of association with friends and family members who are or have been active in gangs, the ability of schools, families, and other social institutions to provide for the needs of youths in socially disorganized areas, and the broad array of reward structures within the community that make gang membership attractive to adolescents.

Social Intervention Programs

Social intervention programs such as detached worker programs, other outreach programs, and preadjudication counseling programs do not appear to have been successful with gangs, and there is some evidence that suggests that such programs may have been counterproductive, may have made the gang problem worse than it was before the introduction of the program. As with community organization programs and social area projects, national support for such efforts seems to be unwarranted, but local funding and evaluation of such programs on specific populations, or to assess the impact of particular innovations in such programs, may be warranted.

Social intervention programs are likely to fail in part because the magnitude of the intervention is typically puny in comparison to the magnitude of the forces that operate on the individual in the neighborhood or community setting. According to Sutherland (1947), the impact of association with criminal or noncriminal others depends on the priority (which came first), duration (how long has the association been occurring), intensity (how important is the association to the individual), and frequency (how often does the association occur) of that association. Spending a few minutes or hours a week with a detached gang worker or counselor seems unlikely to have an impact on adolescents who have spent much of their lives in association with others from whom they have learned that illegal behavior is permissible or tolerable, for pragmatic reasons, under many circumstances.

In addition, the detached gang worker or counselor may, in an attempt to build rapport with the gang, refrain from applying negative sanctions when he or she witnesses illegal behavior. This may be important for building rapport with the gang, but it may also send the message that illegal behavior is, at least up to some point, acceptable. If the detached worker or counselor further emphasizes pragmatic reasons for not engaging in gang delinquency, he or she reinforces the pragmatic, nonmoralistic rhetoric (Hagedorn 1988; Schwendinger and Schwendinger 1985; Short and Strodtbeck 1965) of other gang members, and makes illegal behavior appear to be a tolerable, but not preferred, activity. This, in addition to the unintended reinforcement of gang cohesion discussed earlier, may make detached worker, outreach, and counseling programs the most problematic approach to the reduction of gang membership and gang delinquency.

Opportunity Programs

Results regarding opportunity programs are somewhat mixed, and further confounded by the clear failure of some opportunity programs to implement the changes they intended, often because funding was discontinued. Opportunity in two areas, school and employment, has been singled out by theory (Cloward and Ohlin 1960; Merton 1938), research (Hagedorn 1988; Vigil 1988), and policy recommendations (Duster 1987; Johnstone 1981; Johnstone 1983; Miller 1990) as critical for the reduction of gang activity generally and of gang delinquency in particular.

Employment Opportunity

Hagedorn (1988) asserted that with respect to juvenile gangs, "while full, meaningful employment will not solve all the problems, it would solve most of them." Some writers have suggested that "drying out" the urban areas of impoverishment is critical to eliminating gangs (Johnstone 1981), and that until serious reform is undertaken, impoverished inner-city areas will continue to serve as prime areas for gangs and recruitment to gangs (Johnstone 1983). According to Miller (1990:277), "A particularly vexing reason for the nation's failure to solve its gang problem lies in a pervasive reluctance to face squarely the issue of the social context of gang crime. The social context of gang life and the social characteristics of most gang members entail a set of extremely sensitive issues involving social class and ethnicity that are highly charged in U.S. society, and evoke strong passions." Duster (1987:309) asserted: "The nation is past the point where simple solutions will solve the current problem of unemployment, especially that of inner-city Black youth. No longer will short-term job training or job creation programs suffice. Instead, what is needed are new approaches that will produce a new mix of skills, experience, and qualifications that can provide entry to viable work careers."

The focus on employment needs to be split into two areas: adolescent employment, including employment opportunities for juvenile gang members, and adult employment. *In early and middle adolescence, from ages*

12 to 17, employment is unlikely to reduce, and may even increase, illegal behavior. In later adolescence and early adulthood, from age 18 onward, employment should reduce illegal behavior, especially if the employment is in a job that produces a good income and that provides opportunities for career advancement.

In early and middle adolescence, the culturally appropriate "employment" in the United States and other modern industrial societies is the completion of primary and then secondary education. Any activity, including employment, that distracts the individual from this task potentially constitutes a risk factor for illegal behavior. The money earned from employment potentially makes the adolescent more independent and reduces parental control over the adolescent (Cullen et al. 1985; Wofford 1991). In addition, serious concerns about occupational careers are relatively rare in early and middle adolescence (Schwendinger and Schwendinger 1985; Sullivan 1989), so it is unlikely that they would have any substantial effects on gang membership or gang delinquency.

In later adolescence and early adulthood, however, such concerns become important, and the provision of good job opportunities to late adolescent and early adult gang members may facilitate and hasten their departure from the gang. This may be especially relevant to gang leaders, who tend to be older than other gang members. In support of these recommendations regarding employment, Wofford (1991) provided evidence from the National Youth Survey that employment was positively associated with minor and index offending in adolescence (up to age 17 for index offending, up to age 20 for minor offending), but that employment was negatively associated with minor and serious offending in young adulthood.

Adult employment may have beneficial consequences that are not limited to juvenile gangs. According to O'Hare (1985:22), "obtaining a job or pay raise is by far the most likely path out of poverty, particularly for men and people in households headed by men. Overall, increased earnings account for 80.3 percent of moves out of poverty." O'Hare also notes that job losses or pay cuts are the most common reason for entry into poverty status. Furthermore, adult employment may have a substantial effect on family structure. O'Hare (1985:32) cited evidence that increases in female-headed families were influenced by "the growing economic independence of women and the relatively poor economic situation of black men." Many African American women, it is suggested, may leave a marriage or not get married because of the shortage of

African American men with the ability to support a family. O'Hare also cited evidence that among both African American and European (non-Hispanic) American men, men with higher incomes were more likely to be married. Employment thus appears to influence the family's ability to provide not only material resources, but also resources of time and parental supervision. Insofar as these affect illegal behavior and gang membership for adolescents, employment of adults, particularly parents, may be expected to reduce illegal behavior and gang membership among adolescents.

School Intervention Programs

In early and middle adolescence, and even earlier in childhood, the school may be the most appropriate arena for intervention to reduce gang membership, gang delinquency, and juvenile delinquency generally. Educational attainment, involvement, commitment, and performance are consistently lower among more frequent and serious delinquents than among less frequent and serious delinquents, although their effects appear to operate indirectly, through association with delinquent peers (Elliott et al. 1989; Elliott et al. 1985; Hawkins and Lishner 1985; Hirschi 1969; Kercher 1988).

Although earlier research indicated that dropping out of school was associated with lower rates of illegal behavior for some adolescents (Elliott and Voss 1974), more recent research by Thornberry et al. (1985) indicated that adolescents who drop out of school have higher rates of illegal behavior both before and after they drop out. One explanation for this discrepancy may be the increase in educational "credentials" required for employment (Wilson 1987).

For individuals living in the poorest inner-city areas, access to education may be inadvertently limited by the schools themselves. The broader picture of problems in American primary and secondary education is detailed by the National Commission on Excellence in Education (1983). Specific to impoverished, inner-city, predominantly African American neighborhoods and their schools, Wilson (1987:58) wrote that data on educational attainment in inner-city schools "suggest a shockingly high degree of educational retardation in the inner city. In short, the communities of the underclass are plagued by massive joblessness, flagrant lawlessness, and low-achieving schools, and therefore tend to be avoided by outsiders."

Both for purposes of reducing gang activity and for broader purposes

involving education as a good in and of itself and as a means of opportunity in other areas, changes in schools, particularly inner-city schools,
need to accomplish three objectives: insuring a safe environment for
students (Office of Juvenile Justice and Delinquency Prevention 1989b);
providing an adequate education to students (National Commission on
Excellence in Education 1983); and retaining students long enough to
provide them with an adequate education to compete in a job market
that increasingly requires educational credentials and fundamental literacy and numeracy as prerequisites for most jobs.

There are programs of educational intervention that show promise for
different levels of education. For high school students, Law Related
Education (Johnson and Hunter 1987; Social Science Education Consortium and Center for Action Research 1981), a program involving
cooperative, interactive learning about the criminal law and participation of criminal justice personnel as teachers, appears to have some
favorable effects on delinquency and correlates of delinquency, *if* the
program is properly implemented, but failures in implementation may
produce counterproductive results. At the high school and even more at
the middle school level, Positive Action Through Holistic Education
(PATHE), a program that included active participation of parents and
students as well as staff in some policy decisions, and also included
cooperative learning with heterogeneous groups of students, appears to
help reduce illegal behavior (Gottfredson 1986). Also at the middle or
junior high school level, Gang Resistance Education and Training
(GREAT), a theoretically-based program with an explicit agenda for
evaluation, shows some promise, but a final assessment must await the
results of evaluations that are currently underway. At the elementary
school level, a combined parent training and teacher training intervention in the early grades of elementary school, based on Hawkins and
Weis' (1985) social development model (Hawkins and Lam 1987; Hawkins
et al. 1991) appears promising. At the preschool level, the Perry Preschool project, a Headstart type preschool project (Berrueta-Clement et
al. 1987) has reported favorable results for both educational attainment
and delinquency prevention. Some of these programs, and other programs for delinquency prevention, are reviewed in Dryfoos (1990).

Other Interventions

Programs to provide basic necessities such as shelter, clothing, and
medical care may also have unanticipated consequences, either positive

or negative, for juvenile gangs. An important point about these programs and programs for improving education and employment opportunities is that such programs are not justified solely on the basis of their impacts on juvenile gang membership and delinquency. There are other, even more compelling reasons for their adoption. A second point is that it may be necessary to implement some of these programs on a national rather than a local level, or at least to provide national funding for local programs. This is because the expense of substantial employment provision or educational reform is likely to exceed the financial capacity of local governments, and because the local governments most in need of such programs may be least able to generate sufficient funding.

Gang Suppression Programs

Gang suppression programs may temporarily reduce or displace juvenile gang activity. In the long term, however, they probably do neither. Just as official sanctions appear to be ineffective in reducing delinquent behavior generally, they appear to be ineffective in reducing gang membership and gang delinquency. From a learning theory perspective, this is understandable. Self-report studies indicate that for any given offense, apprehension is unlikely. If deterrence theory is correct, and if certainty of punishment is an important element of deterrence, then the very low certainty of punishment for delinquency prevents official deterrence from having any substantial effect. The infrequency of punishment, and the ability of the individual to bear the punishment if he or she is apprehended, should, according to learning theory, result in a higher, not lower, probability of committing crime. In general, the literature on official deterrence effect indicates little if any deterrent effect (Paternoster 1987).

Informal deterrence is another matter altogether. When the negative sanctions come from the neighborhood or community, from people with whom the adolescent is likely to come into everyday contact, both theory (Cloward and Ohlin 1960) and evidence (Sullivan 1989) suggest that the adolescent will change her or his behavior to avoid those negative sanctions. Part of the reason for the influence of peer groups and relatives on illegal behavior may be the sanctions, verbal (approval or disapproval), physical (corporal punishment), or instrumental (provision or deprivation of money or privileges) (Etzioni 1964), that they apply. Other reasons include modeling and expressions of values, norms, or what Sutherland (1947) called "definitions" favorable or unfavorable to the violation of the law. The individuals with whom an individual interacts on a day to day basis may be far more important in influencing behavior than counselors or outreach workers can ever hope to be.

Drugs and Juvenile Gangs

Spergel (1990) suggested that drug use and drug dealing are neither causes nor consequences of gang involvement in violent activity. Gang violence is just part of historical territorial, status, and other gang conflict. Kleiman and Smith (1990), however, suggested that illegal drug markets do increase gang violence, and that drugs contribute more to the gang problem than gangs contribute to the drug problem. They project that "Drug markets will leave more corpses behind them than markets not so dominated. Routine drug enforcement may have little to contribute to gang control" (Kleiman and Smith 1990:103). Evidence suggests that illegal behavior and gang membership may both precede drug use. Reduction of the availability of illicit drugs would thus be unlikely to affect the probability of joining gangs or of involvement in gang delinquency. It is possible, however, that the availability of illicit drugs increases the likelihood that a social, criminal, or violent gang will evolve into a retreatist gang, and that the drug trade may be instrumental in the evolution of some social or violent gangs into criminal gangs. Illicit drug use also appears to prolong involvement in serious illegal behavior (Huizinga et al. 1989).

What impact would drug legalization have on juvenile gangs? The general issue of legalization has been debated elsewhere (Weisheit 1990; Tonry and Wilson 1990). Briefly, the prohibition against drugs has the effect of inflating prices for drugs, and there is some evidence to suggest that addicts are involved in more illegal activity while they are actively using drugs than when they are not. One interpretation of this is that addicts commit crime to obtain money for drugs. An alternative interpretation is that individuals who are actively involved in crime generally are more likely to be active in drug use, as one form of illegal behavior, even though there is no non-spurious causal link between their drug use and their other illegal behavior. If now-illicit drugs were decriminalized, then (1) their prices would go down and (2) more people would use them with greater frequency.

The effect of legalization of drugs such as marijuana and cocaine on gang activity is likely to be no more profound than the effect of legalization of alcohol was on organized crime. Criminal gangs may simply find a different "racket" (extortion, auto theft) to obtain money, although other options may not be as easy or lucrative as the drug trade. Perhaps more importantly, the general increase in drug use would be reflected in greater use of (legalized) drugs among gang members. Potentially, this could result in a higher proportion of retreatist gangs, relative to the other gang types. Overall, changes in the availability of illicit drugs would probably have little impact on gang membership or gang delinquency. The principal impact would be on the organization of the gang, and particularly on the relative prevalence of different types of gangs.

Gun Control and Gangs

As noted in Chapter 1, gangs have become increasingly well armed. Altercations involving firearms are more likely to result in death than altercations involving other weapons (Wright et al. 1983; Morris and Hawkins 1970). In general, with some qualifications (Conklin 1989: 322–328), the literature on firearms and crime suggests that rates of crime, particularly homicides, would be lower with effective gun control laws. One difficulty with making gun control laws effective, however, is that gun control laws on any but a national level may be circumvented by, for example, purchasing a handgun whose purchase is prohibited or strictly regulated in one jurisdiction (e.g., Massachusetts) in another jurisdiction (e.g., Texas) where its purchase is unregulated or weakly regulated. Klein (1995a:242) observes, "It's hard to be a gang researcher these days without also being strongly in favor of gun control. I mean serious gun control, not just delaying tactics."

With regard to juvenile gangs, it is likely that many of the weapons they use were obtained illegally, but at some point someone obtained them legally. Drying up the available supply of some of the more lethal automatic and semiautomatic weapons might have some impact in reducing gang homicides. Even stricter gun control, especially at a national level, might have an even greater impact, perhaps not decreasing overall levels of gang violence, but decreasing the frequency of lethal violence. As with policies for employment and education, however, the justification for gun control lies not in its probable impact on the juvenile gang problem, but in its probable impact on problems on a much broader scale, problems of violence and homicide generally. If effective gun control can be implemented (and again, past experience and current conditions make this seem unlikely), it should decrease lethal violence generally, and incidentally decrease lethal violence by juvenile gangs.

Conclusion: Future Policy and Its Outcomes

Box 12.1 summarizes Miller's (1990) assessment of why the United States has failed to solve its gang problem. In a more positive vein, Miller suggests that we could make progress in solving the gang problem in the United States by developing a comprehensive national strategy, including a federal office of youth gang control, and by informing efforts in local communities based on a national-level perspective on gangs. In addition, gang control operations should be theoretically informed and empirically evaluated. Miller (1990:280) also concluded that "If youth gangs are a product of the circumstances of the lower class, eliminating or substantially changing these circumstances will eliminate or substantially reduce gang problems."

Our own expectation is that gang policy in the United States will continue to be fragmented, local, usually not informed by theory, sometimes not informed by research (and rarely informed by good, solid program evaluation research). We expect gang suppression to be the most frequently adopted strategy, followed by detached worker and counseling programs, and perhaps outreach programs to schools. These are the programs with the least promise for reducing the problems associated with juvenile gangs. The interventions with the best prospects for addressing the juvenile gang problem are interventions that involve long-term social change, and whose effects on gang membership and gang delinquency are likely to be indirect: programs involving the provision of employment, school reform, and secondarily gun control. We do not expect these programs to be implemented, evaluated, or to receive adequate funding to have any substantial impact on the juvenile gang problem in the United States.

Box 12.1: Why the U.S. has failed to solve its gang problem (Miller 1990:283).

The nation has failed to develop a comprehensive gang control strategy. The problem is viewed in local and parochial terms instead of from a national perspective. Programs are implemented in the absence of demonstrably valid theoretical rationales. Efforts to systematically evaluate program effectiveness have been virtually abandoned. Resources allocated to the gang problem are incommensurate with the severity of the problem. There is no organizational center of responsibility for gang problems anywhere in the United States. There is a deep-rooted reluctance to face up to the implications of the social context of gang life.

Programs that would have a more direct effect, especially on gang delinquency and gang membership, are difficult to conceive. There appears to be little we can do to directly alter patterns of interaction with relatives and friends. There do appear to be some interventions at the microsocial level that hold promise for improving the relationships between adolescents and their families and schools (Hawkins and Lam 1987; Hawkins et al. 1991), but these are likely to affect gang membership and delinquency only indirectly, by affecting patterns of association with gang members and nonmembers, with frequent and serious delinquents as opposed to infrequent or less serious delinquents. For the foreseeable future, absent major changes in social policy, juvenile gangs are likely to continue to form, to spread, and to continue their violent and other illegal behavior at rates comparable to those we see today.

CONCLUSION

Simple projections of past trends would suggest that juvenile activity will continue unabated into the foreseeable future, that juvenile gang violence will remain the same or perhaps escalate, that juvenile gangs will continue to recruit new members from an increasingly large population base, and that with the growth of suburban areas and small towns, juvenile gangs will become present and active in places largely untouched until now by juvenile gang activity. Old policies for coping with juvenile gangs will continue to be supported, despite their failure to make inroads into the gang problem, because of a need to "do something" (Hackler

1985) about the juvenile gang problem. Various new intervention programs, especially at the local level, will be proposed, tested, poorly evaluated, and found to be inadequate to deal with the juvenile gang problem. The outlook based on past trends is grim indeed. It suggests that our efforts at dealing with juvenile gangs are doomed to futility. We would suggest that if we do no better than to continue past efforts at juvenile gang intervention, futility is exactly what we can expect.

In view of past attempts at massive social change, particularly the "Great Society" programs of the 1960s, and in view of the current political climate in the United States, the prospects for implementing the types of changes in employment and education that would affect gang membership and gang delinquency appear dim, at best. Absent such changes, we expect the juvenile gang problem to be with us well into the future. Even if such programs were implemented tomorrow, however, it would take considerable time for their effects to be felt. Given the education, employment histories, and life experiences of the urban minority underclass in the United States today, and the involvement of present-day adolescents in juvenile gangs, it is likely to take three generations, beginning with the current generation of adolescents, before large-scale social programs have any impact on juvenile gangs. In the absence of such programs, however, juvenile gangs and their associated problems will be with us even longer.

Box 12.2: Prospects for the Future (Klein 1995a:187)

So what are the prospects for the future? In the next decade or so, is the gang picture likely to improve? I fear not. First, our approaches to intervention and control are likely to be more of what we have already seen. Second, street gangs are the by-product of urban problems likely to increase in severity. Third, we've allowed—indeed, we could not have prevented—the widespread diffusion of street gang culture. Finally, there are signs that our unique American street gang is emerging in other nations as some of their urban situations come more to resemble ours. . . . I apologize . . . for the pessimism, but I think it is simply realistic. . . .

If our expectations are pessimistic, we are not alone (see Klein's comments in Box 12.2), and our pessimism is based on over five decades of failure in dealing with the juvenile gang problem in the United States. On a more comforting note, like the ghost of Christmas future, we have tried to show not what must be, but what may be.

REFERENCES

Abrahamson, M. 1980. *Urban Sociology.* Second edition. Englewood Cliffs, NJ: Prentice-Hall.

Adams, Stuart. 1967. A cost approach to the assessment of gang rehabilitation techniques. *Journal of Research in Crime and Delinquency 4:*166–182.

Adler, F. 1975. *Sisters in Crime.* New York: McGraw-Hill.

Adler, P.A. and P. Adler 1983. Shifts and oscillations in deviant careers: The case of upper-level drug dealers and smugglers. *Social Problems 31:* 195-207.

Akers, R.L. 1985. *Deviant Behavior: A Social Learning Approach.* Third edition. Belmont, CA: Wadsworth.

Albanese, J.S. 1989. *Organized Crime in America.* Second edition. Cincinnati: Anderson.

Alcorn, D.S. 1978. *A Social Psychological Perspective on Deterrence: Development and Test of a Causal Model.* Ann Arbor, MI: University Microfilms.

Allen, H.E. 1995. The American dream and crime in the twenty-first century: Presidential address to the Academy of Criminal Justice Sciences. *Justice Quarterly* 12:427–445.

Anderson, E. 1994. The code of the streets. *The Atlantic Monthly,* 273: 80–94.

Arboit, K.M. 1995. A process evaluation of the G.R.E.A.T. program in the Torrance Unified School District. Paper presented at the 1995 annual meeting of the American Society of Criminology, Boston.

Armstrong, G. and M. Wilson. 1973. City politics and deviancy amplification. In I. Taylor and L. Taylor (eds.), *Politics and Deviance.* Harmondsworth, England: Penguin.

Asbury, H. 1927. *The Gangs of New York.* Garden City, NY: Garden City Publishing Company.

Augustine, Saint. 1949. *Confessions.* New York: Modern Library.

Bailey, G.W. and N.P. Unnithan. 1994. Gang homicides in California: A discriminant analysis. *Journal of Criminal Justice,* 22:267–275.

Baker, B. 1988. Gang murder rates get worse. *Los Angeles Times,* April 10.

Baker, R. 1988. Homeboys: Players in a deadly drama. *Los Angeles Times,* June 26.

Ball, R.A. and G.D. Curry. 1995. The logic of definition in criminology: purposes and methods for defining "gangs". *Criminology* 33:225–245.

Banerjee, Sumanta. 1980. India/Juvenile gangs. *New Society 51*(902):125.

Banks, K. 1985. A wave of gang violence. *Maclean's* 98 (April 8):50–51.

Barice, B. 1986. A reporter at large: The crazy life. *New Yorker* 62 (November):97–130.

Bartol, C.R. and A.M. Bartol. 1989. *Juvenile Delinquency: A Systems Approach.* Englewood Cliffs, NJ: Prentice-Hall.

Bastian, L.D. 1993. Criminal victimization 1992: A National Crime Victimization

Survey Report. *Bureau of Justice Statistics Bulletin.* Washington, DC: U.S. Department of Justice, Bureau of Justice Statistics.

Bastian, L.D. 1995. Criminal victimization 1992: National Crime Victimization Survey. *Bureau of Justice Statistics Bulletin.* Washington, DC: U.S. Department of Justice, Bureau of Justice Statistics.

Bastian, L.D. and B.M. Taylor. 1991. *School Crime: A National Crime Victimization Survey Report.* Washington, DC: U.S. Department of Justice, Bureau of Justice Statistics.

Baur, E.J. 1964. The trend of juvenile offences in the Netherlands and the United States. *Journal of Criminal Law, Criminology, and Police Science 55:* 359–369.

Beales, R. 1975. In search of the historical child: Miniature adulthood and youth in colonial New England. *American Quarterly 27:* 379-398.

Becker, H.S. 1963. *The Outsiders.* New York: Free Press.

Bellamy, J. 1973. *Crime and Public Order in England in the Later Middle Ages.* London: Routledge and Kegan Paul.

Bernard, H.R. 1988. *Research Methods in Cultural Anthropology.* Newbury Park, CA: Sage.

Bernard, T.J. 1987. Testing structural strain theories. *Journal of Research in Crime and Delinquency 24:* 262–280.

Bernard, W. 1949. *Jailbait.* New York: Greenberg.

Berrueta-Clement, J.R., L.J. Schweinhart, W.S. Barnett, and D.P. Weikart. 1987. The effects of early education intervention on crime and delinquency in adolescence and early adulthood. In J.D. Burchard and S.N. Burchard (eds.), *Prevention of Delinquent Behavior.* Newbury Park, CA: Sage.

Bibb, M. 1967. Gang related services of Mobilization for Youth. In M. Klein (ed.), *Juvenile Gangs in Context: Theory, Research, and Action.* Englewood Cliffs, NJ: Prentice-Hall.

Binder, A., G. Geis, and D. Bruce. 1988. *Juvenile Delinquency: Historical, Cultural, and Legal Perspectives.* New York: Macmillan.

Binder, D. 1990. Violence by skinheads startling East Germans. *New York Times International,* August 21, 1990: A–2.

Bittner, E. 1970. *The Functions of the Police in Modern Society.* Washington, DC: U.S. Government Printing Office.

Bjerregaard, B. and C. Smith. 1993. Gender differences in gang participation, delinquency, and substance abuse. *Journal of Quantitative Criminology 4:* 329-355.

Black, D. and A.J. Reiss. 1970. Police control of juveniles. *American Sociological Review 35:* 63-77.

Blau, J. and P. Blau. 1982. The cost of inequality: Metropolitan structure and violent crime. *American Sociological Review 47:* 114–129.

Bloch, H.A. and A. Niederhoffer. 1958. *The Gang: A Study of Adolescent Behavior.* New York: Philosophical Library.

Block, C.B. 1985. *Lethal Violence in Chicago Over Seventeen Years: Homicides Known to the Police.* Chicago: Illinois Criminal Justice Information Authority, Statistical Analysis Center.

Block, C.R. and R. Block. 1993. *Street Gang Crime in Chicago.* Washington, DC: National Institute of Justice.

Blumstein, A. 1995. Violence by young people: why the deadly nexus? *Juvenile Justice Journal* (August) 2–9.

Blumstein, A., J. Cohen, J.A. Roth, and C.A. Visher. 1986. *Criminal Careers and "Career Criminals," Volume I.* Washington, DC: National Academy Press.

Bobrowski, L.J. 1988. *Collecting, Organizing, and Reporting Street Gang Crime.* Chicago: Special Functions Group, Chicago Police Department, Mimeo.

Bookin-Weiner, H. and R. Horowitz. 1983. The end of the youth gang: Fad or fact? *Criminology 21:*585–602.

Bordua, D.J. 1961. Delinquency subcultures: Sociological interpretations of gang delinquency. *Annals of the American Academy of Political and Social Science 338:* 119–136.

Bogardus, E. 1943. Gangs of Mexican-American youth. *Sociology and Social Research 28:*55–66.

Bouma, D. 1969. *Kids and Cops: A Study in Mutual Hostility.* Grand Rapids, MI: Eerdman Publishing.

Bowker, L. 1978. *Women, Crime, and the Criminal Justice System.* Lexington, MA: D.C. Heath.

Bowker, L. and M.W. Klein. 1983. The etiology of female juvenile delinquency and gang membership: A test of psychological and social structural explanations. *Adolescence 18:*739–751.

Bowker, L.H., H.S. Gross, and M.W. Klein. 1980. Female participation in delinquent gang activities. *Adolescence 15:*509–519.

Braithwaite, J. 1977. Australian delinquency: Research and practical considerations. In P. Wilson (ed.) *Delinquency in Australia: A Critical Appraisal.* St. Lucia, Australia: University of Queensland Press.

Brantingham, P.J. and P.L. Brantingham (eds.). 1981. *Environmental Criminology.* Beverly Hills, CA: Sage.

Breen, L. and M.M. Allen. 1983. Gang program: psychological and law enforcement implications. *FBI Law Enforcement Bulletin 52:*19–24.

Bremner, R.H. (ed.). 1970. *Children and Youth in America: A Documentary History. Volume 1: 1600–1865.* Cambridge, MA: Harvard University Press.

Breznitz, T. 1975. Juvenile delinquents' perceptions of own and others' commitment to delinquency. *Journal of Research in Crime and Delinquency 12:*124–132.

Briar, S. and I. Piliavin. 1965. Delinquency, situational inducements, and commitment to conformity. *Social Problems 13:*35–45.

Brown, W.K. 1977. Black female gangs in Philadelphia. *International Journal of Offender Therapy and Comparative Criminology 21:*221–228.

Brown, W.K. 1978. Graffiti, identity, and the delinquent gang. *International Journal of Offender Therapy and Comparative Criminology 22:*39–45.

Bruman, C. 1983. Boat people in a new land. *Maclean's* 96 (October):19.

Brunner, R. Focal points of juvenile crime: Typology and conditions. In *Juvenile Crime and Resocialization.* Congress Report. Stuttgart, West Germany: Springer-Verlag.

Buerkle, J.V. and R.J. Kleiner. 1966. *The North Philadelphia Community: Aspirations and Values.* Philadelphia: Commission on Human Relations.

Buford, B. 1990. *Among the Thugs.* New York: Vintage Books.

Bullington, B. 1977. *Heroin Use in the Barrio.* Lexington, MA: D.C. Heath.

Bureau of Justice Statistics. 1993. *Federal Criminal Case Processing 1982–91 with Preliminary Data for 1992.* Washington, DC: U.S. Department of Justice.

Burgess, E.W. 1928. The growth of the city. In R.E. Park, E.W. Burgess, and R.D. McKenzie (eds.), *The City.* Chicago: University of Chicago Press.

Bursik, R.J. 1984. Urban dynamics and ecological studies of delinquency. *Social Forces 63:*393–413.

Bursik, R.J. 1988. Social disorganization and theories of crime and delinquency: Problems and prospects. *Criminology 26:*519–551.

Bursik, R.J., Jr., and H.G. Grasmick. 1993. *Neighborhoods and Crime: The Dimensions of Effective Community Control.* New York: Lexington Books.

Burt, C. 1925. *The Young Delinquent.* New York: Appleton.

Bushnell, J. 1990. Introduction: The history and study of Soviet youth subculture. *Soviet Sociology 29:*3–10.

Bynum, J.E. and W.E. Thompson. 1988. *Juvenile Delinquency: A Sociological Approach.* Boston: Allyn and Bacon.

Byrne, J.M. and R.J. Sampson (eds.). 1986. *The Social Ecology of Crime.* New York: Springer-Verlag.

Callahan, C.M. and Rivara, F.P. 1992. Urban high school youth and handguns: A school-based survey. *Journal of the American Medical Association,* 267: (22)3038–3042.

Callahan, P. 1996. Firebombs increasing: violent trend spreads quickly in Denver. *The Denver Post,* January 29, pp. 1A and 4A.

Came, B., P. Lewis, J. Hart, D. Wolff, E. O'Farrell, L. Ogston, G. Allen, A. Gregor, and L. Black. 1989a. A growing menace: Violent skinheads are raising urban fears. *Maclean's 102* (January 23):43–44.

Came, B., L. Gilles, J. Howse, P. Kaihla, B. Wickens, and D. Burke. 1989b. Gang Terror. *Maclean's 102* (May 22):36–39.

Camp, G.M. and C.G. Camp. 1985. *Prison Gangs: Their Extent, Nature, and Impact on Prisons.* Washington, DC: U.S. Government Printing Office.

Campbell, A. 1984a. Girl's talk: The social representation of aggression by female gang members. *Criminal Justice and Behavior 11:*139–156.

Campbell, A. 1984b. *The Girls in the Gang: A report from New York City.* Oxford, England: Basil Blackwell.

Campbell, A. 1987. Self report fighting by females. *British Journal of Criminology 26:*28–48.

Campbell, A. 1990. Female participation in gangs. In C.R. Huff (ed.), *Gangs in America.* Newbury Park, CA: Sage.

Campbell, A. 1991. *The Girls in the Gang.* Second edition. Cambridge, MA: Basil Blackwell.

Campbell, A. and S. Muncer. 1989. Them and us: A comparison of the cultural context of American gangs and British subcultures. *Deviant Behavior 10:*271–288.

Campbell, A., S. Munce, and J. Galea. 1982. American gangs and British subcultures: A comparison. *International Journal of Offender Therapy and Comparative Criminology 26:*76–89.

Campbell, J. 1991. We are the billy boys. In R. Rosen and P. McSharry (eds.), Street Gangs: Gaining Turf, Losing Ground. New York: The Rosen Publishing Group, pp. 1–12.

Canter, R. 1982. Sex differentials in self-reported delinquency. *Criminology 20:*373–393.

Capp, B. 1977. English youth groups and the Pinder of Wakefield. *Past and Present 76:*127–133.

Carlson, M. 1988. The price of life in Los Angeles. *Time 131* (February 22):31.

Carney, J. 1986. Sunbelt import: Youth gangs plague the south. *Time 129* (August 18):17.

Carney, F.J.,'H.W. Mattick, and J.D. Callaway. 1969. *Action on the Streets.* New York: Association Press.

Cartwright, D.S., B. Thomson, and H. Schwartz (eds.). 1975. *Gang Delinquency.* Monterey, CA: Brooks/Cole.

Cavan, R.S. and J.T. Cavan. 1968. *Delinquency and Crime: Cross-Cultural Perspectives.* Philadelphia: Lippincott.

Centers for Disease Control and Prevention. 1992. Morbidity and Mortality Weekly, October 16. Atlanta, GA: National Center for Health Statistics.

Cernkovich, S., P. Giordano, and M. Pugh. 1985. Chronic offenders: The missing cases in self-report delinquency research. *Journal of Criminal Law and Criminology 76:*705–732.

Cervantes, R.C. (ed.). 1992. *Substance Abuse and Gang Violence.* Newbury Park, CA: Sage Publications.

Chaiken, J. and M. Chaiken. 1982. *Varieties of Criminal Behavior.* Santa Monica, CA: Rand Corporation.

Chaiken, J. and M. Chaiken. 1989. Drug use and predatory crime. In J.Q. Wilson and M. Tonry (eds.), *Drugs and Crime.* Chicago: University of Chicago Press.

Chaiken, M. and B.D. Johnson. 1988. *Characteristics of Different Types of Drug Involved Offenders.* Washington, DC: National Institute of Justice.

Chalidze, V. 1977. *Criminal Russia: A Study of Crime in the Soviet Union.* New York: Random House.

Chambliss, W.J. 1973. The saints and the roughnecks. *Society 11:*341–355.

Chavira, R. 1980. West coast story. *Nuestro 4* (May):21.

Chaze, W. 1981. Youth gangs are back—on old turf and new. *U.S. News and World Report 90:*46–47.

Chaze, W.L. 1984. Asian gangs stake out turf in U.S. *U.S. News and World Report 97* (November 5):82.

Chein, I., D.L. Gerald, R.S. Lee, and E. Rosenfeld. 1964. *The Road to H: Narcotics, Delinquency, and Social Policy.* New York: Basic Books.

Chesney-Lind, M. 1973. Judicial paternalism and the female status offender. *Crime and Delinquency 23:*121–130.

Chesney-Lind, M. 1989. Girls' crime and woman's place: Toward a feminist model of female delinquency. *Crime and Delinquency 35:*5–29.

Chin, K. 1986. Chinese triad societies, tongs, organized crime, and street gangs in Asia and the United States. Ph.D. dissertation, University of Pennsylvania.

Chin, K. 1989. Triad subculture and criminality: A study of trials, tongs, and Chinese gangs. New York: unpublished.

Chin, K. 1990. *Chinese Subculture and Criminality: Non-traditional Crime Groups in America.* New York: Greenwood Press.

Chin, K. 1990. Chinese gangs and extortion. In C.R. Huff (ed.), *Gangs in America.* Newbury Park, CA: Sage.

Christiansen, K.O. 1977. Preliminary study of criminality among twins. In K.O. Christiansen and S.A. Mednick (eds.), *Biosocial Bases of Criminal Behavior.* New York: Gardner.

Clark, A.C. 1984. *Profiles of the Future.* New York: Warner Books.

Clark, J.P. and E.P. Wenninger. 1962. Socioeconomic class and area as correlates of illegal behavior among juveniles. *American Sociological Review 27:*826–834.

Clarke, J. 1976. The skinheads and magical recovery of working class communities. In S. Hall, J. Clarke, T. Jefferson and B. Roberts (eds.) *Resistance Through Rituals.* London: Hutchinson.

Clarke, M. 1987. Citizenship, community, and the management of crime. *British Journal of Criminology 24:* (4) 384-400.

Clinard, M.B. 1960. A cross cultural replication of urbanism to criminal behavior. *American Sociological Review 25:*253–257.

Clinard, M.B. and D. Abbott. 1973. *Crime in Developing Countries: A Comparative Perspective.* New York: Wiley.

Clinard, M.B. and R. Quinney. 1973. *Criminal Behavior Systems.* New York: Holt, Rinehart, and Winston.

Cloward, R.A. 1959. Illegitimate means, anomie, and deviant behavior. *American Sociological Review 24:*164–176.

Cloward, R.A. and L.E. Ohlin. 1960. *Delinquency and Opportunity: A Theory of Delinquent Gangs.* New York: Free Press.

Cockburn, J.S. 1977. *Crime in England 1550–1800.* Princeton, NJ: Princeton University Press.

Cohen, A.K. 1955. *Delinquent Boys: The Culture of the Gang.* New York: Free Press.

Cohen, A.K. 1990. Foreword and overview. In C.R. Huff (ed.), *Gangs in America.* Newbury Park, CA: Sage.

Cohen, B. 1969. The delinquency of gangs and spontaneous groups. In T. Sellin and M.E. Wolfgang (eds.), *Delinquency: Selected Studies.* New York: Wiley.

Cohen, S. 1973. Mods and rockers: The inventory of manufactured news. In S. Cohen and J. Young (eds.), *The Manufacture of News.* Beverly Hills, CA: Sage.

Cohen, S. 1980. *Folk Devils and Moral Panics: The Creation of the Mods and Rockers.* Oxford: Martin Robertson.

Cohen, A.K. and J.F. Short. 1958. Research in delinquent subcultures. *Journal of Social Issues 14:*20–37.

Cohen, S. 1972. *Folk Devils and Moral Panics.* London: MacGibbon and Kee.

Cole, G.G. 1986. *The American System of Criminal Justice.* Fourth edition. Monterey, CA: Brooks/Cole.

Coleman, J.S. 1970. *The Circle.* Ludlow, MA: Pro Litho.

Collingwood, T., H. Williams, and A. Doud (eds.) 1976. HRD approach to police diversion for juvenile justice offenders. *Personnel and Guidance Journal 54:* 435-437.

Collins, H.C. 1979. *Street Gangs.* New York: New York City Police Department.

Conklin, J.E. 1989. *Criminology.* Third edition. New York: Macmillan.

Connor, W.D. 1972. *Deviance in Soviet Society: Crime, Delinquency, and Alcoholism.* New York: Columbia University Press.

Cook, T.D. and D.T. Campbell. 1979. *Quasi-Experimentation: Design and Analysis Issues for Field Settings.* Chicago: Rand McNally.

Cooper, B.M. 1987. Motor city breakdown. *Village Voice,* December 1, 23–25.

Cooper, C. 1967. The Chicago YMCA detailed workers: Current status of a prison program. In M.W. Klein (ed.), *Juvenile Gangs in Context.* Englewood Cliffs, NJ: Prentice-Hall.

Cornish, D.B. and R.V. Clarke. 1986. *The Reasoning Criminal.* New York: Springer-Verlag.

Coplon, J. 1988. Skinhead Nation. *Rolling Stone* (540):54–95.

Cortez, A. and M. Robinson. 1996. 5 held in firebomb attacks. *The Denver Post,* February 2, pp. 1A and 20A.

Coser, L.A. 1956. *The Functions of Social Conflict.* New York: Free Press.

Cosgrove, S. 1984. The zoot-suit and style warfare. *History Workshop 18:*77–91.

Covey, H.C. 1992. Book review essay, youth gangs: Three recent books on gangs. *Criminal Justice Review, 17:*118–125.

Cullen, F.T. 1988. Were Cloward and Ohlin strain theorists? Delinquency and Opportunity revisited. *Journal of Research in Crime and Delinquency 25:*214–241.

Cullen, F.T., M.T. Larson, and R.A. Mathers. 1985. Having money and delinquent involvement: The neglect of power in delinquency theory. *Criminal Justice and Behavior 12:*171–192.

Cummings, S. and D.J. Monti. 1993. *Gangs.* Albany, New York: State University of New York Press.

Currie, E. 1985. *Confronting Crime: An American Challenge.* New York: Pantheon.

Curry, G.D. and I. Spergel. 1988. Gang homicide, delinquency, and community. *Criminology 26:*381–405.

Dahmann, J. 1995. An evaluation of Operation Hardcore: A prosecutorial response to violent gang criminality. Pp. 301–303 in M.W. Klein, C.L. Maxson, and J. Miller (eds.), *The Modern Gang Reader.* Los Angeles, CA: Roxbury.

Daniels, P. 1977. How Relevant are Delinquency Theories? In P. Wilson (ed.) *Delinquency in Australia: A Critical Appraisal.* St. Lucia, Australia: University of Queensland Press.

Danker, U. 1988. Bandits and the state: Robbers and the authorities in the Holy Roman Empire in the late seventeenth and eighteenth centuries. In R. Evans (ed.), *The German Underworld: Deviants and Outcasts in German History.* London: Routledge and Kegan Paul.

Dannefer, D. and R.K. Schutt. 1982. Race and juvenile justice processing in court and police agencies. *American Journal of Sociology 87:*1113–132.

Datesman, S. and F.R. Scarpitti. 1977. Unequal protection for males and females in the juvenile court. In T.N. Ferdinand (ed.), *Juvenile Delinquency.* Beverly Hills, CA: Sage.

Davis, A. and M. Haller (eds.). 1973. *The People of Philadelphia.* Philadelphia, PA: Temple University Press.

Davis, J.R. 1978. Neighborhood: The street war. *Terrorists—Youth, Biker, and Prison Violence.* San Diego, CA: Grossmont Press.

Davis, N. 1971. The reasons of misrule: Youth groups and charivaris in sixteenth century France. *Past and Present 50:*41–75.

Dawley, D. 1973. *A Nation of Lords.* Garden City, NY: Anchor.

Dawley, D. 1992. *A Nation of Lords: The Autobiography of the Vice Lords,* Second Edition. Prospect Heights, IL: Waveland Press, Inc.

Decker, S. and K. Kempf-Leonard. 1991. Constructing gangs: The social definition of youth activities. *Criminal Justice Policy Review* 5:271–291.

Decker, S. and B. Van Winkle. 1994. "Slinging dope": The role of gangs and gang members in drug sales. *Justice Quarterly* 11:583–604.

DeFleur, L.B. 1967a. Delinquent gangs in cross-cultural perspective: The case of Cordoba. *Journal of Research in Crime and Delinquency 4:*132–141.

DeFleur, L.B. 1967b. Ecological variables in the cross-cultural study of delinquency. *Social Forces 45:*536–570.

DeFleur, L.B. 1979. Alternative strategies for the development of delinquency theories applicable to other cultures. *Social Problems 17:*30–39.

DeJong, W. 1986. Project DARE: Teaching Kids to Say "No" to Drugs and Alcohol. *NIJ Reports.*

De La Rosa, M.R. and F.I. Soriano. 1992. Understanding criminal activity and use of alcohol and cocaine derivatives by multi-ethnic gang members. In Cervantes, R.C. (ed.), *Substance Abuse and Gang Violence.* Newbury Park, CA: Sage, pp. 24–39.

DeMott, J.S. 1985. Have gang will travel. *Time 126* (December 9):34.

Dimenstein, G. 1991. *Brazil War on Children.* London: Latin America Bureau.

Dolan, E.G. and S. Finney. 1984. *Youth Gangs.* New York: Simon and Schuster.

Donovan, J. 1988. An introduction to street gangs. Paper prepared for Senator Garamondi's office, Sacramento, California.

Downes, D. 1966. *The Delinquent Solution.* New York: Free Press.

Drowns, R.W. and K.M. Hess. 1990. *Juvenile Justice.* St. Paul, MN: West.

Dryfoos, J.G. 1990. *Adolescents at Risk: Prevalence and Prevention.* New York: Oxford University Press.

Dumpson, J.R. 1949. An approach to antisocial street gangs. *Federal Probation 13:*22–29.

Dunford, F. and D.S. Elliott. 1984. Identifying career offenders using self-report data. *Journal of Research in Crime and Delinquency 21:*57–86.

Dungworth, T. 1977. Discretion in the juvenile justice system: The impact of case characteristics on prehearing detention. In T.N. Ferdinand (eds.), *Juvenile Delinquency.* Beverly Hills, CA: Sage.

Dunnett, M.D. 1975. Individualized prediction as a strategy for discovering demographic and interpersonal/psychological correlates of drug resistance and abuse. In *Predicting Adolescent Drug Abuse: A Review of Issues, Methods, and Correlates.* Washington, DC: U.S. Government Printing Office.

Duran, M. 1987. *Specialized Gang Supervision Program Progress Report.* Los Angeles: Los Angeles County Probation Department.

Durkheim, E. 1933 [originally published in 1893]. *The Division of Labor in Society.* New York: Free Press.

Durkheim, E. 1951 [originally published in 1897]. *Suicide.* New York: Free Press.

Duster, T. 1987. Crime, youth unemployment, and the underclass. *Crime and Delinquency 33:*22–29.

Duxbury, E.B. 1993. Correctional interventions. Pp. 427–437 of A.P. Goldstein and C.R. Huff (eds.), *The Gang Intervention Handbook.* Champaign, IL: Research Press.

Ebbe, O.N.I. 1989. Crime and delinquency in metropolitan Lagos: A study of "crime and delinquency" theory. *Social Forces 67:*751–765.

Eisenstadt, S.N. with M. Curelaru. 1976. *The Form of Sociology: Paradigms and Crisis.* New York: Wiley.

Elliott, D.S. 1962. Delinquency and perceived opportunity. *Sociological Inquiry 32:*216–227.

Elliott, D.S. and R.A. Ageton. 1976. The relationship between drug use and crime among adolescents. Appendix to *Drug Use and Crime.* Research Triangle Park, NC: National Institute on Drug Abuse.

Elliott, D.S. and S.S. Ageton. 1980. Reconciling race and class differences in self-reported and official estimates of delinquency. *American Sociological Review 40:*95–110.

Elliott, D.S., S.S. Ageton, and R.J. Canter. 1979. An integrated theoretical perspective on delinquent behavior. *Journal of Research in Crime and Delinquency 16:*3–27.

Elliott, D.S., S.S. Ageton, D. Huizinga, B.A. Knowles, and R.J. Canter. 1983. *The Prevalence and Incidence of Delinquent Behavior 1976–1980.* Boulder, CO: Behavioral Research Institute.

Elliott, D.S. and D. Huizinga. 1983. Social class and delinquent behavior in a national youth panel: 1976–1980. *Criminology 21:*149–177.

Elliott, D.S. and D. Huizinga. 1984. The relationship between delinquent behavior and ADM problems. National Youth Survey Report No. 28. Boulder, CO: Institute of Behavioral Science.

Elliott, D.S., D. Huizinga, and S.S. Ageton. 1985. *Explaining Delinquency and Drug Use.* Beverly Hills, CA: Sage.

Elliott, D.S., D. Huizinga, and S. Menard. 1989. *Multiple Problem Youth: Delinquency, Substance Use, and Mental Health Problems.* New York: Springer-Verlag.

Elliott, D.S. and S. Menard. 1996. Delinquent friends and delinquent behavior: temporal and developmental patterns. Pp. 28–67 in J.D. Hawkins (ed.), *Delinquency and Crime: Current Theories.* Cambridge, England: Cambridge University Press.

Elliott, D.S. and H. Voss. 1974. *Delinquency and Dropout.* Lexington, MA: D.C. Heath.

Elliott, D.S., W.J. Wilson, D. Huizinga, R.J. Sampson, A. Elliott, and B. Rankin. 1995. The effects of neighborhood disadvantage on adolescent development. Report to the MacArthur Research Program on Successful Adolescent Development. Boulder, CO: Institute of Behavioral Science.

Elliott, D.S., W.J. Wilson, D. Huizinga, S. Menard, A. Elliott, and B. Rankin. (Forthcoming). *Beating the Odds.* Chicago: University of Chicago Press.

Empey, L. 1967. Delinquency theory and recent research. *Journal of Research in Crime and Delinquency 4:*28–42.

Empey, L.T. 1982. *American Delinquency: Its Meaning and Construction.* Homewood, IL: Dorsey.

Engel, K. and S. Rothman. 1983. Prison violence and the paradox of reform. *Public Interest 73:*91–105.

English, T.J. 1995. *Born to Kill: America's Most Notorious Vietnamese Gang, and the Changing Face of Organized Crime.* New York: William Morrow and Company.

Erickson, M.L. and J.P. Gibbs. 1978. Objective and perceptual properties of legal punishment and the deterrence doctrine. *Social Problems* 25:253–264.

Erickson, M.L., J.P. Gibbs, and G.F. Jensen. 1977. The deterrence doctrine and the perceived certainty of legal punishments. *American Sociological Review* 42: 305–317.

Erickson, M.L. and G.F. Jensen. 1977. Delinquency is still group behavior! Toward revitalizing the group premise in the sociology of deviance. *Journal of Criminal Law and Criminology 68:*262–273.

Erlanger, H.S. 1979. Estrangement, machismo, and gang violence. *Social Science Quarterly 60:*235–248.

Esbensen, F. 1995. The national evaluation of the Gang Resistance Education and Training (G.R.E.A.T.) program: An overview. Paper presented at the 1995 annual meeting of the American Society of Criminology, Boston.

Esbensen, F. 1996. A national gang strategy. In J.M. Miller and J.P. Rush (eds.), *A Criminal Justice Approach to Gangs: From Explanation to Response.* Illinois: Anderson.

Esbensen, F. and D. Huizinga. 1990. Community structure and drug use: From a social disorganization perspective. *Justice Quarterly* 7:691–709.

Esbensen, F. and D. Huizinga. 1991. Gangs, drugs, and delinquency in a survey of urban youth. Denver Youth Survey Project Report #14. Boulder, Colorado: Institute of Behavioral Research.

Esbensen, F. and Huizinga, D. 1993. Gangs, drugs, and delinquency in a survey of urban youth. *Criminology*

Esbensen, F., D. Huizinga, and A.W. Weiher. 1993. Gang and non-gang youth: Differences in explanatory factors. *Journal of Contemporary Criminal Justice,* 9:(2) 94–116.

Etzioni, A. 1964. *Modern Organizations.* Englewood Cliffs, NJ: Prentice-Hall.

Fagan, J. 1989. The social organization of drug use and drug dealing among urban gangs. *Criminology 24:*439–471.

Fagan, J. 1990. Social processes of delinquency and drug use among urban gangs. In C.R. Huff (ed.), *Gangs in America.* Newbury Park, CA: Sage.

Fagan, J., E. Slaughter, and E. Hartstone. 1987. Blind Justice: The impact of race on the juvenile justice process. *Crime and Delinquency 33:*224–258.

Fagan, J., E. Piper, and M. Moore. 1986. Violent delinquents and urban youths. *Criminology 24:*439–471.

Fain, A.P. 1990. Specific features of informal youth association in large cities. *Soviet Sociology 29:*19–42.

Far Eastern Economic Review. 1989. Chinese Crime Pays. *Far Eastern Economic Review 143* (January 12):30.

Farley, J.E. 1982. *Majority-Minority Relations.* Englewood Cliffs, NJ: Prentice-Hall.

Fattah, D. 1987. The house of UMOJA as a case study for social change. *Annals of the American Academy of Political and Social Science 494:*37–41.

Faust, D.G. 1980. Culture, conflict, and community: The meaning of power on an antebellum plantation. *Journal of Social History 14:*83–97.

Federal Bureau of Investigation. 1993. *Age-Specific Arrest Rates and Race-Specific Arrest Rates for Selected Offenses 1965–1992.* Washington, DC: U.S. Department of Justice.

Feldman, H.W., J. Mandel, and A. Fields. 1985. In the neighborhood: A strategy for delivering early intervention services to young drug users in their natural environments. In A. Friedman and G. Beschner (eds.), *Treatment Services for Adolescent Substance Users*. Rockville, MD: National Institute of Drug Abuse.

Felson, M. and L.E. Cohen. 1980. Human ecology and crime: A routine activity approach. *Human Ecology 8:*389–406.

Ferdinand, T.N. 1966. *Typologies of Delinquency: A Critical Analysis*. New York: Random House.

Ferdinand, T. and E. Luchterhand. 1970. Inner city youth, the police, the juvenile court, and justice. *Social Problems 17:*510–527.

Ferracuti, F., S. Dinitz, and A. de Brenes. 1975. *Delinquents and Nondelinquents in the Puerto Rican Slum Culture*. Columbus, OH: Ohio State University Press.

Feri, E. 1909. *Criminal Sociology*. New York: Appleton.

Finestone, H. 1976. *Victims of Change: Juvenile Delinquency in American Society*. Westport, CT: Greenwood.

Fischer, C. 1975. Toward a subcultural theory of urbanism. *American Journal of Sociology 80:*1319–1330.

Fishman, L. 1995. The Vice Queens: An Ethnographic Study of Black Female Gang Behavior. In M. Klein, C. Maxson, and J. Miller (eds.) *The Modern Gang Reader*. Los Angeles, CA: Roxbury Publishing Company.

Fleisher, M.S. 1994. Youth gangs and social networks: observations from a long-term ethnographic study. Paper presented at the annual meeting of the American Society of Criminology in Miami, Florida, November, 1994.

Foley, M. 1983. Coping strategies of street children. *International Journal of Offender Therapy and Comparative Criminology 27:*5–20.

Fong, R.S., R.E. Vogel, and S. Buentello. 1996. Prison gang dynamics: a research update. Pp. 105–128 in J.M. Miller and J.P. Rush (eds.), *Gangs: A Criminal Justice Approach*. Cincinnati, OH: Anderson.

Fox, J.R. 1985. Mission impossible? Social work practice with black urban youth gangs. *Social Work 30:*25–31.

Francia, L. 1991. The dusty realm of Bagong barrio. In R. Rosen and P. McSharry (eds.), *Street Gangs: Gaining Turf, Losing Ground*. New York: The Rosen Publishing Group, pp. 13–30.

Freed, D. 1995. Policing gangs: Case of contrasting styles. Pp. 288–291 in M.W. Klein, C.L. Maxson, and J. Miller (eds.), *The Modern Gang Reader*. Los Angeles, CA: Roxbury.

Friday, P. and L. Stewart. 1977. *Youth Crime and Juvenile Justice*. New York: Praeger Publishers.

Friedman, C.J., F. Mann, and H. Adelman. 1976. Juvenile street gangs: The victimization of youth. *Adolescence 11:*527–533.

Friedman, C.J., F. Mann, and A. Friedman. 1975. A profile of juvenile street gang members. *Adolescence 10:*563–607.

Friedrichs, R. 1970. *A Sociology of Sociology*. New York: Free Press.

Fry, J.R. 1973. *Locked-Out Americans*. New York: Harper and Row.

Furfey, P. 1928. *The Gang Age*. New York: MacMillan.

Fyvel, T.R. 1963. *The Insecure Offenders*. Harmondsworth, England: Penguin.

Gabrielli, W. and S. Mednick. 1984. Urban environment, genetics, and crime. *Criminology* 22:645–653.

Gallagher, J.P. 1992. As law enforcement crumbles, Russian crime, gangs proliferate. *Chicago Tribune,* September 2: Section 1, page 6.

Gandossy, R.P., J.R. Williams, J. Cohen, and H.J. Harwood. 1980. *Drugs and Crime: A Survey and Analysis of the Literature.* Washington, DC: U.S. Government Printing Office.

Gannon, T.M. 1966. Emergence of the "defensive" gang. *Federal Probation 30:*172–179.

Garrett, M. and J.F. Short, Jr. 1978. Social class and delinquency: Predictions and outcomes of police-juvenile encounters. In P. Wickman and P. Whitten (eds.), *Readings in Criminology.* Lexington, MA: D.C. Heath.

Geis, G. 1965. *Juvenile Gangs.* Washington, DC: President's Committee on Juvenile Delinquency and Youth Crime.

Gelles, R.J. and C.P. Cornell. 1990. *Intimate Violence in Families.* Second edition. Newbury Park, CA: Sage.

Gendreau, P. and R.R. Ross. 1984. Correctional treatment: some recommendations for effective intervention. *Juvenile and Family Court Journal* 34:31–39.

Genelin, M. 1989. *Los Angeles Street Gangs: Report and Recommendations of the Countrywide Criminal Justice Coordination Committee.* Los Angeles: Inter-Agency Task Force.

Gerrard, N.L. 1964. The core member of the gang. *British Journal of Criminology* 4:361–371.

Giallombardo, R. 1974. *The Social World of Imprisoned Girls.* New York: Wiley.

Giallombardo, R. 1980. Female delinquency. In D. Shichor and D.H. Kelly (eds.), *Critical Issues in Juvenile Delinquency.* Lexington, MA: Lexington Books.

Gibbens, T.C. and R.H. Ahrenfeld. 1966. *Culture Factors in Delinquency.* London: Tavistock.

Gibbons, D.C. 1965. *Changing the Lawbreaker.* Englewood Cliffs, NJ: Prentice-Hall.

Gibbons, D.C. 1985. The assumption of the efficacy of middle-range explanation: Typologies. In R.F. Meier (ed.), *Theoretical Methods in Criminology.* Beverly Hills, CA: Sage.

Gibbons, D.C. and D.L. Garrity. 1959. Some suggestions for the development of etiological and treatment theory in criminology. *Social Forces 38:*51–59.

Gibbs, J. 1985. The methodology of theory construction in criminology. In R.F. Meier (ed.), *Theoretical Methods in Criminology.* Beverly Hills, CA: Sage.

Giordano, P.C. 1978. Girls, guys, and gangs: The changing context of female delinquency. *Journal of Criminal Law and Criminology 69:*126–132.

Giordano, P.C. and S.A. Cernkovich. 1979. On complicating the relationship between liberation and delinquency. *Social Problems 26:*467–481.

Giordano, P.C., S.A. Cernkovich, and M.D. Pugh. 1986. Friendships and delinquency. *American Journal of Sociology 91:*1170–1202.

Gist, N.P. and S.F. Fava. 1974. *Urban Society.* Sixth edition. New York: Crowell.

Glaser, D. 1972. *Adult Crime and Social Policy.* Englewood Cliffs, NJ: Prentice-Hall.

Glionna, J.M. 1993. Pals in the posse: Teen culture has seized the word as a hip name for groups; Not all harmless. *The Los Angeles Times* February 26: B-3.

Glueck, S. and E. Glueck. 1950. *Unraveling Juvenile Delinquency.* Cambridge, MA: Harvard.

Glueck, S. and E. Glueck. 1956. *Physique and Delinquency.* New York: Harper.

Glueck, S. and E. Glueck. 1964. *Ventures in Criminology.* Cambridge: Harvard University Press.

Gold, M. 1970. *Delinquent Behavior in an American City.* Belmont, CA: Brooks/Cole.

Gold, M. 1987. Social ecology. In H.C. Quay (ed.), *Handbook of Juvenile Delinquency.* New York: Wiley.

Gold, M. and D.J. Reimer. 1975. Changing patterns of delinquent behavior among Americans 13 to 16 years old: 1967–1972. *Crime and Delinquency Literature 7:* 483–517.

Goldstein, A.P. 1991. *Delinquent Gangs: A Psychological Perspective.* Champaign, IL: Research Press.

Goldstein, A.P. and B. Glick, with W. Carthan and D.A. Blancero. 1994. *The Prosocial Gang: Implementing Aggression Replacement Training.* Thousand Oaks, CA: Sage.

Goldstein, A.P. and C.R. Huff (eds.). 1993. The Gang Intervention Handbook. Champaign, IL: Research Press.

Goldstein, P.J. 1985. The drugs-violence nexus: A tri-partite conceptual framework. *Journal of Drug Issues 15:*493–506.

Goode, E. 1970. *The Marijuana Smokers.* New York: Basic Books.

Gordon, R.A. 1967. Social level, social disability, and gang interaction. *American Journal of Sociology 73:*42–62.

Gordon, R.A., J.F. Short, D.S. Cartwright, and F.L. Strodtbeck. 1963. Values and gang delinquency. *American Journal of Sociology 69:*109–128.

Goring, C. 1972 [originally 1913]. *The English Convict: A Statistical Study.* Montclair, NJ: Patterson Smith.

Gottfredson, D. 1986. An empirical test of school-based environmental and individual interventions to reduce the risk of delinquent behavior. *Criminology 24:*705–731.

Gottfredson, M. and T. Hirschi. 1990. *A General Theory of Crime.* Palo Alto, CA: Stanford University Press.

Green, E. 1970. Race, social status, and criminal arrest. *American Sociological Review 35:*476–490.

Gunst, L. 1989. Johnny-too-bad and the sufferers. *Nation 249*(16):549, 567–569.

Gunst, L. 1995. *Born Fi' Dead: A Journey Through the Jamaican Posse Underworld.* New York: Henry Holt and Company.

Hackler, J.C. 1985. The need to do something. In R.A. Weisheit and R.G. Culbertson (eds.), *Juvenile Delinquency: A Justice Perspective.* Prospective Heights, IL: Waveland Press.

Hagan, J., A.R. Gillis, and J. Simpson. 1985. The class structure of gender and delinquency: Toward a power-control theory of common delinquent behavior. *American Journal of Sociology 90:*1151–1160.

Hagedorn, J.M. 1994. Neighborhoods, Markets, and gang drug organization. *Journal of Research in Crime and Delinquency* 31:264–294.

Hagedorn, J.M., with P. Macon. 1989. *People and Folks.* Chicago: Lake View Press.

Hagedorn, J., P. Macon, and J. Moore. 1986. *Final Report: Milwaukee Gang Research Project.* Milwaukee, WI: Urban Research Center, University of Wisconsin, Milwaukee.

Hall, R.H. 1987. *Organizations: Structures, Processes, and Outcomes.* Fourth edition. Englewood Cliffs, NJ: Prentice-Hall.

Hamm, M.S. 1993. *American Skinheads.* Westbrook, CN: Greenwood Publishing Group, Inc.

Hanawalt, B. 1979. *Crime and Conflict in English Communities, 1300-1348.* Cambridge Massachusetts: Harvard University Press.

Hannan, M.T. and J. Freeman. 1977. The population ecology of organizations. *American Journal of Sociology 82:*929–964.

Hanson, K. 1964. *Rebels in the Streets: The Story of New York Girl Gangs.* Englewood Cliffs, NJ: Prentice-Hall.

Harding, J. 1952. A street corner gang and its implications for sociological and psychological theory. In J.E. Hulett and R. Stagner (eds.), *Problems in Social Psychology.* Urbana, IL: University of Illinois Press.

Hardman, D.G. 1967. Historical perspectives on gang research. *Journal of Research in Crime and Delinquency 4:*5–27.

Hardman, D.G. 1969. Small town gangs. *Journal of Criminal Law, Criminology, and Police Science 60:*173–181.

Harrington, M. 1963. *The Other America: Poverty in the United States.* Baltimore: Penguin.

Harris, M.G. 1988. *Cholas: Latino Girls and Gangs.* New York: AMS Press.

Haskell, M.R. and L. Yablonsky. 1978. *Juvenile Delinquency.* Skokie, IL: Rand McNally.

Hawes, J.M. 1971. *Children in Urban Society.* New York: Oxford University Press.

Hawkins, J.D. and T. Lam. 1987. Teacher practices, social development, and delinquency. In J.D. Burchard and S.N. Burchard (eds.), *Prevention of Delinquent Behavior.* Newbury Park, CA: Sage.

Hawkins, J.D. and D.M. Lishner. 1987. Schooling and delinquency. In E.J. Johnson (ed.), *Handbook on Crime and Delinquency Prevention.* Westport, CT: Greenwood Press.

Hawkins, J.D., D.M. Lishner, and R.F. Catalano. 1985. Childhood predictors and the prevention of adolescent substance use. In C.L. Jones and R.J. Battjes (eds.), *Etiology of Drug Abuse: Implications for Prevention.* Washington, DC: National Institute on Drug Abuse.

Hawkins, J.D., E. von Cleve, and R.F. Catalano. 1991. Reducing early childhood aggression: Results of a primary prevention program. *Journal of the American Academy of Child and Adolescent Psychiatry 30:*208–217.

Hawkins, J.D. and J.G. Weis. 1985. The social development model: An integrated approach to delinquency prevention. *Journal of Primary Prevention 6:*73–97.

Healy, W. 1915. *The Individual Delinquent.* London: Heinemann.

Heller, C. 1966. *Mexican American Youth: Forgotten Youth at the Crossroads.* New York: Random House.

Helmreich, W.B. 1973. Race, sex, and gangs: Black Crusaders—The rise and fall of political gangs. *Society 11*(1):44–50.

Hepburn, J.R. 1978. Race and the decision to arrest: An analysis of warrants issued. *Journal of Research in Crime and Delinquency 15:*54–73.

Higgins, P. and G.L. Albrecht. 1981. Cars and kids: A self-report study of juvenile auto theft and traffic violations. *Sociology and Social Research 66:*29–41.

Himber, C. 1941. *Meet the Gang.* New York: Association Press.

Hindelang, M., T. Hirschi, and J. Weis. 1981. *Measuring Delinquency.* Beverly Hills, CA: Sage.

Hindelang, M. and J. Weis. 1972. The BC–TRY cluster and factor analysis system: Personality and self-reported delinquency. *Criminology 10:*268-294.

Hiner, N. 1975. Adolescence in eighteenth-century America. *The History of Childhood Quarterly 3:* 253-280.

Hirschi, T. 1969. *Causes of Delinquency.* Berkeley, CA: University of California Press.

Hirschi, T. 1987. Review of *Explaining Delinquency and Drug Use* by Delbert S. Elliott, David Huizinga, and Suzanne S. Ageton. *Criminology 25:*193-201.

Holtz, J.A. 1975. The "low-riders" portrait of an urban youth culture. *Youth and Society 6:*495-508.

Hood, R. and R. Sparks. 1970. *Key Issues in Criminology.* New York: McGraw-Hill.

Hopper, C.B., and J. Moore. 1983. Hell on wheels: The outlaw motorcycle gangs. *Journal of American Culture 6:*58-64.

Hopper, C.B. and J. Moore. 1990. Women in outlaw motorcycle gangs. *Journal of Contemporary Ethnography 18:*363-387.

Horowitz, R. 1982. Adult delinquent gangs in a Chicano community: Masked intimacy and marginality. *Urban Life 11:*3-26.

Horowitz, R. 1986. Remaining an outsider: Membership as a threat to research rapport. *Urban Life 14:*409-430.

Horowitz, R. 1987. Community tolerance of gang violence. *Social Problems 34:* 437-450.

Horowitz, R. 1990. Sociological perspectives on gangs. In C.R. Huff (ed.), *Gangs in America.* Newbury Park, CA: Sage.

Horowitz, R. and G. Schwartz. 1974. Honor, normative ambiguity, and gang violence. *American Sociological Review 39:*238-251.

Howell, J.C. 1994. Recent gang research: program and policy implications. *Crime and Delinquency 4:*495-515.

Hotyst, B. 1982. *Comparative Criminology.* Lexington, MA: Lexington Books.

Huff, C.R. 1989. Youth gangs and public policy. *Crime and Delinquency 35:*524-537.

Huff, C.R. (ed.). (1990). *Gangs in America.* Newbury Park, CA: Sage.

Huizinga, D. and D.S. Elliott. 1987. Juvenile offenders: Prevalence, offender incidence, and arrest rates by race. *Crime and Delinquency 33:*206-223.

Huizinga, D., S. Menard, and D.S. Elliott. 1989. Delinquency and drug use: Temporal and developmental patterns. *Justice Quarterly 6:*419-455.

Humphries, S. 1981. *Hooligans or Rebels: An Oral History of Working Class Childhood and Youth, 1889-1939.* Oxford: Basic Blackwell.

Hutchings, B. and S. Mednick. 1977. Criminality in adoptees and their adptive and biological parents: A pilot study. In K.O. Christiansen and S. Mednick (eds.), *Biosocial Bases of Criminal Behavior.* New York: Gardner.

Ianni, F.A.J. 1972. *A Family Business: Kinship and Social Control in Organized Crime.* New York: Russell Sage Foundation.

Igbinovia, P.E. 1985. Soccer hooliganism in Black Africa. *International Journal of Offender Therapy and Comparative Criminology 29:*135-146.

Inciardi, J. 1978. *Reflections on Crime: An Introduction to Criminology and Criminal Justice.* New York: Holt, Rinehart, and Winston.

Inciardi, J.A. 1986. *The War on Drugs: Heroin, Cocaine, Crime, and Public Policy.* Palo Alto, CA: Mayfield.

Jackson, P.G. 1989. Theories and findings about youth gangs. *Criminal Justice Abstracts,* 21:(2)313–329.

Jackson, P.I. 1991. Crime, youth gangs, and urban transitions: The social dislocations of postindustrial economic development. *Justice Quarterly 8:*379–397.

Jackson, R.K. and W.D. McBride. 1985. *Understanding Street Gangs.* Sacramento: Custom Publishing.

Jacobs, J.B. 1974. Street gangs behind bars. *Social Problems 21:*395–409.

Jankowski, M.S. 1991. *Islands in the Street: Gangs and American Urban Society.* Berkeley: University of California Press.

Jansyn, L., Jr. 1966. Solidarity and delinquency in a street corner group. *American Sociological Review 31:*600–614.

Jensen, G.F. 1972. Parents, peers, and delinquent action: A test of the differential association perspective. *American Journal of Sociology 78:*562–575.

Jensen, G.F. and D.G. *Delinquency.* Lexington, MA: D.C. Heath.

Jessor, R. 1976. Predicting time of onset of marijuana use: A developmental study of high school youth. *Journal of Consulting and Clinical Psychology 44:*125–134.

Joe, D. and N. Robinson. 1980. Chinatown's immigrant gangs: The new young warrior class. *Criminology 18:*337–345.

Joe, K.A. 1994. The new criminal conspiracy? Asian gangs and organized crime in San Francisco. *Journal of Research in Crime and Delinquency* 31:390–415.

Johnson, B.D. 1973. *Marijuana Users and Drug Subcultures.* New York: Wiley.

Johnson, C., Webster, B. and Connors, E. 1995. *Prosecuting Gangs: A National Assessment.* Washington, DC: National Institute of Justice.

Johnson, G. and R.M. Hunter. 1987. Using school-based programs to improve students' citizenship in Colorado: A report to Colorado educators. Denver, CO: Colorado Juvenile Justice and Delinquency Prevention Council.

Johnston, L., P.M. O'Malley, and J. Bachman. 1986. *Drug Use Among American High School Students, College Students, and Other Young Adults.* Washington, DC: U.S. Department of Health and Human Services.

Johnston, L.D., P. O'Malley, and L. Eveland. 1978. Drugs and delinquency: A search for causal connections. In D. Kandel (ed.) *Longitudinal Research on Drug Use.* New York: Wiley.

Johnstone, J.W.C. 1978. Social class, social areas, and delinquency. *Sociology and Social Research 63:*49–72.

Johnstone, J.W.C. 1981. Youth gangs and black suburbs. *Pacific Sociological Review 24:*355–375.

Johnstone, J.W.C. 1983. Recruitment to a youth gang. *Youth and Society 14:*281–300.

Jonassen, C.T. 1949. A re-evaluation and critique of the logic and some methods of Shaw and McKay. *American Sociological Review 14:*608–617.

Joseph, J. 1991. In Japan, It's legal. In R. Rosen and P. McSharry (eds.), *Street Gangs: Gaining Turf, Losing Ground.* New York: The Rosen Publishing Group, pp. 153–161.

Juarez, P.D. 1992. The public health model and violence prevention. In R.C. Cervantes (ed.), *Substance Abuse and Gang Violence.* Newbury Park, CA: Sage, pp. 43–59.

Jung, M. 1976. Characteristics of contrasting Chinatowns. *Social Casework 57:*149–154.

Jungk, R. 1959. *Children of the Ashes.* New York: Harcourt, Brace, and World.

Kandel, D.B. 1975. Stages of adolescent involvement in drug use. *Science 190:*912–914.

Kandel, D.B. 1978. *Longitudinal Research on Drug Use: Empirical Findings and Methodological Issues.* New York: Wiley.

Kandel, D.B. 1980. Drug use and drinking behavior among youth. *Annual Review of Sociology 6:*235–285.

Kang, G.E. and T.S. Kang. 1978. The Korean urban shoeshine gang: A minority community. *Urban Anthropology 7:*171–183.

Kantor, D. and W. Bennett. 1968. Orientation of streetcorner workers and their effects on gangs. In S. Wheeler (ed.), *Controlling Delinquents.* New York: Wiley.

Kaplan, H.B., R.J. Johnson, and C.A. Bailey. 1987. Deviant peers and deviant behavior: Further elaboration of a model. *Social Psychology Quarterly 50:*277–284.

Karacki, L. and J. Toby. 1962. The uncommitted adolescent: Candidate for gang socialization. *Sociological Inquiry 32:*203–215.

Keiser, R. 1969. *The Vice Lords: Warriors of the Streets.* New York: Holt, Rinehart and Winston.

Kelly, K. 1991. Youth held without bail in gang death. *Omaha World Herald* 243:1–2.

Kercher, K. 1988. Criminology. In E.G. Borgatta and K.S. Cook (eds.), *The Future of Sociology.* Newbury Park, CA: Sage.

Kiernan, J.P. 1977. Public transport and private risk: Zionism and the black commuter in South Africa. *Journal of Anthropological Research 33:*214–226.

Kitsuse, J.I. and D.C. Dietrick. 1959. Delinquent Boys: A Critique. *American Sociological Review 24:*208–215.

Kleiman, M.A.R. and K.D. Smith. 1990. State and local drug enforcement: In search of a strategy. In M. Tonry and J.Q. Wilson (eds.), *Drugs and Crime.* Chicago: University of Chicago Press.

Klein, M.W. 1967. *A Structural Approach to Gang Intervention: The Lincoln Heights Project.* San Diego: Youth Studies Center.

Klein, M.W. (ed.). 1967. *Juvenile Gangs in Context.* Englewood Cliffs, NJ: Prentice-Hall.

Klein, M.W. 1968a. Impressions of juvenile gang members. *Adolescence 3:*53–78.

Klein, M.W. 1968b. *The Latino Hills Project.* Los Angeles: Youth Studies Center, University of Southern California.

Klein, M.W. 1969a. Gang cohesiveness, delinquency, and a street worker program. *Journal of Research in Crime and Delinquency 6:*135–166.

Klein, M.W. 1969b. Violence in American juvenile gangs. In D.J. Mulvihill, M.M. Tumin, and L.A. Curtis (eds.), *Crimes of Violence.* Volume 13. Staff Report to the National Commission on the Causes and Prevention of Violence. Washington, DC: U.S. Government Printing Office.

Klein, M.W. 1971. *Street Gangs and Street Workers.* Englewood Cliffs, NJ: Prentice-Hall.

Klein, M.W. (ed.). 1988. *Cross-National Research in Self-Reported Crime and Delinquency.* Dordrecht: Kluwer Academic Publishers.

Klein, M.W. 1993. Attempting gang control by suppression: The misuse of deterrence principles. *Studies on Crime and Crime Prevention* 2:88–111.

Klein, M.W. 1995a. *The American Street Gang.* New York: Oxford University Press.

Klein, M.W. 1995b. Street gang cycles. In J.Q. Wilson and J. Petersilia (eds.), *Crime.* San Francisco, CA: Institute for Contemporary Studies.

Klein, M.W. and L.Y. Crawford. 1967. Groups, gangs, and cohesiveness. *Journal of Research in Crime and Delinquency 4:*63–75.

Klein, M.W., M.A. Gordon, and C.L. Maxson. 1986. The impact of police investigations on police-reported rates of gang and non-gang homicides. *Criminology 24:*489–511.

Klein, M.W. and C.L. Maxson. 1985. "Rock" sales in south Los Angeles. *Sociology and Social Research 69:*561–565.

Klein, M.W. and C.L. Maxson. 1989. Street gang violence. In N.A. Weiner and M.E. Wolfgang (eds.), *Violent Crimes, Violent Criminals.* Newbury Park, CA: Sage.

Klein, M.W., C.L. Maxson, and L.C. Cunningham. 1991. "Crack," street gangs, and violence. *Criminology 29:*623–650.

Klein, M.W. and B.G. Myerhoff (eds.). 1967. *Juvenile Gangs in Context: Theory, Research, and Action.* Englewood Cliffs, NJ: Prentice-Hall.

Klein, M.W., C.L. Maxson, and J. Miller (eds.). 1995. *The Modern Gang Reader.* Los Angeles, CA: Roxbury Publishing Company.

Kleiner, R.J., H.R. Stub, and J. Lanahan. 1975. A study of black youth groups: Implications for research, action, and the role of the investigator. *Human Organization 34:*391–394.

Knight, N. 1982. *Skinhead.* London: Omnibus Press.

Knox, G.W. 1978. Perceived closure and respect for the law among delinquent and nondelinquent youths. *Youth and Society 9:*385–406.

Knox, G. 1993. *An Introduction to Gangs.* Berrien Springs, MI: Vande Vere Publishing Ltd.

Kobrin, S. 1969. The Chicago Area Project: A 25 year assessment. In R.S. Cavan (ed.), *Readings in Juvenile Delinquency.* New York: Lippincott.

Kobrin, S., J. Puntil, and E. Peluso. 1967. Criteria of status among street groups. *Journal of Research in Crime and Delinquency 4:*98–118.

Kodluboy, D.W. and L.A. Evenrud. 1993. School-based interventions: Best practices and critical issues. Pp. 257–299 in A.P. Goldstein and C.R. Huff (eds.), *The Gang Intervention Handbook.* Champaign, IL: Research Press.

Kornblum, W. 1987. Ganging together. Helping gangs go straight. *Social Issues and Health Review 2:*99–104.

Kornhauser, R.R. 1978. *Social Sources of Delinquency.* Chicago: University of Chicago Press.

Kratcoski, P.C. and L.D. Kratcoski. 1990. *Juvenile Delinquency.* Third edition. Englewood Cliffs, NJ: Prentice-Hall.

Krisberg, B. 1974a. The politics of delinquency prevention: The urban leadership training program. *Social Policy 5:*53–56.

Krisberg, B. 1974b. Gang youth and hustling: The psychology of survival. *Issues in Criminology 9:*115–131.

Krisberg, B. and J. Austin (eds.). 1978. *The Children of Ishmael: Critical Perspectives on Juvenile Justice.* Palo Alto, CA: Mayfield.

Kuhn, T.S. 1962. *The Structure of Scientific Revolutions.* Chicago: University of Chicago Press.

Kuo, Y. 1973. Identity-diffusion and tai-pau gang delinquency in Taiwan. *Adolescence 8:*165–170.

Labov, T. 1982. Social structure and peer terminology in a black adolescent gang. *Language in Society 2:*391–411.

Lachman, R. 1988. Graffiti as career and ideology. *American Journal of Sociology 94:*229–250.

Lasley, J.R. 1992. Age, social context, and street gang membership: Are "youth" gangs becoming "adult" gangs? *Youth and Society,* 23(4)434–451.

Laub, J. 1983. Urbanism, race, and crime. *Journal of Research in Crime and Delinquency 20:*188–198.

Le Blanc, M. and N. Lanctôt. 1994. Adolescent gang members social and psychological characteristics, gang participation: A selection or activation process? Paper presented at the annual meeting of the American Society of Criminology, Miami, Nov. 1994.

Ledochowski, C. 1991. The skollie gangs. In R. Rosen and P. McSharry (eds.), *Street Gangs: Gaining Turf, Losing Ground.* New York: The Rosen Publishing Group, pp. 101–110.

Lehmann, N. 1986a. The origins of the underclass. *Atlantic Monthly 257:*31–55.

Lehmann, N. 1986b. The origins of the underclass. *Atlantic Monthly 258:*54–68.

Lemert, E.M. 1951. *Social Pathology.* New York: McGraw-Hill.

Leo, J., M. Casey, and R. Woodbury. Parasites on their own people: Gangs are tougher, better armed, and more violent than ever. *Time 126*(July 8):76.

Lerman, P. 1967. Gangs, networks, and subcultural delinquency. *American Journal of Sociology 73:*63–72.

Levin, J. and J. McDevitt. 1993. *Hate Crimes: The Rising Tide of Bigotry and Bloodshed.* New York: Plenum Press.

Likhanov, D. 1991. Dirt: From kazan to Tashkent. In R. Rosen and P. McSharry (eds.), *Street Gangs: Gaining Turf, Losing Ground.* New York: The Rosen Publishing Group, pp. 125–137.

Lipsey, M.W. 1992. The effect of treatment on juvenile delinquents: results from meta-analysis. Pp. 131–143 in F. Losel, D. Bender, and T. Bliesener (eds.), *Psychology and the Law: International Perspectives.* Berlin, Germany: Walter de Gruyter.

Lizzotte, A., J. Tesoriero, T. Thornberry, and M. Krohn. 1994. Patterns of Adolescent Firearms Ownership and Use. *Justice Quarterly* 11:51–74.

Loeb, R. 1973. Adolescent groups. *Sociology and Social Research 58:*13–22.

Loftus, R.P. 1977. The idioms of Japan XVII. *Japan Interpreter 11:*384–394.

Lombroso, C. 1972 [originally 1911]. *Criminal Man, According to the Classification of Cesare Lombroso.* Montclair, NJ: Patterson Smith.

Los Angeles County Sheriff's Department 1995. L.A. style: A street gang manual of the Los Angeles County Sheriff's Department. In M. Klein, C. Maxson, and J. Miller (eds.), *Modern Gang Reader.* Los Angeles: University of Southern California Press, 34–45.

Louwage, F.E. 1951. Delinquency in Europe after World War II. *Journal of Criminal Law, Criminology, and Police Science 42:*53–56.

Lowney, J. 1984. The Wall Gang: A study of interpersonal process and deviance among twenty-three middle-class youths. *Adolescence 19:*527–538.

Lundman, R.J. 1984. *Prevention and Control of Juvenile Delinquency.* New York: Oxford University Press.

Lundman, R.J. 1993. *Prevention and Control of Juvenile Delinquency.* Second edition. New York: Oxford University Press.

Lundman, R.J., R.E. Sykes, and J.P. Clark. 1978. Police control of juveniles: A replication. *Journal of Research in Crime and Delinquency 15:*74–91.

Macy, M.W. 1990. Learning theory and the logic of critical mass. *American Sociological Review 55:*809–826.

Magdol, E. 1973. Against the gentry: An inquiry into a southern lower-class community and culture, 1965–1970. *Journal of Social History 6:*259–283.

Maguire, K. and A.L. Pastore (eds.). 1995. *Sourcebook of Criminal Justice Statistics 1994.* Washington, DC: U.S. Department of Justice, Bureau of Justice Statistics.

Mano, D.K. 1988. There's more to Chinatown. *New York Times* (April 12):42.

Marris, P. and M. Rein. 1973. *Dilemmas of Social Reform.* Second edition. Chicago: Aldine.

Marsh, P. and A. Campbell. 1978. The sex boys on their own turf. *New Society 45:*133–135.

Marsh, P. and A. Campbell. 1978. The youth gangs of New York and Chicago go into business. *New Society 45:*67–69.

Martinez, F.B. 1992. The impact of gangs and drugs in the community. In Cervantes, R.C. (ed.), *Substance Abuse and Gang Violence.* Newbury Park, CA: Sage, pp. 60–73.

Marwell, G., P. Oliver, and R. Prahl. 1988. Social networks and collective action: A theory of critical mass III. *American Journal of Sociology 94:*502–534.

Martindale, D. 1960. *The Nature and Types of Sociological Theory.* Boston: Houghton Mifflin.

Martindale, D. 1979. Ideologies, paradigms, and theories. In W.E. Snizek, et al. (eds.), *Contemporary Issues in Theory and Research: A Metasociological Perspective.* Westport, CT: Greenwood Press.

Matheron, M.S. 1988. China: Chinese triads, the Oriental mafia. *CJ International 4* (3):3, 4, 26–27.

Matza, D. 1964. *Delinquency and Drift.* New York: Wiley.

Matza, D. and G.M. Sykes. 1961. Juvenile delinquency and subterranean values. *American Sociological Review 26:*712–719.

Maxson, C.L., M.A. Gordon, and M. Klein. 1985. Differences between gang and nongang homicides. *Criminology 23:*209–221.

Maxson, C.L. and M.W. Klein. 1983. Gangs: Why we couldn't stay away. In J. Kluegel (ed.), *Evaluating Juvenile Justice.* Beverly Hills, CA: Sage.

Maxson, C.L. and M. Klein. 1994. Investigating gang structures. Paper presented at the annual meeting American Society of Criminology, Miami, 1994.

Mayo, P. 1969. *The Making of a Criminal: A Comparative Study of Two Delinquency Areas.* London: Weidenfeld and Nicolson.

McCall, A. 1979. *The Medieval Underworld.* London: Hamish Hamilton.

McDermott, M.J. and M. Hindelang. 1981. *Juvenile Criminal Behavior in the United States: Its Trends and Patterns.* Washington, DC: U.S. Government Printing Office.

McKinney, K.C. 1988. Juvenile gangs: Crime and drug trafficking. *Juvenile Justice Bulletin.* Washington, DC: Office of Juvenile Justice and Delinquency Prevention.

Mednick, S. and J. Volavka. 1982. Biology and crime: Lee Ellis, genetics, and criminal behavior. *Criminology 10:*43–66.

Meier, R., S. Burkett, and C. Hickman. 1984. Sanctions, peers, and deviance: Preliminary models of a social control process. *Sociological Quarterly 25*:67-82.

Menard, S. 1987. Short-term trends in crime and delinquency: A comparison of UCR, NCS, and self-report data. *Justice Quarterly 4*:455–474.

Menard, S. 1995. A developmental test of Mertonian anomie theory. *Journal of Research in Crime and Delinquency* 32:136–174.

Menard, S. 1992. Demographic and theoretical variables in the age-period-cohort analysis of illegal behavior. *Journal of Research in Crime and Delinquency* 29:178–199.

Menard, S. 1994. A test of Cloward and Ohlin's anomie-opportunity theory. Paper presented at the American Society of Criminology annual meeting, Boston, Massachusetts.

Menard, S. and H.C. Covey. 1988. UCR and NCS: Comparisons over space and time. *Journal of Criminal Justice 16*:371–384.

Menard, S. and D.S. Elliott. 1990. Longitudinal and cross-sectional data collection and analysis in the study of crime and delinquency. *Justice Quarterly 7*:11–55.

Menard, S. and D.S. Elliott. 1994. Delinquent bonding, moral beliefs, and illegal behavior: A three-wave panel model. *Justice Quarterly* 11:173–188.

Menard, S. and D. Huizinga. 1994. Changes in conventional attitudes and delinquent behavior in adolescence. *Youth and Society* 26:23–53.

Mennell, R.M. 1973. *Thorns and Thistles: Juvenile Delinquents in the United States 1825–1945*. Hanover, NH: University Press of New England.

Merton, R.K. 1938. Social structure and anomie. *American Sociological Review 3*:672–682.

Merton, R.K. 1959. Social conformity, deviation, and opportunity-structures: A comment on the contributions of Dubin and Cloward. *American Sociological Review 24*:177–189.

Merton, R.K. 1968. *Social Theory and Social Structure*. Enlarged edition. New York: Free Press.

Messick, H. and B. Goldblatt. 1974. *Gangs and Gangsters: The Illustrated History of Gangs from Jesse James to Murph the Surf*. New York: Ballantine Books.

Mieczkowski, T. 1986. Geeking up and throwing down: Heroin street life in Detroit. *Criminology 24*:645–666.

Miller, W.B. 1958. Lower class culture as a generating milieu of gang delinquency. *Journal of Social Issues 14*:5–19.

Miller, W.B. 1962. The impact of a "total community" delinquency control project. *Social Problems 10*:168–191.

Miller, W.B. 1966. Violent crimes in city gangs. *Annals of the American Academy of Political and Social Science 364*:97–112.

Miller, W.B. 1973. Race, sex, and gangs: The Molls. *Society 11* (1):32–35.

Miller, W.B. 1974. American youth gangs: Past and present. In A.S. Blumberg (ed.), *Current Perspectives on Criminal Behavior*. New York: Knopf.

Miller, W.B. 1976. Youth gangs in the urban crisis era. In J.F. Short, Jr. (ed.), *Delinquency, Crime, and Society*. Chicago: University of Chicago Press.

Miller, W.B. 1977. Rumble this time. *Psychology Today 10* (2):52–88.

Miller, W.B. 1980. Gangs, groups, and serious youth crime. In D. Shichor and D. Kelly (eds.), *Critical Issues in Juvenile Delinquency*. Lexington, MA: Lexington Books.

Miller, W.B. 1981. American youth gangs: Past and present. In A.S. Blumberg (ed.), *Current Perspectives on Criminal Behavior.* New York: Knopf.

Miller, W. 1983. Youth gangs and groups. In Kadish, S.H. (ed.), *Encyclopedia of Crime and Justice.* New York: Free Press.

Miller, W.B. 1989. Book Review of *People and Folks: Gangs, Crime, and the Underclass in a Rustbelt City. American Journal of Sociology 94:*784–787.

Miller, W.B. 1990. Why the United States has failed to solve its youth gang problem. In C.R. Huff (ed.), *Gangs in America.* Newbury Park, CA: Sage.

Mirande, A. and J. López. 1992. Chicano urban youth gangs: A critical analysis of a social problem? *Latino Studies Journal,* 3 (3) 15–28.

Monnet, D.M. 1995. The implementation of the G.R.E.A.T. (Gang Resistance Education and Training) program in Las Cruces, NM. Paper presented at the annual meeting of the American Society of Criminology, Boston, MA.

Monroe, R.R. 1978. *Brain Dysfunctions in Aggressive Criminals.* Lexington, MA: D.C. Heath.

Monsod, J. 1967. Juvenile gangs in Paris: Toward a structural analysis. *Journal of Research in Crime and Delinquency 4:*142–165.

Moore, J.B. 1993. *Skinheads Shaved for Battle: A Cultural History of American Skinheads.* Bowling Green, OH: Bowling Green State University Popular Press.

Moore, J. 1977. A case study of collaboration: The Chicano Pinto Research Project. *Journal of Social Issues 33:*144–158.

Moore, J. 1978. *Homeboys.* Philadelphia: Temple University Press.

Moore, J. 1988. The changing Chicano gangs: Acculturation, generational change, evolution of deviance or emerging underclass? In J.H. Johnson and M.L. Oliver (eds.), *Proceedings of the Conference on Comparative Ethnicity.* Los Angeles: Institute for Social Science Research.

Moore, J.W. 1989. Is there a Hispanic underclass? *Social Science Quarterly 70:*265–284.

Moore, J.W. 1991. *Going Down to the Barrio: Homeboys and Homegirls in Change.* Philadelphia: Temple University Press.

Moore, J.W. 1993. Gangs, drugs, and violence. In S. Cummings and D.J. Monti (eds.). *Gangs: The Origins and Impact of Contemporary Youth Gangs in the United States.* Albany: University of New York Press.

Moore, J., D. Vigil, and R. Garcia. 1983. Residence and territoriality in Chicano gangs. *Social Problems 31:*182–194.

Morales, A. 1992. A clinical model for the prevention of gang violence and homicide. In R.C. Cervantes (ed.), *Substance Abuse and Gang Violence.* Newbury Park, CA: Sage, pp. 105–118.

Morash, M. 1983. Gangs, groups, and delinquency. *British Journal of Criminology 23:*309–331.

Morash, M. and M. Chesney-Lind. 1991. A reformulation and partial test of the power control theory of delinquency. *Justice Quarterly 8:*347–377.

Morganthau, T. 1982. Vietnamese gangs in California. *Newsweek 100:*22.

Morris, N. and G. Hawkins. 1970. *The Honest Politician's Guide to Crime Control.* Chicago: University of Chicago Press.

Muehlbauer, G. and L. Dodder. 1983. *The Losers: Gang Delinquency in an American Suburb.* New York: Praeger.

Mungham, G. 1977. The sociology of violence. *New Society 42:*60–63.

Munoz, I. 1996. Juvenile drug trafficking in El Salvador: Is there an American gang connection? Paper presented at the annual meeting of the Western Society of Criminology, Rohnert Park, California.

Murphy, S. 1978. A year with the gangs of east Los Angeles. *Ms.* 7(1):56–64.

Mydans, S. 1990a. Life in a girls' gang. Colors and bloody. *New York Times* (January 29):1, 12.

Mydans, S. 1990b. Not just the inner city: Well-to-do join gangs. *New York Times National* (April 10):A–7.

Myerhoff, H.L. and B.G. Myerhoff. 1964. Field observations of middle class "gangs". *Social Forces 42:*238–336.

Nagel, I. and J. Hagan. 1982. Gender and crime: Offense patterns and criminal court sanctions. In N. Morris and M. Tonry (eds.), *Crime and Justice: An Annual Review of Research.* Volume 4. Chicago: University of Chicago Press.

National Commission on Excellence in Education. 1983. *A Nation at Risk: The Imperative for Educational Reform.* Washington, DC: U.S. Government Printing Office.

Needle, J. and W.V. Stapleton. 1983. *Reports of the National Juvenile Justice Assessment Centers, Police Handling of Youth Gangs.* Washington, DC: Office of Juvenile Justice and Delinquency Prevention.

Neumeyer, M.H. 1956. International trends in juvenile delinquency. *Social Science Research 41:*94–99.

New York City Youth Board. 1960. *Reaching the Fighting Gang.* New York: New York City Youth Board.

New York Times. 1988a. Police watch over churchgoers after Los Angeles gang shooting. *New York Times* (April 4):A–16.

New York Times. 1988b. Los Angeles dragnet over gang violence leads to 592 arrests. *New York Times* (April 10):30.

Nye, F.I. 1958. *Family Relationships and Delinquent Behavior.* New York: Wiley.

Nye, F.I., J.F. Short, Jr., and V.J. Olsen. 1958. Socio-economic status and delinquent behavior. *American Journal of Sociology 63:*318–329.

O'Brien, R.M. 1985. *Crime and Victimization Data.* Beverly Hills, CA: Sage.

O'Donnell, C.R. 1995. Firearm deaths among children and youth. *American Psychologist* 50:771–776.

O'Hagan, F.J. 1976. Gang characteristics: An empirical survey. *Journal of Child Psychology and Psychiatry 17:*305–314.

O'Hare, W.P. 1985. Poverty in America: Trends and new patterns. *Population Bulletin 40:*1–43. Washington, DC: Population Reference Bureau.

Office of Juvenile Justice and Delinquency Prevention. 1988. *Juvenile Gangs: Crime and Drug Trafficking.* Washington, DC: U.S. Department of Justice.

Office of Juvenile Justice and Delinquency Prevention. 1989a. *Using the Law to Improve School Order and Safety.* Washington, DC: U.S. Department of Justice.

Office of Juvenile Justice and Delinquency Prevention. 1989b. *Weapons in Schools.* Washington, DC: U.S. Department of Justice.

Oliver, P. and G. Marwell. 1988. The paradox of group size in collective action: A theory of critical mass II. *American Sociological Review 53:*1–8.

Oliver, P., G. Marwell, and R. Teixeira. 1985. A theory of critical mass I: Interdependence, group heterogeneity, and the production of collective action. *American Sociological Review 49:*601–610.

Padilla, F. 1992. *The Gang as an American Enterprise.* New Brunswick, NJ: Rutgers University Press.

Paez, A. and F. Shenk. 1983. *Criminal Victimization in the United States: 1973–1982 Trends.* Washington, DC: U.S. Department of Justice.

Palen, J.J. 1987. *The Urban World.* Third edition. New York: McGraw-Hill.

Park, R.E. 1925. The urban community as a spatial pattern and a moral order. *Publications of the American Sociological Society 20:*1–14.

Park, R.E. 1936. Human ecology. *American Journal of Sociology 42:*1–15.

Parks, C.P. 1995. Gang behavior in the schools: Reality or myth? *Educational Psychology Review,* 7:(1)41–68.

Parsons, T. 1977. *The Evolution of Societies.* Englewood Cliffs, NJ: Prentice-Hall.

Paternoster, R. 1987. The deterrent effect of the perceived certainty and severity of punishment: A review of the evidence and issues. *Justice Quarterly 4:*173–217.

Patrick, J. 1973. *A Glasgow Gang Observed.* London: Eyre Methuen.

Patterson, E.B. 1991. Poverty, income inequality, and community crime rates. *Criminology 29:*755–776.

Patterson, G.R. and T.J. Dishion. 1985. Contributions of families and peers to delinquency. *Criminology 23:*63–79.

Pawlak, E.J. 1977. Differential selection of juveniles for detention. *Journal of Research in Crime and Delinquency 14:*1–12.

Paz, O. 1961. *The Labyrinth of Solitude: Life and Thought in Mexico.* New York: Grove Press.

Pearson, G. 1983. *Hooligan: A History of Reportable Fears.* New York: Schocken.

Pennell, S. 1983. *San Diego Street Youth Program: Final Evaluation.* San Diego: Association of Governments.

Perkins, U.E. 1987. *Explosion of Chicago's Black Street Gangs 1900 to Present.* Chicago: Third World Press.

Pfautz, H.W. 1961. Near-group theory and collective behavior: A critical reformulation. *Social Problems 9:*167–174.

Pickett, R.S. 1969. *House of Refuge.* Syracuse: Syracuse University Press.

Piven, F.F. and R.A. Cloward. 1971. *Regulating the Poor.* New York: Pantheon.

Platt, A.M. 1977. *The Child Savers: The Invention of Delinquency.* Second edition. Chicago: University of Chicago Press.

Polk, K., D. Frease, and L. Richmond. 1974. Social class, school experience, and delinquency. *Criminology 12:*84–96.

Pope, C. and W. Feyerherm. 1982. Gender bias in juvenile court dispositions. *Journal of Social Services Research 6:*1-16.

Porché-Burke, L. and C. Fulton. 1992. The impact of gang violence. In R.C. Gervantes, (ed.), *Substance Abuse and Gang Violence.* Newbury Park, CA: Sage, pp. 85–104.

Posner, G. 1991. Truads. In R. Rosen and P. McSharry. (eds.), *Street Gangs: Gaining Turf, Losing Ground.* New York: The Rosen Publishing Group, pp. 111–126.

Prothrow-Stith, D. 1987. *Violence Prevention Curriculum for Adolescents.* Newton, MA: Education Development Center.

Prothrow-Stith, D. and M. Weissmann. 1991. *Deadly Consequences.* New York: Harper Perennial.

Puffer, J.P. 1912. *The Boy and His Gang.* Boston: Houghton Mifflin.

Quicker, J. 1974. The Chicana Gang: A Preliminary Description. Paper presented at the annual meeting of the Pacific Sociological Association, San Jose, California, 1974.

Quicker, J. 1983. *Homegirls: Characterizing Chicana Gangs.* San Pedro, California: International Universities Press.

Raab, S. 1988a. The ruthless young crack gangsters. *New York Times* (March 20):9.

Raab, S. 1988b. Brutal gangs wage war of terror in upper Manhattan. *New York Times* (March 15):B-1.

Rand, A. 1987. Transitional Life Events and Desistance from Delinquency to Crime. In M. Wolfgang, T. Thornberry and R. Figio (eds) *From Boy to Man, From Delinquency to Crime.* Chicago: University of Chicago Press.

Reed, B. 1989. Nazi retreat. *New Republic 200* (April 3):10–11.

Reed, J.P. and R.S. Reed. 1973. Status, images, and consequence: Once a criminal always a criminal. *Sociology and Social Research 57:*460–472.

Reinhold, R. 1988. In the middle of L.A.'s gang warfare. *New York Times Magazine 5:* 22-30.

Reiss, A.J., Jr. 1951. Delinquency as the failure of personal and social controls. *American Sociological Review 16:*196–207.

Reiss, A.J., Jr. 1986. Co-offender influences on criminal careers. In A. Blumstein, J. Cohen, J.A. Roth, and C.A. Visher (eds.), *Criminal Careers and "Career Criminals," Volume II.* Washington, DC: National Academy Press.

Reiss, A.J., Jr. 1994. Doing evaluations in policy research: implications for drug control initiatives. Pp. 18–41 in D.L. MacKenzie and C.D. Uchida (eds.), *Drugs and Crime: Evaluating Public Policy Initiatives.* Thousand Oaks, CA: Sage.

Reiss, A.J., Jr. and A.L. Rhodes. 1961. The distribution of delinquency in the social class structure. *American Sociological Review 26:*720–732.

Reiss, A.J., Jr. and A.L. Rhodes. 1963. Status deprivation and delinquent behavior. *Sociological Quarterly 4:*135–149.

Reuterman, N.A., M.J. Love, and F. Fiedler. 1973. A partial evaluation of Bloch and Niederhoffer's theory of gang delinquency. *Criminology 11:*415–425.

Rice, B. 1977. The new gangs of Chinatown. *Psychology Today 10* (12):60–69.

Rice, R. 1963. A reporter at large: the Persian Queens. *New Yorker* October 19 39:153.

Riis, J. 1984. *The Children of the Poor.* New York: Garret Press.

Ritzer, G.C. 1980. *Sociology: A Multiple Paradigm Science.* Revised edition. Boston: Allyn and Bacon.

Ritzer, G.C. 1981. *Toward an Integrated Sociological Paradigm: The Search for an Exemplar and Image of the Subject Matter.* Boston: Allyn and Bacon.

Robin, G.D. 1964. Gang member delinquency: Its extent, sequence and typology. *Journal of Criminal Law, Criminology, and Police Science 55:*59–69.

Robison, S., N. Cohen, and M. Sachs. 1946. Autonomous groups: An unsolved problem in group loyalties and conflicts. *Journal of Educational Sociology 20:*154–162.

Rockaway, R.A. 1980. The rise of the Jewish gangster in America. *Journal of Ethnic Studies 8:*31–44.

Rodriguez, L.J. 1993. *Always Running: La Vida Loca: Gang Days in L.A.* Willimantic, CT: Curbstone Press.

Roitberg, T. and S. Menard. 1995. Adolescent violence: a test of integrated theory. *Studies on Crime and Crime Prevention* 2:177–196.

Rojek, D.G. and G.F. Jensen (eds.). 1982. *Readings in Juvenile Delinquency.* Lexington, MA: D.C. Heath.

Romig, D.A., C.C. Cleland, and L.J. Romig. 1989. *Juvenile Delinquency: Visionary Approaches.* Columbus, Ohio: Merrill.

Rosario, R. 1980. A tale of two barrios. *Nuestro 4* (May):18–20.

Rosen, R. and P. McSharry (eds.). 1991. *Street Gangs: Gaining Turf, Losing Ground.* New York: Rosen Publishing Group.

Rosenbaum, J.L. 1991. Female crime and delinquency. In S.E. Brown, F. Esbensen, and G. Geis, *Criminology: Explaining Crime and Its Context.* Cincinnati, OH: Anderson.

Rosenberg, M.L. and J.A. Mercy. 1991. Assaultive violence. In Rosenberg, M.L. and Fenley, A. (eds.), *Violence in America: A Public Health Approach.* New York: Oxford University Press, pp. 14–50.

Rosenquist, G.M. and E.I. Megargee. 1969. *Delinquency in Three Cultures.* Austin: University of Texas Press.

Salazar, A. 1992. *Born to Die in Medellin.* Nottingham, England: Russell Press.

Salazar, M.L. 1991. Personal communication: Comments from gang members.

Sampson, R.J. 1985. Structural sources of variation in race-age-specific rates of offending across major U.S. cities. *Criminology 23:*647–673.

Sampson, R.J. 1986. Effects of socioeconomic context on official reactions to juvenile delinquency. *American Sociological Review 51:*876–885.

Sampson, R.J. 1987. Urban black violence: The effect of male joblessness and family disruption. *American Journal of Sociology 93:*348–382.

Sampson, R.J. 1990. Book review of *People and Folks: Gangs, Crime, and the Underclass in a Rustbelt City. Contemporary Sociology 19:*95.

Sampson, R.J. and W.B. Groves. 1989. Community structure and crime: Testing social disorganization theory. *American Journal of Sociology 94:*774–802.

Sanders, W.B. 1970. *Juvenile Offenders for a Thousand Years: Selected Readings from Anglo-Saxon Times to 1900.* Chapel Hill, NC: University of North Carolina Press.

Sanders, W.B. 1981. *Juvenile Delinquency: Causes Patterns, and Reactions.* New York: Holt, Rinehart, and Winston.

Sanders, W.B. 1994. Gangbangs and Drive-Bys: Grounded Culture and Juvenile Gang Violence. New York: Aldine De Gruyter.

Sarnecki, J. 1982. *Criminality and Peer Relations: Study of Juvenile Delinquency in a Swedish Commune.* Stockholm, Sweden: Brottsforebyggande Radet.

Sarri, R.C. 1983. Gender issues in juvenile justice. *Crime and Delinquency 29:*381–397.

Savitz, L., M. Lalli, and L. Rosen. 1977. *City Life and Delinquency-Victimization, Fear of Crime, and Gang Membership.* Washington, DC: Office of Juvenile Justice and Delinquency Prevention.

Schlossman, S. and M. Sedlak. 1983. The Chicago Area Project revisited. *Crime and Delinquency 29:*398–462.

Schrag, C. 1961. A preliminary criminal typology. *Pacific Sociological Review 4:*11–16.

Schrag, C. 1962. Delinquency and opportunity: Analysis of a theory. *Sociology and Social Research 46:*167–175.

Schur, E.M. 1965. *Crimes Without Victims.* New Jersey: Prentice-Hall.

Schur, E.M. 1973. *Radical Nonintervention: Rethinking the Delinquency Problem.* Englewood Cliffs, NJ: Prentice-Hall.

Schwendinger, H. and J. Schwendinger. 1979. Delinquency and social reform: A radical perspective. In L. Empey (ed.), *Juvenile Justice.* Charlottesville: University of Virginia Press.

Schwendinger, H. and J.S. Schwendinger. 1985. *Adolescent Subcultures and Delinquency.* New York: Praeger.

Scott, P. 1956. Gangs and delinquent groups in London. *British Journal of Delinquency 7:*4–21, 25–26.

Scott, P.D. and D.R.C. Wilcox. 1965. Delinquency and the amphetamines. *British Journal of Psychiatry 61:*9–27.

Sears, E. 1989. Skinheads: A new generation of hate-mongers. *USA Today 117* (May 1):24–26.

Shannon, L.W. 1984. *The Development of Serious Criminal Careers and the Delinquent Neighborhood.* Washington, DC: U.S. Department of Justice, Office of Juvenile Justice and Delinquency Prevention.

Shaw, C.R. 1930. *The Jackroller.* Chicago: University of Chicago Press.

Shaw, C.R. 1931. *The Natural History of a Delinquent Career.* Chicago: University of Chicago Press.

Shaw, C.R. 1938. *Brothers in Crime.* Chicago: University of Chicago Press.

Shaw, C.R. and H.D. McKay. 1942. *Juvenile Delinquency and Urban Areas.* Chicago: University of Chicago Press.

Shaw, C.R. and H.D. McKay. 1972. *Juvenile Delinquency and Urban Areas.* Revised edition. Chicago: University of Chicago Press.

Shaw, C.R., F.M. Zorbaugh, H.D. McKay, and L.S. Cottrell. 1929. Delinquency Areas. Chicago: University of Chicago Press.

Sheldon, H.D. 1898. The institutional activities of American Children. *American Journal of Psychology 9:*425–428.

Sheldon, W. 1949. *The Varieties of Delinquent Youth.* New York: Harper.

Sheley, J.F. and J.D. Wright. 1993. *Gun Acquisition and Possession in Selected Juvenile Samples.* Washington, DC: U.S. Department of Justice, Office of Juvenile Justice and Delinquency Prevention.

Sheth, H. 1961. *Juvenile Delinquency in an Indian Setting.* Bombay, India: Popular Book Depot.

Shoemaker, D.J. 1990. *Theories of Delinquency: An Examination of Explanations of Delinquent Behavior.* Second edition. New York: Oxford University Press.

Short, J.F., Jr. 1964. Gang delinquency and anomie. In M.B. Clinard (ed.), *Anomie and Deviant Behavior: A Discussion and Critique.* New York: Free Press.

Short, J.F., Jr. 1968a. *Gang Delinquency and Delinquent Subcultures.* New York: Harper and Row.

Short, J.F., Jr. 1968b. Comment on Lerman's "Gangs, networks, and subcultural delinquency." *American Journal of Sociology 73:*513–515.

Short, J.F. 1974a. Collective behavior, crime, and delinquency. In D.Glaser (ed.), *Handbook of Criminology.* Skokie, IL: Rand McNally.

Short, J.F. 1974b. Youth, gangs, and society: Micro- and macrosociological processes. *Sociological Quarterly 15:*3–19.

Short, J.F., Jr. 1976a. Gangs, politics, and the social order. In J.F. Short, Jr. (ed.), *Delinquency, Crime, and Society.* Chicago: University of Chicago Press.

Short, J.F., Jr. (ed.). 1976b. *Delinquency, Crime, and Society.* Chicago: University of Chicago Press.

Short, J.F., Jr. 1987. Exploring integration of the theoretical levels of explanation: Notes on juvenile delinquency. In *Theoretical Integration in the Study of Deviance and Crime: Problems and Prospects.* Albany, New York: Unpublished proceedings of the Albany Conference, May 7–8. Cited in Bynum and Thompson (1988).

Short, J.F., Jr. 1989. Exploring integration of theoretical levels of explanation: Notes on gang delinquency. In S.F. Messner, M.D. Krohn, and A.E. Liska (eds.), *Theoretical Integration in the Study of Deviance and Crime: Problems and Prospects.* Albany, NY: State University of New York Press.

Short, J.F., Jr. 1990. *Delinquency and Society.* Englewood Cliffs, NJ: Prentice-Hall.

Short, J.F., Jr. and J. Moland, Jr. 1976. Politics and youth gangs: A follow-up study. *Sociological Quarterly 17:*162–179.

Short, J.F., Jr., R. Rivera, and H. Marshall. 1964. Adult-adolescent relations and gang delinquency. *Pacific Sociological Review 7:*59–65.

Short, J.F., Jr., R. Rivera, and R.A. Tennyson. 1965. Perceived opportunities, gang membership, and delinquency. *American Sociological Review 71:*56–67.

Short, J.F., Jr. and F.L. Strodtbeck. 1965. *Group Process and Gang Delinquency.* Chicago: University of Chicago Press.

Shorter, E. 1977. *The Making of the Modern Family.* New York: Basic Books.

Shover, N. 1973. The social organization of burglary. *Social Problems* 20:499–514.

Sibley, J. 1989. Gang violence: Response of the criminal justice system to the growing threat. *Criminal Justice Journal 11:*403–422.

Siegel, L.J. 1989. *Criminology.* Third edition. St. Paul, MN: West.

Siegel, L.J. and J.J. Senna. 1988. *Juvenile Delinquency.* Second edition. St. Paul, MN: West.

Silberman, M. 1976. Toward a theory of criminal deterrence. *American Sociological Review 41:*442-461.

Silver, A. 1967. The demand for order in civil society: A review of some themes in the history of urban crime, police, and riot. In D.J. Bordua (ed.), *The Police: Six Sociological Essays.* New York: Wiley.

Simmel, G. 1955. *Conflict and the Web of Group Affiliations.* New York: Free Press.

Simcha-Fagan, O. and J.E. Schwartz. 1986. Neighborhood and delinquency: An assessment of contextual effects. *Criminology 24:*667–699.

Simon, R. 1975. *The Contemporary Woman and Crime.* Rockville, MD: National Institute of Mental Health.

Skolnick, J.H., T. Correl, E. Navarro, and R. Rabb. 1990. The social structure of street drug dealing. American Journal of Police, 9:1–41.

Smith, G. 1977. Kids, cops and conflict. In P.R. Wilson (ed.), *Delinquency in Australia: A Critical Appraisal.* St. Lucia, Australia: University of Queensland Press.

Snyder, H.N. and M. Sickmund. 1995. *Juvenile Offenders and Victims: A National Report.* Washington, DC: U.S. Department of Justice, Office of Juvenile Justice and Delinquency Prevention.

Social Science Education Consortium and Center for Action Research. 1981. *Law-Related Education Evaluation Project Final Report Phase II Year 1.* Boulder, CO: Social Science Education Consortium and Center for Action Research.

Sorokin, P. 1964. *Contemporary Sociological Theories.* New York: Harper and Row.

Spanier, G. and C. Fisher. 1973. The housing project and familial functions: Consequences for low-income urban families. *Family Coordinator 22:*235–240.

Spencer, J.C. 1964. *Stress and Release in an Urban Estate.* London: Tavistock.

Spergel, I. 1961. An exploratory research in delinquent subcultures. *Social Service Review 35:*33–47.

Spergel, I. 1964. *Slumtown, Racketville, Haulburg.* Chicago: University of Chicago Press.

Spergel, I. 1973. Community based delinquency prevention programs: An overview. *Social Service Review 47:*16–31.

Spergel, I. 1984. Violent gangs in Chicago: In search of social policy. *Social Service Review 58:*199–226.

Spergel, I. 1986. The violent gang problem in Chicago: A local community approach. *Social Service Review 60:*94–131.

Spergel, I.A. 1990. Youth gangs: Continuity and change. In N. Morris (ed.), *Crime and Delinquency: An Annual Review of Research.* Volume 12. Chicago: University of Chicago Press.

Spergel, I.A. 1995. *The Youth Gang Problem: A Community Approach.* New York: Oxford University Press.

Spergel, I.A. and G.D. Curry. 1990. Strategies and perceived effectiveness in dealing with the youth gang problem. In C.R. Huff (ed.), *Gangs in America.* Newbury Park, CA: Sage.

Srivastava, S.S. 1955. Sociology of juvenile ganging. *Journal of Correctional Work 2:*72–81.

Stafford, M. 1984. Gang delinquency. In R.E. Meier (ed.), *Major Forms of Crime.* Beverly Hills, CA: Sage.

Stanfield, R.E. 1966. The interaction of family variables and gang variables in the aetiology of delinquency. *Social Problems 13:*411–417.

Steffensmeier, D.J. and R.H. Steffensmeier. 1980. Trends in female delinquency. *Criminology 18:*62–85.

Stephens, R.D. 1993. School-based interventions: Safety and security. In A.P. Goldstein and C.R. Huff (eds.), *The Gang Intervention Handbook.* Champaign, IL: Research Press.

Stover, D. 1986. A new breed of youth gang is on the prowl and a bigger threat than ever. *American School Board Journal 173:*19–21.

Stover, D. 1987. Dealing with youth gangs in the schools. *Education Digest 52:*30–33.

Strodtbeck, F.L. and J.F. Short, Jr. 1964. Aleatory risks versus short-run hedonism in explanation of gang action. *Social Problems 12:*127–140.

Stumphauzer, J.S., E.V. Veloz, and T.W. Aiken. Violence by street gangs: East Side Story? In R.B. Stuart (ed.), *Violent Behavior: Social Learning Approaches to Prediction, Management, and Treatment.* New York: Brunner-Mazel.

Subcommittee on Juvenile Justice. 1983. *Gang Violence and Control.* Hearings before the Subcommittee on Juvenile Justice of the Committee on the Judiciary. Washington, DC: Subcommittee on Juvenile Justice.

Sullivan, M.L. 1989. *"Getting Paid": Youth Crime and Work in the Inner City.* Ithaca, New York: Cornell University Press.

Sutherland, E.H. 1934. *Criminology.* Second edition. Philadelphia: Lippincott.

Sutherland, E.H. 1947. *Criminology.* Fourth edition. Philadelphia: Lippincott.

Suttles, G. 1990. Book Review—*People and Folks: Gangs, Crime, and the Underclass in a Rustbelt City. Social Forces 68:*1001–1002.

Swart, W.J. 1995. Female gang delinquency: A search for "acceptably deviant behavior." In M. Klein, C. Maxson, and J. Miller (eds.), *Modern Gang Reader.* Los Angeles: University of Southern California Press.

T, Ice, with H. Sigmund. 1994. *The Ice Opinion.* New York: St. Martin's.

Takagi, P. and A. Platt. 1978. Behind the gilded ghetto: An analysis of race, class, and crime in Chinatown. *Crime and Social Justice 9:*2–25.

Takata, S. and R.G. Zevitz. 1990. Divergent perceptions of group delinquency in a midwestern community: Racine's gang problem. *Youth and Society 21:*282–305.

Tannenbaum, F. 1939. *Crime and the Community.* New York: Columbia University Press.

Taylor, C.S. 1990. Gang imperialism. In C.R. Huff (ed.), *Gangs in America.* Newbury Park, CA: Sage.

Taylor, C.S. 1990a. *Dangerous Society.* East Lansing, MI: Michigan State University Press.

Taylor, C.S. 1993. *Girls, Gangs, Women and Drugs.* East Lansing, MI: Michigan State University Press.

Taylor, I. and D. Wall. 1976. Beyond the skinheads: Comments on the emergence and significance of the slam rock cult. In G. Mungham and G. Pearson (eds.), *Working Class Youth Culture.* London: Routledge and Kegan Paul.

Terry, R.M. 1967. The screening of juvenile offenders. *Journal of Criminal Law, Criminology, and Police Science 58:*163–171.

Thomlinson, R. 1976. *Population Dynamics: Causes and Consequences of World Demographic Change.* New York: Random House.

Thompson, D.W. and L.A. Jason. 1988. Street gangs and preventive interventions. *Criminal Justice and Behavior 15:*323–333.

Thompson, P., J. Brown, R. Scott, and L. Poe. 1993. *Developing gang intervention strategies within community based programs: The Portland model.* Paper presented at the 20th National Conference on Juvenile Justice, Seattle, Washington.

Thompson, R. 1984. Adolescent culture in colonial Massachusetts. *Journal of Family History 9:*127–144.

Thornberry, T.P. 1987. Toward an interactional theory of delinquency. *Criminology* 25:863–891.

Thornberry, T.P., M. Moore, and R.L. Christenson. 1985. The effect of dropping out of high school on subsequent criminal behavior. *Criminology 23:*3–18.

Thornberry, T.P., M.D. Krohn, A.J. Lizotte, and D. Chard-Wierschem. 1993. The role of juvenile gangs in facilitating delinquent behavior. *Journal of Research in Crime and Delinquency* 30:55–87.

Thrasher, F. 1927. *The Gang.* Chicago: University of Chicago Press.

Tinklenberg, J. 1973. Drugs and Crime. In *National Commission on Marijuana and Drug Abuse, Drug Use in America: Problem in Perspective*, Volume 1. Washington, DC: U.S. Government Printing Office.

Tittle, C.R. 1975. Labelling and crime: An empirical evaluation. In W.R. Gove (ed.), *The Labeling of Deviance: Evaluating a Perspective.* New York: Wiley.

Tobias, J.J. 1967. *Crime and Industrial Society in the 19th Century.* New York: Schocken Books.

Toby, J. 1957. Social disorganization and stake in conformity: Complementary factors in the predatory behavior of hoodlums. *Journal of Criminal Law, Criminology, and Police Science 48:*12–17.

Toby, J. 1961. Review of *Delinquency and Opportunity. British Journal of Sociology 12:*282–289.

Toby, J. 1967. Affluence and crime. In *Task Force Report: Juvenile Delinquency and Youth Crime.* Washington, DC: President's Commission on Law Enforcement and the Administration of Justice.

Toffler, A. 1970. *Future Shock.* New York: Random House.

Tolan, P. and N. Guerra. 1994. What works in reducing adolescent violence: An empirical review of the field. Boulder, CO: Center for the Study and Prevention of Violence.

Tonry, M. and J.Q. Wilson (eds.). 1990. *Drugs and Crime.* Chicago: University of Chicago Press.

Tracy, P.E. 1987. Subcultural delinquency: A comparison of the incidence and severity of gang and nongang member offenses. Boston: College of Criminal Justice, Northeastern University.

Tracy, P. and E. Piper. 1982. Gang membership and violent offending: Preliminary results from the 1958 cohort study. Philadelphia: Center for Studies in Criminology and Criminal Law, University of Pennsylvania.

Trojanowicz, R.C. 1978. *Juvenile Delinquency: Concepts and Control.* Englewood Cliffs, NJ: Prentice-Hall.

Tromanhauser, E. 1994. The relationship between street gang membership and the possession and use of firearms. Paper presented at the Annual Meeting of the American Society of Criminology, Miami, Florida, November, 1994.

Trostle, L.C. 1986. *The Stoners: Drugs, Demons and Delinquency,* Graduate Dissertation. Claremont, CA: Claremont Graduate School.

Tuck, R. 1943. Behind the zoot suit riots. *Survey Graphic,* 32:313–316, 335.

U.S. Department of Justice. 1988a. *Report on Asian Organized Crime.* Washington, DC: U.S. Government Printing Office.

U.S. Department of Justice. 1988b. Juvenile gangs: Crime and drug trafficking. *Juvenile Justice Bulletin* (September). Washington, DC: Office of Juvenile Justice and Delinquency Prevention.

U.S. Department of Justice. 1989. *The INS Enforcement Approach to Chinese Crime Groups.* Washington, DC: U.S. Government Printing Office.

U.S. Department of Justice. 1991. *Violent Crime in the United States.* Washington, DC: Bureau of Justice Statistics.

U.S. News and World Report. 1979. Youth gangs: They're back, growing worse. *U.S. News and World Report 87* (August 20):46.

U.S. News and World Report. 1989. When gangs move in to fine places. *U.S. News and World Report 106* (June 5):42.

U.S. Senate. 1980. Professional motor vehicle theft and chop shops. Hearings before the Permanent Subcommittee on Investigations, 96th Congress, First Session. Pp. 255–267 in L.D. Savitz and N. Johnston (eds.), *Contemporary Criminology.* New York: Wiley.

Vaz, E.W. 1962. Juvenile gang delinquency in Paris. *Social Problems 10:*23–31.

Vaz, E.W. (ed.). 1967. *Middle-Class Juvenile Delinquency.* New York: Harper and Row.

Velarde, A.J. 1978. Do delinquents really drift? *British Journal of Criminology 18:*23–39.

Vigil, J.D. 1988. *Barrio Gangs.* Austin, TX: University of Texas Press.

Vigil, J.D. 1990. Cholos and gangs: Culture change and street youth in Los Angeles. In C.R. Huff (ed.), *Gangs in America.* Newbury Park, CA: Sage.

Vigil, J.D. 1994. Review of *Juvenile Gangs* by Herbert C. Covey, Scott Menard, and Robert J. Franzese. *Criminal Justice Review* 19:307–308.

Vigil, J.D. and J.M. Long. 1990. Emic and etic perspectives on gang culture: The Chicano case. In C.R. Huff (ed.), *Gangs in America.* Newbury Park, CA: Sage.

Vigil, J.D. and S.C. Yun. 1990. Vietnamese youth gangs in southern California. In C.R. Huff (ed.), *Gangs in America.* Newbury Park, CA: Sage.

Vold, G.B. and T.J. Bernard. 1986. *Theoretical Criminology.* Second edition. New York: Oxford University Press.

Waldorf, D. 1993. Don't be your own best customer—Drug use of San Francisco gang drug sellers. *Crime, Law and Social Change,* 19:1–15.

Walker, S. 1994. *Sense and Nonsense about Crime and Drugs: A Policy Guide.* Third edition. Belmont, CA: Wadsworth.

Wang, A.Y. 1994. Pride and prejudice in high school gang members. Adolescence, 29: 279–291.

Washburn, P.C. 1976. Student protestors and gang delinquents: Toward a theory of collective deviance. *Sociological Focus 9:*27–46.

Wasserstrom, J. 1984. Resistance to the one-child family in modern China. *Modern China 10:*345–358.

Wattenberg, W. and J. Balistrieri. 1950. Gang membership and juvenile misconduct. *American Sociological Review 15:*744–752.

Weber, M. 1947. *The Theory of Social and Economic Organization.* Translated by A.M. Henderson and T. Parsons. Edited by T. Parsons. New York: Free Press.

Weinberg, S.K. 1964. Juvenile delinquency in Ghana: A comparative analysis of delinquents and non-delinquents. *Journal of Criminal Law, Criminology, and Police Science 55:*471–481.

Weiner, N.L. and C.V. Willie. 1971. Decisions by juvenile officers. *American Journal of Sociology 76:*199–210.

Weis, J.G. and J.D. Hawkins. 1981. *Preventing Delinquency.* Office of Juvenile Justice and Delinquency Prevention, U.S. Department of Justice. Washington, DC: U.S. Government Printing Office.

Weisfeld, G. and R. Feldman. 1982. A former street gang leader reinterviewed eight years later. *Crime and Delinquency 28:*567–581.

Weisheit, R. 1990. *Drugs, Crime, and the Criminal Justice System.* Cincinnati: Anderson.

Wellman, B. and B. Leighton. 1979. Networks, neighborhoods, and communities: Approaches to the study of the community question. *Urban Affairs Quarterly 14:*363–390.

Werthman, C. 1967. The function of social definitions in the development of the gang boy's career. In *Task Force Report: Juvenile Delinquency and Youth Crime.* Washington, DC: President's Commission on Law Enforcement and the Administration of Justice.

Werthman, C. and I. Piliavin. 1967. Gang members and the police. In D. Bordua (ed.), *The Police: Six Sociological Essays.* New York: Wiley.

West, D. 1967. *The Young Offender.* New York: International University Press.

West, D. and D. Farrington. 1977. *The Delinquent Way of Life.* London: Heineman.

Weston, J. 1995. Community policing: An approach to youth gangs in a medium-sized city. Pp. 297–300 in M.W. Klein, C.L. Maxson, and J. Miller (eds.), *The Modern Gang Reader.* Los Angeles, CA: Roxbury.

White, H.R., R.J. Pandina, and R.L. LaGrange. 1987. Longitudinal predictors of serious substance use and delinquency. *Criminology 25:*715–740.

Whitehead, J.T. and S.P. Lab. 1990. *Juvenile Justice: An Introduction.* Cincinnati: Anderson.

Whitfield, R.G. 1982. American gangs and British subcultures: A commentary. *International Journal of Offender Therapy and Comparative Criminology 26:*90–92.

Whyte, W.F. 1955. *Street Corner Society.* Chicago: University of Chicago Press.

Williams, D. 1969. Neural factors related to habitual aggression: Consideration of differences between habitual aggressives and others who have committed crimes of violence. *Brain 92:*503–520.

Williams, J. and M. Gold. 1972. From delinquent behavior to official delinquency. *Social Problems 20:*220–229.

Williams, T. 1989. *The Cocaine Kids: The Inside Story of a Teenage Drug Ring.* Reading, MA: Addison-Wesley.

Willis, P. 1973. The triple-x boys. *New Society 23:*693–695.

Willman, M.T. and J.R. Snortum. 1982. A police program for employment of youth gang members. *International Journal of Offender Therapy and Comparative Criminology 26:*207–214.

Willoughby, J. 1991. The Motel people. In R. Rosen and P. McSharry (eds.), *Street Gangs: Gaining Turf, Losing Ground.* New York: The Rosen Publishing Group, pp. 139–152.

Wilmott, P. 1966. *Adolescent Boys of East London.* London: Routledge and Kegan Paul.

Wilson, W.J. 1980. *The Declining Significance of Race: Blacks and Changing American Institutions.* Second edition. Chicago: University of Chicago Press.

Wilson, W.J. 1984. The black underclass. *The Wilson Quarterly 8:*88–99.

Wilson, W.J. 1987. *The Truly Disadvantaged: The Inner City, the Underclass, and Public Policy.* Chicago: University of Chicago Press.

Wilson-Smith, A. 1989. Gang warfare, Soviet style. *Maclean's 102* (May 22):44.

Winfree, L.T., Jr., F.-A. Esbensen, and D.W. Osgood. 1995. Evaluating a school-based gang prevention program: A theoretical perspective. Paper presented at the annual meeting of the Academy of Criminal Justice Sciences, Boston.

Winfree, L.T., Jr. and G.L. Mays. 1996. Family and peer influences on gang involvement: A comparison of institutionalized and free-world youth in a southwestern state. Pp. 35–53 in J.M. Miller and J.P. Rush (eds.), *Gangs: A Criminal Justice Approach.* Cincinnati, OH: Anderson.

Winfree, L.T., Jr., G.L. Mays, and T. Vigil-Backstrom. 1994. Youth gangs and incarcerated delinquents: exploring the ties between gang membership, delinquency, and social learning theory. *Justice Quarterly* 11:229–255.

Winfree, L.T., Jr., T. Vigil-Backstrom, and G.L. Mays. 1994. Social learning theory, self-reported delinquency, and youth gangs. *Youth and Society* 26:147–177.

Wintemute, G.J. 1987. Firearms as a cause of death in the United States, 1920–1982. *The Journal of Trauma,* 27:532–536.

Wofford, S. 1991. A preliminary analysis of the relationship between employment and delinquency/crime for adolescents and young adults. National Youth Survey Report No. 50. Boulder, CO: Institute of Behavioral Science.

Wolfgang, M. 1966. *Patterns in Criminal Homicide.* New York: Wiley.

Wolfgang, M. and F. Ferracuti. 1967. *The Subculture of Violence.* London: Tavistock.

Wolfgang, M.E., R.M. Figlio, and T. Sellin. 1972. *Delinquency in a Birth Cohort.* Chicago: University of Chicago Press.

Wooden, W.S. 1995. *Renegade Kids, Suburban Outlaws: From Youth Culture to Delinquency.* Belmont, CA: Wadsworth.

Woodward, J. 1958. *Management and Technology.* London: Her Majesty's Stationery Office.

Wright, J.D., P.H. Rossi, and K. Daly. 1983. *Under the Gun: Weapons, Crime, and Violence in America.* Chicago: Aldine.

Wright, J.D., J.F. Sheley, and M.D. Smith. 1992. Kids, guns, and killing fields. *Society* 30:84–89.

Yablonsky, L. 1959. The delinquent gang as a near group. *Social Problems* 7:108–117.

Yablonsky, L. 1962. *The Violent Gang.* New York: Macmillan.

Yablonsky, L. 1970. *The Violent Gang.* Revised edition. Baltimore: Penguin.

Yablonsky, L. and M. Haskell. 1988. *Juvenile Delinquency.* Fourth edition. New York: Harper and Row.

Zatz, M.S. 1985. Los Cholos: Legal processing of Chicano gang members. *Social Problems* 33:13–30.

Zatz, M.S. 1987. Chicano youth gangs and crime: The creation of a moral panic. *Contemporary Crisis* 11:129–158.

Zeldes, I. 1981. *The Problem of Crime in the USSR.* Springfield, IL: Charles C Thomas.

Zevitz, R.G. and S.R. Takata. 1992. Metropolitan gang influence and the emergence of group delinquency in a regional community. *Journal of Criminal Justice,* 20:93–106.

Zimring, F.E. 1981. Kids, groups, and crime: Some implications of a well-known secret. *Journal of Criminal Law and Criminology* 72:867–885.

Zu-Yuan, H. 1988. China: Juvenile delinquency and its prevention. *CJ International 4* (5):5–10.

Zucker, M. 1978. Walls of barrio are brought to life by street gang art. *Smithsonian 9* (October):105–110.

NAME INDEX